T0131991

Poverty, Chronic Poverty and Poverty Dynamics

Aasha Kapur Mehta · Shashanka Bhide
Anand Kumar · Amita Shah
Editors

Poverty, Chronic Poverty and Poverty Dynamics

Policy Imperatives

 Springer

Editors
Aasha Kapur Mehta
Indian Institute of Public Administration
New Delhi, India

Anand Kumar
Indian Institute of Advanced Study
Shimla, India

Shashanka Bhide
Madras Institute of Development Studies
Chennai, India

Amita Shah
Center for Development Alternatives
Ahmedabad, Gujarat
India

ISBN 978-981-13-4477-0   ISBN 978-981-13-0677-8   (eBook)
https://doi.org/10.1007/978-981-13-0677-8

Printed on acid-free paper

This Springer imprint is published by the registered company Springer Nature Singapore Pte Ltd.
The registered company address is: 152 Beach Road, #21-01/04 Gateway East, Singapore 189721, Singapore

Foreword

It is widely known among serious poverty researchers globally that India still suffers from widespread, extreme and chronic poverty, in spite of a variety of policy actions implemented over several decades and high economic growth rates during the past 25 years. Many social scientists have devoted their research efforts to find remedial measures to tackle the problem. During the past decade, a group of four researchers, Aasha Kapur Mehta, Shashanka Bhide, Anand Kumar and Amita Shah, actively participated in an IIPA research project on chronic poverty in India, as part of an international venture. This collection of nine essays edited by Aasha Kapur Mehta and her co-authors presents the findings on the different aspects of the current poverty problem in India and suggests a number of public policy actions at the grass-roots level for the eradication of extreme poverty and the associated disabilities afflicting a large proportion of the Indian population, in the framework of three sustainable development goals, SDG1, SDG2 and SDG3.

The review of latest policy measures formulated by NITI Aayog in recent years and the editors' assessment in Chap. 9 preceded by meticulous and painstaking research efforts of the four researchers in collaboration with six others on different aspects of the problem are reported in Chaps. 2–8: trends in poverty incidence (Chap. 2), poverty dynamics (Chap. 3), hunger and poverty (Chap. 4), the twin challenges of chronic poverty and conflict between extremists and state agencies (Chap. 5), structural barriers to rural to urban migration as a coping mechanism (Chap. 6), utter inadequacy of the provision of public health care, with affected families sliding into poverty (Chap. 7) and paucity of educational and skill formation opportunities (Chap. 8). Working of NSAP and MGNREGA programmes of the Government of India is appraised in Chap. 9.

A distinctive merit of the volume is its focus on a proposed systematic approach to identify people mired in poverty in each village and slum and to attend to their needs. Casual agricultural labour, marginalised groups, especially scheduled tribes, too deserve special attention.

By virtue of its comprehensive and careful analysis of a problem of paramount importance at this stage of India's development, this book is a masterpiece of the current decade. Academic researchers in the area of poverty, development economists and policy analysis will find this book extremely useful.

New Delhi, India   K. L. Krishna
April 2018   Former Professor and Head, Department of Economics
                                    Delhi School of Economics, Delhi University
                     and Chairperson, Madras Institute of Development Studies

Preface

Poverty rates have declined over the years but continued persistence of high rates, especially for some regions, and social groups are indicative of the intractability or stubbornness of poverty in such cases and the lack of responsiveness to overall economic growth and development. Sustainable development goal 1 or SDG1 requires that we end poverty in all its forms everywhere. This cannot be achieved unless policies and programmes for poverty alleviation address chronic poverty and the dynamics of poverty. These are the issues that are analysed in this book titled *Poverty, Chronic Poverty and Poverty Dynamics*, which is the last of more than 70 publications brought out by the Chronic Poverty Research Centre, India, head-quartered at IIPA, New Delhi, over more than a decade.

Apart from the India Chronic Poverty Report 2011, which has also been translated into Hindi and Odia, 51 peer-reviewed working papers have been published in the CPRC-IIPA working paper series. Some of the earlier working papers have subsequently been revised and converted into articles in journals such as *World Development, Journal of Human Development, Margin, Economic and Political Weekly, Yojana and Down to Earth* and books such as *Chronic Poverty in India* (2003) published by IIPA and *Chronic Poverty and Development Policy in India* (2006) published by Sage. This book, *Poverty, Chronic Poverty and Poverty Dynamics: Policy Imperatives*, builds on the last lot of working papers published in this series. Additionally, a book titled *Understanding Poverty Dynamics and Eradicating Chronic Poverty* (2014) documented the discussions during a very successful two-day international seminar organised at IIPA as part of this work.

I appreciate the commitment and sustained efforts put in by the core team members of the CPRC India project, Prof. Aasha Kapur Mehta, Prof. Shashanka Bhide, Prof. Anand Kumar and Prof. Amita Shah, as well as the partner institutions where they work, for their support.

Although poverty has declined in the Indian context, it still remains a huge challenge that faces us. As this book cogently argues, unless we try to understand the drivers, sustainers and interrupters of poverty and strengthen the processes that address them, many of those living in poverty today will remain poor and may pass their poverty to their children. This, combined with the size of the problem, demands that we address this challenge on priority. This book is a valuable addition to the literature on this subject and will inform both policy and research in this important field.

New Delhi, India   Tishyarakshit Chatterjee
                                     Director, Indian Institute of Public Administration

Acknowledgements

We place on record our deep gratitude to: The Chronic Poverty Research Centre, UK, headquartered at ODI and DFID for sponsoring and supporting the research on which this book is based; Dr. Andrew Shepherd for providing tremendous support at all stages of the research; the chairpersons, discussants and participants at the seminars at which the earlier drafts of the chapters were presented, especially the International Seminar on Understanding Poverty Dynamics and Eradicating Chronic Poverty held at IIPA in February 2011; the International Conference on Ten Years of War Against Poverty held at the University of Manchester in 2010; the UN Women – IIPA National Consultation on "Reviewing Flagship Programmes from a Gender Lens: ICDS" held at IIPA; the many senior academics who valued and supported our work; the reviewers of working papers and draft chapters for their extremely valuable comments; anonymous peer reviewers for valuable comments on the book proposal; the editors for permitting the use of sections or earlier drafts that we had published in their journals; the management, faculty and administration of the four partner institutions that constitute the CPRC India project, IIPA, NCAER, GIDR and JNU; Dr. T. Chatterjee, Director, IIPA, and his team for administrative support in enabling us to complete the 21 additional publications that were requested of us when we were closing the CPRC project in 2011; Late Mr. G. C. L. Joneja, Late Dr. P. L. Sanjeev Reddy, Mr. B. S. Baswan and Late Dr. Rakesh Hooja for the tremendous support and encouragement that they gave to our research on poverty at IIPA; Indian Institute of Advanced Studies, Madras Institute of Development Studies and Centre for Development Alternatives, with whom the CPRC India core team is presently affiliated; support from NCAER in using panel data, particularly Prof. Hari Nagarajan, for access to the rural panel data from the Rural Economic and Demographic Surveys and several colleagues at NCAER who worked with us on the project; all the authors and co-authors of the nine chapters;

Ms. Nupoor Singh, Associate Editor, Springer, for very useful and constructive suggestions while finalising the chapters; Sanjay Pratap, Research Officer, CPRC; and Sonia Bajaj, Project Assistant, for cheerful research assistance.

Aasha Kapur Mehta
Shashanka Bhide
Anand Kumar
Amita Shah

Contents

1 Introduction 1
   Aasha Kapur Mehta, Shashanka Bhide, Anand Kumar and Amita Shah

2 Poverty Trends and Measures 9
   Aasha Kapur Mehta and Shashanka Bhide

3 A Review of Poverty Dynamics Issues 37
   Shashanka Bhide and Aasha Kapur Mehta

4 Hunger, Under-Nutrition and Food Security in India 55
   N. C. Saxena

5 Addressing Poverty and Conflict: Learning from a Gandhian
   Initiative in Mushahari (Muzaffarpur, Bihar) 93
   Anand Kumar and Kanihar Kant

6 Changing Scenario of Migration and Poverty in India:
   Reflections and Issues 127
   Amita Shah, Itishree Pattnaik and Animesh Kumar

7 Ill Health and Poverty: Policy Imperatives for Achieving SDG3 153
   Aasha Kapur Mehta and Sanjay Pratap

8 Interface Between Education and Poverty in India: Eluding Goals
   and Search for New Perspectives? 195
   Amita Shah, Kiran Banga Chhokar, Sanjay Pratap
   and Itishree Pattnaik

9 Conclusions 241
   Aasha Kapur Mehta and Shashanka Bhide

Index 251

Editors and Contributors

About the Editors

Aasha Kapur Mehta is Professor of Economics at the Indian Institute of Public Administration. She studied at Delhi School of Economics, Jawaharlal Nehru University (JNU), New Delhi, and Iowa State University, USA. She is a McNamara Fellow and a Fulbright Scholar. She was a Member of Working Groups for the 11th and 12th Five-Year Plans; chaired two subgroups; served as Member of the core group of the Cabinet Secretariat Ad hoc Task Force for reviewing RFDs of ministries/departments of Government of India and state governments; and was a Member of Committees constituted by ministries such as MoRD, MoPR, MoSPI and MWCD. She was invited as an expert to assist NITI Aayog in formulating the rural economy chapter for the vision, strategy and action plan document. She has led the work of the Chronic Poverty Research Centre in India for more than a decade. Her publications are on poverty, human and gender development indicators, multidimensional deprivation, gender issues, gender budgeting and data gaps.

Shashanka Bhide is presently Director of Madras Institute of Development Studies (MIDS), Chennai. He was Senior Researcher at the National Council of Applied Economic Research, New Delhi, before joining MIDS. He received his Ph.D. from Iowa State University, USA, and Master's from Indian Agricultural Research Institute, New Delhi. He has worked in the areas of macroeconomic modelling and forecasting, agricultural economics, infrastructure and issues relating to chronic poverty in rural India.

Anand Kumar is Fellow at the Indian Institute of Advanced Study, Shimla, since 2016. Prior to this, he worked as Professor of Sociology at the Jawaharlal Nehru University, New Delhi, from 1998. He received his M.A. in Sociology at the Banaras Hindu University (BHU), Varanasi, in 1972; M.Phil. in Sociology at the Jawaharlal Nehru University (JNU), New Delhi, in 1975; and Ph.D. in Sociology at the University of Chicago in 1986. He was Lecturer in Sociology at BHU from 1979 to 1989 and Associate Professor of Sociology at JNU from 1990 to 1998. He was also India Chair at Albert Ludwig University, Freiburg, Germany, and GSP Scholar at Humboldt University of Berlin, Germany. He was a Fulbright Visiting Scholar at Tufts University from January to May 2013; International Faculty at University of Innsbruck, Austria; GSP Faculty at FLACSO, Buenos Aires, Argentina; and Visiting Professor at NEHU, Shillong; Kashmir University, Srinagar; and Central University of Tripura. He was President of the Indian Sociological Society (2013–2015).

Amita Shah is an economist, with a wide-ranging experience of conducting research on various aspects of development studies. She is presently working with Centre for Development Alternatives (CFDA), Ahmedabad, as Honorary Fellow. Prior to this, she was Professor and Director of Gujarat Institute of Development Research, Ahmedabad. She has worked closely with a number of bilateral and multilateral organisations besides a number of government agencies and ministries at the central and state levels and participated in an informed process of policy formulation. She has extensively undertaken collaborative research both within and outside India. She has published about 100 research papers in professional journals and has co-authored/edited four books. She has been invited as Visiting Fellow/Scholar to academic institutions in UK, China, France, the Netherlands and Canada. She was President of the Indian Society for Ecological Economics (2013–2015).

Contributors

Kiran Banga Chhokar Independent Consultant, Education for Sustainable Development, New Delhi, India

Kanihar Kant Centre for the Studies of Social System, Jawaharlal Nehru University, New Delhi, India

Animesh Kumar UNISDR Regional Office for Asia and Pacific, Bangkok, Thailand

Itishree Pattnaik Gujarat Institute of Development Research (GIDR), Ahmedabad, India

Sanjay Pratap Indian Institute of Public Administration, New Delhi, India

N. C. Saxena Former Secretary, Planning Commission, GOI, New Delhi, India

Acronyms

ADB	Asian Development Bank
AHDI	Augmented Human Development Index
AIDS	Acquired immune deficiency syndrome
AIE	Alternative and Innovative Education
ANM	Auxiliary Nurse and Midwife
ASHAs	Accredited Social Health Activists
AVARD	Association of Voluntary Agencies for Rural Development
AWCs	Anganwadi centres
AWH	Anganwadi helper
AWW	Anganwadi worker
AYUSH	Ayurveda, Yoga, Unani, Siddha and Homeopathy
BACKD	Village belonging to Backward District
BMI	Body mass index
BPL	Below poverty line
BRICS	Brazil, Russia, India, China and South Africa
BY	Base year
CAG	Comptroller and Auditor General
CBHI	Central Bureau of Health Intelligence
CBOs	Community-based organisations
CCUs	Critical care units
CDPOs	Child Development Programme Officers
CED	Chronic energy deficiency
CGHS	Central Government Health Scheme
CHCs	Community Health Centres
CMDR	Centre for Multi-disciplinary Development Research
CMNNDs	Communicable, maternal, neonatal and nutritional diseases
CP	Chronic poor
CPI	Consumer price index
CPRC	Chronic Poverty Research Centre
CPRs	Common property resources

CRM	Common Review Mission
CSE	Centre for Science and Environment
CSS	Centrally Sponsored Schemes
DALY	Disability-adjusted life year
DCT	Direct cash transfer
DDAY	Deen Dayal Antyodaya Yojana
DHs	District hospitals
DIC	District Industries Centre
DISTANCE	Distance from the village to pucca (tarred) road
DOTS	Directly observed treatment short course
DPCE	Daily per capita expenditure
DPEP	District Primary Education Programme
DPOs	District Programme Officers
DPT	Diphtheria, pertussis and tetanus
EC	Emergency case
EDU	Level of Secondary Education captured by number of secondary schools in the village
EG	Economic growth
EGS	Education Guarantee Scheme/Employment Guarantee Scheme
FAO	Food and Agriculture Organization
FMR	Female-to-male ratio
FPS	Fair Price Shops
FRU	First Referral Unit
FTDs	Fever treatment depots
FYP	Five-Year Plan
GDI	Gender Development Index
GDP	Gross domestic product
GER	Gross Enrolment Ratio
GHI	Global Hunger Index
GIA	Level of % gross irrigated area to gross sown area
GOI	Government of India
GSDP	Gross State Domestic Product
HCR	Head count ratio
HDI	Human Development Index
HHDs	Households
HIG	Higher income group
HIV	Human immunodeficiency virus
HIV/AIDS	Human immunodeficiency virus and acquired immune deficiency syndrome
HP	Himachal Pradesh
HR	Haryana
HUNGaMA	Hunger and Malnutrition Report
HUPA	Ministry of Housing and Urban Poverty Alleviation
HW	Health worker
ICDS	Integrated Child Development Services

ICMR	Indian Council of Medical Research
ICRISAT	International Crops Research Institute for the Semi-Arid Tropics
ID	Identity
IFPRI	International Food Policy Research Institute
IGNDPS	Indira Gandhi National Disability Pension Scheme
IGNOAPS	Indira Gandhi National Old Age Pension Scheme
IGNWPS	Indira Gandhi National Widow Pension Scheme
IHDS	India Human Development Surveys
IIPA	Indian Institute of Public Administration
IMR	Infant mortality rate
IRDP	Integrated Rural Development Programme
ISKCON	International Society for Krishna Consciousness
ISS	Institute of Social Studies
ITCs	Industrial Training Centres
ITIs	Industrial Training Institutes
JE	Japanese encephalitis
JNURM	Jawaharlal Nehru National Urban Renewal Mission
J-PAL	Abdul Latif Jameel Poverty Action Lab
JSY	Janani Suraksha Yojana
KBK	Kalahandi, Bolangir and Koraput
KCAL	Kilocalorie
KISS	Kalinga Institute of Social Science
LBW	Low birth weight
LEB	Life expectancy at birth
MCP	Mother and Child Protection
MDG	Millennium Development Goal
MDGs	Millennium Development Goals
MDMS	Midday Meal Scheme
MGNREGA	Mahatma Gandhi National Rural Employment Guarantee Act
MGNREGS	Mahatma Gandhi National Rural Employment Guarantee Scheme
MHRD	Ministry of Human Resource Development
MMR	Maternal mortality ratio
MMUs	Mobile Medical Units
MNCs	Multinational corporations
MOHFW	Ministry of Health and Family Welfare
MoRD	Ministry of Rural Development
MOs	Medical officers
MoSPI	Ministry of Statistics and Programme Implementation
MP	Madhya Pradesh
MPCE	Monthly per capita consumption expenditure
MRP	Mixed recall period
MSP	Minimum Support Price
MT	Million tonnes
MWCD	Ministry of Women and Child Development
NAS	National Accounts Statistics

NCAER	National Council of Applied Economic Research
NCDs	Non-communicable diseases
NCEUS	National Commission for Enterprises in the Unorganised Sector
NCRL	National Commission on Rural Labour
NELM	New economics of labour migration
NFBS	National Family Benefit Scheme
NFHS	National Family and Health Survey
NFSA	National Food Security Act
NGO	Non-governmental organisation
NHM	National Health Mission
NIRD	National Institute of Rural Development
NITI Aayog	National Institute for Transformation of India Aayog
NLEP	National Leprosy Eradication Programme
NMR	Neonatal mortality rate
NNMB	National Nutrition Monitoring Bureau
NP	Non-poor
NPCB	National Programme for Control of Blindness
NREGA	National Rural Employment Guarantee Act
NREGS	National Rural Employment Guarantee Scheme
NRHM	National Rural Health Mission
NRLM	National Rural Livelihood Mission
NSAP	National Social Assistance Programme
NSDP	Net State Domestic Product
NSP	New sputum positive
NSS	National Sample Survey
NSSO	National Sample Survey Organisation
NUEPA	National University of Educational Planning and Administration
NULM	National Urban Livelihood Mission
NVBDCP	National Vector Borne Disease Control Programme
OBC	Other Backward Class
OBCs	Other Backward Classes
OECD	Organisation for Economic Co-operation and Development
OOPE	Out-of-pocket expenditures
OPD	Out-Patient Department
ORS	Oral rehydration salts
P	Poor
PAP	Proportion (per 1000) of ailing persons
PCNSDP	Per capita net state domestic product
PCSDP	Per capita state domestic product
PDS	Public distribution system
PHCs	Primary Health Centres
PLB	Poverty line basket
PMKVY	Pradhan Mantri Kaushal Vikas Yojana
PNCA	Level of net sown area per household
PPP	Public–private partnership/Purchasing Power Parity

PRIs	Panchayati Raj Institutions
PROBE	Public Report on Basic Education
PTR	Pupil–teacher ratio
PUCL	People's Union for Civil Liberties
PWD	Public Works Department
RDA	Recommended Dietary Allowances
RHS	Rural Health Statistics
RIP	Rural Industries Project
RIVER	Rishi Valley Institute for Educational Resources
RJ	Rajasthan
RMCs	Rural marketing centres
RMSA	Rashtriya Madhyamik Shiksha Abhiyan
RNTCP	Revised National TB Control Programme
RSBY	Rashtriya Swasthya Bima Yojana
RSOC	Rapid Survey on Children
RTE	Right to Education
RY	Reference year
SC	Scheduled Caste
SCs	Sub-centres
SCs	Scheduled Castes
SDG	Sustainable Development Goal
SDGs	Sustainable Development Goals
SDP	State Domestic Product
SECC	Socio-Economic Caste Census
SEQI	School Education Quality Index
SN	Supplementary Nutrition
SNP	Supplementary Nutrition Provisioning
SNs	Staff nurses
SRB	Sex ratio at birth
SRS	Sample Registration System
SSA	Sarva Shiksha Abhiyan
ST	Scheduled Tribe
STs	Scheduled Tribes
SWRC	Social Work Research Centre
TB	Tuberculosis
TE	Triennium ending
TFR	Total fertility rate
TP	Transient poor
TPDS	Targeted Public Distribution System
TRIPS	Trade-Related Aspects of Intellectual Property Rights
TSAE	Temporarily staying away for employment
U-5MR	Under-5 mortality rate
U-DISE	Unified District Information System for Education
UEE	Universalisation of Elementary Education
UN	United Nations

UNDP   United Nations Development Programme
UNESCO   United Nations Educational, Scientific and Culture Organization
UNICEF   United Nations Children's Fund
UP   Uttar Pradesh
URP   Uniform Recall Period
USA   United States of America
USD   United States dollar
UTs   Union territories
VET   Vocational education and training
VISIZE   Size of the village captured though number of households
WB   West Bengal
WCD   Women and Child Development
WHO   World Health Organization
WTO   World Trade Organization
WVDP   Whole Village Development Plan

List of Figures

Chapter 4

Fig. 1 Percentage of rural households by selected measures
        of poverty   59
Fig. 2 Per capita annual foodgrain production (kg)   62
Fig. 3 Average per capita daily availability of foodgrains in India
        during the last four decades.   63
Fig. 4 Daily average calorie and protein intake per capita across MPCE
        fractile rural classes in 2011–12   65

Chapter 5

Fig. 1 Map of Muzaffarpur district.   101
Fig. 2 Instruments of Gram Swaraj   107
Fig. 3 Post-conflict programmes in Mushahari.   107
Fig. 4 Land distribution structure in the region   118
Fig. 5 Reasons for incidence of migration   121

Chapter 7

Fig. 1 Selected health outcome indicators: five best and worst
        performing large states in 2015–16.   167

List of Tables

Chapter 2

Table 1	Trends in poverty	11
Table 2	Rural and urban poverty lines 1973–74 to 2011–12: consumption expenditure per capita per month (Rs) in current prices	13
Table 3	Poverty lines adopted for measuring HCR in different periods	15
Table 4	Percentage change in the poverty line per year over the period from the previous survey year to the reporting year	16
Table 5	India poverty head count ratio at $1.90 a day (2011 PPP) (% of population)	17
Table 6	Incidence of poverty across social groups: HCR	19
Table 7	Incidence of poverty across social groups from a panel survey: HCR	19
Table 8	State population below the poverty line, 2011–12	20
Table 9	Spatial concentration of India's poor	21
Table 10	HDI and GDI scores for states/UTs, 2006	22
Table 11	Fifty-two most deprived districts	23
Table 12	State-wise distribution of selected aspirational districts	24
Table 13	Rural households suffering from each of the seven specific deprivations	27
Table 14	Multidimensional poverty index (MPI) and population in multidimensional poverty	29
Table 15	Poverty status and poverty band, 2004–05	32

Chapter 3

Table 1   Drivers, maintainers and interrupters of chronic poverty   41
Table 2   Mobility of households across consumption expenditure
           groups   45

Chapter 4

Table 1   Country global hunger index scores by rank   56
Table 2   Growth in real average per capita monthly expenditure on all
           goods and on food (in Rs) at 1993–94 prices   61
Table 3   Changes in per capita cereal consumption (kg per month) in
           since 1993–94 for different MPCE classes: all-India, rural   61
Table 4   Mean per capita consumption of calories, protein and fats   64
Table 5   Recommended dietary allowance (RDA) for Indians   65
Table 6   Nutrition status of Indian adults, 1975–79 to
           2011–12 (BMI)   67
Table 7   Production, procurement and offtake of foodgrains
           (in million tonnes)   78
Table 8   Provisions for nutritional security and entitlements in the act to
           special groups   79
Table 9   Percentage of severely malnourished children in 2013–14
           according to UNICEF and State Governments   86

Chapter 5

Table 1   Comparative levels of poverty in Bihar and India   114
Table 2   Caste profile of the selected villages   116
Table 3   Occupational distribution in the region   117
Table 4   Incidence of landless and marginal peasants, by caste   119

Chapter 6

Table 1   Migration in India (2007–08): a snap shot   131
Table 2   Migration rates by categories, 1983–2007–08   132
Table 3   Distribution of migrants by MPCE classes
           (per 1000 population)   134
Table 4   Linkages between short duration migration and poverty   136
Table 5   Incidence of seasonal migration across states   141
Table 6   Short-term migration from the sample villages results
           of the logit model   142
Table 7   Flow of migration in Madhya Pradesh   145

Chapter 7

Table 1   Comparing achievements on life expectancy at birth, maternal
           mortality ratio, under-5 mortality rate and neonatal mortality
           rate for selected countries in 2015.   157
Table 2   Tuberculosis, malaria and HIV: comparing India with selected
           countries   158
Table 3   Contribution of disease categories to DALYs and to deaths,
           1990 and 2016 (%)   159
Table 4   Contribution of disease categories to DALYs, 1990
           and 2016 (%)   160
Table 5   Proportion (per 1000) of ailing persons (PAP) during
           last 15 days: rural and urban.   161
Table 6   Number (per 1000) of persons reporting ailment during
           last 15 days by gender   161
Table 7   Proportion (number per 1000) of ailing persons in selected
           states by gender   162
Table 8   Treatment of childhood diseases (children under age
           5 years).   163
Table 9   Anaemia among children and adults   163
Table 10   Contribution of different disease categories to death
           in 2016   164
Table 11   Performance of large states on neonatal mortality rate (NMR),
           under-5 mortality rate (UMR), total fertility rate (TFR), low
           birth weight (LBW) and sex ratio at birth (SRB) in base year
           (BY) 2014–15 and reference year (RY) 2015–16   166
Table 12   Health outcomes and health expenditures in selected
           countries   168
Table 13   Key health financing indicators for India across NHA
           rounds.   169
Table 14   Percentage distribution of persons by coverage of health
           expenditure support for each quintile class of usual monthly
           per capita consumption expenditure in 2014   170
Table 15   Average total medical expenditure (Rs) for treatment per
           hospitalization case (EC) during stay at hospital   170
Table 16   NRHM: targets and achievement on IMR, MMR and other
           indicators.   172
Table 17   Mortality rates due to tuberculosis and measles in India, China
           and Bangladesh.   176
Table 18   Coverage of rural health infrastructure (as on
           31 March 2016)   176
Table 19   Number of sub-centre, PHCs and CHCs functioning
           in India   176
Table 20   Doctors at PHCs   177

Table 21   Number of sub-centres without ANMs or health workers
           (as on 31 March 2016) 178
Table 22   Vacancies of medical officers and staff 179
Table 23   Functional FRUs, 24 × 7 PHCs and CCUs 181
Table 24   Maternal and child health 182
Table 25   Delivery care (for births in the 5 years before the survey) 182
Table 26   Immunization 183
Table 27   Percentage distribution of cases of hospitalized treatment
           received from public sector and private sector hospitals for
           rural and urban areas................................... 184

Chapter 8
Table 1   Broad indicators of education 206
Table 2   Literacy rate in India................................. 208
Table 3   Percentage distribution of persons of age 15 years
           and above by completed level of education................ 209
Table 4   State-wise literacy rate 210
Table 5   Two-way link of literacy and poverty.................... 211
Table 6   Coefficient of correlation between education and poverty 212
Table 7   Two way link of literacy and PCNSDP 213
Table 8   Adult population (age 15 years and above) with secondary
           and higher education, by economic groups, 1995–96 214
Table 9   Poverty and education among social groups 215
Table 10   Education level of household head and dynamics
           of poverty 216
Table 11   Government expenditure on education, 1960–61
           to 2010–11 220
Table 12   Education: Important laws, policies, commissions,
           constitutional provisions and programmes................. 229
Table 13   State-wise poverty ratio, literacy rate and per capita net state
           domestic product...................................... 235

Chapter 9
Table 1   SDG1 – end poverty in all its forms everywhere 242
Table 2   Variation in monthly pension reaching the
           vulnerable (in Rs) 245
Table 3   Employment and wages under MGNREGA in recent years 247

List of Boxes

Chapter 2

Box 1   Below Poverty Line Census Results, 2002 and 2010   25

Chapter 5

Box 1   Jaiprakash Narayan's First Open Letter to the Locals During his
        Mushahari Stay   105

Box 2   Second Open Letter of Jaiprakash Narayan to the Locals
        During his Mushahari Stay   110

Chapter 1
Introduction

Aasha Kapur Mehta, Shashanka Bhide, Anand Kumar and Amita Shah

1 Introduction

Poverty reduction continues to remain an unmet goal even though it has been an important policy objective at both national and global levels. Despite rapid growth, infrastructure development and investments in health and education over a substantial period of time, an unacceptably high proportion of our population continues to suffer severe and multidimensional deprivation and remains vulnerable to losing whatever gains have been made when there are shocks to livelihoods. The need to "end poverty, ignorance, disease and inequality of opportunity" was stressed in the

---

With necessary permissions, this chapter draws on Chapter 1 of the India Chronic Poverty Report (2011); and Mehta (2013) Poverty: Promises Made and Miles to Go, Yojana, August, pp. 47–50.

The views expressed in the book are the authors' and not necessarily of the institutions to which they are affiliated.

A. K. Mehta (✉)
Indian Institute of Public Administration, New Delhi, India
e-mail: aasha2006@gmail.com

S. Bhide
Madras Institute of Development Studies, Chennai, India

A. Kumar
Indian Institute of Advanced Study, Shimla, India

A. Shah
Center for Development Alternatives, Ahmedabad, India

© Springer Nature Singapore Pte Ltd. 2018
A. K. Mehta et al. (eds.), *Poverty, Chronic Poverty and Poverty Dynamics*,
https://doi.org/10.1007/978-981-13-0677-8_1

speeches right from the days of the Constituent Assembly.[1] In his address on Independence Day, 15 August 1947, Dr. Rajendra Prasad asked that Indians resolve to create the conditions to enable all individuals to develop and rise to their fullest stature, such that poverty, squalor, ignorance and ill health would vanish and the distinction between high and low and between rich and poor would disappear. He additionally hoped that religion would be practised freely and would not divide and separate, that untouchability would be forgotten, that "exploitation of man by man" would cease, that those who were "backward" would catch up with others and that there would be no hunger.

Whether we view the above statements as pledges, visions or plans, it is clear that ending poverty, ignorance, disease and inequality of opportunity was identified as a major priority for an independent India. Over the years since Independence, concerns and commitments regarding reducing, ameliorating and eliminating poverty have been expressed repeatedly at the highest level. However, the goal of making poverty, squalor, ignorance and ill health vanish from India has been elusive.

Six decades after Independence, in his Foreword to the Eleventh Plan (2007–12), Prime Minister Manmohan Singh said:

> the benefits of rapid growth, in terms of income and employment, must be "adequately shared by the poor and weaker sections of our society, especially the Scheduled Castes (SCs) and the Scheduled Tribes (STs), Other Backward Classes (OBCs) and minorities". For this, "growth must occur not just in our major cities but also in our villages and small towns. It must be spread across all states and not just limited to some. It must generate sufficient volumes of high quality employment to provide the means for uplift of large numbers of our population from the low income low quality occupations in which too many of them have been traditionally locked." He reiterated that "the higher rate of growth that we have set out for ourselves, coupled with our thrust on the growth process being inclusive, should ensure that the struggle for the removal of chronic poverty, ignorance, and disease will register major gains in the Eleventh Plan."

The Twelfth Plan (2012–17) was subtitled "Faster, More Inclusive and Sustainable Growth". Referring to the official estimates of poverty (based on the Tendulkar Committee recommendations), it notes that:

> There is no doubt that the Tendulkar Committee poverty line represents a very low level of consumption and the scale of poverty even on this basis is substantial.

More recently, the Cabinet Secretariat Press Note dated 1 January 2015 regarding constitution of the NITI Aayog states, "Poverty elimination remains one of the most important metrics by which alone we should measure our success as a nation".

At the turn of the century, the Millennium Development Goals sought to "eliminate extreme poverty and hunger". Today, Sustainable Development Goal 1 (SDG) aims to "end poverty in all its forms everywhere". The international targets associated with SDG1 require the following by 2030:

---

[1]See https://cadindia.clpr.org.in/constitution_assembly_debates/volume/5/1947-08-15. Accessed 15th May 2018.

- Eradicate extreme poverty for all people everywhere, currently measured as people living on less than $1.25 a day.
- Reduce at least by half the proportion of men, women and children of all ages living in poverty in all its dimensions according to national definitions.
- Implement nationally appropriate social protection systems and measures for all, including floors, and achieve substantial coverage of the poor, and the vulnerable, ensure that all men and women, in particular the poor and the vulnerable, have equal rights to economic resources, as well as access to basic services, ownership and control over land and other forms of property, inheritance, natural resources, appropriate new technology and financial services, including microfinance.
- Build the resilience of the poor and those in vulnerable situations, and reduce their exposure and vulnerability to climate-related extreme events and other economic, social and environmental shocks and disasters.

However, SDG1 or "ending poverty in all its forms everywhere" cannot be achieved unless policies and poverty alleviation programmes understand and address poverty, chronic poverty and the dynamics of poverty. This requires that we estimate the extent of poverty accurately, understand the factors that lead to people getting stuck in it and how this can be addressed. It also requires understanding the dynamic nature of poverty or the fact that many of those who are poor are able to move out of poverty as well as the fact that many others who are not poor become impoverished. These are the issues that are examined and addressed in this book.

The book draws on the available literature, including earlier contributions of the authors of the chapters on the poverty dynamics, the process of poverty reduction, persistence of poverty or chronic poverty, escape from poverty and descent into poverty.

2 Poverty Trends, Measures and the SDGs

What is India's performance on poverty reduction? While it is indisputable that poverty has declined, or that numerous initiatives have been undertaken to supplement the means of livelihood of the poor, the reduction has been well below what was anticipated. Regardless of what poverty line is used, it is clear that poverty remains a massive problem in the Indian context. Drawing attention to global references to the "frugality" of India's official poverty line, Chap. 2 points out that India's poverty trends and estimates pertain to extreme poverty. If poverty lines are raised to realistic – instead of subsistence – levels, the percentage of poor will be much larger than the present estimates. It is important to note that a significant proportion of those who are above the poverty line are vulnerable to falling into poverty. The first step in tackling poverty is that we acknowledge the extent of poverty and measure it.

While poverty rates have declined over the years, continued persistence of high rates, especially for some regions and social groups, is indicative of the intractability or stubbornness of poverty in such cases and the lack of responsiveness to overall or average economic growth and development. Chapter 2 discusses these issues and also highlights the multidimensional nature of poverty, its concentration among specific socio-economic groups and geographic locations and the correlates or household-level social and economic characteristics and village or district features that are closely associated with poverty in rural India.

3 Poverty Dynamics

The process of poverty reduction is dynamic and while many of those who are poor are stuck in poverty over a considerable period of time, a large proportion is able to escape from it. Still, others who are not poor become poor due to suffering shocks such as ill health or crop failure due to drought or floods. SDG1 or "ending poverty in all its forms everywhere" cannot be achieved unless policies and programmes for poverty alleviation address chronic poverty and the dynamics of poverty. This requires that we estimate the extent of the problem as well as understand the factors that lead to people getting stuck in poverty, those enabling escape from it and those causing the non-poor to get impoverished. In other words, it requires understanding the dynamic nature of poverty and how this can be addressed. Poverty dynamics and the drivers, maintainers and interrupters of poverty are discussed in Chap. 3.

4 Hunger and Poverty

Poverty has many dimensions, and it is seen in many forms. Ending poverty in all its forms is the running thread that binds all the SDGs together. For example, SDG2 is concerned with ending hunger. Not only is hunger the starkest form of poverty, but it is additionally both a cause and an effect of poverty. Hunger in India has gender and age dimensions too. Women, children and old people are less likely to get full nutritious meals needed for their development when the food is scarce. There are important seasonal variations in nutritional and health status depending on the cycle of agricultural work and extent of dependence of the poor on agricultural work for livelihood. Hunger and starvation also have regional or geographical dimensions. Tribal regions in India have a higher incidence of food insecurity than the non-tribal regions in the same state. Endemic hunger continues to afflict a large proportion of the Indian population, and the puzzles of increased food production, availability of subsidised food and at the same time prevalence of hunger in different forms pose challenges to policies that seek to eliminate hunger. These issues are discussed in Chap. 4.

5 Conflict and Poverty

Chapter 5 of the book draws attention to the conflict that has affected a number of states and districts in India. One of the consequences has been a vicious circle of chronic poverty and conflict between extremists and the state agencies. While there are changes in the level of poverty and the conflicts, understanding the interrelationships is important while designing policies that can lead to significant reduction in poverty.

From the perspective of the political sociology of poverty, there are four major results in such districts. These are radicalisation of economic conflict and marginalisation of parliamentary political organisations; criminalisation of political processes (like elections) and politicisation of criminal activities; flight of capital and decline in the entrepreneurial climate; and externalisation of victims of poverty through migration and ethnic exclusion and such outcomes not beneficial for integrated solutions. It points out that poverty-based conflicts contribute towards at least six forms of deficits in the functioning of any polity in a democratic set-up, i.e., development deficit, governance deficit, legitimacy deficit, democracy deficit, citizenship deficit, and nation-building deficit. The chapter also highlights the importance of finding participatory solutions based on consultations with men and women of various classes, castes and communities and studying the causes of distress and destitution. It then analyses a strategy that was successful in addressing poverty emanating from situations of conflict based on plans for integrated rural development to address the twin challenges of chronic poverty and class violence.

6 Migration as a Coping Mechanism

Migration is a critical coping mechanism among the poor. Chapter 6 draws attention to the structural barriers operating on both the demand and the supply side with regard to migration. In addition to being constrained by lack of education, discrimination and a hostile policy environment that are discussed in the literature, it highlights the persistence of poverty among migrants in India due to the stagnant agricultural and rural economy, limited job expansion in non-farm activities in urban areas and the sociocultural barriers resulting in high non-economic costs and hence low revealed preference for migration among certain segments of population. Whereas the first may get manifested in terms of limited demand and overcrowding, the latter may get reflected in limited supply and/or high reservation price despite the labour surplus situation prevailing in most parts of the rural economy in the country.

It argues that approaches that focus on either supporting migrant workers to facilitate improvements in the outcomes of migration especially in urban areas or on checking distress-related migration from rural areas seem to work in isolation without taking into consideration the continuum between rural and urban areas, economies and poverty. The discussion on migration, with special focus on the poor, must take a dynamic view of the changing realities in both rural and urban areas. This would help in resolving several of the dichotomies in the existing literature on migration, viz. migrants versus non-migrants, distress versus accumulation motives, lifetime versus circular migration, rural versus urban development, preventive versus facilitating migration, and economic versus human welfare. This would necessitate deeper understanding of the changing scenarios in both rural and urban areas and their influence on migration decisions and the outcomes thereof. In the absence of this, merely tracing the extent, pattern and streams of migratory flows may not help in addressing the issue of migration and development in a dynamic context.

7 Ill Health and Poverty

Chapter 7 draws attention to the strong link between SDG1 and SDG3, i.e. "end poverty in all its forms everywhere", and "ensure healthy lives and promote well-being for all at all ages". It argues that unless concerted efforts are made to substantially reduce poverty, disease burden and mortality rates in India, SDG1 and SDG3 will not be achieved either nationally or globally.

The state of health and health care in India is grim. Extreme poverty, disease burden, morbidity and mortality levels are significant. More than half of India's children and women are anaemic, and more than a third of children below the age of five are malnourished. Government spending on health care in India is among the lowest in the world at only 1.15% of GDP. Financial support for medical emergencies is abysmal as 86% of Indians living in rural and 82% in urban areas lack health insurance. Access to public provisioning of health care is limited, and out of pocket expenditure on health is extremely high.

Further, the sudden onset of a long and expensive illness can drive households that are not poor into poverty due to high costs of accessing health care combined with loss of income due to inability to work. Ill health creates immense stress even among those who are financially secure. High health care costs force households to sell the meagre assets they own and additionally borrow money in order to try and save family members who suffer from a serious illness. Since most households do not have insurance, they are forced to borrow at usurious interest rates or sell meagre assets to cover expenses. This can lead to intergenerational transmission of poverty. It is in this context that public provisioning of good quality health care is extremely important.

It presents a comparative status of India's health outcomes and high disease burden, provides an overview of national and state-wise morbidity and spatial differences in health outcomes, draws attention to the extremely low spending on health by the government and reviews the targets set for NRHM in 2005 against achievements in 2012 and 2015–16 in the context of health provisioning and disease burden. It also draws lessons regarding what does and does not work in the context of NRHM and ICDS for achievement of better health and nutrition outcomes.

8 Education and Poverty

Education can provide a pathway out of poverty if basic education is linked with skills and employment opportunities. Hence, Chap. 8 raises concerns regarding access for the chronically poor to education that is inclusive and empowering and that can enable them to exit poverty. It highlights the need to go beyond the dominant perspective on education and the state's role as a provider to it being a stimulator to promote community initiatives. Legislation and statutes are essential, but they need to be accompanied by an empowered community, especially of parents, to demand the rights of their children. In fact, communities could help in various ways other than just being a watchdog for the state machinery to perform and deliver. Identifying and creating space for spontaneous yet latent forces within the communities may help generate such dynamism from within. This may call for changing the value system of what matters in education; increasing the scope for local innovation and initiatives; and above all, creating their agency for making education inclusive and relevant. It also points out that increased privatisation, as envisaged by the recent policy approach, could hardly be an effective solution when it comes to including poor children into quality education on a mass scale.

It stresses the importance of focusing on quality and points out that the purpose of education has to be to empower through attainment of a sense of well-being rather than suffering exclusion at the start of the schooling system.

9 Achieving SDG1

The concluding Chap. 9 summarises the most critical policy issues that need to be addressed. It reviews two of the programmes identified by NITI Aayog as core of the core interventions for achieving an end to poverty in all its forms everywhere and explains why these interventions require considerable strengthening if SDG1 is to be achieved.

What have we achieved and what do need to do if we wish to achieve the SDG1 based elusive goal of ending poverty in India, SDG2 on ending hunger and SDG3 on health? This chapter discusses these issues and offers potential solutions.

---

10 Limitations

In order to retain the focus on dynamics of poverty, the book does not deal with the implications of some of the more recent approaches to the implementation of poverty reduction strategies that rely far more on technology and financial innovations.

A large proportion of those in poverty are the "working poor", for whom the state has not been able to meet its requirement to secure the right to an adequate means of livelihood. Hence, programmes for ameliorating poverty are important. However, the book does not address the implications of provision of subsidised goods and services in kind to the poor rather than cash support. The behavioural or motivational aspects of utilisation of resources within households or within social and economic groups may have an impact on the effectiveness of the poverty reduction programmes. These issues are not addressed in the present volume.

Chapter 2
Poverty Trends and Measures

Aasha Kapur Mehta and Shashanka Bhide

1 Introduction

It is undeniable that there has been a reduction in the proportion of India's population in poverty over the last five decades during which it has been measured and tracked in the country. However, the high incidence of poverty, the large number of those who are poor, combined with the multiple deprivations that the poor experience, makes this the most important development challenge that faces us.

Research, carried out by the scholars and other professionals, has highlighted which segments of the population are more vulnerable to poverty – seen across social groups, geographical locations, gender or the age groups. Governments and others have attempted to address these issues over the years through a plethora of programmes and policies, moving from targeted and single objective approaches to more universal and 'convergence-oriented' approaches. The global efforts to reduce poverty have been articulated in the Millennium Development Goals and more recently the Sustainable Development Goals.

With necessary permissions, this chapter draws on Chap. 2 of the India Chronic Poverty Report (2011); Mehta and Bhide (2010); Mehta (2013); and Mehta (2017).

A. K. Mehta (✉)
Indian Institute of Public Administration, New Delhi, India
e-mail: aasha2006@gmail.com

S. Bhide
Madras Institute of Development Studies, Chennai, India

© Springer Nature Singapore Pte Ltd. 2018
A. K. Mehta et al. (eds.), *Poverty, Chronic Poverty and Poverty Dynamics*,
https://doi.org/10.1007/978-981-13-0677-8_2

The persistence of poverty in certain specific socio-economic and regional groups of population has also meant that it is not only one generation of household members that suffer from poverty, but that children in these poor households may also grow up as poor. This intergenerational persistence of deprivations makes the goal of poverty reduction ever more imperative.

In this chapter, we provide a brief review of the estimates of poverty to highlight the scale and complexity of the challenge of poverty reduction before the country.

In Sect. 2 of this chapter, we discuss the trends in the poverty head count ratio as well as poverty lines and methods used to measure it. Section 3 draws attention to the fact that poverty is concentrated in certain parts of India, among particular social groups and among certain occupations. An understanding of the geographical, sociological and economic concentrations of poverty is important for an assessment of the type of policy approaches that can reach the poor. Section 4 of the chapter identifies the factors that explain the incidence of poverty. Section 5 outlines the importance of initial conditions in explaining the limited impact of growth on poverty reduction. Section 6 draws attention to the bands of vulnerability presented by the National Commission for Enterprises in the Unorganised Sector (NCEUS). Section 7 concludes the chapter.

2 Trends in Poverty: Incidence and Determinants

The head count ratio (HCR), or percentage of population below the poverty line, is an important indicator of the extent of poverty in a country. Before a problem can be addressed, the size of the problem must be known. The HCR is used to track progress in reducing poverty as well as design programmes to alleviate it. How many Indians are poor? What is the percentage of India's population that is below the poverty line? The answer to these questions depends on how poverty is measured.

Traditionally, discussion regarding the extent of poverty and poverty trends in India is based on estimates of the head count ratio determined on the basis of household sample surveys conducted on a quinquennial basis by the National Sample Survey Organisation (NSSO). The official poverty estimates, patterns and trends in poverty are determined on the basis of analysis of data on household consumption expenditures on which poverty lines are juxtaposed to separate the poor from the non-poor and determine the extent of poverty. Detailed data on consumer expenditure from nationally representative samples are available from the early 1970s to the present at intervals of approximately 5 years.[1]

---

[1]The National Sample Surveys began in the 1950s with the launching of the first nationwide survey of household expenditures in 1950.

Table 1 Trends in poverty

Year	No. of poor (in million)			% population below poverty line			% of rural poor in total poor
	Rural	Urban	Total	Rural	Urban	Total	
1973–74 (L)	261.3	60.0	321.3	56.44	49.01	54.9	81.3
1977–78 (L)	264.3	64.6	328.9	53.07	45.24	51.3	80.4
1983 (L)	252.0	70.9	322.9	45.65	40.79	44.5	78.0
1987–88 (L)	231.9	75.2	307.1	39.09	38.20	38.9	75.51
1993–94 (L)	244.0	76.3	320.3	37.27	32.26	36.0	76.2
2004–05 (L)	220.9	80.8	301.7	28.3	25.7	27.5	73.2
1993–94 (T)	328.0	74.4	402.4	50.1	31.5	45.2	80.6
2004–05 (T)	325.8	81.4	407.2	41.8	25.7	37.2	80.0
2009–10 (T)	278.2	76.4	354.7	33.8	20.9	29.8	78.5
2011–12 (T)	214.1	51.6	265.7	25.7	13.7	21.9	80.6
2009–10 (R)	325.93	128.6	454.6	39.6	26.4	38.2	71.7
2011–12 (R)	260.52	102.47	362.99	30.9	26.4	29.5	71.8

Notes (1) 'L' refers to the methodology recommended by the Expert Group headed by Prof. Lakdawala for the measurement of poverty; 'T' refers to the methodology recommended by the Expert Group headed by Prof. S. R. Tendulkar; 'R' refers to the methodology recommended by the Expert Group headed by Prof. C. R. Rangarajan. We have not included here the estimates for 1999–00 because of the changes in the recall period used to elicit responses from the households on their expenditures in this round as compared to the previous rounds. The estimates for 1993–94 for Tendulkar methodology are from Dev (2013, Annexure Table A 12.4)

Ten large sample consumer surveys have been conducted by the NSS on a quinquennial basis since 1973–1974. Poverty measured in terms of HCR registered a sustained decline over the 30-year period from 1973–74 to 2004–05, during which it halved from 54.9 to 27.5%. It declined further to 21.9% in 2011–12 (Table 1). However, it is important to note that the estimates of poverty presented in Table 1 are based on poverty lines computed by using three different methods. Estimates for 1973–74 to 2004–05 are based on the recommendations of the Lakdawala Committee (Planning Commission 1979); for 1993–94 to 2011–12 on the Tendulkar Committee (Planning Commission 2009); and for 2009–10 and 2011–12 on the Rangarajan Committee (Planning Commission 2014). These are discussed in Sect. 1 below.

Whether 27.5% of India's population was in poverty in 2004–05 or whether the estimate was 37.2% depends on the poverty line that is applied. If the poverty line is computed on the basis of the method suggested by the Lakdawala Committee, then 27.5% of the population was in poverty in 2004–05. If, however, the methodology suggested by the Tendulkar Committee is used to compute the poverty line, 37.2% Indians were living in poverty in this year. The basis for computing the poverty lines that lead to these different estimates of the percentage of the population that is in poverty is outlined in the section below.

2.1   The Poverty Line

Planning Commission constituted a Task Force to estimate poverty in 1977. On the basis of a systematic study of nutritional requirements, the Task Force submitted a report in which it recommended separate national-level poverty lines for rural and urban areas.

Based on observed consumer behaviour in 1973–74, it estimated that, on average, consumer expenditure of Rs 49.63 per capita per month was associated with a calorie intake of 2400 per capita per day in rural areas. Correspondingly, Rs 56.76 per capita per month was associated with a calorie intake of 2100 per capita per day in urban areas. The poverty line for subsequent years was estimated by adjusting the poverty line for the base year of 1973–74 for inflation (Planning Commission 1979).

In 1989, the Planning Commission constituted an Expert Group to review the methodology used for the assessment of poverty (Planning Commission 1993). It recommended:

- Continuation of the calorie-based consumption expenditure as a cut-off to determine the proportion of population below the poverty line;
- Disaggregation of national poverty lines into state poverty lines and then updating them using the Consumer Price Index (CPI) for industrial workers in urban areas and the CPI for agricultural labour in rural areas;
- Discontinuation of adjustment for the difference between NSS estimates of mean consumption expenditure and the National Accounts Statistics (NAS) estimate, because of increasing divergence between the two and because the adjustment increased the level of consumption expenditure for all households and decreased the estimated rate of poverty as compared with unadjusted data.

However, questions have remained regarding the adequacy of the poverty line that has been adopted. A large body of the literature questions the accuracy of official estimates of poverty on various counts: consumption patterns underlying the rural and urban poverty line basket (PLB) remain tied down to those observed in 1973–74; changes in the consumption pattern of the poor are not reflected in the poverty lines; use of the CPI for agricultural labourers understates the price rise for the rural population and hence the extent of rural poverty relative to urban poverty; the state is assumed to provide basic social services of health and education [although private expenditure on education and health was covered in the base year of 1973–74, no account has been taken either of the increase in the proportion of this in total expenditure over time or of its proper representation in available price indices (Planning Commission 2009)]. There are issues of consistency between the national accounts and sample survey data; deviation of the official poverty lines from their original definition based on minimum calorie norms; unrealistically large ratios of official rural–urban poverty lines in subsequent years compared with the

Table 2 Rural and urban poverty lines 1973–74 to 2011–12: consumption expenditure per capita per month (Rs) in current prices

Year	Rural poverty line (Rs per capita per month)	Urban poverty line (Rs per capita per month)
1973–74 (Lakdawala)	49.3	56.76
1977–78 (Lakdawala)	56.4	70.33
1983 (Lakdawala)	89.5	115.65
1987–88 (Lakdawala)	115.2	162.16
1993–94 (Lakdawala)	205.84	281.35
1999–00[a]	327.56	454.11
2004–05 (Lakdawala)	356.30	538.6
2004–05 (Tendulkar)	446.68	578.80
2009–10 (Tendulkar)	673	860
2009–10 (Rangarajan)	801	1198
2011–12 (Tendulkar)	816	1000
2011–12 (Rangarajan)	972	1407

Note [a]Estimates for 1999–00 are based on the mixed recall period (MRP) method and are not comparable with estimates for earlier years which are based on the uniform recall period (URP) or Lakdawala method

Sources Planning Commission various years; Press Information Bureau various years; Tendulkar Committee Report (Planning Commission 2009), Rangarajan Committee Report (Planning Commission 2014)

initial 1973–74 ratio; lack of comparability of estimates from the 1999–00 survey of consumer expenditure and subsequent surveys due to changes in method, etc.[2]

Sen (2005) argued that these poverty lines are 'not arbitrary figures, but have been derived from age-sex-occupation-specific nutritional norms by using the all-India demographic data from the 1971 Census…based explicitly on estimates of the normative nutritional requirement of the average person in the rural and urban areas of the country separately'.

Table 2 presents Planning Commission estimates of poverty lines separately for rural and urban areas over the period from 1973–74 to 2011–12. Poverty lines for the period 1973–74 to 1993–94 and 2004–05 are computed on the basis of the Lakdawala Committee method; for 2004–05, 2009–10 and 2011–12 on the basis of the Tendulkar Committee method; and for 2009–10 and 2011–12 also based on the Rangarajan Committee method. These poverty lines have been used to determine incidence of poverty at different points of time since 1973–74.

Two fundamental problems have been raised in the literature with regard to the poverty lines. First is the lack of correspondence of poverty lines to consumption of 2400 kcal in rural and 2100 kcal in urban areas (Mehta and Venkatraman 2000; Sen 2005; Srinivasan 2007; Patnaik 2007, 2010). Second, while dietary requirements are calculated on a 'scientific' basis according to bodily needs, this is not

---

[2]Himanshu (2010); Mehta and Shah (2001, 2003); Popli et al. (2005); Ray and Lancaster (2005).

applied to the non-food component of the poverty threshold so there is no guarantee of meeting basic non-food needs (Saith 2005). Serious concerns have been expressed especially regarding state budgetary allocations to and provisioning of health care (NRHM 2005). Ill health, and the need to spend large amounts on health care, exacerbates the suffering of those who are already poor and leads those who are not poor to poverty.[3]

Further, if nutrition is the underlying criterion of the poverty line, then it is shown from the same survey data which is used to define poverty line that even the population well above the poverty line may not be consuming the minimal requirement of calories.

In view of all of the above critiques and differences in views, the Planning Commission set up an Expert Group headed by Professor S. D. Tendulkar to re-examine the issue and suggest a new poverty line and poverty estimates. The Tendulkar Committee Report (Planning Commission 2009) recommended four major changes in the methodology for estimating poverty incidence:

1. A conscious move away from the calorie anchor while testing for the adequacy of actual food expenditure near the poverty line to ensure certain aggregate nutritional outcomes;
2. Using the same consumption basket for the rural poor as for the urban poor, but applying prices prevailing in rural areas to estimate the poverty line for rural areas. This exercise was done for each state, and estimates of the poor were then built to the national level for rural and urban areas;
3. A price adjustment procedure based predominantly on the same data set that underlies the poverty estimation and hence corrects for problems associated with externally generated and population segment-specific price indices with out-dated price and weight bases used so far in official poverty estimations;
4. Explicit provision in price indices for private expenditure on health and education, which has been rising over time, and testing for their adequacy to ensure certain desirable educational and health outcomes.

The Lakdawala Committee-based poverty line was set at Rs 356.30 per capita per month for rural areas and Rs 538.60 per capita per month for urban areas for 2004–05. The Tendulkar Committee raised the poverty line for 2004–05 from:

1. Rs 356.30 per capita per month based on previous assessment to Rs 446.68 or by Rs 90 per capita per month (rural);
2. Rs 538.60 per capita per month to Rs 578.80 or by Rs 40 per capita per month (urban).

The HCR correspondingly increased from 27.5 to 37.2% in 2004–05. In other words, small increases in the poverty line led to a massive increase in the estimated population in poverty of almost 10 percentage points, with 407.2 million people living below this subsistence-level poverty threshold.

---

[3]Duggal (2009); Mehta (2007, 2009); Mehta and Gupta (2005).

The Tendulkar Committee changed the basis for computing the poverty line. From the cut-off level of expenditure at which households are generally able to obtain food items that provide a certain number of calories of nutrition, the cut-off level of expenditure has now been delinked from the calorific intake of 2400 kcal in rural and 2100 kcal in urban areas. A miniscule amount has been added to accommodate consumption of certain basic services such as health, education and housing. The distinction between rural and urban requirements in computing the poverty line has also narrowed. There was dissatisfaction with the Tendulkar Committee methodology as well. Hence, the Rangarajan Committee was constituted in June 2012 and it redefined the poverty line.

Application of the Tendulkar Committee method to estimate poverty results in 29.8% of India's population or 355 million people living in poverty in 2009–10. In comparison, estimation of poverty based on application of the Rangarajan Committee method results in 38.2% of the population or 455 million Indians being in poverty in 2009–10 and 30% of the population or 363 million poor in 2011–12. It can therefore be concluded that small increases in this subsistence-level poverty line lead to massive increases in the proportion of the population that is estimated to be in poverty.

The trends show that when the methodology for defining the poverty line changed, the poverty lines, as well as the difference between the rural–urban poverty lines, changed considerably. For instance, application of the methodology recommended by the Tendulkar Committee to the poverty line for 2004–05 led to a 25% increase in the poverty line for rural areas and a 7.5% increase in the poverty line for urban areas, relative to those defined as per the methodology proposed by Lakdawala Expert Group. The Rangarajan Expert Group's approach led to an increase in the poverty line defined by Tendulkar Expert Group by 19% and 39.3% in 2009–10 for the rural and urban areas (Tables 3 and 4).

Table 3 Poverty lines adopted for measuring HCR in different periods

Year	Lakdawala Expert Group (Planning Commission 1993)		Tendulkar Expert Group (Planning Commission 2009)		Rangarajan Expert Group (Planning Commission 2014)	
	Rural	Urban	Rural	Urban	Rural	Urban
Consumption expenditure per capita per month (Rs) in current prices						
2004–05	356	539	447 (25.5%)	579 (7.5%)		
2009–10			673	860	801 (19.0%)	1198 (39.3%)
2011–12			816	1000	972	1407

Note Figures in parentheses indicate percentage change in poverty line between different rounds of revisions over the previous definition

Table 4 Percentage change in the poverty line per year over the period from the previous survey year to the reporting year

Reporting year	Percentage change in poverty line per year from the previous year to the reporting year					
	Rural	Urban	Rural	Urban	Rural	Urban
1977–78	1.48	2.35				
1983–84	3.34	3.67				
1987–88	2.78	3.74				
1993–94	4.29	4.07				
1999–2000	3.42	3.53				
2004–05	0.73	1.49				
2009–10			3.62	3.50		
2011–12			4.27	3.33	4.29	3.55

Note These are annualised rates of change based on the rates of poverty reported in Table 2

As shown in Table 1, significant changes in poverty lines have led to a sharp increase in the estimated percentage of the population that is classified as poor. However, the reduction in HCR using different approaches to define poverty line has been of similar order of magnitude when such poverty lines are available for the same time periods. For instance, the Rangarajan Expert Group methodology indicates a reduction in HCR by 8.7 percentage points between 2004–05 and 2011–12. The Tendulkar approach indicates a decline in HCR by 7.9 percentage points. Between 1993–94 and 2004–05, using Lakdawala methodology, the incidence of poverty for the aggregate population fell by 8.5 percentage points and for the same period HCR fell by 8 percentage points using the Tendulkar methodology. Hasan et al. (2013, p. 2) point out that the poverty rates are measured by expenditure, and expenditures have gone up for every percentile of the population when adjusted for price changes over time and across space.

The decline in HCR between 2004 and 2011 reported by the World Bank (Table 5) is comparable to the decline seen in the estimates by the Tendulkar approach. However, the decline of almost 10 percentage points between 2009 and 2011 is greater than that based on the estimates by Tendulkar (7.9%) and Rangarajan (6.7%) approaches. Hasan et al. (2013, p. 3) note the same pattern.

A Task Force on the Elimination of Poverty in India was set up by NITI Aayog on 16 March 2015 under the Chairmanship of Dr. Arvind Panagariya, Vice Chairman, NITI Aayog. The Task Force prepared a paper titled 'Eliminating Poverty: Creating Jobs and Strengthening Social Programs' (NITI Aayog 2016). The Task Force concluded that tracking poverty over time and space was the principal objective behind the measurement of poverty. It suggested the consideration of four options for tracking extreme poverty:

(i) Continue with the Tendulkar poverty line;
(ii) Switch to the Rangarajan or other higher rural and urban poverty lines;
(iii) Track progress over time of the bottom 30% of the population;

(iv) Track progress along specific components of poverty such as nutrition, housing, drinking water, sanitation, electricity and connectivity.

However, a decision in this regard is yet to be taken. The latest official estimate of poverty that is available is for 2011–12 based on the Tendulkar method. Additionally, estimates have been provided by the Committee headed by Prof. Rangarajan.

2.2   Global Standards for Measuring Extreme Poverty

The World Bank estimates of poverty were initially set at PPP $1 a day in 1990 and were the average of the poverty lines of the poorest 15 countries. This became the 'standard for measuring extreme poverty in the world' and the basis of MDG 1 to halve poverty by 2015 (Ravallion et al. 2008).

This was revised or adjusted each time a new set of PPPs were produced by the International Comparison Program – PPP $1.08 in 1993, PPP $1.25 a day in 2005 and PPP $1.90 in 2015.

Ravallion (2010) responding to Deaton (2010) points out that in 2005, $1.25 a day was the average line of the poorest 15 countries. Further, $1.00 a day at 2005 prices was very close to India's official poverty line and that 'India's official line is low by developing country standards', and it is a 'frugal line'.

The decline in the HCR based on this 'frugal line' that is representative of 'extreme' poverty for India is shown in Table 5. It is interesting to note that while the decline is 7.7 percentage points over 11 years between 1993 and 2004, it is 7.1 percentage points over 5 years between 2004 and 2009 and a massive 9.9 percentage points over only 2 years between 2009 and 2011.

Commenting on the PPP $1.90 per day that has been adopted by the SDGs Hickel (2015) points out that

$1.90 is not enough for basic human survival.... this amount of money is inadequate to achieve even the most basic nutrition. The US Department of Agriculture calculates that in 2011 the very minimum necessary to buy sufficient food was $5.04 per day. And that's not taking account of other requirements for survival, such as shelter and clothing.

He further points out that

The World Bank picked the $1.90 line because it's the average of the national poverty lines of the very poorest countries in the world, like Chad and Burundi. ...The bank itself admits that poverty in Latin America, for example, should be measured at about $6 a day. And yet for some reason it persists with the $1.90 line.

Table 5   India poverty head count ratio at $1.90 a day (2011 PPP) (% of population)

Year	1983	1987	1993	2004	2009	2011
HCR at $1.90 a day (2011 PPP)	53.9	44.8	45.9	38.2	31.1	21.2

Source World Bank available at: https://data.worldbank.org/indicator/SI.POV.DDAY

If we want to stick with a single international line, we might use the "ethical poverty line" devised by Peter Edward of Newcastle University. He calculates that in order to achieve normal human life expectancy of just over 70 years, people need roughly 2.7–3.9 times the existing poverty line. In the past, that was $5 a day. Using the bank's new calculations, it's about $7.40 a day. As it happens, this number is close to the average of national poverty lines in the global south.

Yet the SDGs use the $1.90 line to measure poverty even though it is an 'implausibly low threshold', perhaps because a 'more honest approach would force us to face up to the fact that the global economy simply is not working for the majority of humanity'.

The World Bank is now reporting poverty rates for all countries using two new international poverty lines: a lower middle-income international poverty line, set at $3.20/day, and an upper middle-income international poverty line, set at $5.50/day.

Regardless of what poverty line is used, it is clear that poverty remains a massive problem in the Indian context. If poverty lines are raised to realistic – instead of subsistence – levels, the percentage of poor will be much larger than the present estimates. A significant proportion of those who are above the poverty line are vulnerable to decline into poverty. The first step in tackling poverty then is that we acknowledge the extent of poverty and measure it. The potential for divergence of attention from addressing the poverty challenge because of the rise in the overall economic growth remains significant.

3 Social, Spatial and Occupational Concentration of Poverty

Estimates of incidence of poverty across social groups by the Planning Commission (2013a, b) also reflect large variations. The pattern of changes between 2004–05 and 2011–12 shows that the decline in poverty was faster in the case of Scheduled Castes than for Scheduled Tribes and Other Backward Castes. The pace of decline in HCR for all these three social groups exceeded that for the rural population as a whole and that for each of these groups in urban areas also. The incidence of poverty remains higher for ST, SC and OBC than for the 'other category' in both rural and urban areas in 2004–05 and 2011–12 (Table 6).

Findings of a panel study by Thorat et al. (2017) are presented in Table 7. These are for around the same period as the estimates provided in the Planning Commission report (Table 6). However, the reduction is somewhat greater for ST in this study and the incidence of poverty remains the highest for ST among the major social groups.

Table 6 Incidence of poverty across social groups: HCR

Social group	Rural			Urban		
	2004–05	2011–12	Decline from 2004–05 to 2011–12 (percentage points)	2004–05	2011–12	Decline from 2004–05 to 2011–12 (percentage points)
Scheduled Tribes	62.3	45.3	17.0	35.5	24.1	11.4
Scheduled Castes	53.5	31.5	22.0	40.6	21.7	18.9
Other Backward Castes	39.8	22.6	17.2	30.6	15.4	15.2
Others	27.1	15.5	11.6	16.1	8.2	7.9
All groups	41.8	25.7	16.1	25.7	13.7	12.0

Source Planning Commission (2013a). Available at: planningcommission.gov.in/reports/genrep/rep_pov1303.pdf (downloaded on 31 October 2017) and own estimates

Table 7 Incidence of poverty across social groups from a panel survey: HCR

Social group	2005	2012	Decline from 2005 to 2012 (percentage points)
Scheduled Tribes	65	42	23
Scheduled Castes	47	27	20
Other Backward Castes	38	20	18
Others	26	14	8
All groups	38	21	17

Source Based on Thorat et al. (2017)

Spatial Concentration of Poverty[4]

Geographical factors are important, and the chronically poor are likely to be concentrated in the poorest states in India, which may also ironically be abundant in natural resources and in districts where multidimensional deprivation is significant. Poverty persists in almost all states. However, the proportion of the poor who suffer long-duration poverty and intergenerational transmission is likely to be significantly higher in those parts of the country that have consistently suffered greater incidence of severe poverty and multidimensional deprivation over many years. Poor states, in terms of per capita state domestic product, have in general remained poor compared with others – and the inequalities among the states have certainly not diminished over time (Bandyopadhyay 2001; Shepherd et al. 2004).

As can be seen from Table 8, states/UTs with 30% or more of their population in poverty in 2011–12 are Chhattisgarh, Dadra and Nagar Haveli, Jharkhand,

[4]This section draws on Chap. 1 of Mehta and Shepherd (2006) and Mehta (2003).

Table 8 State population below the poverty line, 2011–12

State	HCR (%)	State	HCR (%)
Chhattisgarh	39.9	Tripura	14.0
Dadra and Nagar Haveli	39.3	Meghalaya	11.9
Jharkhand	37.0	Tamil Nadu	11.3
Manipur	36.9	Uttarakhand	11.3
Arunachal Pradesh	34.7	Haryana	11.2
Bihar	33.7	J&K	10.3
Orissa	32.6	Delhi	9.9
Assam	32.0	Daman and Diu	9.9
Madhya Pradesh	31.6	Puducherry	9.7
Uttar Pradesh	29.4	Andhra Pradesh	9.2
Chandigarh	21.8	Punjab	8.3
Karnataka	20.9	Sikkim	8.2
Mizoram	20.4	HP	8.1
West Bengal	20.0	Kerala	7.1
Nagaland	18.9	Goa	5.1
Maharashtra	17.4	Lakshadweep	2.8
Gujarat	16.6	A & N Islands	1.0
Rajasthan	14.7	All India	21.9

Source Planning Commission Press Note on poverty estimates 2011–12 dated 22 July 2013

Manipur, Arunachal Pradesh, Bihar, Orissa, Assam and Madhya Pradesh. Uttar Pradesh has 29.4% of its population in poverty.

The regional concentration of poverty has also been recognised in various policies since the early days of planning. For example, the Second Five-Year Plan (1956–1960) articulated balanced regional development as a key goal for India's development effort (Bhide and Srinivasan 2004). Drèze and Srinivasan (1996), in World Bank (1997), illustrate variations in poverty incidence within a state but, even so, high levels of poverty have persisted in Bihar, Orissa, Madhya Pradesh and Uttar Pradesh.

More than one-third of India's poor are located in Uttar Pradesh and Bihar (Table 9), in 2011–12. Just four states – Uttar Pradesh, Bihar, Madhya Pradesh and Maharashtra – account for more than half (52%) of India's poor. Panda (2008) points to the contiguous nature of 'high poverty states'.

Those who suffer poverty are deprived not just in terms of calorific intake and income, but in many dimensions. Table 10 presents HDI estimates for India and states/union territories (UTs) for 2006.

The scores on the Human Development Index and Gender Development Index also follow the pattern of the incidence of poverty. The lowest scores on HDI and GDI were achieved by Bihar, Uttar Pradesh, Madhya Pradesh, Orissa, Rajasthan, Chhattisgarh and Jharkhand. Most of these are states in which there is high income poverty.

Table 9 Spatial concentration of India's poor

State	(%) of India's poor located in state	State	(%) of India's poor located in state
Uttar Pradesh	22.17	J&K	0.49
Bihar	13.28	Uttarakhand	0.43
Madhya Pradesh	8.68	Manipur	0.38
Maharashtra	7.34	HP	0.21
West Bengal	6.86	Tripura	0.19
Orissa	5.13	Arunachal Pradesh	0.18
Karnataka	4.81	Nagaland	0.14
Jharkhand	4.61	Meghalaya	0.13
Chhattisgarh	3.86	Mizoram	0.09
Rajasthan	3.81	Chandigarh	0.09
Gujarat	3.79	Dadra and Nagar Haveli	0.05
Assam	3.75	Puducherry	0.04
Tamil Nadu	3.06	Goa	0.03
Andhra Pradesh	2.92	Sikkim	0.02
Haryana	1.07	Daman and Diu	0.01
Kerala	0.89	A & N Islands	0.00
Punjab	0.86	Lakshadweep	0.00
Delhi	0.63	All India	100.00

Source Computations based on Planning Commission Press Note on poverty estimates 2011–12 dated 22 July 2013

On the basis of incidence of poverty and certain other development parameters, the Planning Commission set up an Expert Committee in 1997 to identify the 100 most backward and poorest districts in the country. The broad parameters adopted to analyse the causes of backwardness included indicators of deprivation (poverty ratio) and social and economic infrastructure. Social infrastructure in rural areas was viewed in terms of: (1) availability of safe drinking water; (2) basic health facilities; and (3) housing facilities.

The Committee found that Bihar and Jharkhand had more than a third, or 38, of the poorest districts; Madhya Pradesh and Chhattisgarh 19; Uttar Pradesh and Uttarakhand 17; Orissa 4; and Rajasthan 2. It is important to note, though, that some of these districts were also found in Maharashtra (10), West Bengal (4), Karnataka (1), Haryana (1), Himachal Pradesh (1), Dadra and Nagar Haveli (1) and Sikkim (2).

Table 10 HDI and GDI scores for states/UTs, 2006

State	HDI score	GDI score	State	HDI score	GDI score
Bihar	0.507	0.479	Sikkim	0.665	0.659
Uttar Pradesh	0.528	0.509	Tamil Nadu	0.666	0.655
Madhya Pradesh	0.529	0.516	Himachal Pradesh	0.667	0.664
Orissa	0.537	0.524	Punjab	0.668	0.663
Rajasthan	0.541	0.526	Dadra and Nagar Haveli	0.677	0.673
Chhattisgarh	0.549	0.542	Mizoram	0.688	0.687
Jharkhand	0.574	0.558	Maharashtra	0.689	0.677
Andhra Pradesh	0.585	0.574	Lakshadweep	0.697	0.635
Jammu and Kashmir	0.590	0.568	Nagaland	0.700	0.677
Assam	0.595	0.585	Daman and Diu	0.700	0.697
Karnataka	0.622	0.611	Manipur	0.702	0.699
Meghalaya	0.629	0.624	Andaman and Nicobar Islands	0.708	0.692
Gujarat	0.634	0.624	Pondicherry	0.725	0.706
West Bengal	0.642	0.622	Delhi	0.740	0.701
Haryana	0.643	0.632	Goa	0.764	0.747
Arunachal Pradesh	0.647	0.642	Kerala	0.764	0.745
Uttarakhand	0.652	0.647	Chandigarh	0.784	0.763
Tripura	0.663	0.626	All India	0.605	0.590

Source Government of India (2009)
Note HDI refers to the Human Development Index and GDI refers to the Gender Development Index

While spatial inequalities exist at all levels of disaggregation, the extent of these varies with choice of indicator and the geographical space over which comparisons are made. Multidimensional deprivation was estimated for about 379 districts in 15 large states of India based on data for the early 1990s, using variables for which data were available at the district level and that reflect long-duration deprivation (Mehta 2003; Mehta et al. 2004). For example, persistent spatial variations in the IMR could be considered to reflect persistent deprivation in the means of accessing health care. This could be a result of several factors, such as inability to obtain medical care because of lack of income; lack of available healthcare facilities in the vicinity; poor quality drinking water, resulting in waterborne diseases that cause mortality; lack of roads and public transport that enable quick transportation to hospitals in case of emergency; or all of the above. Similarly, illiteracy could be considered a persistent denial of access to information, knowledge and voice. Low levels of agricultural productivity may reflect a poor resource base; low yields owing to lack of access to irrigation and other inputs; poor quality of soil resulting from erosion; or lack of access to resources for investment because of lack of

Table 11 Fifty-two most deprived districts

State	District	State	District
Assam (1)	Dhubri	Madhya Pradesh	West Nimar
Bihar (4)	Araria		Tikamgarh
	Kishanganj	Orissa (4)	Ganjam
	Palamu		Kalahandi
	Sitamarhi		Koraput
Madhya Pradesh (24)	Bastar		Phulbani
	Betul	Rajasthan (9)	Banswara
	Chhatarpur		Barmer
	Damoh		Bhilwara
	Datia		Dungarpur
	East Nimar		Jalore
	Guna		Jhalawar
	Jhabua		Pali
	Panna		Sirohi
	Raisen		Tonk
	Rajgarh	Uttar Pradesh (11)	Bahraich
	Ratlam		Banda
	Rewa		Basti
	Sagar		Budaun
	Satna		Etah
	Sehore		Gonda
	Shahdol		Hardoi
	Shajapur		Lalitpur
	Shivpuri		Shahjahanpur
	Sidhi		Siddarthnagar
	Surguja		Sitapur

Source Mehta (2003) and Mehta et al. (2004)

collateral or adverse climatic or market conditions. Poor quality of infrastructure reflects persistent denial of opportunities for income generation and growth.

While different lists of backward districts are available, Table 11 lists the 52 districts that suffer from the highest levels of persistent deprivation that are common to HDI and Augmented HDI (AHDI) methods of estimation. All the districts are from six of the seven states identified as having extensive rural poverty (Nath 2006).

Multiple deprivations that historically marginalised groups suffer make it harder for them to escape poverty, as different forms of poverty tend to be mutually reinforcing. Regions that are particularly likely to have large numbers of chronically poor people include tribal and forested (or degraded forest) regions, much of which are in the central and eastern 'poverty heartlands' and in semi-arid areas (Mehta and Shah 2001).

Table 12 State-wise distribution of selected aspirational districts

State	Number of districts	State	Number of districts
Andhra Pradesh	3	Manipur	1
Arunachal Pradesh	1	Meghalaya	1
Assam	7	Mizoram	1
Bihar	13	Nagaland	1
Chhattisgarh	10	Odisha	8
Gujarat	2	Punjab	2
Haryana	1	Rajasthan	5
Himachal Pradesh	1	Sikkim	1
Jammu and Kashmir	2	Tamil Nadu	2
Jharkhand	19	Telangana	3
Karnataka	2	Tripura	1
Kerala	1	Uttar Pradesh	8
Madhya Pradesh	8	Uttarakhand	2
Maharashtra	4	West Bengal	5

Source NITI Aayog (2018)

Bagchi (2018) mentions a recent study by Singh, Arora and Siddiqui[5] in which they find a huge improvement in India's multidimensional poverty between 2005–06 and 2015–16, due to the performance of southern states, i.e. Kerala, Tamil Nadu, Karnataka, Telangana and Andhra Pradesh. However, multidimensional poverty remains high in Bihar, Jharkhand, Uttar Pradesh, Rajasthan and Odisha (29%).

NITI Aayog has identified 115 aspirational districts based on 49 indicators across five sectors that include health and nutrition, education, agriculture and water resources, financial inclusion and skill development, and basic infrastructure. These districts are being encouraged to catch up with the best district in their state and aspire to become the best district in the country. States with the highest number of such districts are Jharkhand 19 districts, Bihar 13, Chhattisgarh 10 and Madhya Pradesh, Odisha and Uttar Pradesh 8 districts each (Table 12).

The BPL Census

For implementation purposes, however, other measures, such as a census of household regarding the ownership of assets by the household or economic activities of household members, have been used to identify the poor. Hence, the Ministry of Rural Development (MoRD) conducted a Below Poverty Line (BPL) Census in 1992, 1997 and 2002 in association with states/union territories, to identify rural households that need assistance through various ministry programmes.

[5]See http://www.thehindu.com/news/national/southern-comfort-indias-global-poverty-rank-improves/article23866587.ece.

The MoRD BPL Census 2002 was based on an indicator-based scoring approach to classify households as poor and non-poor. The scorecard had 13 questions on various aspects, like size of landholding, type of house, availability of clothing, ownership of consumer durables, food security, access to sanitation, education attainment, migration. Each question had five scores, from zero to four, and the household was given a total score out of a maximum possible of 52. The BPL status of each household is on MoRD's website. As was the case with methods used prior to the BPL Census 2002, the scorecard method used in this Census too was critiqued on a large number of grounds.

Vardhan (2010) re-administered the BPL scorecard to all households in two villages in February 2010 to determine the change in household status over time (Box 1)

Box 1: Below Poverty Line Census Results, 2002 and 2010

The MoRD BPL Census 2002 scorecard was re-administered to all households in two villages in February 2010. The data on all 13 dimensions were analysed for households in Juvvalapalem and Thippalakatta villages in Guntur district, Andhra Pradesh, for two points in time, 2002 and 2010. It was possible to identify houses that had exited poverty, those that had entered it and those that had persisted in it, and to analyse the factors leading to such movements. Using a cut-off score of 20 for declaring a household poor, 21% of households were found to be chronically poor. Some salient observations were:

- Many households around the poverty line had been vulnerable to shocks and influenced by enablers in moving above and below the line. Their entry or exit from poverty cannot be said to be relatively permanent. These are transient poor and vulnerable households, excluded from chronic poverty calculations.
- Children seem to be most impacted by the economic movements of a household. All households that had exited poverty showed an improvement in children's access to education without them having to contribute to family income; the reverse was true for households that entered poverty.
- Sanitation and access to health care are important in entry, exit and persistence of poverty. Among households without access to sanitation facilities, poor households formed a disproportionately large group.
- A total of 59% of households that had exited poverty showed an increase in the score on migration. Linkages with the urban economy might be driving the escape from poverty in rural India.
- Other factors for exit from poverty are enablers (like access to credit, favourable agro-climatic conditions, alternative asset base) and more secure livelihoods (in terms of reduced market risks or more days of work).

- Low literacy/educational attainment is connected to persistence of poverty. A total of 89% of households that had remained poor showed no change in educational attainment status (qualification of the most literate adult).
- Other factors for persistence are unsecure livelihoods and poor asset base of households. This indicates that self- and wage employment programmes will help chronically poor households.
- Shocks related to health and agro-climatic conditions are the most common reasons for entry into poverty. Poor public healthcare delivery and inefficient implementation of women and child welfare programmes are detrimental.
- Being non-poor is associated with multidimensional wellness. Each parameter contributed almost equally between 5 and 10% to the total score. For poor households, the contributions of each of the parameters varied between 2 and 24%.

Source Vardhan (2010).

In May 2011, Union Cabinet approved BPL Census along with Caste Census for both rural and urban areas. The Saxena Committee (2011) and Hashim Committee (2012) reports provide details regarding the methodology suggested for identifying the poor for rural and urban areas, respectively. The methodology developed used a mechanism for automatic inclusion and automatic exclusion based on the criteria given below. The remaining households are graded to identify the poorest among them. SECC 2011 shows that three-fourths (74%) of the total households are located in rural areas.

SECC 2011: Rural Areas

Automatic exclusion: A household is automatically excluded from the BPL category if it has any of the following: motorised 2 or 3 or 4 – wheeler/fishing boat; mechanised 3 or 4 – wheeler agricultural equipment, Kisan Credit Card with a credit limit of over Rs 50,000; any household member is a government employee; non-agricultural enterprise registered with government; a member of the household earns above Rs 10,000 per month; income tax payee or a professional tax payee; house with three or more rooms with pucca walls and roof; ownership of a refrigerator, landline phone, more than 2.5 acres of irrigated land with 1 irrigation equipment, 5 acres or more of irrigated land for two or more crop seasons or 7.5 acres of land or more with at least one irrigation equipment.

Automatic inclusion: A household is automatically included among the BPL category if it lacks shelter; is destitute or lives on alms; depends on manual scavenging; belongs to a Primitive Tribal Group; and is a legally released bonded labourer.

Table 13 Rural households suffering from each of the seven specific deprivations

	Deprivation criteria	Number of rural households	Per cent rural households (%)
D1.	Households with one or less room, kuccha walls and kuccha roof	2.38 crore	13.28
D2.	No adult member in household between age 18 and 59	65.33 lakh	3.64
D3.	Female-headed household with no adult male member between 16 and 59	69.43 lakh	3.86
D4.	Households with differently abled member with no other able-bodied adult member	7.20 lakh	0.40
D5.	SC/ST households	3.87 crore	21.56
D6.	Households with no literate adult above age 25 years	4.22 crore	23.52
D7.	Landless households deriving a major part of their income from manual labour	5.40 crore	30.04
	Households with any one of the seven deprivations	8.73 crore	

Source SECC website http://secc.gov.in/reportlistContent. Accessed 17 May 2018

The remaining households are graded to determine the poorest on the basis of seven deprivation criteria. The **deprivation criteria** are households with only one room, kuccha walls and kuccha roof; no adult members between ages of 16 and 59; female-headed households with no adult male member between 16 and 59; households with a disabled member and no able-bodied member; SC/ST households; households with no literate adult above 25 years; and landless households deriving a major part of their income from manual casual labour. As many as 8.73 crore out of 17.97 crore rural households, or 48.58% households report at least one deprivation (Table 13).[6]

Casual agricultural labour is the largest group that is stuck in poverty (Bhide and Mehta 2003; Mehta et al. 2011). This pattern has been corroborated by the data collected by the Socio-Economic Caste Census. Landless households dependent on manual casual labour constitute 30% of all households. This category of households additionally suffers from several of the seven deprivations mentioned above. These are 'working poor' for whom the state has not been able to meet its requirement to secure the right to an adequate means of livelihood.

The results of SECC 2011 are being used by the Ministry of Rural Development while implementing programmes in rural areas.

[6]See http://secc.gov.in/reportlistContent. Accessed 17 May 2018.

SECC 2011: Urban Areas

The methodology suggested for identifying the poorest in urban areas is similar to that for rural areas (see Planning Commission 2012). The indicators suggested for determining exclusion, inclusion and scoring criteria are listed below.[7]

Automatic exclusion: If the number of dwelling rooms exclusively in possession of the household is 4 or above (dwelling rooms as specified in the Report) that household will be excluded. Secondly, the household possessing any one of the assets, i.e. '4 wheeler motorised vehicle', 'AC set' and 'computer or laptop with Internet', will also be excluded. Besides the households possessing any three of the following four assets, i.e. refrigerator, telephone (landline), washing machine, two wheeler motorised vehicle will also be excluded.

Automatic inclusion: Households facing various kinds of deprivations and vulnerabilities, viz. residential, social and occupational vulnerabilities, would be automatically included in the BPL list.

i. **Residential vulnerability**: If the household is 'houseless' as defined in the Report or the household has a house with roof and wall made of plastic/polythene or the household having only one room or less with the material of wall being grass, thatch, bamboo, mud, un-burnt brick or wood and the material of roof being grass, thatch, bamboo, wood or mud, then that will be automatically included.

ii. **Occupational vulnerability**: The household having no income from any source; any household member (including children) engaged in a vulnerable occupation like beggar/rag picker, domestic worker (who are actually paid wages) and sweeper/sanitation worker/mali); and all earning adult members in a household are daily wagers or irregular wagers; then, that household should be automatically included.

iii. **Social vulnerability**: If there is no member of the household aged 18 years and above (child-headed household) or there is no able-bodied person aged between 18 and 60 years in the household or all earning adult members in a household are either disabled, chronically ill or aged more than 65 years, then that household should be automatically included.

Scoring index: In the third and final stage, the remaining households will be assigned scores from 0 to 12 based on various indicators of residential, social and occupational vulnerabilities. Those households with scores from 1 to 12 are to be considered eligible for inclusion in the BPL list in the increasing order of the intensity of their deprivations meaning thereby that those with higher scores are more deprived.

[7]See Planning Commission (2012). Available at: http://planningcommission.nic.in/reports/genrep/rep_hasim1701.pdf.

Table 14 Multidimensional poverty index (MPI) and population in multidimensional poverty

MPI Year	Country	Survey source	Data for year	Multidimensional poverty index (MPI = H*A)	Headcount ratio: population in multidimensional poverty (H)	Intensity of deprivation among the poor (A)
2011	India	DHS	2005/06	0.283	53.7	52.7
2017	India	IHDS	2011/12	0.191	41.3	46.3
2011	Brazil	WHS	2003	0.039	8.5	46.0
2011	Brazil	PNDS	2006	0.011	2.7	39.3
2016	Brazil	PNAD	2014	0.021	5.3	40.6
2013	China	WHS	2002	0.056	12.5	44.9
2015	China	CFPS	2012	0.023	5.2	43.2
2017	China	CFPS	2014	0.017	4.0	41.3
2010	South Africa	WHS	2003	0.014	3.1	38.1
2011	South Africa	NIDS	2008	0.057	13.4	42.3
2014	South Africa	NIDS	2012	0.044	11.1	39.5
2017	South Africa	NIDS	2014/15	0.036	9.2	39.1
2011	Sri Lanka	WHS	2003	0.021	5.3	38.7

Source Oxford Poverty Human Development Initiative. Available at: http://ophi.org.uk/multidimensional-poverty-index/global-mpi-2017/. Accessed 18 May 2018

International Measures of Multidimensional Deprivation

The Oxford Poverty and Human Development Initiative 'counts the different types of deprivation that individuals experience at the same time, such as a lack of education or employment, or poor health or living standards'. Based on this, a multidimensional index of poverty (MPI) is constructed. The 2017 MPI shows that the per cent of India's population in multidimensional poverty declined from 53.7% in 2005–06 to 41.3% in 2011–12 though the data are collected from different surveys. However, the per cent of India's population in multidimensional poverty is far higher than that in Brazil (5.3% in 2014), China (4% in 2014), South Africa (9.2% in 2014–15) and Sri Lanka (5.3% in 2003) (Table 14).

4 Factors Affecting the Incidence of Poverty

As pointed out earlier, the regional and household social characteristics significantly differentiate the incidence of poverty. The persistence of this pattern reflects the vulnerability of these segments of the society to the poverty trap.

The results of the panel or longitudinal surveys of rural households reported in Bhide and Mehta (2011) and Dhamija and Bhide (2011) show that Scheduled Caste and Scheduled Tribe status, large household size and large proportion of children among household members were consistently associated with severe poverty (households with consumption expenditure 25% or more below the poverty line) in each of three rounds of the survey in 1970–71, 1981–82 and 1998–99 in rural India.

The findings of the above-mentioned studies show that access to land, livestock and village-level infrastructure and urban linkage (relatively large urban population of the district), irrigation and village size are statistically significant and have a negative impact on the incidence of poverty in two out of three rounds of the survey.

Using the NSS data for 2004–05 and 2011–12 and following the Tendulkar approach to the poverty line, Chatterjee et al. (2016) highlight the fact that measured by the traditional consumption expenditure norm to define poverty line, there was a sharp reduction in the percentage of poor in the population and a decline in the absolute number of poor between the two rounds by about 130 million. The paper also points out that using an internationally comparable poverty line of 1.9 PPP dollars (2011 base year) per capita per day, the data show a sharp decline in poverty during the period. Nevertheless, the paper notes that India continues to have a proportionately larger number of the world's poor – 26% – and the largest number in absolute terms. Further, India's success in reducing the proportion of poor by a consumption measure does not translate into improvements in the other dimensions of poverty – under-5 mortality and under nutrition. The under-5 mortality rate in India was higher than Nepal, Bangladesh and Vietnam. We may note that India remains among the low-ranked countries in a range of human development indicators. In the recent 2017 Global Hunger Index of IFPRI, India ranks among the lowest in Asia. The faster pace of poverty reduction is a significant achievement, in comparison with the past record but much remains to be done to improve the living conditions of the poor. Chatterjee et al. note that 'many households that escaped poverty after 2005 still had consumption levels that were precariously close to the poverty line in 2012'.

Besides the vulnerability of social and regional groupings also noted above, the study by Chatterjee et al. (2016) indicates that:

- 'In the case of households belonging to Scheduled Tribes and Scheduled Castes, the non-monetary deprivation of well-being such as health and education status was also greater than other caste groups.
- Poor in the low-income states, who were sizable in number, also were faced with the prospects of limited opportunities for income mobility as well.
- Growth of agriculture which was an important driver of poverty reduction is not any different from the growth impact of the other sectors on poverty reduction.
- Cities, more than the sectors, drive poverty reduction, but in this sense it is the non-farm sectors that provide higher income levels for the households than agriculture, which is the major source of livelihood for the rural areas.
- Jobs, more than income transfers, mattered for the households who escaped poverty'.

The analysis presented by Chatterjee et al. (2016) points to the key role urbanisation has played in reducing poverty during the period 2005–2012. Urban growth has provided increasing number of jobs, including for the poor. The sharp reduction in the incidence of poverty between 2005 and 2012 has been attributed primarily to (1) increase in wage rates for the unskilled workers, which emerged as demand for unskilled labour increased as construction activity in both rural and urban areas expanded (2) rise in agricultural commodity prices which in turn led to an increase in demand for workers in farming and (3) withdrawal of women from labour market for a variety of reasons.

Urbanisation and economic growth are seen to be the key drivers of poverty reduction during 2005–12. However, the study does caution on the continued vulnerabilities of a significant part of the population to any income shocks.

5 Growth and Incidence of Poverty

The limitations of the 'trickle-down effects' of the growth process translating into benefits for the poor have been widely recognised. Beginning from the seminal work of Ahluwalia (1978) in which he drew attention to the poverty-reducing effect of agricultural growth, further research by a number of scholars has pointed to the complex set of factors that affect poverty trends and patterns. Economic growth at a broad level, or even sectoral growth, while important, may not necessarily lead to poverty reduction. The work of Rao et al. (1986) and Sen (1996) highlights the many factors that influence the pattern of poverty and poverty reduction with implications for the linkages between growth and poverty reduction.

The impact of growth on poverty reduction, even in the case of agricultural growth, has been shown to be nuanced. Rao et al. (1986) draw attention to the positive effects of irrigation and rural electrification but note that the effect of roads and fertiliser use is not conclusive. Productivity of agricultural output per hectare is associated with lower HCR, but productivity per person is associated with higher HCR. Higher agricultural prices are seen to be associated with higher HCR. The vulnerability of agricultural labour to poverty has also been highlighted.

Examining the period 1960–61 to 1993–94, Sen (1996) finds that the initial conditions with respect to irrigation, female literacy and infant mortality are significant factors influencing poverty reduction. He also finds that the effect of relative prices (agriculture relative to overall) on poverty is more important than the overall inflation rate. Hasan et al. (2013, p. 12) also note that one of the explanations for lower impact of economic growth on poverty reduction witnessed in India when compared to other countries such as China, Vietnam and Indonesia is the set of initial conditions of human development. Additionally, the structure of economic growth in India has been such that employment growth has occurred in sectors where productivity growth rate is slower.

The need for more purposeful policies for poverty reduction, rather than relying merely on economic growth, has been articulated by a wide range of studies [Gaiha (1989, 1995), Jha (2000), Krishna et al. (2005), Bhalla and Hazell (2003)]. Hasan et al. (2013) point to the role of the structural changes that lead to poverty reduction. Faster output growth in sectors that employ more labour has a greater impact on poverty reduction than otherwise.

6 Bands of Vulnerability or Poverty

The National Commission for Enterprises in the Unorganised Sectors (NCEUS) presents the concept of a poverty band, so as to be able to explore the realities hidden behind the concept of a poverty line (Table 15). It estimates that 76.7% of the Indian population in 2004–05 lived on average per capita daily expenditure of just Rs 16, with the maximum expenditure just Rs 24. Moreover, of the total population, 36% were in the 'vulnerable' category. A single exogenous shock (such as death or disability of a breadwinner, serious sickness of a child or others or marriage expenses) could pull them back into the official 'poverty' group (Kannan 2010).

This picture, constructed on the basis of DPCE, reveals that every fifth Indian had only Rs 12 or less to spend each day in 2004–05. Further, three of four persons were in the poor and vulnerable categories in terms of daily consumer expenditure. High- and middle-income categories held 4 and 19.3% of the population, respectively. While estimates of this pattern are not available for more recent surveys, the estimated HCR from the 2011–12 expenditure survey remains at least 20% or 260 million population.

Table 15 Poverty status and poverty band, 2004–05

Serial no.	Poverty status	% of population	DPCE (Rs)
1	Extremely poor	6.4	9
2	Poor	15.4	12
3	Marginally poor	19.0	15
4	Vulnerable poor	36.0	20
5	Middle income	19.3	37
6	High income	4.0	93
7	Poor and vulnerable (1–4)	76.8	16
8	All	100.0	46

Note DPCE = Daily Per Capita Expenditure
Source Kannan (2010)

7 Conclusions

In this chapter, we have presented estimates of poverty over time and patterns of incidence of poverty across socio-economic groups of population and geographical or regional variations in the incidence of poverty.

While poverty rates have declined over the years, continued persistence of high rates, especially for some regions and social groups, is indicative of the intractability or stubbornness of poverty in such cases and the lack of responsiveness to overall or average economic growth and development.

The multidimensional nature of poverty has been highlighted in the studies which have examined the deprivations of many minimal sets of necessities experienced by the poor as also of those who may be slightly above the 'poverty line' that is adopted to estimate the size of the population which is poor. Deprivation of health, education and shelter has been both an effect and a cause of economic or consumption poverty.

The studies examining the correlates of poverty point to a number of household-level social and economic characteristics and a few features of the village or district that are closely associated with the economic status of the households in rural India. Continued prevalence of this pattern over time also suggests that the dynamics of economic changes has not been sufficiently in favour of the disadvantaged to change the structure of poverty. The interaction between economic growth at the macro-level and incidence of poverty has also been a subject of a large number of studies.

Many of those living in poverty today will remain poor over time and may pass their poverty to their children. This, combined with the size of the population which is poor, demands that we address the poverty challenge on priority. Accurately estimating the number of poor is important but is not enough. We also need to understand how many people are stuck in poverty and why? What are the factors that explain the persistence of poverty? How can these be addressed? How many people have moved out of poverty? What enabled them to move out of poverty? Did they manage to stay out of poverty? How many people who were not poor have become poor? What are the shocks that they suffered that led to their impoverishment? How can these be prevented from pushing people into poverty? These issues are discussed in the next chapter.

References

Ahluwalia, M. S. (1978). Rural poverty and agricultural performance in India. *Journal of Development Studies, 14*(3), 289–323.

Bagchi, S. (2018, May 12). Southern comfort: India's global poverty rank improves. *The Hindu.* Available at: http://www.thehindu.com/news/national/southern-comfort-indias-global-poverty-rank-improves/article23866587.ece.

Bandyopadhyay, S. (2001). *Twin peaks, convergence empirics of economic growth across Indian states*. Discussion Paper 2001/142. Helsinki: World Institute for Development Economics Research United Nations University.

Bhalla, G. S., & Hazell, P. (2003, August 16–22). Rural employment and poverty: strategies to eliminate rural poverty within a generation. *Economic and Political Weekly, 38*(33).

Bhide, S., & Mehta, A. K. (2003). *Issues in chronic poverty: Panel data based analysis* (CPRC-IIPA Working Paper No. 6). New Delhi: IIPA.

Bhide, S., & Mehta, A. K. (2011). *Economic growth and poverty dynamics* (CPRC-IIPA Working Paper No. 36). New Delhi: IIPA.

Bhide, S., & Srinivasan, J. T. (2004). *Development policies, priorities and sustainability perspectives in India. Social and Economic Change Monograph* (Vol. 6). Bangalore: Institute for Social and Economic Change.

Chatterjee, U., Murgai, R., Narayan, A., & Rama, M. (2016). *Pathways to reducing poverty and sharing prosperity in India. Lessons from the Last Two Decades.* Washington, DC: The World Bank.

Deaton, A. (2010). Price indexes, inequality and the measurement of world poverty. *American Economic Review*.

Dev, M. (Ed.). (2013). *India development report 2012–13*. New Delhi: Oxford University Press.

Dhamija, N., & Bhide, S. (2011). *Dynamics of chronic poverty: Variations in factors influencing entry and exit of chronic poor* (CPRC-IIPA Working Paper No. 39). New Delhi: IIPA.

Drèze, J. P., & Srinivasan, P. V. (1996). *Poverty in India. Regional estimates 1987–88* (Working Paper No. 36). Centre for Development Economics, Delhi School of Economics.

Duggal, R. (2009, August). Sinking flagships and health budgets in India. *Economic & Political Weekly, 44*(33), 15–21.

Gaiha, R. (1989). Are the chronically poor also the poorest in rural India? *Development and Change, 20*(2), 295–322.

Gaiha, R. (1995). Does agricultural growth matter in poverty alleviation? *Development and Change, 26*(2), 285–304.

Government of India. (2009, August). *Report of the expert group to advise the Ministry of Rural Development on the methodology for conducting the Below Poverty Line (BPL) census for 11th five year plan*. New Delhi: Ministry of Rural development.

Hasan, R., Lamba, S., & Sen Gupta, A. (2013, November). *Growth, structural change, and poverty reduction: Evidence from India* (South Asia Working Paper Series, No. 22). Manila: Asian Development Bank.

Hickel, J. (2015). The Guardian, International Edition. https://www.theguardian.com/global-development-professionals-network/2015/nov/01/global-poverty-is-worse-than-you-think-could-you-live-on-190-a-day, downloaded March 25, 2018.

Himanshu, R. (2010, January). Towards new poverty lines for India. *Economic & Political Weekly, 45*(1), 2–8.

Jha, R. (2000). *Reducing poverty and inequality in India: Has liberalisation helped? Research paper 2000/204*. Helsinki: World Institute for Development Economics Research, United Nations University.

Kannan, K. P. (2010). Estimating and identifying the poor. *Journal of Human Development, 4*(1), 91–98.

Krishna, A., Kapila, M., Porwal, M., & Singh, V. (2005). Why growth is not enough: Household poverty dynamics in Northeast Gujarat, India. *Journal of Development Studies, 41*(7), 1163–1192.

Mehta, A. K. (2003). Multidimensional poverty in India: District level estimates. In A. K. Mehta, S. Ghosh, D. Chatterjee, & N. Menon (Eds.), *Chronic poverty in India*. New Delhi: Chronic Poverty Research Centre and Indian Institute for Public Administration.

Mehta, A. K. (2007). *Gender budgeting, alternative economic survey*. New Delhi: Daanish Books.

Mehta, A. K. (2009, May). Global financial crisis, healthcare and poverty. *Mainstream, 47*(21), 9.

Mehta, A. K. (2013). *Poverty: Promises made and miles to go, yojana*. August, pp. 47–50.

Mehta, A. K. (2017). Poverty Eradication: Why do we always fail? In Richard Mahapatra & Sunita Narain (Eds.), *State of India's environment 2017*. New Delhi: Centre for Science and Environment.

Mehta, A. K., & Bhide, S. (2010). Poverty and poverty dynamics in India, estimates, determinants and policy responses. Presented at a Conference in Manchester on Ten Years of War Against Poverty. Available at: http://www.chronicpoverty.org/publications/details/poverty-and-poverty-dynamics-in-india.

Mehta, A.K., & Gupta, S. (2005). *The impact of HIV/AIDS on women care givers in situations of poverty: Policy issues*. New Delhi: United Nations Development Fund for Women South Asia and Institute of Public Administration.

Mehta, A. K., & Shah, A. (2001). Chronic poverty in India: Overview study (Working Paper 7). Manchester and New Delhi: Chronic Poverty Research Centre, University of Manchester and Indian Institute of Public Administration.

Mehta, A. K., & Shepherd, A. (Eds.). (2006). *Chronic poverty and development policy in India*. New Delhi: Sage.

Mehta, J., & Venkatraman, S. (2000, July 1–7). Poverty statistics. *Economic and Political Weekly, 35*(27).

Mehta, A. K., Panigrahi, R., & Sivramkrishna, S. (2004). *Operationalizing multidimensional concepts of chronic poverty: An exploratory spatial analysis* (CPRC-IIPA Working Paper No. 18). New Delhi: IIPA.

Mehta, A. K., Shepherd, A., Bhide, S., Shah, A., & Kumar, A. (2011). *India chronic poverty report: Towards solutions and new compacts in a dynamic context*. New Delhi: Indian Institute of Public Administration.

Nath, N. C. B. (2006). Political perspectives on chronic poverty. In A. K. Mehta & A. Shepherd (Eds.), *Chronic poverty and development policy in India*. New Delhi: Sage.

National Rural Health Mission (NRHM). (2005). Mission document 2005–2012. New Delhi: National Rural Health Mission, Ministry of Health and Family Welfare. Available at: http://www.pbnrhm.org/docs/mission_doc.pdf.

NITI Aayog. (2018, April). List of 115 aspirational districts. Available at: https://pmawards.gov.in/public/List-of-Aspirational-Districts.pdf. Government of India.

NITI Aayog. (2016). Eliminating poverty: Creating jobs and strengthening social programs, Occasional Paper No. 2, 21st March. Government of India.

Patnaik, U. (2007, July 28–August 3). Neoliberalism and rural poverty in India. *Economic and Political Weekly, 42*(30).

Patnaik, U. (2010, January 23–29). Trends in urban poverty under economic reforms: 1993–94 to 2004–05. *Economic and Political Weekly, 45*(4).

Planning Commission. (1979). *Report of the task force on projections of minimum needs and effective consumption demand*. New Delhi: Perspective Planning Division, Planning Commission.

Planning Commission. (1993). *Report of the expert group on estimation of proportion and number of poor (Lakdawala Committee)*. New Delhi: Perspective Planning Division, Planning Commission.

Planning Commission. (2009). *(Tendulkar Committee) Report of the expert group to review the methodology for estimation of poverty*. New Delhi: Planning Commission.

Planning Commission. (2012). *Report of the expert group to recommend the detailed methodology for identification of families living below poverty line in the urban areas*. New Delhi: Perspective Planning Division, Planning Commission.

Planning Commission. (2013a). *Poverty estimates for social groups 2004–05 and 2011–12*. Available at: planningcommission.gov.in/reports/genrep/rep_pov1303.pdf (downloaded on October 31, 2017).

Planning Commission. (2013b). Press note on poverty estimates 2011–12 dated 22 July 2013.

Planning Commission. (2014). *(Rangarajan Committee) Report of the expert group to review the methodology for estimation of poverty*. New Delhi: Planning Commission.

Popli, G., Parikh, A., & Palmer-Jones, R. (2005, October). Are the 2000 poverty estimates for India a myth, artefact or real? *Economic & Political Weekly, 40*(43), 22–28.

Rao, C. H. H., Gupta, D. B., & Sharma, P. S. (1986). Infrastructural development and rural poverty in India: A cross sectional analysis. In J. W. Mellor & G. M. Desai (Eds.), *Agricultural change and rural poverty: A variation on a theme by Dharam Narain*. New Delhi: Oxford University Press.

Ravallion, M. (2010, April). *Poverty lines across the world* (Policy Research Working Paper 5284). The World Bank Development Research Group. Available at: http://documents. worldbank.org/curated/en/298951468174919253/pdf/WPS5284.pdf.

Ravallion, M., Chen, S., & Sangraula, P. (2008). *Dollar a day revisited* (Policy Research Working Paper Series 4620). The World Bank.

Ray, R., & Lancaster, G. (2005, January). On setting the poverty line based on estimated nutrient prices. *Economic & Political Weekly, 40*(1), 1–7.

Saith, A. (2005, October 22–28). Poverty lines versus the poor. *Economic and Political Weekly, 40* (43).

Sen, A. (1996, September 1–7). Economic reforms, employment and poverty: Trends and options. *Economic and Political Weekly, 31*(35).

Sen, P. (2005, October 22–28). Of Calories and Things. *Economic and Political Weekly, 40*(43).

Shepherd, A., Anderson, E., & Kyegombe, N. (2004). *India's "poorly-performing" states. Background Paper*. Overseas Development Institute: London.

Srinivasan, T. N. (2007, October 13–19). Poverty lines in India: Reflections after the Patna Conference. *Economic and Political Weekly, 42*(41).

Thorat, A., Vanneman, R., Desai, S., & Dubey, A. (2017). Escaping and falling into poverty. *World Development, 93,* 413–426.

Vardhan, M. H. (2010). *Factors causing persistence of poverty, entry into it and escape from it: An exploratory analysis based on fieldwork in 2 villages of Andhra Pradesh*. B.E. (Hons) thesis, Birla Institute of Technology and Science.

World Bank. (1997). *India, achievements and challenges in reducing poverty* (Report 16483-IN). New Delhi: Country Operations, Industry & Finance Division, Country Department II, South Asia Region: World Bank.

Chapter 3
A Review of Poverty Dynamics Issues

Shashanka Bhide and Aasha Kapur Mehta

1 Introduction

The literature on poverty has primarily focused on those who are poor at a given time rather than on how long they have been poor or when and how they became impoverished or escaped impoverishment. There is much less research on the 'dynamics of poverty' – movement into and out of poverty, or lack of it or on understanding the processes and factors that determine these changes. A major concern is that a large proportion of those who are poor in India are stuck in poverty or are chronically poor. In addition to income or consumption poverty, those who are stuck in poverty suffer deprivation in multiple dimensions such as low levels of literacy and education, poor health, malnutrition, diseases related to unsafe drinking water, lack of access to sanitation, clean fuels and livelihood-related opportunities. The massive number of those who are poor, combined with the fact that many of them will remain poor over time and poverty may be transmitted to their children, makes this the most important development challenge facing India. This chapter discusses the dynamics of poverty in the country and tries to understand these issues by reviewing empirical studies that have examined poverty dynamics in the Indian context.

With necessary permissions, this chapter draws on Chap. 3 of the India Chronic Poverty Report (2011), CPRC IIPA working papers 6, 28, 36, 39 and 47; Mehta and Bhide (2010). "Poverty and Poverty Dynamics in India, Estimates, Determinants and Policy Responses", presented at a Conference in Manchester on Ten Years of War Against Poverty, available at: http://www.chronicpoverty.org/publications/details/poverty-and-poverty-dynamics-in-india; and Mehta (2013) Poverty: Promises Made and Miles to Go, Yojana, August, pp. 47–50.

S. Bhide (✉)
Madras Institute of Development Studies, Chennai, India
e-mail: shashankabhide@gmail.com

A. K. Mehta
Indian Institute of Public Administration, New Delhi, India

© Springer Nature Singapore Pte Ltd. 2018
A. K. Mehta et al. (eds.), *Poverty, Chronic Poverty and Poverty Dynamics*,
https://doi.org/10.1007/978-981-13-0677-8_3

Continued high levels of poverty in specific regions or social groups imply that channels of upward income mobility or better livelihood-generating options are missing for certain areas and groups. This aspect of poverty has led to the need for examining types of poverty dynamics under different situations to improve our understanding of the 'drivers' of poverty, 'interrupters' of poverty and 'chronic poverty'. An assessment of dynamics of poverty – 'entry', 'escape' or 'trapped' – requires an assessment of the prevailing conditions of the population at different points of time.

The basic framework that has been used to explain changes in the levels of poverty can be captured as follows:

$$\begin{pmatrix} P \\ NP \end{pmatrix} t = \begin{pmatrix} p11 & p12 \\ p21 & p22 \end{pmatrix} \begin{pmatrix} P*(1+r)^j \\ NP*(1+r)^j \end{pmatrix} t - j$$

Or, abstracting from population growth,

$$P_t = p11 * P_{t-j} + p12 * NP_{t-j}$$

$$NP_t = p21 * P_{t-j} + p22 * NP_{t-j}$$

where

P_t = number of poor in year t
NP_t = number of non-poor in year t
r = annual rate of growth of population between the two periods, assumed here to
     be the same for the poor and the non-poor
$p11$ = proportion of population that remains poor between period $t - j$ and t
$p12$ = proportion of non-poor in $t - j$ who become poor in year t
$p21$ = proportion of poor in year $t - j$ who become non-poor in year t
$p22$ = proportion of non-poor in year $t - j$ who remain non-poor in year t

The above specification involves a number of simplifying assumptions including the one about a uniform population growth and constant probabilities of change applied to the incremental population of the poor over time. These assumptions can be relaxed when adequate information is available to reflect the differential rates and probabilities.

In the case of analysis which considers poverty incidence for a given year, the formulation does not distinguish between whether the household that is poor this year was also poor earlier and whether a previously non-poor household is still non-poor or has become poor. Nor does it identify whether a household that is non-poor in this year was poor earlier or was non-poor earlier too.

In such an analysis, we have

$$P_t = \text{HCR}_t * \text{Population}_t \tag{1}$$

where HCR is the Head Count Ratio or the percentage of poor among the total population.

The specification may then provide HCR for different categories of the population. Empirical analysis has focused on determinants of HCR.

Poverty dynamics examines the probabilities of movement of households or population across income categories. These probabilities may not remain constant across different categories of population or over time for the same category of population. In this framework, it would be of interest to examine the following:

$$CP_t = p11 * P_{t-j} \tag{2}$$

$$TP_t = p12 * NP_{t-j} \tag{3}$$

$$P\_NP_t = p21 * P_{t-j} \tag{4}$$

$$NP\_NP_t = p22 * NP_t \tag{5}$$

where CP = chronic poor or those who have remained poor in both the years, TP = transient poor, who were non-poor earlier (in year $t - j$) but are now poor (in year t), P_NP, who were poor earlier and escaped poverty and NP_NP, those who were above the poverty line in both the years. Dynamics or changes in poverty status over time may also be defined in terms of 'spells' of poverty: whether households experienced poverty for more than a few spells (one or more periods) between the two years under consideration.

The perspectives obtained from specification of incidence of poverty in a dynamic framework provide insights into differentiation of factors that lead individuals or population groups into poverty or help them escape from poverty.

This paper is organised into five sections. Section 2 discusses the drivers, maintainers and interrupters framework for understanding the determinants of poverty and poverty dynamics and what is driving the changes. Section 3 reviews the dynamics of poverty and its determinants, and Sect. 4 provides a review of the modelling framework adopted in assessing future scenarios of poverty reduction. The final section provides a summary and concludes the chapter.

2   Drivers, Maintainers And Interrupters[1]

High levels of poverty have persisted in India (see Chap. 2) despite high economic growth rates. Depending on growth alone to make a dent on either rural or urban poverty will take too long. It is therefore important for policy to take cognisance of poverty dynamics. Poverty dynamics recognises the existence of processes through

---

[1]This section is based on Chap. 3 of the India Chronic Poverty Report (2011) and Mehta (2013) Poverty: Promises Made and Miles to Go, Yojana, August, pp. 49–50.

which the poor either escape from poverty or fail to escape it and the non-poor either remain non-poor or become poor. Longitudinal studies provide valuable evidence regarding the scale of persistent poverty and poverty dynamics in India (Gaiha 1988; Singh and Binswanger 1993; Mehta and Bhide 2003; Bhide and Mehta 2004). Analysis of a rural panel data set covering about 3000 households across the country draws attention to the significant scale of incidence of chronic poverty. The estimates also indicate that a sizeable proportion of non-poor households may fall into poverty, while a large proportion of those who are poor manage to escape from it (Bhide and Mehta 2011).

Forces that cause a non-poor household to become poor are termed 'drivers', the factors that enable poor households to become non-poor are termed 'interrupters', and the factors that keep poor households in poverty are termed 'maintainers' (Hulme et al. 2003). Analysis of panel data and a review of the literature point to factors that act as 'drivers' forcing people into poverty. These could be related to the sudden onset of a long-term and expensive illness, a disaster such as a flood or earthquake, a failed crop, a failed investment or a policy change that leads to a loss of livelihood or reduction in income. Similarly, there are factors that 'maintain' people in poverty. These include illiteracy, living in a remote geographic location that provides a few livelihood opportunities, poor access to healthcare facilities, forced sale of assets to meet a crisis, indebtedness and bonded labour – any of which could force people to get stuck in poverty. 'Interrupters' are factors that can enable escape from poverty. These include access to diversified income sources, linkages with urban areas, improvements in rural infrastructure, accumulation of human, physical and financial assets, access to water for irrigation and increase in wages (Bhide and Mehta 2003; Mehta and Shepherd 2006). Table 1 lists a number of 'drivers', 'maintainers' and 'interrupters' of poverty that require policy attention.

Research shows that since poverty is concentrated in identified spatial locations there is a 'geography of poverty'. There is also a 'sociology of poverty', since the proportion of those who are poor is higher among certain social groups. Additionally, there are identifiable occupational features of the poor: 'they are concentrated in agricultural labour and artisanal households in rural areas, and among casual labourers in urban areas' (Government of India 2008). Poverty is associated with structural factors such as low wages; insecure, casual employment; low-productivity smallholder agriculture; and low social status of Scheduled Caste (SC) and, especially, Scheduled Tribe (ST) households living in the poorest and most multi-dimensionally deprived states and regions. A higher concentration of poverty in certain geographic regions and types of households and greater vulnerability of certain groups together point to the need for effectively addressing these dimensions of the poverty conundrum that maintain people in poverty.

Table 1 Drivers, maintainers and interrupters of chronic poverty

Drivers	Maintainers	Interrupters
Health shock	Illiteracy/lack of skills	Diversification of income
Sudden disability	Poverty/disability/old age	Intensive farming/crop diversification
Large social expenditure	Social exclusion	Off-farm work/new job
High-interest borrowing	Geography (remoteness)	Urban linkages
Investment failure	Drink/drug addiction	Improved rural infrastructure
Crop failure	Poor healthcare facilities	Kinship networks
Natural disaster	Larger household size	Asset accumulation
Loss of productive assets	Lack of job information	Marketable skills/linkages
Macro policy change	Forced sale of assets	Information network on job opportunities
Loss of job	Indebtedness	Decrease in dependency
Social and class conflict	Bonded labour	Increase in wages
	Governance failure	Access to credit
		Social safety networks

Source: Mehta et al. (2011), p. 56 adapted from Bhide and Mehta (2004), p. 3 and 4

3 Dynamics of Poverty: Entry, Escape And Traps[2]

The relatively 'low' level of the poverty line – in the sense that the expenditure considered in defining the poverty status of the households covers only the minimal requirements of the population – also suggests that there is a need to focus on channels of income mobility as much as extending safety nets to the vulnerable groups of population. Without achieving higher and more stable income levels, the poor may be severely and adversely affected in the event of shocks such as ill health, decline in the price of outputs or job losses. These are the issues, which have been the subject of studies focusing on the dynamics of poverty. How do households or individuals fall into poverty, escape poverty, get trapped in poverty or remain non-poor?

---

[2]With necessary permission, this section builds on Mehta and Bhide (2010). 'Poverty and Poverty Dynamics in India, Estimates, Determinants and Policy Responses', presented at a Conference in Manchester on Ten Years of War Against Poverty.

As noted earlier, the dynamic view of poverty suggests that at a general level, the population at any given time would be composed of poor and non-poor. The poor would include those who have been poor for some time as well as those who were not poor earlier but have now become poor. The non-poor would include those who were non-poor for some time as well as those who were poor earlier and have successfully escaped poverty. Those who have been 'poor for some time and continue to be poor' are the 'chronic poor'. Are strategies to get the chronic poor out of poverty different from the strategies to prevent households from falling into poverty? There are clearly 'structural' barriers in both instances of poverty in the dynamic perspective. Calvo and Dercon (2009) have argued that the challenge is to identify the people who are likely to stay poor in the future.

What are the relative positions of different groups of poor in terms of chronicity of poverty? While periodic independent or fresh cross-sectional surveys of households with respect to consumption expenditure or income provide an assessment of trends in the pattern of incidence of poverty, such as the persistence of high rates of HCR in specific population or geographic groups, they do not shed light on whether the persistence in the incidence of poverty is due to the 'entry of new poor' or 'continued existence in poverty'.

Panel data on households provide a valuable basis for examining the dynamics of poverty: what changes are experienced by the households in their income status and which factors are associated with this income mobility. Alternative qualitative methods have also evolved to assess poverty dynamics in place of panel or repeated surveys of the same households. The 'synthetic' or 'pseudo'-panels may also address some issues relating to poverty or income dynamics.

3.1 Poverty Persistence, Entry and Escape: Findings of Panel Data-Based Studies

The NCAER National Rural Household Surveys

In one of the early studies referring to the period of 1968–70, based on a national-level rural household survey conducted by the National Council of Applied Economic Research (NCAER), Gaiha (1988) provided estimates of changes in the levels of poverty for a panel of sample households over a 3-year period of 1968–1970. Distribution of households during the two periods showed that about 33% of the households remained poor at the beginning of the period and at the end of the survey period. About 13% of the households who were non-poor at the beginning of the survey period became poor, and 24% of the households who were poor exited poverty in the third year of the survey. The survey pointed to considerable mobility across the 'poverty line', although a third of the households were 'chronically poor' over the 3-year period. The study concludes that 'the escape from poverty was not a result of growth trickling down to the poor; instead, it was largely an outcome of the direct involvement of a section of the cultivating poor in the growth process itself, initiated by the new agricultural technology'.

In a follow-up survey (Rural Economic and Demographic Survey) of the same households in 1981–82 by NCAER (1986a), it was reported that the extent of persistence remained significant even over the long period of a decade. The churn, exit from and entry into poverty remained greater in scale than the estimates provided by Gaiha (1988) for the late 1960s. The caveats on the findings arising from the nature of the panel and measurement of poverty should be borne in mind, but the significant scale of exit from and entry into poverty points to the need for examining these processes of change.

To reiterate, a significant third of the sample rural households remained poor for over a decade. These findings find some corroboration from the cross-sectional studies, although the cross-sectional studies do not capture the dynamics: between 1973–74 and 1983, HCR in rural areas estimated from NSS data declined by 16 percentage points (Government of India 1979) and by about 11 percentage points by the Expert Group methodology (Government of India 1993). However, HCR remained high at 40–45% in both the estimates (Bhide and Mehta 2011).

The assessment of dynamics of poverty from the NCAER's survey of rural households was reported by Bhide and Mehta (2005) using data from the additional round of the survey in 1998. The chronicity of poverty was found to be higher as about 39% of the poor households remained poor between 1981–82 and 1998–99. The chronic poor were about 24% of the total sample – lower than the estimated 33% in the previous decade.

Dhamija and Bhide (2009) analysed the rural panel data from all three rounds of the NCAER surveys. They report that slightly more than half the poor households remained poor between 1970–71 and 1981–82 and also between 1980–81 and 1998–99.

The analysis cited above also points to the extent to which poor households move out of poverty and the non-poor enter into poverty.

There are, therefore, forces that enable poor households to escape from poverty, and at the same time there are also processes that bring households into poverty over time. From the numbers observed during the two surveys, fortunately, the forces which bring the non-poor into poverty seem to be weaker than the forces which lead the poor out of poverty.

Other Panel Data-Based Studies

World Bank (1997) drew attention to the importance of safety nets to assist the households in dealing with unforeseen shocks which may drive them into poverty and also refer to a few longitudinal village studies that report poverty dynamics. Important among a few panel data-based studies are the findings of Singh and Binswanger (1993) based on a six-village panel study in South India. They found that around '38% of all households (and 63% of those in poverty) were chronically poor'. Similarly, Gaiha and Deolalikar (1993) also found persistence of poverty for this panel. Gaiha and Imai (2003) used panel data for 183 households belonging to five sample villages in Andhra Pradesh and Maharashtra in India for 1975–84 and found that large segments of rural households experienced long spells of poverty (over 3 years) even without negative crop shocks. However, occurrence of crop shocks led to an increased proportion of households experiencing short spells of poverty (1–2 years).

Using qualitative techniques of enquiry, involving 25-year recall for 6,376 households in 35 villages in the state of Rajasthan, Krishna (2017) found that 17.8% of households were stuck in poverty while 11.1% were able to move out of it. Further, while 7.9% households descended into poverty, 63.2% remained non-poor. Rajasthan is a state that has experienced a decline in poverty. Shah and Sah (2003) also corroborate the findings on the magnitude of the long-term poverty using qualitative methods in two tribal villages in Madhya Pradesh. They found that about 58% of the sample households were in chronic poverty. Further, all the severely poor were also chronically poor.

The IHDS Rural and Urban Panel: 2005–12

Thorat et al. (2017) report the findings of a new nationally representative panel study of over 38,000 households covering both rural and urban areas for the period of 2005–2012. They note that 'cross-sectional analysis of poverty that misses the churning of exits and entrance into poverty also misses the importance of steady income for protecting households from poverty'. They find that the majority of the poor in wave 2 (61%) were also poor in wave 1. However, 36% of the rural households who were poor in 2005 remained poor in 2012 and 29 percent of urban households who were poor in 2005 remained poor in 2012. In the urban areas, 'chronic poverty' is estimated at 8% in the India Human Development Survey (IHDS) panel.

Citing the IHDS data (of 2011–12), Krishna (2017) notes:

- 13% of all Indians had monthly per capita incomes below Rs 500.
- 22% had Rs 500–1000.
- 30% had Rs 1000–2000.
- 3% of people had more than Rs 10,000.

The layered society may be seen in terms of the rural–urban differentiation, which Krishna (2017) emphasises. Proximity to urban areas, size of land holding, inability of rural migrants to the urban areas to find longer term employment there and lack of jobs in the formal sector of the economy are some of the factors seen to be leading to the segmentation of opportunities for the poor to escape poverty.

Krishna (2017) notes that 'the ladder leading upward is broken in many places'. What is needed to help in moving up the ladder is high-quality education, clear career pathways, role models in the neighbourhood, information about careers, changing attitudes and beliefs (that hold back individual's development).

Based on studies in Karnataka, Rajasthan and Andhra Pradesh, over different periods during 1995–2012, Krishna (2017) points to the severe consequences to entry into professional education due to multiple disadvantages comprising of being

Table 2 Mobility of households across consumption expenditure groups

Status in 2005	Status in 2012			
	Poor	Vulnerable	Middle class	Total
Poor	15.3	15.9	5.7	36.9
Vulnerable	8.2	18.3	13.8	40.3
Middle class	1.5	6.7	14.6	22.8
Total	25.0	40.9	34.1	100.0

Source Based on data reported in Chatterjee et al. (2016). The numbers are adjusted in the largest category of 'vulnerable' column to round off the total percentage of households to 100

poor; rural and belonging to SC or ST; being a woman. He also notes that the multiple disadvantages are common as over 75% of the SC and 90% of ST are rural.

The study by Chatterjee et al. (2016), using IHDS data, shows that, at all levels of expenditure, a larger proportion of households (urban and rural) moved to higher levels of consumption expenditure than those whose expenditures declined. The pattern of changes in consumption expenditure groups is summarised in Table 2.

The findings show that 58.5% ((36.9 − 15 − 3)/36.9) of the households who were poor in 2005 moved to higher consumption expenditure group, i.e., 'vulnerable' or 'middle class' in 2012. However, most of the poor in 2005 were in the 'vulnerable' category or above the poverty line but close to it. During the same period, 20% of those households who were 'vulnerable' became poor and 34% moved into the 'middle-class' category. In other words, although many of those who were poor did become 'non-poor' during the period of 2005–2012, nearly half of those who became non-poor were 'vulnerable' and a significant proportion could become poor if subjected to shocks that reduce income.

3.2   Characteristics of Chronic Poverty

Analysis of panel data shows that dependence on casual agricultural labour, land-lessness, illiteracy (Gaiha 1989), poorer quality land, poorer resource base, lower risk-bearing capacity, (Singh and Binswanger 1993) household size and belonging to a Scheduled Tribe or ST (Bhide and Mehta 2008) are among the characteristics of the chronic poor that make it difficult for them to escape poverty. The ST households are characterised by remote habitations much more than the others. More than the caste status, occupation, assetlessness and inability to benefit from opportunities in nearby urban economies influence the persistence of poverty (Bhide and Mehta 2008).

3.3 Factors Reducing Persistence or Enabling Exit from Poverty

A study of panel households in the semi-arid tropical regions by Deb et al. (2014) covering two villages from Telangana and four from Maharashtra during the period of 1975–1984, 1989 and 2001–2011 found that pathways out of poverty included proximity to new factories and cities, involvement in education, migration and diversification opportunities. The study notes, 'agricultural opportunities are not necessarily the main factors shaping village development'.

Bhide and Mehta (2008) examine the factors or characteristics that explain escape from poverty. Across three types of assets considered, they find while the initial conditions pertaining to cultivable land do not explain movement out of poverty, assets such as own house, income generation from livestock and increased cultivable land are important in enabling escape from poverty. Bhide and Mehta (2004) also draw attention to the importance of initial conditions such as literacy of the household head, proximity to large urban population and infrastructure in escaping from poverty or reducing the incidence of poverty.

Dhamija and Bhide (2009) find that better village infrastructure, percentage of urban population of the district, ownership of agricultural land and having irrigated agricultural land are poverty interrupters, as they increased the probability of households escaping poverty. The Scheduled Caste or Scheduled Tribe status of the household reduces the probability of escape from poverty as compared to the other social groups. These are also among the factors cited by Chatterjee et al. (2016) and Krishna (2017) using alternate data sets and methods of data collection.

The factors commonly responsible for the escape from poverty in the study by Krishna (2017) were (a) diversification of income, (b) private sector employment, (c) public sector employment, (d) government or NGO assistance and (e) irrigation. Diversification of income was a common factor in all three states. Public sector employment was important, and private sector employment was relatively more common in Gujarat than in the other states.

Improving the quality of education in the rural areas comes up in Krishna's (2017) work as the key builder of capacity to escape from poverty. He concludes that realisation of the potential of urbanisation will require more investments in rural India.

Chatterjee et al. (2016) noted that the following factors can help the poor to escape from poverty. 'Non-farm wage employment' was the 'main ticket' out of poverty. 'Regular jobs' were a key feature of the households that escaped from poverty and helped in enabling them to remain 'non-poor'. Non-farm casual jobs helped the households to escape poverty, but a large number of those in casual non-farm employment also fell into poverty.

The steep rise in the wages of casual labour helped many of those who were poor to escape from poverty.

Urban areas create more jobs and therefore help in reducing poverty. However, this also implies that low-income states, which are less urbanised, need a differentiated strategy.

The analysis by Chatterjee et al. (2016) reiterates some of the factors that influence the dynamics of poverty that were identified by the earlier studies (Bhide and Mehta 2011; Dhamija and Bhide 2009) based on use of panel data for the rural households in the country. However, the paper provides more recent evidence, highlights additional important aspects of factors impacting the income mobility of households and particularly emphasises the role of urbanisation in poverty reduction. The paper also argues for creation of 'suitable jobs' for women to improve their participation in labour force as this is one additional source of income that can help households to increase their earnings.

Taken together, the above findings highlight the role of village-level infrastructure, rural–urban linkages and possession of assets as poverty interrupters or in assisting the poor in escaping from poverty or reducing the probability of downward mobility of households on the poverty scale. Put differently, improvements in the development of village-level infrastructure, job opportunities – implied by greater urban linkages – and assets enable the poor to move out of poverty.

3.4   Factors Leading to Entry into Poverty

Downward mobility is a significant aspect of poverty dynamics, and several factors drive people into poverty. For instance, the sudden onset of a long-term and expensive illness exacerbates the suffering of those who are already poor and drives many of those who are non-poor into poverty. For those who work in the unorganised sector, ill health is often associated with having to forego income owing to inability to work. It drains the household of its financial resources and may lead to debt at usurious interest rates to cover expenses (Bhide and Mehta 2003; Mehta and Gupta 2005). This is also mentioned in Krishna (2003), Noponen (1991) and Sen (2003).

Other factors that lead to entry into poverty include social expenses (Krishna 2003), disasters, loss of natural or human or financial assets or adverse market conditions (Sen 2003; Noponen 1991), severe crop shocks (Gaiha and Imai 2003) and lack of job opportunities, assets. (NCAER 1986a,b; Singh and Binswanger 1993). Noponen (1991) also draws attention to the repeated economic shocks suffered by poor households.

The analysis of factors influencing entry into poverty reported by Dhamija and Bhide (2009) shows that better village infrastructure and household size are the only variables that decrease the probability of a household entering into poverty. Another set of factors that reduce the household's poverty status from becoming more severe are village-level infrastructure, village population, percentage of urban population of the district, ownership of house or livestock and irrigation. The latter set of factors do not influence non-poor households in entering into poverty, but they reduce the probability that a marginally poor household will become severely poor.

Weaker infrastructure, urban linkages and lack of assets increase the vulnerability of poor households to further shocks that may increase the severity of poverty. The Scheduled Caste households are more likely to enter into poverty compared with the other social groups.

Krishna (2017) provides a number of insights in his studies of households conducted around 2003–04 based on data pertaining to the previous 25 years through the recall method. In the study of rural households in Andhra Pradesh, Gujarat and Rajasthan, he finds that common factors leading households into poverty are (a) poor health- and health-related expenditures, (b) marriage-, dowry- and new household-related expenditures, (c) funeral-related expenses and (d) drought, irrigation failure and crop disease.

Thorat et al. (2017) find that 'traditional caste and religious differences remain a major impediment for escaping poverty and pose an equally strong risk for falling into poverty. In contrast, educational attainment and a salaried position offer protection against the danger of falling into poverty but offer somewhat less help once there. Urban location offers similar protection against falling into poverty but almost no advantage in escaping poverty'. But even in this study, the shocks that drive households into poverty at the household level do not seem to have been covered to explain entry into poverty: the health shocks, macroeconomic shocks during the intervening periods (related to employment or price changes) and financial shocks. As the study by Deb et al. (2014) notes, the land owned by the households reduced to almost half between 1975 and 2011.

Thorat et al. (2017) consider the role of a wide range of factors in influencing poverty dynamics. Although they do not examine the factors influencing 'chronic poverty', they examine the factors influencing entry into poverty and exit. The study points to the advantages of urban location, physical capital assets, human capital (in the form of education) and social capital (membership in formal/informal organisations) as protection against entry into poverty. The study points out that reaching a certain minimum level of income (above poverty) is important for the factors to effectively 'protect against slipping into poverty'.

4 Assessing Future Prospects of Poverty Reduction

Policy statements have repeatedly aimed at 'eliminating poverty', but the goal has remained elusive. Observed reduction in the incidence of poverty, measured using a rather narrow yardstick of a minimum level of consumption, over time has been a basis for assessing future scenarios for the incidence of poverty.

The rate of economic growth, composition of economic growth, urbanisation, infrastructure development and progress in improving health and education have been the criteria to assess the future levels of poverty.

The Millennium Development Goals set a goal of halving the extreme poverty ratio during the 15-year period from 2000 to 2015. This required an understanding of what drives changes in poverty so that policies could identify instruments to design strategies to achieve the desired goal. Nevertheless, the strategies that have been adopted in India rely on multiple instruments and approaches, given the scale of the problem and its complexity. From a 'beneficiary-oriented welfare pro-gramme' approach, the policies saw a change to adoption of the 'rights-based approach' in the first decade of the twenty-first century. From reliance on just the government machinery, the approach changed to including the participation of non-government organisations in the implementation of the development pro-grammes aimed at poverty reduction. Finally, we now have the move towards cash transfers rather than the delivery of subsidised goods and services. The method-ologies used for assessing the future scenarios of poverty do not capture all the changes in the policies and approaches of the government. What they do is to incorporate the recent trends.

Bhide and Dash (2011) refer to a number of studies that have considered the relationship between incidence of poverty and factors influencing poverty. The factors have ranged from initial level of income and income inequality, economic growth rate, changes in income inequality, initial levels of human capital, land distribution, quality of human capital (incorporating health, education and skills), urbanisation, stage of development (composition of economic output), changes in relative prices – particularly the rise in food prices and public expenditure.

The evidence from panel data also points to the factors that either accelerate or decelerate income mobility of the households.

It is, therefore, not merely economic growth but a host of initial conditions and the trajectories of different variables, which influence the poverty scenario that unfolds in the future periods. Studies by Fan et al. (1999) use a model to estimate and assess rural poverty. Virmani (2008) provides an analysis of incidence of poverty taking into account initial level of income (GDP), economic growth rate (GDP growth rate) and consumption share of the lower 40% of population, all at the level of states. The Planning Commission also provided projections of poverty rates over the perspective plan periods (Planning Commission 1998).

Taking into account the previous studies, Bhide and Dash (2011) estimate a measure of HCR as the dependent variable and per capita GSDP, ratio of GSDP from primary sectors to overall GSDP, consumption inequality (and its square), road density and HDI for rural and urban areas separately at the state level for the period of 1973–74 to 2004–05 excluding the data for 1999–00.

The model used for assessing the future scenarios relating to poverty was:

$$Ln\ (HCR/1 - HCR) = f\ [Ln\ (GSDP/POP), (GSDP\_PRI/\ GSDP),\ LnHDI,\ Ln\ Infra]$$

(6)

The model was estimated for rural and urban poverty using state-level data in a balanced panel fixed effects framework for the period 1973–74 to 2004–05 excluding 1999–00.

Based on a range of assumptions relating to the explanatory variables for the projection period, the study projected HCR of 21.5% for 2011–12 for rural and urban areas combined, close to the actual estimate of 21.9%. However, the projections for rural areas at 21.6% were lower than actuals at 25.7% while they were much higher for urban areas at 21.4% compared to the actual HCR of 13.7% in 2011–12. Errors in the projection of independent variables, separately for rural and urban areas, may have led to the deviation between the projected and achieved poverty reduction.

As we had noted earlier, the assessments of poverty using merely the correlates of poverty and structure of population in poverty are incomplete without reflecting the dynamics of poverty. The pattern of dynamics illustrated by the rural panel surveys of 1971–81 and 1981–98 shows that over long periods, as many as 50% of the poor households have remained poor. The analysis presented by Krishna (2017) suggests that the 'ladders' needed for exit from poverty are not working. It is difficult to examine the trends in poverty from 1993–94 to 2011–12 because of changes in methodology adopted in official statistics in measuring incidence of poverty. However, taking note of the fact that the extent of reduction in poverty broadly matches whichever methodology is adopted, one can extend the trends in HCR over the period from 2004–05 to 2011–12 applying the reductions seen from subsequent approaches. The sharp reduction in rural HCR by 16% points over 7 years (2004–05 to 2011–12), therefore, requires an assessment of whether this reflects a sharp reduction in the long term or chronic poverty or a temporary respite. Whether the impact of urbanisation, articulated in the work of Chatterjee et al. (2016), has been strong enough to reduce chronic poverty in the rural areas needs further analysis.

5   Summary and Conclusions

While the empirical analysis of incidence of poverty has highlighted many of the structural characteristics of the society and economy in perpetuating poverty, the studies of poverty dynamics highlight the vulnerabilities of the households that are barely above the poverty line and the 'ladders' that need to be there for the poor to move out of poverty in a sustained manner.

Measurement and analysis of the incidence of poverty and changes in the incidence of poverty are both important for designing strategies for achieving the goal of eliminating poverty. While the measures have remained inadequate in capturing the deprivation and suffering that the poor experience, implementation of policy measures and assessment of the impact of policies require the use of appropriate indicators. Such indicators should include factors affecting poverty dynamics in order to design poverty reduction policies and assess their impact.

In this chapter, we have drawn attention to the insights from studies of poverty dynamics that complement the analysis of incidence of poverty. While the latter point to the correlates of poverty in terms of characteristics of individuals, house-holds, rural and urban locations and regions of residence, the former examine the processes by which the correlates help the poor escape poverty or lead to persis-tence of it. The incidence of poverty – at minimal levels of income – has declined over the years, but the chronicity of poverty is still significant. Programmes such as employment guarantee, subsidised food, health insurance, crop insurance, old age pension, etc., aim to provide a protective umbrella for the households that are at low levels of income so that they do not slip further down the income and consumption ladder. However, helping the lower income households to access and utilise opportunities for increasing their incomes and well-being remains equally relevant.

Urbanisation, infrastructure, education, good health and geography are seen to be the ladders to enable the poor escape from poverty. However, there is a need to invest in good quality education, health care and infrastructure so that these steps in the ladder are accessible to the poor, who need them most to escape from poverty.

The analysis points to the increased need for examining the dynamics of poverty or more broadly income mobility, to understand the strategies that can assist the poor to move out of poverty in a sustained manner and to protect the non-poor from falling into poverty. Poverty dynamics may also encompass other dimensions of poverty which point to how sustainable the observed income mobility would be. In this sense, expanding the household surveys from cross section to longitudinal and from income or consumption indicators to those covering health, education and habitation would be essential to understand the prospects for further reduction in poverty as the public policies aim to improve these indicators and achieve the SDGs.

References

Bhide, S., & Dash, R. (2011). Prospects for poverty reduction in India. CPRC-IIPA Working Paper No. 47, IIPA, New Delhi.

Bhide, S., & Mehta, A. K. (2003). Chronic poverty in rural India using panel data: Issues and findings. Paper presented at a conference on staying poor, chronic poverty and development policy. Manchester, 7–9 April.

Bhide, S., & Mehta, A. K. (2004). Correlates of incidence and exit from chronic poverty in rural India: Evidence from panel data, CPRC and IIPA.

Bhide, S., & Mehta, A. K. (2005). Tackling poverty through panel data: Rural poverty in India 1970–1998. Working Paper 28. Manchester and New Delhi: Chronic Poverty Research Centre, University of Manchester and Indian Institute of Public Administration.

Bhide, S., & Mehta, A. K. (2008). Economic growth and poverty dynamics. Working Paper 36. Manchester and New Delhi: Chronic Poverty Research Centre, University of Manchester and Indian Institute of Public Administration.

Bhide, S., & Mehta, A. K. (2011). Dynamics of poverty, in India chronic poverty report, towards solutions and new compacts in a dynamic context. In A. K. Mehta, A. Shepherd, S. Bhide, A. Shah, & A. Kumar (Eds.). New Delhi: IIPA.

Calvo, C., & Dercon, S. (2009). Chronic poverty and all that: The measurement of poverty over time. In T. Addison, D. Hulme, & R. Kanbur (Eds.), *Poverty dynamics, interdisciplinary perspectives*. New York: Oxford University Press.

Chatterjee, U., Murgai, R., Narayan, A., & Rama, M. (2016). Pathways to reducing poverty and sharing prosperity in India, lessons from drivers of change, dynamics of rural livelihoods and poverty in SAT India. *Research Bulletin* (p. 50), No. 26. Patancheru 502 324, Telangana, India: International Crops Research Institute for the Semi-Arid Tropics.

Deb, U., Bantilan, C., & Anupam, G. V. (2014). Drivers of change, dynamics of rural livelihoods and poverty in SAT India. *Research Bulletin*, No. 26, Patancheru, Telangana, India: International Crop Research Institute for the Semi Arid Tropics (ICRISAT).

Dhamija, N., & Bhide, S. (2009). Dynamics of chronic poverty: variations in factors influencing entry and exit of chronic poor. Working Paper 39. Manchester and New Delhi: Chronic Poverty Research Centre, University of Manchester and Indian Institute of Public Administration.

Fan, S., Hazell, P., & Thorat, S. K. (1999). Linkages between Government spending and poverty in rural India. Research report #110, International Food Policy Research Institute, Washington, DC.

Gaiha, R. (1988). Income mobility in rural India. *Economic and Cultural Change, 36*(2), 2–8 January.

Gaiha, R. (1989). On estimates of rural poverty in India: An assessment. *Asian Survey, 29*(7), 687–697.

Gaiha, R., & Imai. (2003). Vulnerability, shocks and persistence of poverty—estimates for semi-arid rural South India. University of Delhi, and University of Oxford.

Gaiha, R., & Deolalikar, A. B. (1993). Persistent, expected and innate poverty: Estimates for semi arid rural South India. *Cambridge Journal of Economics, 17*(4), 409–421.

Government of India. (1979). Report of the task force on projections of minimum needs and effective consumption demand. New Delhi: Perspective Planning Division, Planning Commission.

Government of India. (1993). Report of the expert group on estimation of proportion and number of poor. New Delhi: Perspective Planning Division, Planning Commission.

Government of India. (2008). Eleventh five-year plan: Inclusive growth. New Delhi: Planning Commission.

Hulme, D., Moore, K., & Shepherd, A. (2003). Chronic poverty: Meanings and analytical frameworks. In A. K. Mehta, S. Ghosh, D. Chatterjee, & N. Menon (Eds.), *Chronic poverty in India*. New Delhi: IIPA.

Krishna, A. (2003). Escaping poverty and falling into poverty: Who gains, who loses, and why? In *Conference on Staying Poor, Chronic Poverty and Development Policy*. Manchester, 7–9 April.

Krishna, A. (2017). *Broken ladder, the paradox and potential of India's one billion*. Gurgaon: Penguin Random House India.

Mehta, A. K., & Bhide, S. (2003). Issues in chronic poverty: Panel data based analysis. Working Paper, No. 6. New Delhi: CPRC-IIPA.

Mehta, A. K., & Bhide, S. (2010). Poverty and Poverty Dynamics in India, Estimates, Determinants and Policy Responses. Presented at a Conference in Manchester on Ten Years of War Against Poverty. Available at: http://www.chronicpoverty.org/publications/details/poverty-and-poverty-dynamics-in-india.

Mehta, A. K., & Gupta, S. (2005). *The Impact of HIV/AIDS on Women Care Givers in Situations of Poverty: Policy Isssue* New Delhi: United Nations Development Fund for Women South Asia and Institute of Public Administration.

Mehta, A. K. & Shepherd, A. (2006) (Eds). Chronic poverty and development policy in India, New Delhi: Sage.

Mehta, A. K., Shepherd, A., Bhide, S., Shah, A., & Kumar, A. (2011). *India chronic poverty report: Towards solutions and new compacts in a dynamic context* (p. 56). New Delhi: Indian Institute of Public Administration.

National Council of Applied Economic Research (NCAER). (1986a). Changes in household income, inter-class mobility and income distribution in rural India: A longitudinal study, 1970–71 to 1981–82. Unpublished report. New Delhi: NCAER.

National Council of Applied Economic Research (NCAER). (1986b). Demographic and economic interrelationships in rural India: A longitudinal study, 1970–71 to 1981–82. Unpublished report. New Delhi: NCAER.

Noponen, H. (1991). The dynamics of work and survival for the urban poor: A gender analysis of panel data from Madras. *Development and Change, 22*(2), 233–260.

Planning Commission. (1998). *Ninth Five Year Plan*. New Delhi: Planning Commission.

Shah, A., & Sah, D. C. (2003). Chronic poverty in a remote rural district in South West Madhya Pradesh: A multidimensional analysis of its extent and causes. Working Paper 5. Manchester and New Delhi: Chronic Poverty Research Centre, University of Manchester and Indian Institute of Public Administration.

Singh, R. P., & Binswanger, H. (1993). Income growth in poor dryland areas of India's semi-arid tropics. *Indian Journal of Agricultural Economics, 48*(1), 51–64.

Sen, B. (2003). Drivers of escape and descent: Changing household fortunes in rural Bangladesh. *World Development, 31*(3), 513–534.

Thorat, A., Vanneman, R., Desai, S., & Dubey, A. (2017). Escaping and falling into poverty. *World Development, 93,* 413–426.

Virmani, A. (2008). Growth and poverty: policy implications for lagging states. *Economic and Political Weekly*, January. pp. 54–62.

World Bank. (1997). India, achievements and challenges in reducing poverty. Report 16483-IN. New Delhi: Country Operations, Industry & Finance Division, Country Department II, South Asia Region, World Bank.

Chapter 4
Hunger, Under-Nutrition and Food Security in India

N. C. Saxena

1 Introduction

In the past two decades since India achieved high economic growth, a curious problem has haunted the country and vexed its policy makers: India's rising GDP has had little impact on food security[1] and the nutrition levels of its population. Per capita availability as well as consumption of food grains has declined; the cereal intake of the bottom 30% of the population continues to be much less than that of the top two deciles of the population, despite the latter group's better access to fruits, vegetables and meat products; the calorie consumption of the bottom half of the population has been consistently going down since 1987; the percentage of under-nourished stunted children was as high as 39% in 2014; and more than half of India's women and three-quarters of its children are anaemic, with little decline in these estimates in the past eight years, resulting in maternal mortality and under-weight babies. As part of the world community, India had pledged to halve hunger by 2015, as stated in the Millennium Development Goal 1, but the available data shows that this target has not been met.[2]

With necessary permissions, this chapter draws heavily from Saxena (2011). It also draws on the author's other previous articles.

[1]The commonly accepted definition adopted at the 1996 World Food Summit is: food security is achieved when all people, at all times, have physical and economic access to sufficient, safe and nutritious food to meet their dietary needs and food preferences for an active and healthy life.
[2]http://www.hrln.org/hrln/pdf/rtf/reports/Hunger%20under%20nutrition%20and%20food%20security%20in%20India.pdf.

N. C. Saxena (✉)
Former Secretary
Planning Commission, GOI, New Delhi, India
e-mail: naresh.saxena@gmail.com

There is a link between nutritional status and human effort and productivity. Hunger affects the ability of individuals to work productively, to think clearly and to resist disease. Hunger may lead to low output and hence poor wages. Hunger is thus both a cause and an effect of poverty. Hunger in India has gender and age dimensions too. Women, children and old people are less likely to get full nutritious meals needed for their development. There are important seasonal variations in nutritional and health status depending on the cycle of agricultural work. Hunger and starvation also have regional and geographical dimensions. Tribal regions in India have a higher incidence of food insecurity than the non-tribal regions in the same state. Agriculture has brought uneven development across regions and is characterised by low levels of productivity and the degradation of natural resources in tribal areas, leading to low per capita crop output and reduced gathering from common property resources (CPRs).

In short, all indicators point to the hard fact that endemic hunger continues to afflict a large proportion of the Indian population. The International Food Policy Research Institute shows India suffering from alarming hunger, ranked 80 out of the 104 developing countries studied, much below Vietnam and Nepal, countries poorer than India in 2015, and 100 out of 119 countries in 2017 as shown in Table 1.

Hunger can also be equated with chronic food insecurity, as both refer to a situation in which people consistently consume diets inadequate in calories and essential nutrients. This often happens as a result of the inability to 'access' food because of lack of purchasing power. Destitution, leading in extreme cases to starvation deaths but in any case to a life in misery, is more endemic among certain groups. These include persons with disabilities, persons with stigmatising illnesses such as leprosy or HIV/AIDS, the elderly and the young who lack family support, and single women. Social and employment factors causing destitution include being in a scheduled caste population, or tribal population, or being a manual scavenger, beggar, sex worker, landless labourer or artisan. Persons displaced by natural disasters or development projects are also often in this group. Because of the prolonged deprivation of sufficient food and recurring uncertainty about its availability,

Table 1 Country global hunger index scores by rank

Rank 2015	Rank 2017	Country	1990	1995	2000	2005	2015	2017
21	29	China	25.1	23.2	15.9	13.2	8.6	7.5
37	46	Thailand	28.4	22.3	17.6	13.6	11.9	10.6
49	64	Vietnam	44.6	38.8	30.3	24.6	14.7	16.0
58	72	Nepal	44.5	40.3	36.9	31.6	22.2	22.0
69	84	Sri Lanka	31.3	29.7	27.0	25.9	25.5	25.5
73	88	Bangladesh	52.2	50.3	38.5	31.0	27.3	26.5
80	100	India	48.1	42.3	38.2	38.5	29.0	31.4

IFPRI (2015, 2017)

these people are forced to lose their dignity through foraging and begging, debt bondage and low-end, highly underpaid work; self-denial; and sacrifice of other survival needs like medicine or children's education. Thus, they transfer their misery to the next generation (Mander 2008).

This paper examines the hunger and nutrition situation prevailing in the country and reviews the obligations and initiatives taken by the Government of India (GOI) to ensure food and nutritional security through various policies and schemes.

Section 2 of the paper looks at various forms of hunger and makes a distinction between explicit hunger and chronic or endemic hunger, which manifests itself in a lower intake of essential calories, proteins, fats and micro-nutrients, resulting in the underdevelopment of the human mind and body. It examines data, both from government and other sources, on various dimensions of hunger, including self-reported hunger. It also discusses India's record in improving its position on various indicators generally used to measure hunger, such as food intake, calorie consumption, Body Mass Index (BMI), under-nourishment among children, child mortality and Global Hunger Index (GHI).

Section 3 analyses various policies and programmes that affect food security both at the micro- and macro-levels, such as agricultural production, the Public Distribution System, the Mid-Day Meals Scheme and the Integrated Child Development Services (ICDS) programme for improving child malnutrition.[3] The paper ends with a discussion of accountability, which is a cross-sectoral issue.

2 Types and Dimensions of Hunger

There are essentially two types of hunger (Gopaldas 2006). The first is overt (or raw) hunger, or the need to fill the belly every few hours. Hunger in simple terms is the desire to consume food. It can also be termed as self-reported hunger, whereby people judge their own ability to fulfil the physiological urge to satisfy their hunger (Saxena 2011).

The second type of hunger occurs when the human body gets used to having less food than necessary for healthy development and after a while does not even demand more food. If people have always eaten less than their needs, their bodies adjust to less food in what is known as biostasis (Krishnaraj 2006). It is also possible to fill up the stomach with non-nutritious food, which does not provide the required calories or micro-nutrients[4] like vitamins, iron, iodine, zinc, and calcium that are required in tiny amounts. Another situation could be when the essential

---

[3]http://www.hrln.org/hrln/pdf/rtf/reports/Hunger%20under%20nutrition%20and%20food%20security%20in%20India.pdf.

[4]Deficiency in micro-nutrients is often referred to as endemic hunger. However, micro-nutrients do not work unless the person is consuming sufficient calories, protein, etc.

calories, proteins, fats and micro-nutrients are not absorbed in the body due to ill-health and poor hygiene. In all such cases, hunger is not articulated.

This second kind of hunger may be termed chronic or endemic hunger, as it is not felt, recognised or voiced by children or adults. Chronic hunger does not translate into hunger pangs, but into subtle changes in the way the human body develops. For instance, an underfed child may be underweight or stunted for his or her age, if not consuming sufficient calories and fats. If the child is deficient in Vitamin A, he or she will not be able to see properly at dusk ('night blindness'), and respiratory ailments may also occur. In severe Vitamin A deficiency, the child may go totally blind. In the case of iron-deficiency anaemia, the child will slow down both mentally and physically, perform poorly in school and experience chronic tiredness. In the case of iodine deficiency, there will be mental retardation. In its severe form, a goitrous lump may grow at the base of the neck. Thus, prolonged hunger means that a predetermined 'physiological requirement' or 'human potential', defined in terms of norms for calorie and other essential nutrients and growth standards, is not reached.

Subjective hunger, or the first kind of hunger, is a matter of articulation – people or populations have to indicate in some fashion that they are going hungry. Self-reported hunger is also difficult to measure, since perceptions of hunger differ from one person to another. Therefore, objective indicators, such as calorie consumption, BMI, stunting and lack of sufficient variety in food intake, offer a better measure for hunger, as it is perfectly possible to have a full belly and yet display every symptom of under-nutrition.

2.1 Self-reported Hunger

Surveys on self-reported hunger depend on the responses of the head of the household, often a man, who would not be sufficiently aware of the quantity and content of meal left for his wife and other female members of the house (Kundu 2006: 120). Moreover, he may not like to admit that he cannot provide even two square meals to his dependants. Pride, self-image and dignity are issues here, which lead to a deep sense of shame and reluctance on the part of heads of households to publicly admit their incapacity to provide for their families. This may result in under-reporting on the number of meals family members are able to afford (GOI 1993: 53). Despite this limitation, a United Nations Development Programme (UNDP) survey (2008) of 16 districts in the seven poorest states of India showed that for 7.5% of respondents' access to food is highly inadequate, and for another 29% of the households it is somewhat inadequate. A West Bengal Government survey also reported that 15% of families were facing difficulties in arranging two

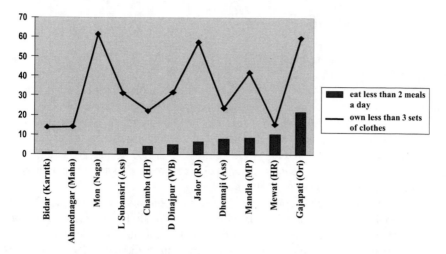

Fig. 1 Percentage of rural households by selected measures of poverty. *Source* UNDP (2007)

square meals a day year round.[5] These figures are gloomier than those in the National Sample Survey Organisation (NSSO) survey of the Ministry of Statistics and Programme Implementation, which claim a drastic decline in self-reported hunger in India from 16.1% in 1983 to 0.9% in 2011–12.[6]

In another survey (UNDP 2007) in selected districts by Pratham, a voluntary organisation, rural residents were asked about the number of meals they consumed on most days in a year and the number of clothes the young women in their families possessed. The results are shown in Fig. 1.

The figure shows that the those consuming less than two meals a day varied from one to 23% in the rural areas of selected districts, while the number of women having just one or two sets of clothes was as high as 60% in some districts.

Hunger has many faces: insufficient food intake, calorie deficiency, loss of energy, increased susceptibility to disease, shortfalls in nutritional status, disability and premature death. No single indicator can provide a complete picture, and a variety of different indicators such as food and calorie consumption, BMI, low weight and height among children, and anaemia among women and children should be used in analysing different aspects of the problem. Dietary diversity, rather than just the consumption of food staples, needs to be measured. Some aspects of hunger, such as the stability of food consumption between seasons and between years, are generally not captured by the existing data.

---

[5]Roy Rajat 2008: Endemic Hunger in West Bengal, Economic & Political Weekly May 3.
[6]Kumaran (2008) and NSSO (2014b): Nutritional Intake in India, 2011–12, NSS 68th Round, Ministry of Statistics and Programme Implementation, New Delhi.

2.2   Food Insecurity

Hunger and malnutrition are caused by a large number of factors, of which availability and access to a balanced diet are important. NSSO data shows that per capita cereal consumption in India is lower than the desired norm (NSSO 2014a), and it has shown a decline over time. As regards changes in expenditure on food over the years, two trends are observed. First, while consumption expenditures in both rural and urban regions rose, this was not reflected in a commensurate rise in expenditure on food (Saxena 2013, 2016a, b). As shown in Table 2, the growth in food expenditure has been significantly lower than the increase in overall expenditure on all goods during the period of analysis.

Thus, the average per capita food expenditure during the period 1993–2010 increased only by 0.2% annually in rural India and fell slightly by 0.1% per annum in the urban areas (Saxena 2013, 2016a, b). Examination of the consumption expenditure data shows that consumption expenditure increased by about 130% during 2004–5 to 2011–12, with most of the increase occurring for non-food items such as education, conveyance, durable goods and medicine. It is to be noted here that during 2004–05, expenditure on food items was higher than non-food expenditure by about 20%. However, this trend got reversed by 2011–12 with non-food expenses exceeding food expenses by about 5%. One may argue that this could indicate shift to more sedentary lifestyle needing less calories. However, the second trend negates this hypothesis for the poor, as the decile-wise data (Table 3) clearly shows that the hard-working poor consume much less cereal (the cheapest form of food) than the non-poor. It also shows a declining trend in the annual per capita consumption of cereals, for all classes of people.

Table 3[7] clearly shows that as India moved to greater prosperity in the last twenty years the cereal consumption of the rural rich went down, but there was no increase for the poor. At any given point of time, the cereal intake of the bottom 10% in rural India continues to be about 15–40% less than the cereal intake of the top decile of the population, despite better access of the latter group to fruits, vegetables and meat products. Their sedentary lifestyle too should be taken into account while assessing the difference between the two groups (Saxena 2016a, b). Food needs of the non-poor may be declining because labour-saving devices are becoming increasingly available in the household, in the workplace and in transportation (NSSO 2014b). For the upper segment of population, the decline in cereal consumption may be attributed to a diversification in food consumption, easy access to supply of other high-value agricultural commodities, changed tastes and preferences, and consumption of more expensive non-foodgrain products. Higher economic growth and per capita incomes thus contribute to reduction in per capita demand for cereals for the rich (Saxena 2011).

---

[7]It is likely that eating out for all classes has increased. Cereal content of meals taken outside at own cost or at public cost is hardly known and is not fully captured in the NSSO data.

Table 2 Growth in real average per capita monthly expenditure on all goods and on food (in Rs) at 1993–94 prices

Years	Average per capita expenditure		Average per capita food expenditure	
	Rural	Urban	Rural	Urban
1993–94	281.4	458.0	177.8	250.3
2009–10	347.5	637.8	184.8	244.9
Annual rate of growth 1993–94 to 2009–10	1.3	2.1	0.2	-0.1

Source Gupta (2012)

Table 3 Changes in per capita cereal consumption (kg per month) in since 1993–94 for different MPCE classes: all-India, rural

Year	Monthly per capita cereal consumption (kg) in population percentile class										
	0–10	10–20	20–30	30–40	40–50	50–60	60–70	70–80	80–90	90–100	Average
1993–94	10.5	12.0	12.6	13.2	13.3	13.7	14.1	14.4	14.6	15.4	13.4
1999–00	10.5	11.6	12.3	12.6	12.9	13.0	13.4	13.5	13.7	14.0	12.7
2004–05	10.4	11.3	11.7	12.0	12.2	12.4	12.6	12.8	12.7	13.1	12.1
2009–10	10.2	10.6	11.1	11.1	11.5	11.4	11.7	11.8	12.1	12.1	11.3
2011–12	10.4	10.8	11.0	11.1	11.5	11.5	11.5	11.6	11.5	11.7	11.2

NSS 68th Round, Report No. 555

However, for those who are around or below the poverty line, this has to be understood as a distress phenomenon, as with marginal increase in their incomes over time they are forced to cut down on their food consumption to meet other pressing demands that were not considered important in the past (Saxena 2010). For instance, as more schools open, the poor too wish to send their children to schools, where expenses are incurred on clothes, books, etc., despite the school fees being met by government. These expenses would thus become a new item on the household budget, and food expenditure may be curtailed to make room for it. Fighting sickness leads to another chunk of essential expenses, for which opportunities did not exist in the past, as there were no doctors in the vicinity. The share of fuel and light in total consumer expenditure has risen from under 6 to 10% in both rural and urban areas between 1972–73 and 2004–05. Finally, the rural labouring masses have to spend on transport in order to earn their livelihoods (Saxena 2013, 2016a, b). The food budget of the poor has been squeezed out because the cost of meeting the minimum non-food requirements has increased (Sen 2005). Thus, it is not possible for households around the poverty line to purchase their initial food basket within their current food budget.

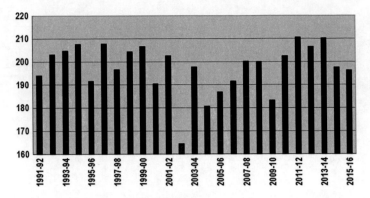

Fig. 2 Per capita annual foodgrain production (kg)

There are also issues at the macro-level. According to the central government, foodgrain production in India has remained almost stagnant[8] during the last two decades, as shown in Fig. 2 (Economic Survey 2016).

From this stagnant production, India has been exporting on an average 7 million tonnes of cereals per annum, causing availability to decline further from 510 g per day per capita in 1991 to 401 g in 2013 (Economic Survey 2016). At the macro-level, foodgrains availability in India is calculated as 87.5% of gross production (the rest is estimated as requirement for seeds, farm animal feed and waste) plus net imports minus changes in government stocks. Assuming no net change in private stocks, this can be taken as a good proxy for per capita foodgrain consumption in the country. Considering five-year averages, India saw a rise in the foodgrains availability[9] per head from 433 g during 1973–77 to 479 g in the early 1990s. However, since then there has been a slide to a low of 445 g per head per day by 2012, a level not seen since the drought years of the 1970s (see Fig. 3).

This has adversely affected the cereal intake of the bottom 30% which, as shown in Table 2, continues to be significantly less than the cereal intake of the top decile of the population. Their expenditure on health, education, liquor, tobacco, transport and fuel has also gone up. Food is still needed, but not demanded as they get used to eating less food and, in the process, get stunted and malnourished. Endemic hunger (often hidden) continues to afflict a large proportion of Indian population (Saxena 2013, 2016a, b).

[8]Production of other forms of food, such as fruits, vegetables, poultry, and livestock products, has increased at a faster rate, but on the whole, there is no improvement in food and nutritional security (Chand and Jumrani 2013).

[9]One of the reasons for decline in availability is the increase in government stocks.

Fig. 3 Average per capita daily availability of foodgrains in India during the last four decades

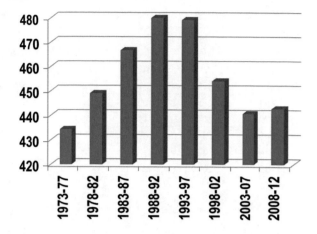

2.3   Calorie Consumption

In this section, we focus on calorie deficiency – caused by not consuming the energy required by the body to see how the situation has changed over the years in India.

As is well known, the official norm of nutritional requirement has been fixed (GOI 1979) at 2400 kcal/day and 2100 kcal/day for rural and urban areas (the difference being attributed to the lower rates of physical activity in the urban areas), respectively.[10] Although these figures have not been revised, an Expert Group chaired by Rangarajan (Government of India 2014) recommended in 2014 lower energy requirement of 2155 kcal per person per day in rural areas and 2090 kcal per person per day in urban areas. The protein and fat requirements were estimated as 48 and 28 g per capita per day, respectively, in rural areas; and 50 and 26 g per capita per day in urban areas (Rangarajan and Dev 2014).

The mean per capita consumption of calories, protein and fats as calculated by various NSS rounds is shown in Table 4.

Thus, in spite of India's rapid economic growth, there has been a sustained decline in per capita calorie and protein consumption between 1983 and 2009–10; fats are the only major nutrient group whose per capita consumption is unambiguously increasing. This unexpected decline of per capita calorie consumption despite reduction in poverty is often referred to as 'calorie consumption puzzle' in India.

---

[10]The average calorie norm of 2110 kcal per capita per day prescribed by the Food and Agriculture Organisation (FAO) for South Asia (Bajpai et al. 2005) in the 1980s is much lower than the 2400 kcal norm that has been typically used by the GOI. The latest calorie norm used by the FAO for India is 1820 kcal (Menon et al. 2008), which would reduce the percentage of under-nourished people to only 17.5 (Chand and Jumrani 2013) in 2010–12.

Table 4 Mean per capita consumption of calories, protein and fats

Year	Calories (kcal)		Protein (g)		Fats (g)	
	Rural	Urban	Rural	Urban	Rural	Urban
1983	2240	2070	63.5	58.1	27.1	37.1
1987–88	2233	2095	63.2	58.6	28.3	39.3
1993–94	2153	2073	60.3	57.7	31.1	41.9
1999–2000	2148	2155	59.1	58.4	36.0	49.6
2004–05	2047	2021	57.0	57.0	35.4	47.4
2009–10	2020	1946	55.0	53.5	38.3	47.9
2011–12	2099	2058	56.5	55.7	46.0	58.0

NSSO (2014b)

However, the declining trend got arrested in 2011–12. This increase in both calorie and protein consumption is explained as due to improvements in PDS system and faster agricultural growth between 2004–05 and 2011–12 (Kolady et al. 2016). Some writers (Smith 2013) allude it to improvement in methodology as 2011–12 survey collected additional information on meals taken away from home. These had positive effects on the reversal of the declining trend of mean calorie intake in India.

These figures are the average for the entire population that includes infants, etc., too; calorie consumption for an adult worker would be much higher than the norm given above. The recommended dietary allowances (RDAs) as assessed by ICMR for various age groups and actual calorie intake are shown in Table 5 (Ramachandran 2013). The ICMR recommendations take into account the fact that body weight and physical activity are major determinants of energy requirement, and therefore ICMR has provided recommendations for energy requirements for the reference man (60 kg, moderately active) and reference woman (55 kg, moderately active) and children (+2SD of the NNMB weight for age).[11]

While interpreting the above data, it should be kept in mind that Indians of all age groups weigh far less than the reference weight used for deriving the RDA norm. However, the calorie gap would still be significant even if actual average weights are taken into account. The gap between the requirements and the intake is highest among pregnant and lactating women and in adolescent girls and boys. Bridging the gap in pregnant and lactating women is of paramount importance as this would benefit both the mother and the child (Ramachandran 2013).

As regards intake by different decile groups, similar to the pattern of food consumption, calorie and protein intake of the poorest three deciles even in 2011–12 was about 30–50% less than the consumption of the top decile, despite the poor needing more energy to compensate for harder manual work, as shown in Fig. 4.

---

[11]icmr.nic.in/final/rda-2010.pdf.

Table 5 Recommended dietary allowance (RDA) for Indians

Group	Reference weight (kg)	RDA for ref wt person (kcal/day)	Actual intake (kcal/day)	Gap
Adult man	60	2730	2000	730
Adult woman	55	2230	1738	492
Pregnant		350 more	1726	854
lactating		500 more	1878	852
1–3 years	12.9	1060	714	346
4–6 years	18	1330	978	352
7–9 years	25.1	1690	1230	460
Boys				
10–12 years	34.3	2190	1473	717
13–15 years	47.6	2750	1645	1105
16–17 years	55.4	3020	1913	1107
Girls				
10–12 years	35	2010	1384	626
13–15 years	46.6	2330	1566	764
16–17 years	52.1	2440	1630	810

Source http://icmr.nic.in/final/rda-2010.pdf

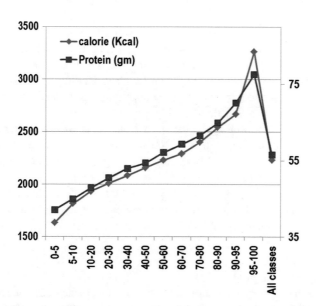

Fig. 4 Daily average calorie and protein intake per capita across MPCE fractile rural classes in 2011–12. *Source* NSSO (2014b)

2.4 BMI

A widely used measure of nutritional status is a combination of weight and height measurements known as the Body Mass Index (BMI). Low body weight, associated with low intakes, is an indication that people are not reaching their growth potential and hence is essentially a sign of continued hunger and nutritional distress. The BMI is defined as weight in kilograms divided by height in metres squared. A BMI of below 18.5 for adults indicates chronic energy deficiency (CED), the result of an intake of calories and other nutrients less than the requirement for a period of several months or years. Low BMI is associated with functional changes such as reduced work capacity for manual work and increased susceptibility to infection.[12]

The prevalence of chronic energy deficiency for adult women has declined from 52% during 1975–79 to 34% during 2011–12, while that of overweight/obesity has increased from 5 to 14% during the same period (Meshram et al. 2016). Median intakes of most of the nutrients have increased over the same period, although they were below recommended levels. This increase in overweight/obesity may be attributed to increased consumption of fatty foods, sedentary lifestyle and improved socio-economic status.[13] There is a need to educate the community about regular physical exercise, low intakes of fats and oils, and a balanced diet.

Data from community-based cross-sectional studies carried out by the National Nutrition Monitoring Bureau (NNMB) in Ten Indian states[14] for various years is shown in Table 6.

At the other end, 14% of women are overweight or obese, as are 12% of men. Thus, India faces today what is known as the triple burden of malnutrition – the coexistence of inadequate calorie intake and under-nutrition among a large section of the population, excess intake of dietary energy leading to obesity and related health issues among another section of the population, and pervasive micro-nutrient deficiencies (Narayanan 2015).

Predictably the percentage of women in rural areas with a BMI below 18.5 in 2004–05 was 41.2 according to the NNMB, which is twice that among urban women, at 22.7 (Arnold et al. 2004). Regarding age distribution, the percentage of women with a BMI below 18.5 ranges from 41.7 for the age group 15–19 to 43.2 for 20–24, 39.4 for 25–29, 35.1 for 30–34 and 31.1 for 35–49. Ironically, it is at the most vulnerable ages, when their reproductive demands are highest, that women are most deficient. So much for India's esteem for mothers!

---

[12]icmr.nic.in/ijmr/2015/august/9.pdf.

[13]https://www.cambridge.org/core/journals/public-health-nutrition/article/trends-in-nutritional-status-and-nutrient-intakes-and-correlates-of-overweightobesity-among-rural-adult-women-1860-years-in-india-national-nutrition-monitoring-bureau-nnmb-national-surveys/A67E56D436D88D02109DBA208059C3B0.

[14]Andhra Pradesh, Karnataka, Kerala, Tamil Nadu, Maharashtra, Madhya Pradesh, Orissa, Uttar Pradesh, Gujarat and West Bengal.

Table 6   Nutrition status of Indian adults, 1975–79 to 2011–12 (BMI)

	Proportion (%) of adults with BMI below 18.5					
	1975–79	1988–90	1996–97	2000–01	2004–05	2011-12
Men	56	49	46	37	33	35
Women	52	49	46	39	36	34

Source Deaton and Drèze (2008) and NNMB (2012)

2.5   Under-nourished Children

Just as for adults, for children too, the anthropometric indicators of nutritional status in India are among the worst in the world. As is well established, the hunger dimension is quantified by measuring underweight, stunting and wasting rates among children because these indirectly reflect inadequate access and lack of affordability of a balanced diet. According to the National Family Health Survey, the proportion of underweight children remained virtually unchanged between 1998–99 and 2005–06 (from 47 to 46% for the age group 0–3). The hunger and malnutrition report (popularly known as HUNGaMA) released by the Prime Minister in January 2012 showed that the number of malnourished children in the 112 rural districts of India was 42% whereas stunting was even higher at 59% (HUNGaMA 2012). Evidence shows that stunted children enrol later in school, perform less well and complete fewer grades; this leads to reduced capabilities and income-earning capacity in adult life and perpetuates the inter-generational cycle of poverty and deprivation in families and communities. This is an unacceptable loss (Chambers and Medeazza 2013).

The latest RSOC[15] data (UNICEF 2014) however shows modest improvement in several indicators. Prevalence of stunting as a measure of under-nutrition among children under-five in India got reduced from 48% in 2005 to 39% in 2013. Initiation of breastfeeding within an hour of birth has improved from 25 to 45% during 2005–13 but remains much below the required threshold of 90% coverage for saving lives and reducing stunting. Current levels of child malnutrition in India are however still higher than those in sub-Saharan Africa.

Children also suffer most because of problems of inadequate diet, poor early care practices and lack of hygiene. With 39% of its child population malnourished and stunted, India's demographic dividend – a large young generation being born each year – will not pay off. Specifically, the return of the investments currently being made in elementary education will be halved because of under-nutrition, which thus remains India's greatest development challenge and a question mark on India's credibility as a global player.

The consequences of stunting are serious, irreversible and lifelong. The losses in physical growth and brain development associated with chronic under-nutrition during the first two years of life can never be regained. The 2013 Lancet nutrition

---

[15]Rapid Survey on Children.

series (Black et al. 2013) estimated that stunting causes about one million child deaths annually worldwide, due to weakened immunity. Furthermore, the children who survive under-nutrition do not often meet their full human potential. Stunted children are more likely to have poor cognition and learning performance in childhood than their well-nourished counterparts. In adulthood, they face diminished productivity and increased risk of nutrition-related chronic diseases, such as obesity, diabetes and hypertension. It ultimately robs the affected poor communities and countries of critical human capital development and undermines investments in health, education and economic growth (Mebrahtu and Sethi 2016).

When one looks at the Indian states, unlike calorie consumption, which is only weakly correlated with poverty, child malnutrition has a strong correlation with poverty (see Table 9). Poorer states such as Madhya Pradesh, Bihar and Jharkhand show a high degree of malnutrition, whereas better-off states such as Punjab, Haryana, Tamil Nadu and Kerala have a comparatively better performance on this indicator.

Emerging economies have demonstrated that child under-nutrition can be drastically reduced: Thailand (Garg and Nandi undated) reduced the percentage of underweight children by half (from 50 to 25%) between 1980 and 1986; Brazil reduced child under-nutrition by 75% (from 20 to 5%) from 1990 to 2006; and China reduced child under-nutrition by 68% (from 25 to 8%) between 1990 and 2002 (UNICEF 2009). Even Viet Nam, a country poorer than India, has seen a reduction in underweight children from 41% in 1996 to 25% in 2006.[16] Therefore, nutrition improvement at national scale is possible. However, economic growth is not enough; it needs to be coupled with effective policy and budgetary action, particularly for the most vulnerable: the youngest, the poorest and the excluded.

2.6   Factors Other Than Food that Lead to Malnutrition

Less well understood than hunger is the nagging problem of under-nutrition among children that leads to them not achieving normal height and weight for their age. The commonly held belief that food insecurity is the primary or even sole cause of malnutrition is misplaced. Even the National Food Security Act, 2013 provides that every pregnant woman and lactating mother shall be entitled to one free meal a day during pregnancy and six months after the childbirth; and maternity benefit of rupees one thousand per month for a period of six months. Thus, the focus is still on food, and not on health and care-related interventions. Consequently, the existing response to malnutrition in India has been skewed towards food-based interventions and has placed little emphasis on schemes addressing the other determinants of malnutrition (Gragnolati et al. 2006).

---

[16]http://www.unsystem.org/scn/Publications/SCNNews/scnnews36.pdf (accessed on 7 July 2014).

Child malnutrition starts very early in life, and often, it is an inter-generational issue. Adolescent girls who are themselves underweight give birth to low weight babies. The child-rearing practices in India unfortunately are highly unscientific, as giving colostrum to the newborn, exclusive breastfeeding for first six months of a child's life, and complementary feeding several times a day after six months are not commonly practised. In the 100 districts studied in the HUNGaMA report, 51% mothers did not give colostrum to the newborn soon after birth and 58% mothers fed water to their infants before six months. Besides, due to bad quality of water and lack of toilets children are exposed to stomach infections, develop diarrhoea and start losing weight. At this stage, they need proper medical care which unfortunately is not available. Then the mothers have to work long hours away from home without any support system and are unable to afford health care (Saxena 2016a, b).

India's age-old habit of defecating in the open – which distinguishes it from many other developing countries – makes matters worse. The proportion of Indians who do this has fallen from 55% a decade ago to 45%, but that is more than enough to help spread diseases, worms and other parasites that make it more difficult to absorb nutrients even when food is abundant. Poor public hygiene may account for much of India's failure to make faster improvements in nutrition.

Thus, there are other factors too that cause malnutrition and hunger, especially among children (Saxena 2011), such as:

- Low status of women in Indian society, their early marriage, low weight at pregnancy and illiteracy leading to low weight of newborn babies.
- Poor childcare practices, such as not immediately starting breastfeeding after birth, no exclusively breastfeeding for the first five months, irregular and insufficient complementary feeding afterwards and lack of quick disposal of child's excreta.
- Poor supply of government services, such as immunisation, access to medical care and lack of priority to primary health care in government programmes.

These factors combined with poor food availability in the family, unsafe drinking water and lack of sanitation lead to high child under-nutrition and permanent damage to their physical and mental capabilities.

2.7 Child Mortality

Mortality in early childhood is measured by Infant mortality rate (the probability of dying before the first birthday) and by under-five mortality (the probability of dying between birth and fifth birthday). All rates are expressed per 1000 live births. India is surely to miss achieving the Millennium Development Goals in respect of these indicators. Infant mortality rate (IMR) under MDGs was targeted to be reduced from 81 in 1990 to 27 by 2015, but the decline has been to only 40 in 2013. Wide differences exist between the attainments of health goals in the better-performing states as compared to the low-performing states. IMR in the poorest 20% of the population is 2.5 times higher than that in the richest 20% of the population. It is clear that national averages of health indices hide wide disparities in public health facilities and health standards in different parts of the country. Given a situation in which national averages in respect of most indices are themselves at unacceptably low levels, the wide inter-state disparity implies that, for vulnerable sections of society in several states, access to public health services is nominal and health standards are grossly inadequate.

Malnutrition in children weakens their immune system, making them more susceptible to disease and less able to fight off infection. It has been estimated that a child is almost ten times more likely to die from key diseases if he or she is severely underweight, and two and a half times more likely to die if he or she is moderately underweight, as compared to an average weight child (Black et al. 2013). Given the fact that more than 3.5 million children die globally on account of under-nutrition, it emerges as a major factor leading to child deaths. Therefore, under-five mortality has been taken by IFPRI as the third indicator for measuring the Hunger Index, as discussed below.

3   Composite Hunger Index by IFPRI

Calorie intake refers to the most proximate aspect of hunger, but it neglects other effects of hunger, such as low weight and mortality. These are captured by the Global Hunger Index (GHI), which was designed to capture three dimensions of hunger: lack of economic access to food, shortfalls in the nutritional status of children and child mortality, which is to a large extent attributable to malnutrition (Weismann et al. 2007). Accordingly, the GHI includes the following three equally weighted indicators: the proportion of people who are food-energy deficient according to UN Food and Agriculture Organisation (FAO[17]) estimates, the proportion of children under the age of five who are underweight according to World Health Organisation (WHO) estimates, and the under-five mortality rate as estimated by UNICEF. Since 2015, stunting and wasting have replaced figures for underweight children, as stunting and wasting are considered better indicators for under-nourishment. The weightage of calorie intake and mortality has remained at one-third each whereas for both stunting and wasting it is one-sixth each now. The GHI ranks countries on a 100-point scale. Zero is the best score (no hunger), and 100 is the worst.

---

[17]According to FAO, after a decline of 20 million in the number of undernourished people between 1990–92 and 1995–97, the number of hungry people in India increased from 201.8 million in 1995–97 to 212.0 million in 2001–03.

The GHI recognises the interconnectedness of these dimensions and therefore captures performance on all four of them. The Index has been an effective advocacy tool which has brought the issue of global and national hunger to the fore in policy debates, especially in developing countries. The ranking of nations on the basis of their index scores has been a powerful tool to help focus attention on hunger, especially for countries like India which underperform on hunger and malnutrition relative to their income levels.

IFPRI estimated that the hunger index for India had declined from 48.1% in 1990 to 29.0% in 2015 (see Table 1), although India still continued to be in the category of nations where hunger was 'alarming'. Worse, its score was poorer than that of many sub-Saharan African counties, which have a lower GDP than India's. This indicates continued poor performance at reducing hunger in India.

The IFPRI report in 2008 estimated the hunger index for 17 major states in India, covering more than 95% of the population. All 17 states had GHI scores that are well above the 'low' and 'moderate' hunger categories. Twelve of the 17 states fall into the 'alarming' category, and one – Madhya Pradesh – into the 'extremely alarming' category. The study concluded that GHI scores are closely aligned with poverty, but that there was little association with state-level economic growth. High levels of hunger are seen even in states that are performing well economically, such as Gujarat and Karnataka.

4   Analysis of Major Programmes and Policy Options

In the foregoing sections, we have discussed some of the dimensions of hunger and its implications for the healthy development of body and mind. Governments have been running many policies and programmes that aim to improve the hunger situation in India, but unfortunately these are not doing very well, as discussed in this section.

Agricultural Production
Hunger and malnutrition are caused by a large number of factors, of which availability and access to a balanced diet are crucial. The consumption basket of the underprivileged households in India is likely to be cereal-centric and not necessarily balanced. In addition to cereals, they should consume adequate quantity of nutritious foods like pulses, coarse grains, fruits, vegetables, dairy products, egg, fish and meat, etc. High market prices as well as lack of awareness deter them from including these essential items in their diet. Public policy thus needs to ensure both production (or availability through imports) and access of all households to nutritious foods.

The current agricultural scene in India has three features that distinguish it from the earlier 'green revolution' phase (1970–85). First, the policy approach to agriculture since the 1990s has been to secure an increase in production through subsidies on inputs such as power, water and fertiliser, and by increasing the MSP rather than through building new capital assets in irrigation, power and rural infrastructure (Saxena 2012a). According to the Planning Commission, budgetary subsidies in agriculture increased from around 3% of agricultural GDP in the late 1970s to about 7% in the early 2000s. During the same period, public investment in agriculture declined from 3.4% of agricultural GDP to 1.9% (Bisaliah 2007).

This has shifted the production base from low-cost regions to high-cost ones, causing an increase in the cost of production, regional imbalances, and an increase in the burden of storage and transport of food grains. The equity, efficiency and sustainability of the current approach are questionable. The subsidies do not improve income distribution nor the demand for labour (Saxena 2004, 2012a). The boost in output from the subsidy-stimulated use of fertiliser, pesticides and water has the potential to damage aquifers and soils – an environmentally unsustainable approach that may partly explain the rising costs and slowing growth and productivity in agriculture, notably in Punjab and Haryana. Although private investment in agriculture has grown, this has often involved macro-economic inefficiencies (such as private investment in diesel-generating sets instead of public investment in electricity supply). Public investment in agriculture has fallen dramatically since the 1980s and so has the share of agriculture in the total gross capital formation. Instead of promoting low-cost options that have a higher capital: output ratio, the present policies have resulted in excessive use of capital on farms, such as too many tube wells in water-scarce regions.

Second, the intensity of private capital is in fact increasing for all classes of farmers, but at a faster pace in the 'green revolution' areas and for larger farmers. Thus, fertilisers, pesticides and diesel accounted for a mere 14.9% of total inputs in 1970–71 but 55.1% in 1994–95. For large-scale farmers in commercialised regions the contribution of purchased inputs may now have become as high as 80%. But the proportion of output sold has increased at a much slower rate than the proportion of monetised inputs, including hired labour. The implication of this is a resource squeeze in agriculture. Whereas the need for resources to purchase these inputs has been increasing, the marketable surplus has been increasing at a slower rate to contribute to this, as the growth of non-farm employment has become very sluggish. It is not surprising that the repayment of loans is such a problem in Indian agriculture and has even led to suicides in some cases. A better strategy would be to concentrate on small and marginal farmers, and on eastern and rainfed areas where returns to both capital and labour are high. The need is also for better factor productivity in agriculture and for new technologies, which would be more labour-intensive and would cut cash costs.

Whereas the use of capital has increased among small and marginal farmers, markets in eastern and central India continue to be imperfect. Therefore, the poor farmers are forced to sell part of their product to pay their loans (mostly from informal sources) for purchased seeds, water and fertiliser, but they do not get a good price and market conditions benefit the trader and moneylender more than they benefit the producer.

Last, groundwater, as opposed to surface and sub-soil water (through shallow wells), has become the main source of irrigation. As a result, nearly 30% of the blocks in the country are presently classified as semi-critical, critical or overexploited (mostly in 'green revolution' areas), as groundwater use exceeds the rate of groundwater recharge. As there is no effective control over digging of tube wells in water-scarce regions, farmers are borrowing money from informal sources at high-interest rates to dig tube wells, but many such borings fail, leading to indebtedness, and even suicide. Since sinking a borewell involves a heavy investment upfront, only the rich or the affluent farmer goes in for it, whereas the small farmer continues to depend on the shallow dugwell that has been in existence for decades. Borewells drain much larger quantities of water, usually from the same aquifers that feed the dug wells. So in a village the small farmer is adversely affected when richer farmers install borewells fitted with electric motors. The affluent farmers owning borewells and electric motors corner most of the benefit of electricity subsidy too. Ironically, they in turn sell their surplus water to the adjacent small farmers at commercial rates. The built-in biases of the green revolution strategy now stand exposed (Saxena 2012a).

The impact of these factors has been increasing landlessness, sharpened inequalities (both inter-state and inter-class), and stagnation in production. The index number of agricultural production rose by 4.4% annually during the 1980s, but dropped to 2.8% from 1990–91 to 1996–97, and the growth rate further plummeted to just 1.4% in the next two decades (Various Economic Surveys). This has also resulted in a slower increase in real agricultural wages,[18] with the poorer states showing no increase or even a decline in wages. In addition, the casualisation of a mass of rural workers without any safety nets, the feminisation of agricultural labour accompanied by low wages, and the persistence of child labour are all worrying trends (Saxena 2011).

The stagnation is despite the soaring annual cost of food subsidies, which rose from Rs 61 billion in 1996–97 to Rs 310 billion in 2007–08 to Rs 1350 billion in 2014–15. If subsidies on free/subsidised rural power and fertilisers are added, the figure may well reach a staggering Rs 2000 billion, or about Rs 70 per day per poor rural family.[19]

5 What Needs to Be Done?

It is thus obvious that Indian agriculture is in a serious crisis and needs several innovative policy interventions. From the point of view of production of nutritious foods which are not today in the diet of a large number of households, these can be divided into two categories. One, such as milk, egg, fish, meat, fruits and vegetables, where production has rapidly increased in the last three decades but demand

---

[18]Rural wages increased significantly during 2004 and 2012 because of better agricultural growth, and demand from construction industry and NREGA, but have again fallen sharply after 2012.

[19]www.chronicpoverty.org/uploads/publication_files2/CPRC-IIPA%2044-new.pdf.

has increased even faster resulting in high prices and making these items out of ordinary people's reach. And the other, such as pulses, millets and coarse cereals, where per capita production has been declining because farmers do not find these crops profitable, and government too has not prioritised their production. Obviously, we need different strategies to ensure their availability at affordable prices.

Per capita consumption of fruits and vegetables has increased rapidly over the past two decades, though it is mostly confined to the well-off sections. In 2011–12, production of fruits and vegetables was 2.7 and 2.6 times that of the output level two decades ago,[20] i.e. in 1991–92. This expansion was much higher than that for cereals, where the output level in 2011–12 was 1.5 times that of 1991–92. A similar and more marked difference may be seen in the most recent past decade (2001–02 to 2011–12) where output of fruits and vegetables has increased by 80 and 69%, respectively, over 2001–02, while output of cereals has grown by 17% in the same period. However, there is considerable wastage and spoilage in fresh produce as also sharp variation in prices during the season.

Because of increasing demand, the rate of increase in the prices of fruits and vegetables has been higher than that for cereals especially in recent years and is a major contributor to the sharp increase in the inflation level for primary food, which is greater than that of manufactured products and appears to be a driving force behind the higher inflationary pressure.

On the other hand, the per capita availability of pulses declined steadily from about 69 g per day in 1961 to 51 g per day in 1971, and to about 43 g per day in 2013 (Economic Survey 2016), due to sluggish growth in production since the 1960s. Pulses production increased only by about 47% to about 18.5 million tonnes in the triennium ending (TE) 2013–14 from about 12.5 million tonnes in TE 1960–61. Similar is the story of coarse cereals and millets. However, production of rice and wheat has gone up by over 225 and 808% to 106 and 95 million tonnes, respectively, over the same period. But the story on the price front is similar to that of fruits and vegetables. Prices of major pulses like tur (red gram), moong (green gram) and urad (black gram) in their split forms (dals) have been trading above Rs 150 per kilogram (kg) since June 2015 in most markets across the country, forcing the ordinary people to cut down consumption of protein-rich pulses.

The following policy measures would help in improving availability of nutritious foods at affordable prices.

Build infrastructure – The most important intervention needed is more investment in irrigation, power and roads in poorer regions. It is essential to realise the potential for production surpluses in central and eastern India, where most poor

---

[20]Report of the committee on encouraging investments in supply chains including provision for cold storages for more efficient distribution of farm produce, Development Policy Division, Planning Commission, New Delhi, May 2012.

people live. Many states in this region do not benefit from the MSP for rice, as the state machinery to buy paddy is not efficient. A basic focus of policy should, therefore, be to ensure effective price support in states and areas with future production potential.

Water is a critical input for achieving higher agricultural growth and ensuring greater food security. Only about 40% of the cultivated area in India is currently irrigated. Greater emphasis should be placed on shifting the balance in favour of surface irrigation and on the more effective use of existing irrigation systems.

Examine redundant laws – The ban or restrictions on land leasing limit the access to land by poor and landless rural households and they drive tenancy underground. They also limit the productivity of land use.

Regulated markets were supposed to improve efficiency, but many official market committees, like those in UP, Punjab and Haryana, make it illegal for farmers to sell through alternative channels, such as directly to millers. The markets have thus emerged as taxing mechanisms, rather than helping farmers get the best price. This needs to be changed and farmers should be allowed to develop direct contact with large (and even corporate) buyers, with a complete ban on exports (Saxena 2012a).

The present extraction rates for both wheat and rice are about 10–30% below the international standards because of the reservation of agro-processing units for the small-scale sector, which uses inefficient technologies. Therefore, licensing controls on flour mills and other food processing industries should be removed. Food processing units, especially for rapeseed and groundnuts, should be de-reserved from the small-scale industries list. On the whole, laws and controls have repressed private foodgrain marketing, undercutting its potential contribution to long-term food security.

Improve value chains – As regards horticultural produce and other perishable farm items, farmers hardly get 20–40% of the high retail price (ADB 2010). A World Bank study on the value chains of mangoes, lychees and potatoes in Bihar shows that a significant amount of the consumer price is lost in transport and wastage; for mangoes, the farmers receive 34%, for lychees 42% and for potatoes only 16% of the consumer price (World Bank 2007). This is on account of the large deficiencies in the logistics system in between the farm to the final consumer. The push to build up storage capacity through cold chains has not been successful in vegetables and is limited for fruits. More investment is required in developing modern supply chains and logistics services, such as cold chains, reefer vans and warehouses, specialised to handle high-value commodities. The private sector has a greater role to play in terms of investments in value chains and strengthening the firm–farm linkages critical for scaling up processing and retailing operations.[21]

---

[21]http://indiagovernance.gov.in/files/food-and-nutrition-security.pdf.

Promote kitchen gardens – Many farmers have homestead farms in which drumsticks, curry leaves, custard apples, papayas, shoe flowers, *begonia, basak,* etc., can easily be grown. Nutrition gardens can be an important resource to supplement diversity in the family's nutrition. Household kitchen waste can be used as compost for these gardens. A different mix of crops can be planted based on local conditions (Welthungerhilfe 2014).

Promote production of pulses and millets – Because of emphasis on wheat and paddy crops since Independence, area and production of key nutritional food crops such as pulses and coarse cereals have experienced a decline. On the consumption side, as pulses have been the main source of protein, the decline in their per capita availability has caused protein deficiency especially among the poor who cannot afford other expensive sources of protein. Therefore, governments must increase indigenous production of these protein and micro-nutrient-rich crops, by promoting extension services as well as better varieties through research and offering producers a remunerative price. This will also need better soil and water management, as described below.

Reduce dependence on groundwater in rainfed areas – There is a huge pressure on groundwater resources in India, and this is felt even more during periods of drought; hence, large investments are needed in building efficient irrigation systems and water conservation strategies in rainfed regions, through conjunctive use of surface and groundwater. The main thrust of the programmes to combat the impact of climate change in rainfed areas should be on activities relating to rainwater harvesting, soil conservation, land shaping, pasture development, vegetative bunding and water resources conservation on the basis of the entire compact micro-watershed which would include both cultivated and uncultivated lands. Agriculture in semi-arid regions has to move from traditional crop-centric farming to agri-pastoral-farm forestry systems (fruit trees, shrubs, perennial grasses and small ruminants).[22]

Similarly in regions with plenty of groundwater, such as eastern UP, Bihar and West Bengal, one should promote pedal pumps that can help improve production of vegetables for small farmers with pumps driven by human beings, as has been successfully tried in Bangladesh and parts of Kenya.

Change cropping pattern in low rainfall regions – There is political reluctance to control water-hungry crops in low rainfall regions, such as sugarcane in Maharashtra and paddy in Punjab. One would need to reduce unrestricted mining of groundwater and ensure stricter implementation of environmentally sound cropping patterns. Drip irrigation and water sprinkler approach, mulching and bed plantation, construction of tanks and check dams should be promoted for water harvesting and conservation.

---

[22]inclusion.skoch.in/story/875/has-rural-india-seen-a-turnaround-lately-1175.html.

Promote peoples' participation – Government of India has announced several programmes in soil and water conservation, but when undertaken by the Agriculture Departments, these remain departmental in approach with no involvement of the people. Maintenance of the created assets suffers, as beneficiaries are not motivated to assume responsibility for maintenance. Watershed development programmes cannot succeed without full participation of project beneficiaries and careful attention to issues of social organisation. Moreover, collective capability is required for management of commons and for new structures created during the project. Disregard of peoples' participation is a legacy of the 'PWD culture' governing civil works.

If rain is captured with peoples' participation, drought can be banished from India in ten years maximum. Unfortunately, the slogan of 'more crop per drop' has so far remained an empty rhetoric, 'an ideology without a methodology'.

Use common lands for promoting Food Forests – A food forest is typically comprised of seven layers, the uppermost layer is comprised of tall trees – typically large fruit and nut trees. Between the tall canopy layer trees, there is a layer of low growing, typically dwarf fruit trees. The combination of trees and plants includes trees, shrubs, perennial vegetables, herbs (also often called weeds!) and climbers, all interacting in a natural way that minimises direct competition and also pest problems and is imitating a productive natural young forest system. In addition, the system mulches itself! There is no need for digging, as the plants themselves break up the soil with their roots, and the mulch from their leaves adds all the nutrients they need (Welthungerhilfe 2014).

Empower women – 79% of rural female workers are still in agriculture. Despite women's vital contribution to agriculture and allied sectors in India, they lack control over productive assets (land, livestock, fisheries, technologies, credit, finance, markets, etc.), face biases due to socio-cultural practices, experience gender differentials in agricultural wages and decisions concerning crop management and marketing (Saxena 2012b).

Ownership of land is concentrated mostly in male hands in our patriarchal society. It has been estimated that in India, landownership in favour of women is not more than 2% (Agarwal 1995). Lack of entitlement to land (and other assets such as house, livestock and so on) is a severe impediment to efficiency in agriculture for women cultivators because in the absence of title women cannot get credit or be entitled to irrigation and other inputs, especially technology. In addition to improved production, the clinching argument in favour of land titles to women is the stability and security it provides, shift to nutritious crops that it would entail, the protection it affords from marital violence, and the bargaining power it gives women in household decision-making and in the labour market for wages. However without title to land, women are not recognised, even by the state, as clients for extension services or as candidates for membership in institutions such as cooperative societies (Saxena 2012b). A campaign needs to be launched to implement succession laws in a gender-sensitive manner.

Table 7 Production, procurement and offtake of foodgrains (in million tonnes)

	1997–98	2007–08	2012–13	2015–16
Food subsidy in billion (00 crores) Rs	79	313	850	1350
Production of foodgrains	192	231	255	252
Procurement of foodgrains	23.6	51.6	69.1	62.4
Distribution through FPS	17	33.5	51.4	49.6
Welfare schemes	2.1	3.9	4.3	4.1

5.1 PDS

With a network of more than 5 lakh Fair Price Shops (FPSs) claiming to distribute annually commodities worth more than Rs 80,000 crore to about 16 crore families,[23] the PDS in India is perhaps the largest distribution network of its type in the world. PDS is operated under the joint responsibility of the central and state governments, with the former responsible for procurement, storage, transportation (up to the district headquarters) and bulk allocation of foodgrains.

The state governments are responsible for distributing these foodgrains to consumers through a network of Fair Price Shops. This responsibility includes identification of families below poverty line (BPL), issue of BPL cards and supervision and monitoring of the functioning of the Fair Price Shops. States are also responsible for movement of foodgrains from the district headquarters to the PDS shop, which requires storage at the sub-district level. As food was always a non-plan subject, such an infrastructure is often weak in the poorer states. Changes in production, procurement and offtake of foodgrains over the years are shown in Table 7.

All is not well with the Public Distribution System in India. Weaknesses in the distribution system include ration cards being mortgaged to ration shop owners, large errors of exclusion of BPL families and inclusion of non-BPL families, prevalence of ghost cards, with weaknesses in the delivery mechanism leading to large-scale leakages and diversion of subsidised grains to markets and unintended beneficiaries. As per the 2004–05 NSS round, households in the bottom quintile obtained only 17% of their foodgrains consumption from PDS for the country as a whole. The percentage varied from 2% for Bihar, 6% for UP to 50% for Tamil Nadu and 68% for Karnataka. A recent evaluation of TPDS by NCAER (2015) showed that Assam cardholders never get their full quota of grain because FPS dealers deduct 3–4 kg per card. The dealers admitted this was true; they justified this deduction as the cost of transport was never reimbursed by government.

Fortunately, many states have tried to improve the PDS in the last ten years. It had always worked quite well in Tamil Nadu, Kerala, Himachal Pradesh and Andhra Pradesh, but now states like Chhattisgarh, Orissa and Rajasthan (Khera 2011) have undertaken state-level PDS reforms by extending coverage, improving

---

[23]Many of them get kerosene only.

delivery and increasing transparency. Due to these efforts, leakage of rice and wheat implied by NSSO estimated consumption and amounts released for PDS have come down from 55% in 2004–05 to 43% in 2007–08 to 30% in 2011–12 (Himanshu and Sen 2011; NSSO 2014b).

Among the poorer states, best results are seen in Chhattisgarh because of replacement of private dealers by panchayats and SHGs, increased commissions, coverage of more than 80% families under the scheme as opposed to only 40% who are officially recognised as BPL by GOI, and regular monitoring and grievance redressal mechanism that leads to swift action if foodgrain does not reach the people.

Other states have followed in Chhattisgarh's footsteps, with similar results. An interesting example is Orissa, especially the 'KBK region' (undivided Kalahandi, Bolangir and Koraput districts), which used to be known mainly for starvation deaths. Today, the KBK region has near-universal PDS, which seems to work quite well. A recent study found that PDS cardholders in Koraput get 97% of their rice entitlements under the system (Outlook March 22, 2014). Much remains to be done to extend these gains across the country, especially in states like UP that show little willingness to reform themselves.

5.2 Food Security Act, 2013

In September 2013, GOI enacted a new National Food Security Act. The main beneficiaries of the Act and their entitlements are summarised in Table 8.

Although the Act seeks to cover 67% of the total population (75% rural and 50% urban), in actual practice the coverage would be much more, as GOI has promised to the richer states which had almost universal coverage that their quota (which

Table 8 Provisions for nutritional security and entitlements in the act to special groups

Target group	Entitlement
Holders of Antyodaya cards	35 kg per household as before, wheat/rice/coarse grain and millets at Rs 2/3/1 per kg
75% of rural and 50% urban population minus those covered above	5 kg per unit of wheat/rice/coarse grain and millets at Rs 2/3/1 per kg
Pregnant woman/lactating mother	Meal, free of charge, during pregnancy and six months after childbirth, maternity benefit of Rs 1000 per month for a period of six months
Children (6 months–6 years)	Age appropriate meal, free of charge, through the local Anganwadi
Children suffering from malnutrition	Meals through the local Anganwadi, free of charge
Children (6–14 years)	One mid-day meal, free of charge, every working day, in all schools run by local bodies, Government and Government aided schools, up to class VIII

would have come down to about half of what they get now, if the Food Security law was strictly followed) would not be reduced, thus increasing the overall coverage to about 75% of the total. Their state-wise number has been determined by GOI but identification of eligible households is left to state governments.

However, implementation of the Act is so far disappointing. According to GOI's calculation, the annual offtake should be at least 55 million tonnes (MT), if each state covered the entire entitled population, but as shown in Table 7, it was only 49.6 MT in 2015–16, which was even less than what was distributed in 2012–13. The scheme of providing maternity benefit of Rs 1000 per month for a period of six months to pregnant and lactating women has not been made universal; it runs in only 53 out of a total 680 districts in India.

Push for millets through PDS – The Food Security Act, 2013 enjoins upon state governments to include millets in PDS, but it has not happened in most states. More effective policy advocacy is needed by the civil society on this issue.

5.3   Cash Transfers

With a view to reduce leakages, Chandigarh administration decided in September 2015 to substitute food by direct cash transfers to the peoples' bank accounts. However, the experiment has not been very popular. Before September 2015, there were 55,917 cardholders in Chandigarh benefitting from TPDS. According to GOI's own calculation (given on page 26, Monthly Bulletin, July 2016), the number of persons to benefit from NFSA should have now increased to about 95,000 households. However, the cash transfer programme unfortunately reduced the number of eligible cardholders from 55,917 to only 41,167 because for the rest their bank accounts had not been seeded with their Aadhaar numbers. Those who got left out got neither food grains (since the 93 ration shops in Chandigarh were closed down), nor cash transfers, leaving them disgruntled.

The Union Department of Food and Civil Supplies maintains that Aadhaar was never compulsory for cash transfers, but the Chandigarh Administration insisted on this. According to them, Aadhaar is important to authenticate identity and ensure that money goes only into the beneficiary's account.

Even having an Aadhaar-linked bank account does not ensure that money reaches regularly. A survey[24] by the Delhi-based Centre for Equity Studies of 200 beneficiaries in December 2015 revealed that 40% had not got their payments, forcing them to buy rations on credit – something that Seetha,[25] a senior journalist, also corroborated and heard the same complaint even in May 2016 from several

[24]http://indiatogether.org/articles/rationtocashaharshtransitionpoverty/; print. Also see http://thewire.in/16373/opting-out-of-the-jam/.
[25]Modi's DBT Review 1: Chandigarh Stumbles But Project Needs Support http://swarajyamag.com/economy/arbitraryinclusionsandexclusionsmakeitaroughrideforcashtransferspilotinchandigarh.

beneficiaries. A survey on the working of the programme by the Abdul Latif Jameel Poverty Action Lab (JPAL), commissioned by the central government and Niti Aayog (but is not in the public domain), is also reported to have indicated that 30% of the beneficiaries with Aadhaar-seeded bank accounts had not got their money. Seetha came across several cases where money had come only for a couple of months and the transfer was irregular. For daily wage earners, making multiple trips to the bank to check on payments is an extra burden. Not all of them have smartphones or are subscribed to mobile alerts to check the status of payments.

While most states are as of now not comfortable with cash transfer (and their consent is mandatory under law), large-scale substitution of PDS by direct cash transfer (DCT) as being planned by the Ministry is not feasible for another reason. Foodgrains purchased from the farmers through MSP mechanism need an outlet for distribution. Introducing DCT nationally would mean that GOI would have to end the state procurement regime. That is neither politically feasible, nor can it be in the realm of consideration by any government in India, given that more than half of the population is still dependent on agriculture. DCT may also result in substantial price rise in the open market in food deficit regions, as private trade would have a vested interest in gaining from such a rise. PDS (even with 30% leakages) at least ensures that GOI would stock sufficient grain in all districts all the time. Selling 60 million tonnes of grain in the open market is also fraught with scope of grand corruption at the GOI level, which would be very different from the petty corruption that exists as of now in the PDS at the district level.

5.4 Reducing Leakages Through Technology

There is however an intermediate solution to reduce leakages. The root cause of corruption in PDS is the dual pricing system, as FPS dealers get grain at a highly subsidised price. In the new proposed model, Government would abolish the dual pricing system and sell stocks to the fair price shop dealer at the market price, say Rs 24 for wheat. The consumer would go to him with only two rupees in cash as before and with her/his AADHAAR card to buy a kg of wheat but the rest 22 Rs would get transferred from government to the shopkeeper's bank account. Under the new model, it is not necessary for the beneficiary to have a bank account or to possess a smartphone. Unlike Chandigarh and Puducherry, where the pilot for cash transfer faces problems of ensuring timely transfer of subsidy to the consumers' accounts, the subsidy amount in the proposed model would be transferred to the shop owner, and not to the beneficiary, thus vastly reducing the number of bank account transfers that need to be monitored.

The main bottleneck is still the last-mile transfer. Although Jan Dhan has been successful in opening bank accounts for a large number of people, bank branches are far away from most people and the banking correspondence system is not widespread or efficient. The proposed model will reduce the necessity of opening 160 million (which is the total number of households eligible for subsidised grain) Aadhaar-seeded bank accounts to just about half a million of the shopkeepers. In all probability, they would already be having an Aadhaar-based bank account.

The proposed model will also enable the beneficiaries to get rations from shops of their choice (also when they are out of hometown), get better service and do not make compromises (by way of leakages) on the quantity and quality of the purchases.

5.5   School Meals

One of India's greatest successes in public interventions in the social sector, the Mid-Day Meal Scheme provides daily meals for millions of children, leading to greater school attendance figures, as well as improved nutrition for the children. It has been able to feed more than 120 million children every day for more than 10 years, and the popular programme's relative success has been recently documented in economic research, clearly showing the positive impact on enrolment, attendance, retention and nutrition (Khera 2013). The success has also been in its scale and regularity, consistently feeding millions of children on a daily basis. Apart from its success in bringing children to school and keeping them there, the nutritional successes are marked, with a study by Afridi (2010) finding positive nutritional effects among children in Madhya Pradesh; when comparing nutrient intake on a school day with a non-school day, she found that 'nutrient intake of programme participants increased substantially by 49–100%', while deficiency in protein intake was reduced by 100% and iron deficiency by 10%. This was achieved for a very small cost of Rs 5 for every child every day. Furthermore, it is popular with parents, making it easier to convince their children to go to school, and it is also a source of employment for tens of thousands of destitute women (Khera 2013).

The scheme is by no means perfect, and the tragedy in Bihar in 2013, where 23 children died from eating food through the MDMS, has highlighted some of the long-standing issues in implementation. Foremost of those concerns have been food quality, hygiene and accountability, as well as lack of proper infrastructure and sufficient staff, caste issues and issues regarding the nutritive quality of food; state governments have made efforts in dealing with these issues, although progress has been slow (Khera 2013).

5.6 Nutrition Programmes for Children Below 5 Years[26]

For children, government runs in every village a programme called Integrated Child Development Services (ICDS). As on 31 January 2013, 13,31,076 centres, called Anganwadi centres[27] (AWCs), are operational across 35 states/UTs, covering 93 million beneficiaries under supplementary nutrition and 35 million 3–6 years children under pre-school component. The Twelfth Five-Year Plan (FYP) has allocated Rs 1236 billion to ICDS – a three-fold increase from the previous FYP. However, in addition to general problems of governance and delivery that affect all programmes, ICDS, the main programme to address malnutrition is particularly doing quite poorly. We discuss some field studies.

5.6.1 ICDS – Some Evaluations

A comprehensive evaluation of ICDS (Planning Commission 2011) concluded that despite the fact that outlay for the ICDS was increased from Rs 121 billion in the X Plan (2002–07) to Rs 444 billion in the XI Plan (2007–12), the outcomes were most disappointing. Only 19% of the mothers reported that the AWC provides nutrition counselling to parents. More than 40% of the funds meant for supplementary nutrition (SN) are siphoned off; for FY 2008–09, the amount of SN allocation diverted is estimated at Rs 29 billion. Although 81% of children below six years of age were living in an area covered by the Anganwadi centres only 31% children received SN and only 12% children received it regularly (Planning Commission 2012a, b). Only 38% of pregnant women and lactating mothers, and 10% of adolescent girls received supplementary nutrition.

An evaluation of ICDS in Gorakhpur by the National Human Rights Commission (Saxena 2013) showed that despite Supreme Court orders[28] to provide hot cooked meals, all centres supplied only packaged ready-to-eat food, containing only 100 cal, as against a norm of 500 cal, and 63% of food and funds were misappropriated. The food being unpalatable, half of it ends up as cattle feed. People have started calling it 'Pashu Ahaar' rather than 'Paushtik Ahaar'. In addition to Ministerial-level corruption, even the AWWs are deeply involved in malpractices and share 2000 rupees per centre every month with their supervisors routinely. The ready-to-eat food is produced in poor hygiene conditions. Some of the ingredients shown on the bags containing the finished product were not found in stock at the time of visit and the stock of maize was only enough to meet 25% of the daily requirement.

---

[26]This and the next section draw heavily from author's previous article published as Saxena 2016.

[27]These are generally one or two room structures, where children gather for about four hours every morning for various ICDS activities.

[28]http://hrln.org/2006-pucl-vs-union-of-india-and-others-civil-writ-petition-196-of-2001/.

However, such reports, though few, are hardly discussed in state Assemblies, as they meet now for fewer than 30 days a year. We need a new law making it compulsory for Parliament and Assemblies to meet for at least 150 days a year.

Comptroller and Auditor General of (CAG) India's performance audit[29] in 2013 revealed how ICDS was failing to help infants and young children. The audit, covering the period 2006–07 to 2010–11, found that 52% of Anganwadis surveyed lack toilets, and 32% don't have drinking water. Around 61% Anganwadis did not have their own buildings and 25% were functioning from semi-pucca or open or partially covered spaces. Medicine kits are not available in 33–49% of Anganwadis. The audit also revealed 33–45% gap between eligible beneficiaries and actual recipients of supplementary nutrition. CAG noted distribution of sub-standard food by the AWCs as 'ready-to-cook mixes' were unpalatable. Audit found that some of these items had sticky texture which became inedible within minutes of preparation. The Audit further found that there was no system of watching expiry of food items.

5.7 Governance Issues

Although governance has several dimensions, for this paper we restrict our discussion to its relevance to the capacity of governments to design, formulate and implement policies and programmes, including accountability of government employees who should be held responsible for their actions. On all these dimensions, the record of ICDS and related health programmes is quite poor: the design of ICDS is flawed, it is poorly delivered, and the staff fudges the reported data so as to avoid responsibility for high malnutrition (Saxena and Srivastava 2009). We discuss these below.

ICDS design needs a change – The ICDS has not yet succeeded in making a significant dent in reducing child malnutrition, as the programme has placed priority on food supplementation rather than on nutrition and health education interventions, and targets children mostly after the age of three when malnutrition has already set in (Saxena 2014b). Very little of the ICDS resources, in terms of funds and staff time, are spent on the under-three child (Planning Commission 2012a, b), and this low priority must be reversed.

Therefore, the focus in ICDS programme, government's main intervention, should be on components that directly address the most important causes of under-nutrition in India, specifically improving mothers' feeding and caring behaviour, improving household water and sanitation, strengthening referrals to the health system and providing micro-nutrients. The basic nature of the programme should be changed from centre-based to outreach-based, as the child under three

---

[29]http://articles.timesofindia.indiatimes.com/2013-03-06/india/37499356_1_cag-audit-icds-malnourished-children and http://zeenews.india.com/news/nation/substandard-food-being-distributed-by-anganwadis_834305.html (accessed on 7 July 2014).

cannot walk to the centre and has to be reached at his/her home. Another advantage of visiting homes is that the entire family, not just the mothers, are sensitised and counselled.

Discourage 'ready-to-eat' food in Supplementary Nutrition Provisioning (SNP) – Government of India should discourage the distribution of manufactured 'ready-to-eat' food, as it leads to grand corruption at the Ministerial level, but unfortunately GOI has encouraged such tendering by laying down the minimum nutritional norms for 'take-home rations' (a permissible alternative to cooked meals for young children), including micro-nutrient fortification, thus providing a dangerous foothold for food manufacturers and contractors, who are constantly trying to invade child nutrition programmes for profit-making purposes. This may have the unintended consequence of supplementing micro-nutrients without consultation with medical professionals as well as leaving the door open for large-scale centralised corruption and subversion of the programme through the back-door entry of private non-descript contractors (Saxena 2014b, 2016a).

ICDS should learn from the success of hot freshly cooked mid-day meals programme that runs fairly well even in states not known for efficiency, whereas the supply of packaged food in ICDS even in efficient states is not popular with the children, besides being irregular and discouraging local participation. For children below the age of three years, nutritious and carefully designed locally prepared take-home rations based on locally procured food should be the recommended option, but there could be centre-specific variations. If fortified milk powder is to be provided, it must be manufactured by a well-known manufacturer. Before inviting financial bids, states must invite technical bids in a transparent manner so that unscrupulous contractors who get into the racket of supplying packaged food through bribes are eliminated. Children can eat only small quantities of food and therefore need fat-rich food to obtain necessary calories. In the absence of oil supplies, there is almost no fat content in the food being given whereas for children below three, almost 40% of their calorie requirement should come from fats. This aspect gets totally unfulfilled in the current SNP.

The best solutions to child malnutrition are based on access to diverse local nutritious diets which will meet calorie, protein and micro-nutrient requirements. This can be done successfully with engagement of local communities in the supply of Supplementary Nutrition. Evidence is that this has led to increased demand for the programme, better community monitoring as well as supported livelihoods of thousands of women.

Improve reporting system – Officials at all levels spend a great deal of time in collecting and submitting information, but these are not used for taking corrective and remedial action or for analysis, but only for forwarding it to a higher level, or for answering Assembly/Parliament Questions. Field staff reports only on activities; it is not involved in impact assessment, or in qualitative monitoring. The concept of stakeholder monitoring is unknown. No indicators exist for assessing public participation or their awareness. Reporting system in the state governments needs overhauling, as at present many reports are not credible (Saxena 2007a, b, 2014a).

Malaria deaths (and so are malnutrition deaths) are under-reported, while immunisation achievements are over-reported.

ICDS too faces substantial operational challenges, such as lack of accountability due to lack of oversight and an irresponsible reporting system. It appears that state governments actively encourage reporting of inflated figures from the districts, which renders monitoring ineffective and accountability meaningless. Each Anganwadi centre reports on the number of malnourished children category-wise, but these figures are neither verified independently by the states nor being used for assessing the effectiveness of the programme. The practice is so widely prevalent in all the states, presumably with the connivance of senior officers, that the overall percentage of severely malnourished children, in case of 0–3 years according to the data reaching GOI from the states is only 2%, as against 9.4% reported by UNICEF in a recent survey (Table 9). The field officials are thus able to escape from any sense of accountability for reducing malnutrition. Figures from some states show their children to be as healthy as in Denmark and Sweden!

One district collector, when confronted with this kind of bogus figures, told the author that reporting correct data is 'a high-risk and low-reward activity'! Dr Manmohan Singh as Prime Minister termed government's performance as a 'national shame', but he was not able to persuade the states to accept that the problem exists!

Staff vacancies – There are massive vacancies due to which their effectiveness is limited. As per the Ministry's website, the sanctioned strength of CDPOs and Supervisors in March 2013 is 9034 and 54,103 in the country, but only 5985 and 34,639, respectively, were in position. Thus, more than one-third of these positions are vacant. In Bihar, for instance, 90% of the Supervisors' posts were vacant. Only 64% of AWWs received their salary either regularly or with a delay of one month, the rest reported delay of two to six months in getting their meagre salaries (Planning Commission 2011).

Unresponsive bureaucracy – Absenteeism of field staff is rampant though seldom measured. Many ICDS centres are often closed or function irregularly. Referral services for severely malnourished children are very weak as primary health care system does not function satisfactorily.

Lack of decentralization – Very few state governments involve local bodies in implementation of programmes relating to health, nutrition and hygiene.

Table 9 Percentage of severely malnourished children in 2013–14 according to UNICEF and State Governments		State government	UNICEF
	Andhra Pradesh	0.8	4.7
	Gujarat	0.8	10.1
	Jharkhand	0.5	16.0
	Madhya Pradesh	2.1	12.0
	Orissa	1.4	11.0
	Uttar Pradesh	0.8	12.9
	West Bengal	0.7	8.9
	India	2.1	9.4

Empowering local panchayats to deal with the problems relating to hunger and malnutrition will certainly help achieve convergence and meet the challenges of poor delivery in many parts of the country (Saxena 2014a).

Non-functional childcare system in urban India – ICDS runs very poorly in urban slum areas because of lack of space for setting up of centres. In urban slums, the problems of appallingly low-rent allocations (Rs 1000 per month for Delhi, for instance) for hiring spaces and non-availability of government buildings need to be addressed urgently to fill the gap in universalising services for slum populations. In the short term, temporary structures can be put up to provide toilets in those slums where either due to legal issues or space constraints, it is not possible to put up permanent structures.

Weak links with sanitation – Only 40% households in rural India use toilets. Besides, due to bad quality of water and lack of toilets children are exposed to stomach infections, develop diarrhoea and start losing weight. Evidence is now sufficient to conclude that open defecation is an important cause of child stunting. Children's height matters because the same early life health and net nutrition that help children grow tall also help them grow into healthy, productive, smart adults. Open defecation is particularly harmful where population density is high – so children are more likely to encounter germs from faeces – which means that India's widespread open defecation and high population density constitute a double threat. Lack of medical attention further aggravates malnutrition.

Learn from International experience – Thailand has been one of the most outstanding success stories of reducing child malnutrition in the period 1980–1988 during which child malnutrition (underweight) rate was effectively reduced from 50 to 25%. This was achieved through a mix of interventions including intensive growth monitoring and nutrition education, strong supplementary feeding provision, high rates of coverage ensured by having high human resource intensity, iron and vitamin supplementation and salt iodization along with primary health care. The programme used community volunteers (with no honorarium) on a huge scale (one per 20 children), and involved local people, so as to instil self-reliance and communicate effectively with target groups. Communities were involved in needs assessment, planning, programme implementation, beneficiary selection and seeking local financial contributions. Inter-village competition in reducing the number of under-nourished children was encouraged, and villages were rewarded for their success.

This has significance for nutrition programmes in India as the levels of per capita GDP, proportion of women in agricultural workforce and child malnutrition rates around 1980 in Thailand were similar to what we had in India in 1992.

Re-examine the role of the Ministry – When the new Ministry of Women and Child Development was set up, it was expected that it would take a holistic view of the problems of women and children and keep a watchful eye on the activities of all other Ministries, such as health, education, labour, drinking water and sanitation that deal with the subjects impinging on children's welfare. It would develop systems that inform GOI, for instance, how and why children are malnourished. On the other hand, it has been observed that the new Ministry took a minimalist view of its responsibility and reduced itself to dealing with the ICDS only without critically monitoring the lack of other inputs needed for reducing malnutrition. Such ostrich-like attitude defeats the purpose for which the Ministry is created. It was expected that the MWCD would generate field reports that look at the access of children to health, water and sanitation, and how it affects malnutrition. Continuous measurement of the critical inputs alone will put pressure on other Ministries and their field administration to improve all services holistically. However, in the present circumstances, advocacy is not a popular agenda with the MWCD officials.

5.8 Summing Up

The Indian State implements massive food, livelihood and social security programmes – some of the largest in the world – which theoretically support vulnerable people from even before their birth to their survivors after death. On paper, expectant mothers are fed in ICDS centres, along with infants, children up to the age of six and adolescent girls. Children in school get school meals. As adults, women receive maternity support and bread earners are guaranteed 100 days of wage employment in public works; and if identified as poor, they can buy subsidised cereals from a massive network of half a million ration shops. The aged – and in many states, widows and disabled people – are given pensions. And if an earning adult dies prematurely, the survivor is entitled to a lump sum payment of ten thousand rupees.

This looks good on paper but the ground reality is different. These programmes are plagued by corruption, leakages, error in selection, delays, poor allocations and little accountability. They also tend to discriminate against and exclude those who most need them, by social barriers of gender, age, caste, ethnicity, faith and disability; and State hostility to urban poor migrants, street and slum residents, and unorganised workers. In Rangpur Pahadi, a slum area just two kms away from Vasant Kunj (Delhi), people living since 1984 have not been given even voter ID or any ration card. Thus, their very existence is denied by the Delhi Government! Therefore, not only do we need to identify the excluded and run special programmes for them, but improve monitoring and accountability for all programmes that impinge on hunger (Saxena 2013).

However, implementation as discussed in this paper needs improvement. Higher public investment in nutrition-based programmes needs to be accompanied by systemic reforms that will improve the quality of public expenditures and overhaul the present system of service delivery, including issues of control and oversight. At the same time, ICDS should correct the design flaws, focus more on the younger age group, on community participation, and strengthening of convergence with related health and sanitation programmes (Saxena 2016a, b).

Problems of lack of coordination between the Ministries (Women and Child, Health, Water and Sanitation) cannot be resolved by passing laws or by incorporating goals of minimising stunting and under-nutrition in the Food Security Act. The experience of both Right to Education and Right to Employment shows that problems of bad design, inadequate funding and poor implementation require administrative and not legal action (Saxena 2016a, b).

Development is an outcome of efficient institutions rather than the other way around. The focus must therefore be shifted from maximising the quantity of development funding to maximising development outcomes and the effectiveness of public service delivery. Concerted policy action is needed to improve the hunger indicators of marginalised groups, of women and children, and of the 300 million poor increasingly concentrated in the poorer states. This requires additional resources, as well as better policies and sound delivery mechanisms.

In the ultimate analysis, the constraints to overcoming malnutrition and hunger are rooted in bad policies, faulty design, lack of appropriate monitoring and evaluation, poor governance and lack of political will. Action is needed on all the fronts. Economic growth alone is insufficient to bring about significant reductions in the prevalence of malnourishment among children, or improvement in health of the poor. Without a major shakeup in agricultural policy and an improvement in design of the ICDS and food-related programmes as well as in the effectiveness of its implementation, the attainment of the goal of fast reduction in hunger and malnutrition looks unlikely (Saxena 2016a, b).

References

Afridi, F. (2010). Child welfare programs and child nutrition: Evidence from a mandated school meal program in India. *Journal of Development Economics, 92*(2), 152–165.

Agarwal, Bina. (1995). *A field of one's own: Gender and land rights in South Asia.* Cambridge, UK: Cambridge University Press.

Bajpai, N., Sachs, J. D., & Volavka, N. (2005). *India's challenge to meet the millennium development goals.* Center on Globalization and Sustainable Development (CGSD), Working Paper No. 24. New York: Earth Institute at Columbia University.

Bisaliah, S. (2007). *Capital formation in Indian agriculture: Growth, composition, determinants and policy directions.* Manila: Asian Development Bank.

Black, R. E., Victora, C. G., Walker, S. P., Bhutta, Z. A., Christian, P., de Onis, M., et al. (2013). Maternal and child undernutrition and overweight in low-income and middle-income countries. *The Lancet, 382*(9890), 427–451.

Chambers, R., & Medeazza, G. V. (2013). Sanitation and stunting in India: Undernutrition's blind spot. *Economic & Political Weekly, 48*(25). June 22, 2013.

Chand, R., & Jumrani, J. (2013). *Food security and undernourishment in India: Assessment of alternative norms and the income effect* (Policy Brief 38). Delhi: ICAR—National Centre for Agricultural Economics and Policy Research.

Deaton, A., & Drèze, J. (2008). *Nutrition in India: Facts and interpretations.* Princeton, NJ: Princeton University Press.

Arnold F., Nangia, P., & Kapil, U. (2004). Indicators of nutrition for women and children: Current status and recommendations. *Economic and Political Weekly, 39*(7). February 14, 2004.

Economic Survey. (2015–16). *Ministry of finance.* New Delhi: Government of India.

Garg, S., & Nandi, S. (undated). Reducing child malnutrition: Thailand Experience (1977–86). In *A Review of International Literature.* http://www.righttofoodindia.org/data/garg-nandi07thailand-reducing-child-malnutrition.pdf.

Gopaldas, T. (2006). Hidden hunger: The problem of and possible interventions. *Economic and Political Weekly, 41*(34). August 26, 2006.

Government of India. (1979). *Report of the task force on projection of minimum needs and effective demand.* Perspective Planning Division. Planning Commission, New Delhi.

Government of India. (1993). *Report of the expert group on estimation of proportion and number of poor.* Perspective Planning Division, Planning Commission. New Delhi.

Government of India. (2014). *Report of the expert group to review the methodology for measurement of poverty.* Chaired by C. Rangarajan, Planning Commission, Government of India, New Delhi.

Gragnolati, M., Bredenkamp, C., Shekar, M., Gupta, M. D., & Lee, Y.-K. (2006). *India's undernourished children: A call for reform and action.* Health, Nutrition and Population (HNP) Discussion Paper, Washington, D.C.: The World Bank.

Gupta, S. (2012). Food expenditure and intake in the NSS 66th round. *Economic & Political Weekly, 47*(2). January 14, 2012.

Himanshu, &, Sen, A. (2011). Why not a universal food security legislation? *Economic & Political Weekly, 46*(12). March 19, 2011.

HUNGaMA. (2012). Fighting hunger & malnutrition. At http://www.naandi.org/CP/HungamaBKDec11LR.pdf. Accessed on 7 July 2014. URL not available.

IFPRI. (2015). *Global hunger index, armed conflict and the challenge of hunger,* International Food Policy Research Institute: October.

IFPRI. (2017). *Global hunger index: The inequalities of hunger.* Washington, DC: International Food Policy Research Institute; Bonn.

Khera, R. (2011). Revival of the public distribution system: Evidence and explanations. *Economic & Political Weekly, 46*(44 & 45). November 5, 2011.

Khera, R. (2013). Mid-day meals: Looking ahead. *Economic & Political Weekly, 48*(10). August 10, 2013.

Kolady, D., Srivastava, S., & Singh, J. (2016). *Can agricultural growth explain the reversal of a declining trend in per capita calorie consumption in India?* Paper presented at Agricultural & Applied Economics Association Annual Meeting, Boston, Massachusetts, July 31–August 2.

Krishnaraj, M. (2006). Food Security, agrarian crisis and rural livelihoods: Implications for women. *Economic & Political Weekly, 41*(52). December 30, 2006.

Kundu, A. (2006). Food security system in India: Analysing a few conceptual issues in the contemporary policy debate. In N. Srivastava & P. Sharma (Eds.), *Protecting the vulnerable poor in India: The role of social safety nets.* World Food Programme: New Delhi.

Kumaran M. (2008) Hunger and under-nutrition in post-liberalisation rural India—A review. *Dissertation.* New Delhi: Jawaharlal Nehru University.

Mander, H. (2008). Living with hunger: Deprivation among the aged, single women and people with disability. *Economic and Political Weekly, 43*(17). April 26, 2008.

Mebrahtu, S., & Sethi, V. (2016). Nutrition—Budget disconnect. *CBGA Budget Track, 11.* February.

Menon, A., Deolalikar, A., & Bhaskar, A. (Eds.). (2008). *The India state hunger index: Comparisons of hunger across states.* New Delhi: IFPRI. October 14, 2008.

Meshram, I. I., Balakrishna, N., Sreeramakrishna, K., Rao, K. M., Kumar, R. H., Arlappa, N., et al. (2016). Trends in nutritional status and nutrient intakes and correlates of overweight/obesity among rural adult women (≥ 18–60 years) in India: National nutrition monitoring bureau (NNMB) national surveys. *Public Health Nutrition, 19*(5), 767–776.

Narayanan, S. (2015). Food security in India: The imperative and its challenges. *Asia & the Pacific Policy Studies, 2*(1), 197–209.

NCAER. (2015). *Evaluation study of targeted public distribution system in selected states.* Sponsored by Department of Food and Public Distribution, Ministry of Consumer Affairs, Food and Public Distribution, Government of India, New Delhi.

NNMB. (2012). *Diet and nutritional status of rural population, prevalence of hypertension and diabetes among adults and infant and young child feeding practices-report of third repeat survey.* NNMB Technical Report No. 26, National Nutrition Monitoring Bureau, National Institute of Nutrition, Indian Council of Medical Research, Hyderabad.

NSSO. (2014a). *Level and pattern of consumer expenditure, 2011–12* (Report No. 555). NSS 68th Round, Ministry of Statistics & Programme Implementation, Government of India. New Delhi. February.

NSSO. (2014b). *Nutritional intake in India, 2011–12* (Report No. 560). NSS 68th Round, Ministry of Statistics & Programmme Implementation, National Statistical Organisation, National Sample Survey Office, Government of India. New Delhi. October.

Planning Commission. (2011). *Evaluation report on integrated child development services (ICDS), Program evaluation organisation.* Government of India. New Delhi. At http://planningcommission.nic.in/reports/peoreport/peo/peo_icds_vol1.pdf.

Planning Commission. (2012a). *Report of the working group on nutrition for the 12th five year plan (2012–17).* Government of India. New Delhi: Ministry of Women and Child Development.

Planning Commission. (2012b). *Report of the committee on encouraging investments in supply chains including provision for cold storages for more efficient distribution of farm produce,* Development Policy Division, May 2012. At http://nccd.gov.in/PDF/DSCC_Report_final.pdf.

Ramachandran, P. (2013). Food & nutrition security: Challenges in the new millennium. *Indian Journal of Medical Research, 138,* 373–382.

Rangarajan, C., & Dev, S. M. (2014). *Counting the poor: Measurement and other issues.* Mumbai: Indira Gandhi Institute of Development Research. December. At http://www.igidr.ac.in/pdf/publication/WP-2014-048.pdf.

Saxena, N. C. (2004). Synergizing government efforts for food security. In M. S. Swaminathan & P. Medrano (Eds.), *From vision to action.* Madras: East West Books.

Saxena, N. C. (2007a). *Outlays and outcomes* (Seminar, Issue no 574). June 2007. At http://www.india-seminar.com/2007/574/574_naresh_c_saxena.htm.

Saxena, N. C. (2007b). Rural poverty reduction through centrally sponsored schemes. *Indian Journal of Medical Research, 126,* 381–389. October 2007, At http://icmr.nic.in/ijmr/2007/October/1015.pdf.

Saxena, N. C. (2010). *Food security in India, inclusion.* July–September 2010. At http://inclusion.skoch.in/story/509/food-security-in-india-809.html.

Saxena, N. C. (2011). Hunger, under-nutrition and food security in India. *CPRC-IIPA Working Paper 44.* New Delhi: Chronic Poverty Research Centre, University of Manchester and Indian Institute of Public Administration. At http://r4d.dfid.gov.uk/PDF/Outputs/ChronicPoverty_RC/CPRC-IIPA44.pdf.

Saxena, N. C. (2012). Hunger and malnutrition in India, standing on the threshold: food justice in India. *IDS Bulletin, 43*(S1), July 2012. Brighton: IDS.

Saxena, N. C. (2012a). *Agriculture in crisis: Some policy suggestions, inclusion.* April–June 2012. At http://inclusion.skoch.in/story/379/agriculture-in-crisis–some-policy-suggestions-679.html.

Saxena, N. C. (2012b). *Women, land and agriculture in rural India.* New Delhi. At http://www.unwomen.org/~/media/field%20office%20esesia/docs/publications/southasia/reportstudies/06_economic%20empowerment/un_women_land_agriculture_in_rural_india%20pdf.ashxv=1&d=20141202T120141.

Saxena, N. C. (2013). Right to food: Food security in India. *Journal of the National Human Rights Commission, 12,* 85–109. At http://www.nhrc.nic.in/Documents/Publications/nhrc_journal_2013.pdf.

Saxena, N. C. (2014a). *Challenges of good governance.* India International Centre, New Delhi: Occasional Publication 62. At http://www.iicdelhi.nic.in/writereaddata/Publications/635545990407436238_OP%20-%2062.pdf.

Saxena, N. C. (2014b). *Children of a lesser god* (Seminar, Issue no. 661). September, 2014. At http://www.india-seminar.com/2014/661/661_n_c_saxena.htm.

Saxena, N. C. (2016a) Governance challenges to reducing hunger and malnutrition in India. In S. Desai, A. Thorat, D. Chopra, & L. Haddad (Eds.), *Undernutrition in India and public policy.* New York: Routledge. Summary of this paper has also been published in CBGA edited Budget

Track on Nutrition, volume 11, February 2016. At http://www.cbgaindia.org/wp-content/uploads/2016/03/Budget-Track-on-Nutrition-Compressed.pdf.

Saxena, N. C. (2016b). *An effective bureaucracy* (Seminar, Issue no. 681), May 2016. At http://www.india-seminar.com/2016/681/681_n_c_saxena.htm.

Saxena, N. C., Sheila, V., & Harsh M. (2014). *Review on food and nutrition security: India's domestic story and scope to build global partnerships.* Knowledge Partnership Programme—PIE Global, UK Aid. Available online at http://ipekpp.com/admin/upload_files/Report_1_15_Review_4510453616.pdf.

Saxena, N. C., & Srivastava, N. (2009). ICDS in India: Policy, design and delivery issues. *IDS Bulletin, 40*(4), 45–52.

Sen, P. (2005). Of calories and things: Reflections on nutritional norms, poverty lines and consumption behaviour in India. *Economic & Political Weekly, 40*(43), 4611–4618. 22 October.

Smith, L. C. (2013). The great Indian calorie debate: Explaining rising undernourishment during India's rapid economic growth. IDS Working Paper 430, Institute of Development Studies.

UNDP. (2007). *People's participation in generating district human development report cards.* PAHELI: New Delhi.

UNDP. (2008). *Study on perception of disadvantaged in seven states of India,* New Delhi.

UNICEF. (2009). *Tracking progress on child and maternal nutrition: A survival and development priority,* November. New York.

UNICEF. (2014). *Rapid survey on children (RSOC) 2013–14 national report.* Ministry of Women and Child Development. New Delhi: Government of India. At http://wcd.nic.in/sites/default/files/RSOC%20National%20Report%202013-14%20Final.pdf.

Welthungerhilfe. (2014). Improving nutrition outcomes in rural livelihood programmes in South Asia, South Asia Regional Office New Delhi.

Weismann, D., Sost, A. K., Schoeninger, I., Dalzell, H., Kiess, L., Arnold, T., & Collins, S. (2007). The challenge of hunger 2007: Global hunger index: Facts, determinants, and trends. Measures being taken to Reduce acute undernourishment and Chronic Hunger. International Food Policy Research Institute, Concern.

Farrington, J., & Saxena, N. C. Food security in India. Available at: http://www.odi.org.uk/publications/working_papers/wp231/wp231_references.pdf.

World Bank. (2007). Bihar agriculture: Building on emerging models of success. Agriculture and rural development sector unit. South Asia Region, *Discussion Paper Series* (Report No. 4). Washington, D.C.: The World Bank.

Chapter 5
Addressing Poverty and Conflict: Learning from a Gandhian Initiative in Mushahari (Muzaffarpur, Bihar)

Anand Kumar and Kanihar Kant

1 Introduction: Poverty, Conflict and Beyond

There is a general understanding about the existence of a close relationship between poverty and conflict because people in poverty live in stressful settings with high proclivity towards conflict. The marginalised in society may not all be poor but the poor are certainly marginalised. Poverty is an issue of social perceptions which are forever changing. It is an end product of a social process and has both a historical and a contemporary context.[1]

Poverty and conflict are widely understood to be closely interconnected with recurring occasions for a variety of sociopolitical conflicts. They are due to

---

With necessary permission, this chapter draws on Chap. 4 of the India Chronic Poverty Report and CPRC-IIPA working paper 42. We are grateful to the Chronic Poverty Research Centre (CPRC) for valuable comments and suggestions on the first draft of this paper. We would like to thank Aasha Kapur Mehta and Andrew Shepherd for their kind cooperation in completing this work. We are also grateful to the participants of the CPRC-IIPA workshop in New Delhi for useful questions and comments. An earlier version of this paper was presented at a seminar of the Centre for the Study of Social Systems, Jawaharlal Nehru University, New Delhi. Fieldwork was carried out by Dr. Haridwar, Shri Surendra Kumar and Shri Vishwanand. The final draft became possible with the help of Shri Manish Tiwari and Shri Pradeep Kumar Jaina. We also received valuable help from Shri Bharat Kumar and Shri Sanjay Pratap.

[1]Kumar (2013).

A. Kumar (✉)
Indian Institute of Advanced Study, Shimla, India
e-mail: anandkumar1@hotmail.com

K. Kant
Centre for the Studies of Social System, Jawaharlal Nehru University,
New Delhi, India

© Springer Nature Singapore Pte Ltd. 2018
A. K. Mehta et al. (eds.), *Poverty, Chronic Poverty and Poverty Dynamics*,
https://doi.org/10.1007/978-981-13-0677-8_5

(a) class-related destitution, (b) socio-ethnic discriminations and (c) politico-legal deprivations. Poverty makes countries more vulnerable to civil war and armed conflicts. It promotes weakening of government institutions and efficacy of political authority. High levels of unemployment and inequalities in conjunction with lack of quality education and inclusive development create fertile grounds for political conflicts and social violence due to the generation of social fragmentation and economic polarisation. At the same time, there is no necessary correlation between poverty and conflict on a long-term basis. Why? It has been observed that there is no uniformity in the making of post-conflict trajectories of politics and economics of poverty. There is probability of a variety of responses towards episodes of poverty-related conflicts and sociopolitical mobilisations of the poor from: (i) the state, (ii) the political community and (iii) victims of poverty. It ranges from brutal repression to better redistribution and resource mobilisation.

In other words, there is existence of poverty–conflict nexus in most of the nation states of the modern world system leading to a spectrum of post-conflict situations including 'conflict trap', compounded poverty, re-configuration of social categories and political coalitions, reform of governance and introduction of new social welfare policies and programmes. Therefore, it is meaningful to have a critical approach towards variability of relations between poverty and conflict.[2] This chapter is organised around the realities of poverty–conflict nexus. It is divided into two parts where a general discussion about poverty and conflict will be followed by a narrative of a Gandhian trajectory which was evolved as a response to Maoist class violence in rural part of Muzaffarpur district of Bihar in the 1970s.

This case study is significant for three reasons: (i) it was the first 'face-to-face' engagement between forces of non-violent social reconstruction on Gandhian lines (also known as Sarvodaya approach) and the proponents of Maoist methods of politico-economic liberation of victims of class exploitations ('power grows out of barrel of a gun'); (ii) it was a case of convergence of Gandhian voluntary organisations, Maoist activists, state power and development experts beyond 'law and order approach' towards poverty-related conflicts; and (iii) it created a new model of anti-poverty programmes with communitarian thrust (also known as Integrated Rural Development Programme or IRDP).

About the Key Concepts
Let us first state what we mean by the concepts of poverty, conflict, state, government and political culture in this discussion. In a general sense, poverty is a condition in which people lack what they need to live, but the limits of 'need to live' are a matter of definition. If poverty is defined in absolute terms – what people need to physically survive – it is relatively simple to define the point at which people become poor. But the experience of poverty also depends on how much people have related to other people in their society and the cultural value that defines 'good life'. Understanding poverty is a major aspect in the study of social stratification and inequality. But most theories of poverty focus on the

---

[2]See Marks (2016), Borooah (2008), Mehta (2011).

characteristics of the poor, rather than the relationship between poverty and the dynamics of wealth accumulation in a given society.[3]

Conflict perspective is one of the major approaches in political sociology of poverty-related theories and analyses. It assumes that social life is shaped by groups and individuals who compete with one another over various resources and rewards resulting in particular patterns of distribution of wealth and power. These patterns give shape to the logic of everyday life and interaction. They also create organising principles of relation between castes, classes, gender, races, nations and regions of the world. The work of Karl Marx and his critique of capitalism has been most influential in the study of social conflict where it is argued that the basic conflict in society is economic and it rests upon the unequal ownership and control of property. But Max Weber has argued for a broader view encompassing economic relations as well as factors such as race, ethnicity and religion. The contributions of Marx and Weber have helped in furthering the understanding of sociology of conflict in more complex realities of large corporations and deeply diversified societies. The writings of Ralf Dahrendorf, Lewis Coser, Randall Collins, Michael Foucault and Eric Hobsbawm have been among the other major influences in this context.[4]

Here, state is defined by its authority to generate, maintain and apply collective power in society. It is organised around a set of social functions including resolving various kinds of sociopolitical and economic conflicts. The state is also expected to continuously engage in the welfare of the population in ways that are beyond the means of the individual such as implementing public health measures, providing mass education and looking after the needs of the resource-less sections of the society. According to a significant stream of conflict perspective, the state also operates in the interest of various dominant groups, such as privileged, social, castes, classes, races, religions and gender. It is important to remind that state is not the same as government, although the terms are often used interchangeably outside of sociology and political science. The state is a social institution which means that it consists of social blueprint for how various functions ought to be accomplished. A government, however, is a particular collection of people who at any given time occupy the positions of authorities within a state. In this sense, governments regularly come and go, but barring revolutions, the state endures and is slow to change.[5]

Political culture is understood as the accumulated store of the symbols, beliefs, values, attitudes, norms and other cultural facts and products that shape and govern political life in a society. It is sociologically significant to know how various aspects of political culture affect political behaviour and outcomes. What are the different patterns of relationship between political culture and various types of political

---

[3]Johnson (2000, pp. 233–4).

[4]For further readings, see Randall (1975), Lewis (1964), Dahrendorf (1959), Michel (1980), Eric (2011).

[5]Johnson, ibid. p. 305.

system such as democracy and authoritarianism? It is also relevant to understand the characteristics of the socialisation process through which political culture is passed from one generation to the next.[6]

Poverty and Conflict in the Contemporary World System

Poverty and conflict in the contemporary world system are to be understood in the context of imperatives of modernisation of economic and political processes and institutions. Modern economies have an organic relationship with the industrial revolution and industry-led urbanisation. The process of economic modernisation has been identified with the following characteristics:

1. Increasing inequalities of income and opportunities;
2. A widening of the inter-sectoral productivity gap;
3. A continual decline in the share of value added and arising in profit; and
4. A faster widening wage gap between the skilled and the unskilled labour force.

Experiences from several countries show that the decline in rural poverty is associated with a significant decline in the proportion of the labour force engaged in agriculture and its increasing absorption in the non-farm sector. But the pace of diversification of agriculture in post-colonial nation states known as Southern economies has been slow. Consequently, the proportion of the labour force dependent on agriculture is quite high and growth in agricultural productivity has been slow. It is exacerbated by inadequate roads, markets, power, and low literacy and skills levels. It is also important to underline that growth alone is not sufficient to prevent people from falling back into the poverty trap. Growth must be complemented by, for example, improvements in mother/child care facilities, nutrition and health care for children, women and the aged. Indices of human development, such as level of literacy, gender disparities and provision of basic needs like drinking water and health care show generally poorer performance in the less-developed nation states and among socially disadvantaged groups.

There are at least six major zones of stress and conflict around the problems of poverty due to the impact of political economy of contemporary pattern of industrialisation and development. These are (i) social security, (ii) health, (iii) environment, (iv) equity, (v) culture and (vi) ethics. There is increasing income poverty and less entitlement for the poor as the WTO rules have contributed towards marginalising indigenous people and Southern countries through curtailed social security benefits and increased tax burdens. There are new insurgencies, secessionist movements and war against terrorism. The health-related situation has been affected by the spread of new epidemics and shrinkage of public health services. Provisions of TRIPS have created prohibiting impact upon manufacture of cheap drugs in poor countries, and MNCs have restricted access to life-saving medicines. There is an increase in environmental crisis due to irreversible ecological disruption

---

[6]The concept of political culture has been elaborated in the writings of several political sociologists including Almond and Verba (1963), Peter and Thomas (1967), Lucian and Verba (1965), Skocpol (1979) and Kymlicka (2002).

caused by reduced state control over manufacture and release of toxic products, lifting of trade bans and release of GM crops.

The issue of equity has been a rallying point because of increased disparity of income and opportunities among different sections and economic sectors. There is no way out of the stark discrimination in the trade terms between north and south countries. There is no prevention of widening gap between the rich and the poor within most of the countries and between nations. There is erosion of cultural diversity due to marginalisation of local languages and homogenisation of food cultures due to the pressures of American industry. There is a wave of consumerism causing importation of American lifestyle and global corrosion of the ideal of simplicity. There is increasing intolerance of multi-culturalism causing shrinking of job opportunities for the migrant labour force. Ethically, there is double danger of more pervasive corruption and increased violation of human rights. Extensive privatisation has promoted abolition of employees' rights and led to drastic layoffs. There are more 'development refugees' and more undemocratic laws to stifle political opposition. There is increase in flouting the UN directives about the rights of vulnerable sections of society including children, women, physical challenged and the aged sections of the society.[7]

Poverty-induced conflicts can be classified into two categories: (i) constitutional and (ii) extra-constitutional. The constitutional forms of conflicts are found to go through three stages. It begins with 'voice'. Then there are 'protests'. Finally, there are 'resistance' activities by the aggrieved sections of the society. There is use of legitimate methods ranging from submitting petitions to going for strikes and other forms of civil disobedience. It may or may not lead to negotiations and settlements. On the other hand, poverty-related conflicts may also follow extra-constitutional path. Here, formation of 'underground' groups, rural and urban guerrilla activities, internal wars and other 'extremist' activities like insurgency and terrorist attacks is most frequent forms of conflict.

What is the significance of poverty-based conflicts from the perspective of a social order and its political sociology? It contributes towards at least six forms of deficits in the functioning of any polity in a democratic setup. These are (i) development deficit, (ii) governance deficit, (iii) legitimacy deficit, (iv) democracy deficit, (v) citizenship deficit and (vi) nation-building deficit. A society confronted with poverty-related conflicts gets caught between the proponents of law and order approach and advocates of inclusive and sustainable development. If 'law and order' line is adopted to deal with poverty-related conflicts, there are two most likely outcomes. There is enlargement of protest activities furthering the problems of stability and development. Or there is suppression of protest activities with unpredictable consequences for development programmes.

Such conflicts create doubts about claims of good governance as the victims of poverty are found to be questioning the priorities of government implying 'neglect' of the problems of the poor. Any democratic government is expected to be engaged

---

[7]Deb (2009).

in poverty alleviation in meaningful ways on a regular basis. Therefore, poverty-related conflicts raise questions about the gap between promises and performance of a given government leading to erosion of legitimacy. It is also well-established understanding that poverty and democracy cannot coexist for a long time because continuity of poverty is contradictory for deepening of democracy. Democracy has become conceptualised in such a way where there is a necessary correlation between its political aspect, social aspect and economic aspect. The issue of citizenship deficit is related to the necessity of meaningful economic participation of all members of society in order to promote citizenship building. Victims of poverty do not enjoy 'full' citizenship due to their economic vulnerabilities. The challenge of nation building includes accommodating the needs and aspirations of all sections of citizens including the victims of poverty. So, if there is a durable conflict between the victims of poverty and better off sections of society it acts as 'speed breaker' for nation building which is contingent upon growth of 'we' feeling among all citizens.

The challenge of growing disconnect between growth and human development has been a major cause of conflicts among socially marginalised groups and within especially remote areas. It is argued by social scientists that a situation of 'relative deprivation' is more conducive to poverty-related conflict than political economy of 'absolute deprivation'. Similarly, a sudden decline in fulfilling the expectation of the victims of poverty is found to generate more conflicts than a situation of 'hopelessness'. There has been a growing intensity of grassroots social actions and increasing challenge to established politics and dominant social groups about the need to prioritise five dimensions of public policies and welfare programmes: (i) diversification and development of physical and social infrastructure to raise agricultural productivity; (ii) public investment in remote areas where poverty is concentrated; (iii) fiscal reforms and a reduction of inessential expenditures to enable greater access to institutional credit; (iv) active participation of the people in decision-making to improve governance and decision-making processes and (v) active participation of the people in programme and policy implementation processes.[8]

1.1   The Mushahari Experience

Mushahari is significant as it opened the floodgates to the possibility of armed struggle in Bihar: it has been called the 'Srikakulam of the North' (Louis 2002).[9] The conflict created a situation of face-to-face struggle between Maoists and Gandhians, which resulted in a new approach to poverty-related conflicts (Narayan 1970a). The post-conflict Sarvodaya (Gandhian) reform process attracted the

---

[8]Rao (2006).

[9]Srikakulam was the site of a clash between Maoists and the Congress-led state apparatus.

attention of the nation's policymakers, who used the experiences of Mushahari in the formulation of nationwide programmes for poverty eradication in later years. The Mushahari Project was studied by experts of the Reserve Bank of India and the Planning Commission, resulting in the launch of the Integrated Rural Development Programme (IRDP) to address the causes of poverty in rural India.

Poverty-related social conflicts take place within a framework of caste/class, market, state and community. As such, their resolution involves a number of initiatives for change. Conflict settings differ from situation to situation in terms of the relative significance of the above factors, so it is important to have an understanding of the context-specific nature of each conflict site as well as the features of the post-conflict situation.

Poverty and related social issues and processes are dealt with in the study of social stratification and inequalities. The sociology of poverty is associated with analysing poverty within societies and among them. However, research focuses mostly on the characteristics of the poor, rather than the relationship between poverty and the processes of capital formation, accumulation of wealth and immiserisation and pauperisation (Amin 2006; Field 1982; Myrdal 1968; Osberg 1991).

Poverty is also a focus in development sociology, which is concerned with a set of economic, technological and sociocultural considerations. A given society is divided into two or more groups by measuring their incomes and understanding their orientations using a set of questions. The most frequently asked questions in the context of economy and society are: how much do people earn? How much do they produce? How much do they save? How fast does production increase compared with population increases? How can modern industrial techniques be best applied to raise productivity? Who are the people who are going to initiate this change? Why and how do these changes in peoples' attitude come about? How do these people get the will to economise? Why did they not have it before? What happens when these changes start? (Feinstein 1964).

Such a developmental approach requires convergence with a 'conflict perspective' to make sense of poverty-related conflicts and post-conflict situations. In general, the conflict perspective assumes that social life is shaped by groups and individuals who struggle or compete with one another over various resources and rewards, resulting in particular distributions of wealth, power and prestige. These interactions develop not only the patterns of everyday life and interaction but also larger patterns, such as those of class, gender, ethnic, caste and racial inequalities, and those surrounding relations among regions within a nation and between nations of the modern world system. Social conflict holds many factors, including gender, class, caste, ethnicity and religion (Bottomore 1975; Collins 1975; Coser 1964). Poverty-related conflicts in rural communities are often associated in different proportions with: social injustices, including caste discriminations, sexual violence; cultural marginality (low caste status, illiteracy, customary deprivations, etc.) and chronic poverty.

An enquiry into the Mushahari case of poverty-related violence and the post-conflict face of society must be organised into four parts to be able to arrive at a meaningful understanding:

- Contextualising the Mushahari experience;
- Explaining the Sarvodaya response, known as the Mushahari Project, to the challenges of poverty and violence;
- Analysing the strengths and weaknesses of the post-conflict Gandhian intervention as conceptualised and implemented under the leadership of Jaiprakash Narayan; and
- Reviewing the Mushahari experience after several decades later.

2 Contextualising the Mushahari Experience

2.1 Background to Mushahari Block

Bihar was a part of the Bengal Presidency under the colonial rule. It was subjected to economic exploitation and underdevelopment through the permanent settlement system of the East India Company. Unlike other comparatively enlightened administrations, the rajas in Bihar seem to have paid little attention to education. The strong nationalist movement against colonialism was nurtured to a large extent in Bihar. Two particular personalities were key to the evolution of political consciousness in Bihar and deepening the roots of mass mobilisation – Mahatma Gandhi and Swami Sahajanand Saraswati. Gandhi led a peasant movement against the indigo planters in 1917–1918, known famous as the Champaran Satyagraha (non-violent resistance). This integrated Bihar into the nationalist political framework around the Indian National Congress. The first President of the Republic of India, Dr. Rajendra Prasad, came into national politics as an organiser of the Gandhian Satyagraha in Champaran. A decade later, Swami Sahajanand Saraswati led the political workers of Bihar to organise peasants of Bihar under the banner of Kisan Sabha (the All India Peasants Union). If Gandhi sensitised Bihar and the nation about the agonies of indigo cultivators in 1917, Swami Sahajanand mobilised the peasants of Bihar against the evils of the zamindari system in the 1930s. The foundation conferences of the Congress Socialist Party and the Kisan Sabha took place in Patna in 1934 and 1936, respectively. These two organisations played a historic role in the anti-colonial struggles and peasant movements of India.

Bihar was applauded as the best-governed state in India in the 1950s. It was the first state to pass legislation for the abolition of zamindari, yet land reforms and agricultural wages remained two of the most fundamental challenges from the colonial past for governance and development in the state at the end of the 1960s.

Politically, the period between 1964 and 1970 was a phase of mobilisation of the masses for political change. There were years of famine (1965–1966), land struggles (1964–1970) and a general election (1967). It was a phase of political turmoil at the state level: for the first time since independence, a non-Congress coalition came into power. Thus, this was a period of deep deprivations, growing unrest, high expectations and significant changes in the political setting, in which the politics against poverty found more support than before. This accelerated the pace of mass mobilisation as well as of poverty-related conflicts. Rising expectations led to an eruption of violent conflicts in Naxalbari (West Bengal), Srikakulam (Andhra Pradesh) and Mushahari (Bihar). Naxalbari saw an encounter between different groups of Marxists. Srikakulam was the site of a clash between the Maoists and the Congress-led state apparatus. Mushahari became the site of a face-to-face conflict between Maoists and Gandhians.

Muzaffarpur district was carved out of Tirhut district in 1875. The district is named after Muzaffar Khan, a revenue farmer who founded the principal town of the district. It has an area of 3175.91 km^2 and a rich historical background. A part of the famous kingdom of Vaishali, Muzaffarpur has also been a centre of many important events in modern Indian history, including the famous bombing case of 1908 involving the great martyrs Khudiram Bose and Prafulla Chandra Chaki. It was a centre of active support for the Champaran Satyagraha of Mahatma Gandhi in 1917 under the guidance of Acharya JB Kripalani, then a teacher of political science at LS College (Fig. 1).

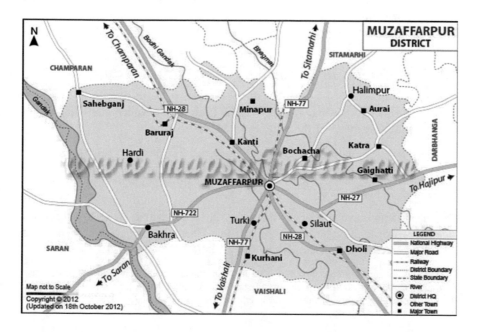

Fig. 1 Map of Muzaffarpur district. *Source* www.mapsofindia.com

The district has two subdivisions, 16 blocks, 387 panchayats and 1,808 villages. With a population of 48.01 lakh, Muzaffarpur is the third most populated district of Bihar as per the 2011 census. The district has a subtropical climate characterised by hot summers, wet monsoons and dry winters. The rural population is dependent almost entirely on agriculture and allied activities. The main trade is in wholesale cloth and food grains.

The predominance of the agriculture sector and the continued rise in population of about 3% per annum since 1951 (AVARD 1971) without any appreciable expansion in industrial activities led to a decline in the land to person ratio in Muzaffarpur district to a level as low as 2.28 acres per rural household. According to Ministry of Agriculture (Government of India Agriculture 2015) 96.91% land-holdings, covering 75.50% of the cultivable area in the state, are below 2 ha (approx 5 acres). Merely, 0.03% of all landholdings and 0.75% of cultivable land area in the state are with persons having holdings of 10 ha (25 acres) or more. Mushahari is the most populated block of Muzaffarpur, located in the rich alluvial plains of north Bihar. Its neighbouring districts are Patna (north), Darbhanga (east) and East Champaran and Saran (west). Budhi Gandak River is to the north, causing frequent floods in the villages of Mushahari block. The block has 112 villages, organised into 25 panchayats. In Mushahari block, nearly 70% of the cultivating households operate holdings below 2.5 acres. Almost all holdings in the villages of the block, small or big, were fragmented mainly due to partition in the family. The proportion of scheduled castes in the population of Mushahari was above 15%, and almost all of them are engaged in agricultural activities as landless labourers.

2.2 The Conflict in Mushahari

Let us begin with a well-known observation of Jaiprakash Narayan (1970a, b) about the outstanding features of the villages of Mushahari:

> My first experience on coming face to face with the reality of Mushahari was to realize how remote and unreal were the brave pronouncements of Delhi or Patna from the actuality at the ground level. Ultimately what meets the eye are utter poverty, misery, backwardness, frustration and loss of hope.

This depressing statement about the situation in Mushahari in 1970 can be read together with the 2006 remarks of the Bihar People's Union for Civil Liberties (PUCL) about the overall trends regarding conflict in rural Bihar:

> The cause of rural conflicts has often been the poor implementation of the provisions of the Land Ceiling Act and the Minimum Wages Act. At times when the conflict turns into bloody clashes the policy of the government has been to let the people fight it out between themselves.

Mushahari attracted the attention of Sarvodaya workers of the whole country because the Naxalites issued a death threat in May 1970 to two eminent Gandhians, Shri Badri Babu and Shri Gopal Mishra, leaders of Gram Swaraj Samiti (self-reliant village system administration). Acharya Vinoba Bhave rushed his close associate, Nirmala Deshpande, to an ailing Jaiprakash Narayan to request urgent intervention. He took no time to reach Muzaffarpur to take stock of the situation, opting to stay in Mushahari block for several months with his wife Prabhavati to open dialogue with all the concerned sections of the village communities, including the supporters of the Naxalite movement.

Mushahari block witnessed the first eruption of violent conflict between 1968 and 1972 as a result of rural poverty and socio-economic injustices. The first reported incident was the forcible harvesting of crops in April 1968 in Gangapur Village, after the landlord and his hired men were driven away. This unprecedented action boosted the morale of the peasants in the nearby villages, who came mainly from the lower castes. There ensued a struggle between the panic-stricken landlords and Kisan Sangram Samitis, during which six landowners were killed, 16 were injured, property worth Rs. 20,000 was confiscated, documents were destroyed, and ornaments mortgaged to landlords were seized and returned to the people. Police camps were set up in the villages to forestall trouble. The main issue in the initial phase of the Mushahari conflict, which had spread from Gangapur to other villages of Mushahari and Muzaffarpur, was occupancy rights over land. When the government machinery retaliated by attacking the leaders and the cadres and their property, many more peasants joined the struggle. In the ensuing struggle, a number of peasant leaders were killed (Louis 2002).

Mushahari block had a relatively large agricultural labour population (Narayan 1970a, b). The average for the whole district of Muzaffarpur was only 33.3%, whereas agricultural labourers with their dependents made up 39.2% of the total rural population of this block. If we add to this number the other landless labourers who sought a livelihood in the town, landless labourers and their dependents would not be less than 45% of the total rural population. Scheduled castes formed 25.2% of the population, and almost all are landless labourers. The daily wage was 1–1.5 kg of paddy or coarse grain. On an average, the wage of 'attached' labourers was half of what was prescribed. Overall, the situation was characterised by a lack of land for many in the area; an uncommon dominance of the landowning families; exceptionally low wages, particularly for attached labourers; a high degree of unemployment; extreme poverty of agricultural labourers and a general climate of discontent.

In his analysis of the situation, Jaiprakash Narayan stressed that the responsibility for the eruption of violent conflict between the landowners and the rural poor in the villages of Mushahari could not be exclusively laid at the door of the Naxalites. He identified the following forces and societal factors as responsible for the crisis (1970): big farmers (cheating the Land Ceiling Act); gentlemen (grabbing government land and village commons); landowners (denying the legal rights of the sharecroppers); clever men (taking away the land of weaker sections by fraud or force); upper caste men (ill treating scheduled caste men and women); moneylenders (usurious interests and seizers of the land of the poor); politicians and administrators (aiding and abetting the above in these wrongs); courts of law (denying a fair deal to the weaker sections); system of education (ill-educated youth); system of planning (unemployment of youth); the party system (reducing democracy to a farce).

3 Sarvodaya Response to the Challenges of Poverty and Maoist Violence: The Mushahari Plan

The Mushahari Plan owes its origin to the unwavering resolve and dedication of Jaiprakash Narayan to a modest programme of action in response to a lack of any serious effort to tackle the ugly and distressing problem of rural chronic poverty and related conflicts. The backdrop was the growing challenge of Naxal or Maoist violence in Mushahari, where a number of murders, dacoities and death threats took place between 1968 and 1970. The Mushahari Plan was proposed to achieve the goals of area development planning in a manner that would help in providing gainful employment to the dispersed and disorganised rural poor. It suggested that poverty-related conflicts in rural communities were often associated in different proportions with social injustices, including caste discrimination, sexual violence, and cultural marginality, such as low caste status, illiteracy or customary deprivations.

Jaiprakash Narayan visited Mushahari in June 1970, at the height of Naxal violence. During his efforts to bring peace in the region, he realised the paramount need to tackle the problem of widespread poverty. He asked the Association of Voluntary Agencies for Rural Development (AVARD), a Gandhian rural development organisation, to prepare an integrated block-level development plan. The Sarvodaya workers were persuaded to form a local voluntary organisation named the Muzaffarpur Development Agency to implement the plan in Mushahari block and to gradually replicate it in other blocks. The local branch of the Bank of Baroda was motivated to provide loans for agriculture, allied activities, artisans and retail traders. By 1973, the Naxalite violence had ebbed to a large extent and the initial results of the Mushahari Plan were quite encouraging. In 1974, the Government of India launched the Rural Industries Project (RIP) in Muzaffarpur district, which was entrusted to the Muzaffarpur Development Agency. In 1978, the RIP was merged with the District Industries Centre (DIC). The DIC in Muzaffarpur continued to be managed by Muzaffarpur Development Agency (MDA) until recently.

What were the prominent features of the Mushahari Plan in response to the conflicts and poverty? It was a five-year plan designed to harness the growth potentialities of the area through a phased programme of agro-industrial development leading to a self-generating economy. The plan also had political and sociocultural components to promote community spirit through participatory decision-making and consensual changes for conflict resolution.

According to the plan, two related factors were aggravating the problems of poverty and underdevelopment: first, land shortage or excessive pressure on land;

and second, inequalities in landholdings. Therefore, the major objective of the plan was to ensure rapid expansions in employment, outputs and incomes, with a view to establish a minimum level of living in the area. The plan had a total outlay of about Rs. 2.4 crores and was designed to generate, by the end of the plan period, an additional annual income or net output (valued at 1970–71 prices) to the tune of about Rs. 1.12 crores, the value of net output per Rs. 1000 investment being 465 (or 46.5%). The rural credit scheme was probably one of the first initiatives of its kind in which institutional credit was used as an important input for sustainable development.

The Sarvodaya initiative received a positive response from government sources in its first 5 years. Apart from the RIP (1974) and the DIC, two more significant schemes converged with the initiative in Mushahari block. Based on the recommendation of the National Commission on Agriculture (1972), the Whole Village Development Plan (WVDP) was conceived in the Fifth Five-Year Plan, implemented in 52 villages of seven districts in four states, out of which 23 were in Mushahari block. The programme involved diversification of agriculture and creation of income-generating assets through bank loans and subsidies. It is significant to recognise that the WVDP was the precursor of the IRDP. Similarly, with a view to ensuring backward and forward linkages for rural artisans, the All India Handicrafts Board launched a scheme to set up rural marketing centres (RMCs) at the block level to provide an effective link with the market for raw materials and finished goods. Out of the 14 RMCs envisaged under the scheme, four were entrusted to the MDA and performed satisfactorily for some time. The other ten, entrusted to several other agencies, could not be started.

The Mushahari Plan was conceived within the Gandhian framework of Gram Swaraj (self-reliant village system). The requisites were: (1) provision of land for the landless through voluntary donations from the landowner class; (2) setting up of a Gram Sabha (village council) for self-governance; (3) creation of a Gram Kosh (village fund) for credit support to the villagers and (4) formation of a Gram Shanti Sena (village peace force) for the protection of the village (see Box 1). It was suggested that rural reconstruction through the organisation and development of Gram Swaraj would bring out the hidden constructive power of the village in the form of people power (Lokshakti) that it would not take long to change the condition of the villages and that this could establish the rule of the village. The Gandhians took the conflict of Mushahari as a challenge requiring a response not of 'revenge' but of change.

Box 1: Jaiprakash Narayan's First Open Letter to the Locals During his Mushahari Stay

Friends,

Staying in the Salha, Naroli and Budhagra Panchayat of your block since 9th June, I have been discussing with you about the organization and development of Gram Swaraj. I feel that my approach and the discussions on Gram Swaraj have been appreciated by you. Accepting this idea, most of the brothers of village have signed on the Gramdan declaration. My heartiest thanks to them and I also thank those brothers who have donated land in favour of the Beegha-Kattha principle. I hope that after giving careful thought to the idea of Gramdan, they will soon join the Gramdan movement.

Requisites for Gram Swaraj are: (1) arranging Beegha-Kattha for the landless; (2) setting up of Gram Sabha; (3) collecting village fund; (4) setting up of Gram Shanti Sena for the protection of the village.

I have been discussing about these programmes with you all. The hidden constructive power of the community will come out in the form of people's power through them and it won't take long to change the present condition of the villages. This could establish the rule of the village. Some of you still do not have faith in this idea, and their heart is not open for this thought. Our efforts to convince such people will go on till the time they willingly accept the idea of Gram Swaraj.

Today on 17th July, I am going out for some necessary work, but my friends will continue to work among you. I will be returning on 4th August and will visit rest of the panchayats. Again, I would like to inform you that till the time the work of this block does not get completed – I'm going to stay here. I believe that the remaining people will donate their BeeghaKattha and will facilitate the path of Gram Swaraj by forming Gram Sabha with the consent of all.

Jaiprakash Narayan

Jaiprakash Narayan turned his mission into a struggle for social and economic justice through radicalisation of the Sarvodaya programmes of Gram Swaraj. The organisation required initiatives in three directions: economic, political and social. These initiatives were taken through a wide variety of instruments (see Fig. 2).

The Mushahari conflict proved to be a mirror for the Gandhian workers as it demonstrated the declining significance of Sarvodaya work among rural communities, particularly in the context of injustices against the poor. It forced them into innovations in terms of their approach towards socio-economic problems. It was after a month-long process of consulting the men and women of various classes, castes and communities and studying the causes of distress and destitution that Jaiprakash Narayan, Prabhavati Devi and the band of Gandhian colleagues came forward with the triple programme of Gram Sabha, Gram Kosh and Gram Shanti Sena to create a new framework to address the problems of pauperisation and poverty-related conflict without allowing escalation of caste/class violence. This was reconciliation through reconstruction. Figure 3 presents the multidimensionality of the programmes launched by the Gandhians in Mushahari in an environment of terror and violence between 1970 and 1972.

Like any major programme of planned social change, the Mushahari Plan had its share of successes and failures. It was thoroughly scrutinised by a variety of people, including social scientists, journalists and political observers at the inception stage.

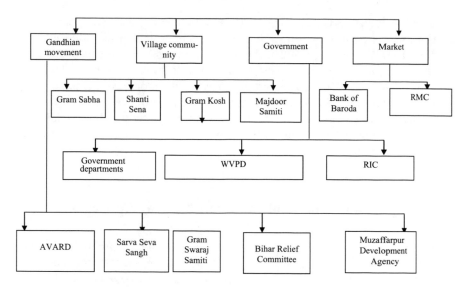

Fig. 2 Instruments of Gram Swaraj

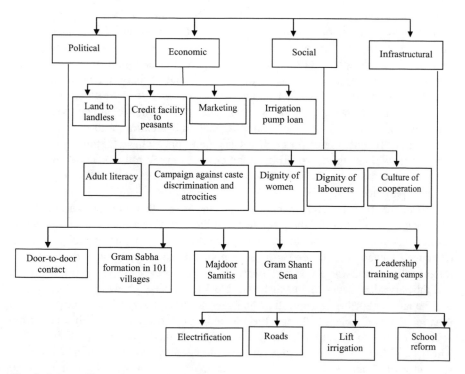

Fig. 3 Post-conflict programmes in Mushahari

Jaiprakash Narayan, Avinash Bhai, Acharya Rammoorthy and many others from the Gandhian circle also presented their critique and evaluations at different points in time. Overall, it was agreed that the post-conflict work of the Gandhians under the leadership of Jaiprakash Narayan at Mushahari did weaken the Naxalite forces in north Bihar in the 1970s. It is further agreed that it promoted internal criticism within the ranks of the Sarvodaya Movement as well as political parties about their orientation and engagements with the problem of rural poverty and the condition of the poorer sections in the regions of Bihar and the rest of India (Avinash 2006; Das 1992; Kumar 2006).

4 Strengths and Limits of the Gram Swaraj Approach

There have been three phases in the Mushahari mission in response to the challenge of Naxal violence. The first phase (1970–1979) was one of the most significant initiatives for non-violent socio-economic transformation to meet the challenge of rural poverty and related violence. The second phase (1980–1988) suffered from a lack of leadership, as Jaiprakash Narayan passed away in October 1979, as well as active discouragement by the state agencies after a number of direct and indirect central investigations, particularly by the Kudal Commission. No instance of any impropriety was noted in any of the investigation reports undertaken by the official agencies. The third phase (1988–2005) was a period of benign neglect and gradual decline. It is regrettable that such a historic initiative between Gandhians and Naxalites on poverty and conflict was not allowed to evolve any further by the state after Jaiprakash Narayan passed away and after the changes of government at the centre and in Bihar in 1979–1980. Any exercise of evaluation of this endeavour on post-conflict reconstruction through a Gandhian approach of 'community-centred inclusive social change', instead of 'conflictive revenge', must be undertaken with an awareness of the drastic difference between the circumstances of the three phases of the experience.

There are two grounds for assessing the strengths and weakness of the Mushahari intervention by the proponents of the Gram Swaraj approach to conflict resolution. First, was it able to reorient rural society from a path of violent conflict (revenge) towards a process of sociopolitical and economic reconstruction (change)? Second, was the Gram Swaraj work (as evolved by Jaiprakash Narayan and the Sarvodaya workers in Mushahari block) replicated elsewhere in later years?

The answer to the first question has been an unequivocal 'yes': the Gandhian intervention was able to change the direction of anti-poverty mobilisation from social violence to developmental reconstruction through people's participation in Mushahari block. There was no recurrence of class/caste violence on any side after the entry of Gram Swaraj workers, in spite of the fact that the rest of Bihar continued to sink deeper into chronic poverty and caste-/class-based group killings.

How did the Mushahari villages find their way out of violence and destruction? Reorientation of the villagers of Mushahari block was achieved through the four-point programme, which promised inclusive as well as holistic development. Land to the landless labourers, formation of the village committee for a communitarian mechanism of village governance (Gram Sabha), creation of a village fund to provide microcredit services to needy households and creation of village volunteer force (Shanti Sena) to maintain security of the villages from external threats were the four pillars of the programme. Within the first 24 months after Jaiprakash Narayan's arrival in June 1970, 101 Gram Sabhas were constituted in the Mushahari block. These proved to be the catalytic agents for implementing the development projects as well as conflict resolution processes.

Some of the obvious strengths of the Gram Swaraj work in the post-conflict Mushahari block were: (1) the charismatic leadership of Jaiprakash Narayan; (2) the open-minded engagement of the Sarvodaya workers with various sections of the village community; (3) an integrated development scheme (Mushahari Plan) with a specific organisational system and the Muzaffarpur Development Agency; (4) cooperation of the village elite, political organisations and the rural poor and (5) active association of the state machinery at the district and province levels.

(a) Creating and developing a zone of non-violent social transformation in an atmosphere of poverty and violence were the most outstanding aspect of this process. Jaiprakash Narayan presented a new definition of the situation, one which avoided the 'blame game' and rejected the 'revenge road'. It was achieved as a result of a three-step process of constructive work: community building through an inclusive process of awareness about the root causes of crisis and conflicts through the central Gram Sabha as a people's instrument;
(b) Identifying the basic needs of various sections and resource mobilisation for their fulfilment (drinking water, credit fund, proper wages, land ownership records, schools for children, health needs, electrification, negation of violence and atrocities, corruption-free role of police and bureaucracy) and presenting a holistic plan for inclusive reforms and development; and
(c) Mutually complementary roles for voluntary groups, state agencies, interest groups, market forces and the village community through the Gram Swaraj programme around an integrative scheme of development of agricultural and non-agricultural activities. A consensus was created about: what was wrong in the present setting of economic and social relations; who was responsible for this; the consequences of an unjust approach and the solution to the major causes of conflicts and crisis.

The approach promoted a new perspective in the post-conflict Mushahari block, one which resisted the wrong practices of the village elite. It also encouraged the construction of instruments of dialogue and negotiations and discouraged the path of caste/class violence.

The approach promoted a new perspective which discouraged justifying the wrong practices of the village elite. It also encouraged people to avoid the path of violence in the context of conflict resolution by creating instruments of dialogue and negotiations.

Now let us look at the limits and weakness of the Gram Swaraj approach. It could be asked, if the Mushahari Plan was so effective in more than 150 villages of north Bihar that there was a wave of constructive activism and words of optimism after June 1970, why it was not replicated in the other parts of Bihar which kept on sinking further in the vicious cycle of pauperisation, conflict and carnage. One of the obvious factors was the dramatic change in the role of the state apparatus between 1970 and 1975, from active encouragement to destructive interference owing to the Bihar Movement led by Jaiprakash Narayan between 1974 and 1977 and the Emergency Rule imposed to control it from 26 June 1975 till the national elections of 1977. The Mushahari Plan received some renewed support during the Janata Party regime between 1977 and 1979, as this was brought into existence as a result of the blessings of Jaiprakash Narayan and his Sarvodaya colleagues. But the return to power of Indira Gandhi created many new obstructions to the further evolution of the Gram Swaraj work, as there were continuous enquiries into all programmes led by Jaiprakash Narayan and his supporters between 1980 and 1988–1989. The second factor was related to the imprisonment of Jaiprakash Narayan and his later passing away on 8 October 1979. There was no alternative to his charisma and capacity in the Sarvodaya movement. Third, there was a decline in interest in the alternate sections of the village community in Gram Swaraj works after the end of the Naxal threat in the area. It was found that the landowning sections of the villages were not sincere about their expected contribution to the well-being of agricultural workers, small peasants and village development. Most of them did not keep their commitments regarding voluntary donations of land for the landless, return of loans and withdrawal of cases against the poorer section of the village community. Finally, the issue of proper wages was approached without sincerity, considered a 'breach of trust' by Gram Swaraj activists, including Jaiprakash Narayan (see Box 2).

Box 2: Second Open Letter of Jaiprakash Narayan to the Locals During his Mushahari Stay
Dear Friends,

I am writing this open letter to you with great sorrow and anxiety. If my health would have been alright and if I would not have taken the decision of one year rest, then I would have travelled in each of the villages and talked to you directly. Till now 101 'Gram Sabhas' have been formed in the Mushahari block. In many villages 'Gram Shanti Sena' (village peace committees) have also been formed and many training camps for peace volunteers have been organized. Gram Sabha members and office bearers have also been elected in many places. One block committee has also been formed but due to political rivalry no office bearers have been elected in the block committee, only a coordinator has been nominated.

After I started work in Mushahari, electricity reached many villages and many farmers have installed electric pumps for irrigation in their lands. Bihar Relief Committee has installed more than hundred of hand-pumps in the lands of many poorer farmers. Due to my intervention Bank of Baroda has sanctioned loans of thousands of rupees for tobacco cultivation. A few water ponds have also been improved due to AVARD's initiative. A few roads have been constructed. Diesel pumps have been set up on boats to lift water from Gandak River for irrigation of the nearby fields. Many poor families have been provided free hand-pumps. In Harijan settlements several hand-pumps have been installed for drinking water. Many tenants have received land entitlement papers. AVARD has prepared a comprehensive plan for inclusive development of the block. 'Padyatras' have been organized many times in many villages of the block. Many training camps have been organized for the primary and secondary school teachers to increase their efficiency and it is still going on. Shri Joytibhai Desai has travelled from far away Gujarat on number of occasions for this purpose for invaluable guidance. Many personalities associated with Sarvodaya movement have visited the area. The atmosphere of terror that was widespread in the area before I arrived has now become a thing of the past. Violence and vandalism if not completely abolished has definitely become marginal.

But I feel all these efforts have gone in vain. Gram Sabhas have only been formed on paper and only a few are functional to the extent that there are occasional meetings. The conditions of Gramdan have not been fulfilled even after the formation of Gram Sabhas. Land has been redistributed only to a few people in a few places according to the Beegha-Kattha principle. Gram Kosh has been created due to the efforts of Avinash Bhai and others in a very few villages largely due to the contributions from the poorer farmers and agricultural workers only. Madhopur was one of the villages where the work initially picked up very well. Large amount of land was redistributed. Some money for Gramkosh was also collected. Many people volunteered in village road constructions, but some laxity has surfaced here also which is so prevalent in the area. Only a small percentage of the people who had taken loan for hand-pumps or tobacco cultivation have repaid and that too partially. Most disappointing is the fact that those people who got help from Electricity Department, Bihar Relief Committee and Bank of Baroda due to my personal intervention or AVARD were the most lax in fulfilling their commitment. The established politicians of the area talk big when they are on stage but very few have worked earnestly for Gram Swaraj beyond taking the post or making personal benefits.

When I started the development work many of my Sarvodaya friends had cautioned that the stage is not ripe for this sort of work because people might sign Gramdan declaration and a few Gram Sabhas may also be formed on the paper due to the hope of some benefits of development but when their interest will be fulfilled the same people will become inactive and it is possible that they start opposing Gram Swaraj from behind the scene. But I had overruled such views. I was of the opinion that changes in the village orientation and the society at large should be simultaneous with development work as it will help in realizing the vision of Gram Swaraj sooner. Social and intellectual transformation and economic development will complement each other. Harmonization in the villages and rapid pace of development will expedite positive changes in the orientation of the peoples as well as the society. But now I feel that my expectation were helpless and those friends who have cautioned me were eventually proved correct.

Thus keeping in mind these circumstances, I have taken the following decisions:

(1) Such villages where the Gram Sabhas are not functioning and do not start to function soon then those villages would be deleted from the name of Gram Sabhas and no developmental work would be undertaken there.

(2) In the villages where the Gram Sabha office bearers have not donated land on the Beegha-Kattha basis and did not contribute to the Gramkosh in a regular manner they will have to vacate their posts. In their place only such people will be appointed who show commitment towards the reconstruction and development of the villages. In the villages, only such families will be included in the development work who have made voluntary land donation on the basis of Beegha-Kattha (if only they have land) and contributed for the Gramkosh. Only those villages will be chosen for holistic and integrated development where people have signed the declaration for Gramdan and have fulfilled the conditions associated with it.

In other words, the change in the role of the state, the death of the leader and a lack of commitment in the upper sections of village communities were three major limitations to the Gram Swaraj approach in Mushahari. These factors together became responsible for preventing a great experiment from opening a constructive path of conflict resolution through change. Although new optimism and activism existed in the villages of Mushahari block after June 1970, this limited its replication in other areas. This was exacerbated by the period of interference and decline (1980–1988), when there was an atmosphere of helplessness and hopelessness, and government programmes failed to provide justice to peasants and agricultural labourers.

5   Poverty and Society in Mushahari: The Post-conflict Scene

This exploration of the post-conflict face of poverty and society in Mushahari block of villages of Muzaffarpur (Bihar) can be concluded with an overview of the present situation after decades of violent conflict followed by the Gram Swaraj campaign. It is also necessary to present a brief outline of the overall situation of poverty, politics and society in Bihar.

Between 1983 and 2011, the proportion of persons below the poverty line in Bihar as a percentage of persons below the poverty line in India decreased from 14.31 to 13.29%. In rural areas, the share declined from 16.58 to 14.79%, and in urban areas, it increased from 6.25 to 7.13% (Table 1). Thus, the reduction in poverty rates during this time period was very varied in both rural and urban areas of Bihar. From 1983 till 2000 there was a constant reduction in poverty estimates for India in absolute numbers as well as percentage terms. However, in the case of Bihar, there was a decline in poverty in 1987–88 followed by an increase in 1993–94. The most radical shift in calculation of poverty estimates happened in 2004–05 when the Planning Commission of India formed an expert group under the chairmanship of Prof. Suresh D. Tendulkar to review the methodology for estimation of poverty in India. The committee submitted its report in 2009 and computed poverty lines and poverty ratios for 2004–05 onwards. Tendulkar committee recommended a shift away from (i) calorie consumption-based poverty estimation; (ii) a uniform poverty line basket (PLB) across rural and urban India; (iii) a change in the price adjustment procedure to correct spatial and temporal issues with price adjustment and (iv) incorporation of private expenditure on health and education while estimating poverty. All this lead to a jump in both absolute number of poor persons as well as percentage of poor both for Bihar and India. But in 2011, based on Tendulkar committee recommendations, there is a perceptible decline in poverty for India and Bihar (see Table 1).

Bihar was identified as a least developed Indian state at the beginning of the new millennium, faring poorly on almost every scale of human development when ranked against the other states. Only 10% of the population resides in urban areas. Just one-half of the population is literate. The situation among the marginalised communities (Dalits and tribal people) is far worse. The creation of Jharkhand has further impoverished the state, having been robbed of access to mineral resources. The pressure on the agrarian economy has become acute, as indicated by the fact that the population density in rural Bihar (880 persons per km^2) is about three times that of rural India as a whole. The process of liberalisation which started in 1991 has also not brought any tangible benefits to Bihar. There was a worsening of per capita income in the state in the 1990s. In 1961, the average income of a person from the state was about two-thirds of that of an average Indian; by 2004, this had fallen to less than one-third (Sridhar 2007).

In order to understand the situation in the villages in Mushahari block 25 years after the passing away of Jaiprakash Narayan, surveys were conducted in four villages in Mushahari block. The villages that were selected on the basis of targeted random sampling are Madapur Chaube, Madhopur, Taraura Gopalpur and Akbarpur. Questionnaires were administered to a total of 951 households of the villages: 158 from Madapur Chaube, 320 from Madhopur, 377 from Taraura Gopalpur and 96 from Akbarpur. Data collection was carried out in 2005–2006.

Madapur Chaube is situated southwest of and is 15 km away from Mushahari town. Madapur Chaube has the characteristics of an interior rural village, with most

Table 1 Comparative levels of poverty in Bihar and India

| Year | Persons below poverty line (lakhs) | | | | | | Bihar's share of poor in India (%) | | |
| | Bihar | | | India | | | | | |
	Rural	Urban	All	Rural	Urban	All	Rural	Urban	All
1983	417.7 (64.37)	44.35 (47.33)	462.05 (62.22)	2519.57 (45.65)	709.4 (40.79)	3228.97 (44.48)	16.58	6.25	14.31
1987–1988	370.23 (53.63)	50.7 (48.73)	420.93 (52.12)	2318.79 (39.09)	751.59 (38.20)	3070.49 (38.86)	15.97	6.74	13.71
1993–1994	450.86 (58.21)	42.49 (34.50)	493.35 (54.96)	2440.31 (37.27)	763.37 (32.36)	3203.68 (35.97)	18.48	5.57	15.40
1999–2000	376.51 (44.30)	49.13 (32.91)	425.64 (42.60)	1932.43 (27.09)	670.07 (23.62)	2602.5 (26.10)	19.48	7.33	16.36
2004–05[a]	445.04 (55.7)	40.89 (43.7)	485.79 (54.4)	3266.63 (41.8)	807.49 (25.7)	4054.09 (37.2)	13.62	4.95	11.98
2011–12[a]	320.40 (34.06)	37.75 (31.23)	358.15 (33.7)	2165.50 (25.7)	528.75 (13.7)	2693.25 (21.9)	14.79	7.13	13.29

[a]The 2004–05 and 2011–12 figures are based on Tendulkar committee methodology
Source Radhakrishna and Ray (2005) and press note on poverty estimates published by Planning Commission (2013)

of the population depending on agriculture-related professions. It has high incidence of migration, for a variety of reasons. Madhopur is situated southeast of Mushahari and has a combination of urban and rural characteristics. It was one of the favourite villages of Jaiprakash Narayan. Taraura Gopalpur is situated north of Mushahari. Most of the population depends on daily wage earnings. Their livelihood is governed by fluctuations in the availability of employment opportunities in neighbouring villages and towns. This is a multi-caste and hetero-religious village, approximately 6 km away from Muzaffarpur city. Akbarpur is situated midway between Madhopur and Taraura Gopalpur. It is approximately 10 km away from Mushahari block headquarters. Agricultural labourers inhabit this village. There are only two peasant households with marginal landholdings. This village received developmental inputs under Jaiprakash Narayan, and there was mobility among the landless labourers and sharecropper categories.

The average size of a household is 7.4 in Akbarpur, 8.8 in Madapur Chaube, 5.7 in Madhopur and 5.7 in Taraura Gopalpur. The average size of household is smaller in the larger villages than in the smaller villages. This requires further study, as there was no clear association between landholding and family size. Most of the agricultural labourers were found to belong to smaller households. In all the four villages, women's share in the workforce is greater in bigger size households. On the whole, the share of male members in the workforce is bigger in small-sized households.

5.1 Caste and Village Profile

Bihar is a caste-based society, with castes among the Muslims also. Table 2 gives us a clear picture of the caste profile of the villages in question. It also gives us the female–male ratio, number of persons per household as well as household size, for specific castes. Household size is further categorised into lowest, middle and highest categories. Tatmas are the most populous caste in the region, with a population of 14.2%, followed by Bhumihars (9.6%) and Chamars (6.7%). The female–male ratios are strikingly high among the Julahas (1571), Lohars (1056), Kahar, Kanu and Nunia, all at 1024 (Table 2). The lowest is recorded is among the Dhunias (645). There are great variations in household size also. Thus, we can see how difficult it is to bring a particular region covering only four villages under one single frame and generalise on the basis of this.

5.2 Incidence of Chronic Poverty

The disabled, the elderly, female-headed households and widows are victims of social as well as cultural exclusion, which is a significant and persistent feature of chronic poverty, along with diminishing capability (Brady 2003). Women take charge of running the household in two situations: either the male has migrated away from the village to earn a livelihood or the woman is a widow or a deserted person. Most female-headed households belong to the vulnerable sections of society, and the women are victims of social exclusion. According to the data, female-headed households account for 18.3% of the total of 951 households in the selected villages. There is very significant ratio of female-headed households in the reference region.

Four castes, Mali, Dhobi, Mehtar and Musehar, are not included in the list. M-Momin (9.3%), Julaha (5.6%) and Muslim (6.3%) in the Muslim community and Yadav (9.1%), Kanu (8.3%), Kushwaha (8.2%), Pasi (7.0%), Lohar (ironsmiths) (6.8%), Dusadh (6.2%), Kahar (6.0%), Mallah (5.9%) and Tamoli (5.8%) are above the poverty line and the rest are below the line. The Bhumihar are found to be at the average level in terms of old persons. A caste analysis of incidence of old persons shows: (1) marginal communities and most poor communities have no incidence of old persons; (2) the highest percentage of females who are old belong to most backward Muslim as well as Hindu communities.

5.3 Occupations and Unemployment

The employed are classified into eight categories: cultivation, agricultural labour, non-agricultural work, industrial work, self-employment, services, traditional

Table 2 Caste profile of the selected villages

S. No.	Caste/ religion	Caste distribution (%)	Female to male ratio[a]	No. persons/ household	Household size		
					Lowest	Middle	Highest
1	Bhumihar	9.6	963	6.6	1	7	22
2	Brahmin	1.9	933	7.25	4	7	11
3	Chamar	6.7	938	5.3	2	6	11
4	Dhobi	1.6	792	5.9	2	6	17
5	Dusadh	3.7	907	4.7	1	5	9
6	Halwai	0.6	947	5.3	3	5	7
7	Hazzam	1.7	789	6	4	6	9
8	Kahar	1.4	1024	6.9	3	8	15
9	Kanu	2.8	1024	6.2	2	7	17
10	Kumhar	3.2	806	6.1	2	7	13
11	Kurmi	3.3	968	5.5	2	6	15
12	Kushwaha	1.0	968	6.1	1	7	14
13	Lohar	1.2	1056	5.3	2	6	10
14	Mali	0.7	905	5	3	6	7
15	Mallah	11.9	903	7.8	2	8	23
16	Mehtar	Neg.[b]	750	7	7	7	7
17	Musehar	Neg.[b]	667	5	5	5	5
18	Muslim	18.2	934	7.2	2	8	21
19	M-Dhunia	0.8	645	5.1	3	5	7
20	M-Julaha	0.6	1571	7.2	5	8	11
21	M-Momin	0.7	720	7.2	1	7	10
22	Nunia	2.8	1024	7.4	1	8	19
23	Pasi	0.9	966	4.8	2	5	7
24	Tamoli	1.1	971	5.3	1	6	9
25	Tatma	14.2	957	6.1	1	7	14
26	Teli	5.3	851	7.5	2	8	27
27	Yadav	2.2	650	6.6	4	7	10
	Total		922	6.2	2	7	13

[a]FMR (female-to-male ratio) denotes females per 1000 males in the community
[b]Less than 0.1 is denoted by negligible
Source Data based on field survey done in the four selected villages in Mushahari block in 2005–06

professions and non-specified occupations. In this area, the majority of the population is engaged in agricultural labour, followed by cultivation. The livelihoods of 36.7% of males and 23.8% of females depend directly on agriculture and cultivation (Table 3).

Table 3 Occupational distribution in the region

S. No.	Workforce category	Out of total workforce[a] in the region (%)		
		Male	Female	Total
1	Uneducated unemployed	10.4	5.6	8.1
2	Educated unemployed	10.7	6.4	8.7
3	Cultivation	15.6	12.0	13.4
4	Agricultural labour	21.1	11.8	17.0
5	Non-agricultural work	19.2	3.5	11.9
6	Industrial work	3.4	4.2	3.5
7	Self-employment	8.9	3.6	5.8
8	Services	4.4	2.5	3.0
9	Traditional professions	6.3	4.3	5.3
10	Non-specified	0.0	46.1	23.3
11	Total	100.0	100.0	100.0

[a]Here, all such persons (male/female) who are above the age of 18 years and not disabled as well as those not engaged in higher education are recognised as part of the workforce
Source Data based on field survey done in the four selected villages in Mushahari block in 2005–06

5.4   Landholding in the Region

Bihar has seen major large-scale voluntary land distribution. Marxists and socialists gave the slogan of land to tillers, while Gandhian thinkers like Acharya Vinoba Bhave launched the Bhoodan (donation of land) movement, later taken up by Jaiprakash Narayan.

But as can be seen from Fig. 4, more than half (54.15%) of the households that are engaged in agriculture are landless or have less than half an acre of land while 13.25% of households are marginal peasants, owning between 0.50 and 2.49 (2.5) acres of land and engaged in agricultural occupations. Small peasants comprise 4.1% of all households in the region and have 2.5–5.0 acres of land. Only 0.74% of all households are in the category of middle peasant, with 10–25 acres of land. Big peasants are at only 0.21%, with 25–50 acres of land.

Land distribution by caste
Muslim (19.8%), Chamar (17.56%), Tatma (9.16%), Dusadh (8.40%) and Nunia (6.11%) account for 61% of households without land. Only 5.6% of households in this category belong to the upper castes (Table 4).

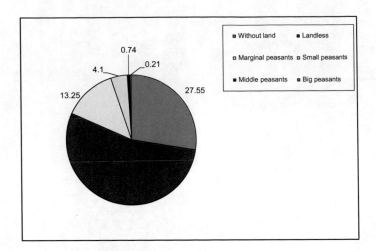

Fig. 4 Land distribution structure in the region. *Source* Data based on field survey done in the four selected villages in Mushahari block in 2005–06

According to a village survey done in the four selected villages, Dhunia, Dusadh, Hazzam, Nunia and Chamar are the most vulnerable persons among the rural communities in terms of landlessness. Also, among the landless are 93.75% of Brahmin households and 29.2% of Bhumihar households. These findings regarding the upper castes the Bhumihars and Brahmins refute the notion that upper castes are landlords and well off families.

On average, two-fifths of all households of Musehar, Chamar, Pasi, Tatma, Dhunia, Julaha, Momin, Nunia and Dusadh are vulnerable to chronic poverty in the region. Musehar and Pasi are victims of chronic poverty. More than half a century has passed since independence but their socio-economic situation remains static.

Of all households, Bhumihar (28.57%), Kurmi (12.7%), Mallah (11.9%), Dusadh (8.73%) and Yadav (7.14%) comprise 69% of all households of marginal peasants. Within each caste, 40.45% of Bhumihar households, 45% of Yadav, 60% of Kushwaha, 29% of Kumi and only 1.3% of Chamar are marginal peasants. In rural Bihar, more than 90% of marginal peasants suffer from poverty and above 60% of marginal peasants carry the attributes of chronic poverty.

Out of all households, 4.1% are small peasants. Small landholding size is an indicator of the fluctuating economic life of villagers. During a good monsoon year, small peasants are secure. In years of flood and drought, the small peasant economy is not stable and people suffer acute misery. More than half of small peasants come from the Bhumihar caste and 41% from backward castes, with only 7.69% from the Muslim community. Big peasants are least in evidence: the share of middle and big peasants is less than one per cent in the region.

Table 4 Incidence of landless and marginal peasants, by caste

S. No.	Castes/religion	Without land (%)		Landless (0.0–0.5) (%)			Marginal (0.5–2.5) (%)	
		Of total households within landholding size	Out of total households	Out of total households within landholding size	Out of total households	Out of total households within landholding size	Out of total households within landholding size	Out of total households
1	Bhumihar	3.82	11.24	3.11	17.98	28.57	40.45
2	Brahmin	2.29	37.50	1.75	56.25	0.79	6.25
3	Chamar	17.56	59.74	5.83	38.96	0.79	1.30
4	Dhobi	2.67	43.75	1.36	43.75	1.59	12.50
5	Dusadh	8.40	45.83	2.91	31.25	8.73	22.92
6	Halwai	0.76	28.57	0.97	71.43	0.00	0.00
7	Hazzam	4.58	70.59	0.58	17.65	1.59	11.76
8	Kahar	1.15	25.00	1.55	66.67	0.00	0.00
9	Kanu	–	–	4.66	88.89	2.38	11.11
10	Kumhar	3.82	31.25	2.91	46.88	4.76	18.75
11	Kurmi	3.44	16.36	5.83	54.55	12.70	29.09
12	Kushwaha	0.38	10.00	0.58	30.00	4.76	60.00
13	Lohar	2.29	42.86	1.36	50.00	0.79	7.14
14	Mali	–	–	1.36	87.50	0.79	12.50
15	Mallah	3.05	8.60	11.84	65.59	11.90	16.13
16	Mehtar	–	–	–	–	0.79	100.00
17	Musehar	–	–	0.19	100.00	–	–
18	Muslim	19.08	32.47	18.25	61.04	5.56	4.55
19	M-Dhunia	3.05	80.00	0.39	20.00	–	–
20	M-Julaha	–	–	0.97	100.00	–	–
21	M-Momin	–	–	1.17	100.00	–	–

(continued)

Table 4 (continued)

S. No.	Castes/religion	Without land (%)	Landless (0.0–0.5) (%)			Marginal (0.5–2.5) (%)	
		Of total households within landholding size	Out of total households	Out of total households within landholding size	Out of total households	Out of total households within landholding size	Out of total households
22	Nunia	6.11	69.57	1.17	26.09	0.79	4.35
23	Pasi	0.00	0.00	2.33	100.00	–	–
24	Tamoli	1.91	38.46	1.36	53.85	0.79	7.69
25	Tatma	9.16	16.90	22.52	81.69	1.59	1.41
26	Teli	5.73	34.88	4.08	48.84	3.17	9.30
27	Yadav	0.76	10.00	0.97	25.00	7.14	45.00
	Total	100.00	27.55	100.00	54.15	100.00	13.25

Source Data based on field survey done in the four selected villages in Mushahari block in 2005–06

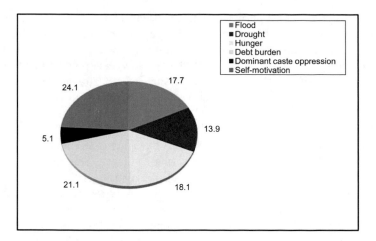

Fig. 5 Reasons for incidence of migration

5.5   Migration

Bihar is vulnerable to natural disasters such as floods and droughts. Of all migration in the four villages studied, 17.7 and 13.9% are the results of flood and droughts, respectively. Hunger is a direct indicator of poverty: 18.1% migrated because of hunger and lack of opportunities for a livelihood to sustain themselves and their families particularly in lean agricultural season. More than one-fifth of migrants are forced to leave because of their burden of debts. Around one-quarter are self-motivated and 5.1% migrated as a result of oppression by dominant castes (Fig. 5).

5.6   Summing Up

This section has underlined a few aspects of poverty and society in post-conflict Mushahari villages that are significant in the context of the dynamics of chronic poverty. First of all, it is observed that most of the children of the scheduled castes are dropping out in the primary stage of education. Musehars (100%) and Julaha (72%) are most serious victims of this problem. Such children may enter adulthood as victims of transmission of inter-generational poverty.

Second, the largest numbers of illiterate unemployed persons are from the Tanta and Mallah castes, whereas the largest numbers of educated unemployed are found among the Bhumihars, who are the dominant caste of the block.

Third, there are large numbers of landless households among the Chamars (80%) and Brahmins (65%). A large section of Yadav (45%) and Kushwaha caste (60%) households are in the marginal peasant category. Only a very small proportion of households (1.12%) are in the category of big peasants.

Fourth, a significant proportion of the small and marginal peasant households from Mallah and Muslim communities are engaged in leasing-in land from other communities for agriculture. Therefore, any study about rural poverty and mobility has to take both facts into account: both the land ownership pattern and the facts about who is 'leasing out' and who is 'leasing-in' land for agriculture. This is changing the traditional pattern of relations between castes and land ownership in favour of the other backward castes and the most backward castes and against the forward castes.

Fifth, a significant proportion of households have members engaged in migration to meet the challenges of survival in Mushahari villages. This includes Chamars (45% of the whole caste), Bhumihars (17%) and Yadavs (10%). In other words, migration as a way out of poverty-related problems is a common practice in all sections in different proportions.

Sixth, there has been a significant decline in incidence of inter-caste and inter-clan violence since the early 1970s. There is more use of channels of negotiation than brute force in conflict situations. However, there has been a growth in the crime–politics nexus in rural settings in recent years. This is affecting the youth of nearly every community and represents a new source of tension and conflict between and within major caste groups in the villages. Meanwhile, there is only a superficial presence of democratic institutions in the rural Mushahari villages. There appears to be no functional scheme of rural development in the area. There is an immediate need for schemes to promote irrigation facilities, agro-based small-scale industries, marketing centres and employment-generating programmes.

6   Towards Conclusions

In short, in 1970, Mushahari was a block of villages with a very high presence of agricultural workers with exceptionally low wages and a high degree of unemployment. The area was marked by extensive poverty and underdevelopment. The political system was organised around dominance of landlords. After three decades, there has been a change in the political power of the other backward castes and the social status of the most backward castes and the scheduled castes owing to a variety of forces, including the legacy of the Gram Swaraj work, democratic changes in the rural polity and spread of caste consciousness. Certainly, the era of dominance of landlords and the upper castes has ended. These villages have entered the phase of dominant caste democracy, which includes the possibility of sociopolitical mobility among the other backward classes and the capacity for resistance among the marginal groups, including the scheduled castes. But poverty has continued to dominate village life owing to a persistent lack of infrastructure improvement, natural calamities like floods and droughts and socio-economic challenges like malnutrition, caste deprivations, illiteracy, unemployment and the crime–politics nexus. Modernisation of agriculture, migration and leasing-out and leasing-in of land has emerged as three major coping strategies among those suffering from pauperisation in the area.

As such, it is obvious that the changes in the political sociology of Bihar and Muzaffarpur, including the villages of Mushahari block, have been quite significant in the post-conflict period since the 1970s, as reflected in the change of regimes and representatives. But they have failed to change the political economy of the people dependent on the rural economy, particularly agriculture.

The endeavour to understand the post-conflict face of poverty and society in the context of Mushahari block leads to a number of conclusions, which deserve further exploration through a comparative study of post-conflict sites in other parts of Bihar:

- There are a number of reasons for the continuity of poverty and discontent in the villages of Mushahari block in the post-conflict period, despite the consensus on the need for attention to the root causes of poverty and the development initiatives of the Mushahari Plan. These reasons are related to the changing nature of four major components in conflict resolution: the state, market forces, caste/class conflict and the community system. We have to ask whether the people's power-based Gram Swaraj approach became a victim of the party rivalries involved in the politics of power.
- Furthermore, all observers, including the Gandhians and Maoists, suggest that there is a high correlation between the institutional collapse of the democratic system and the eruption of violent conflict in Mushahari block and other areas with similar settings. Politics fighting poverty is being replaced by a nexus of politicians, bureaucrats, rich farmers and contractors, who are together promoting institutional decay. On the other hand, village communities, particularly the poorer sections, have demonstrated their capacity to engage creatively with each other to address the challenge of poverty through political innovations and economic initiatives, as experienced during the Mushahari Project led by Jaiprakash Narayan and other Sarvodaya workers. Is there a need for further study of the role of the power elite in the context of the continuity of poverty in post-conflict societies?
- This study has demonstrated the marginality of the impact of the Gram Swaraj work in the long run through empirical facts about the presence of deep poverty in the villages of Mushahari today. This suggests that there is a need for further comprehensive study on similar developmental initiatives on rural poverty in order to obtain a better understanding of their strengths and limits in responding to the challenges of conflict for justice through poverty alleviation.
- The study also demonstrates the expansion of poverty-related problems beyond the polarities of the caste system. The impact of Mandalisation[10] of the

---

[10]Mandalisation refers to the policy of providing reservation to the other backward classes (non-upper castes who are considered above the category of the scheduled castes) in government jobs which has resulted in the consolidation of the middle castes into a 'power block' in elections in North Indian states like Uttar Pradesh, Bihar, Rajasthan and Madhya Pradesh in particular.

discourse of power on poverty and destitution demands further enquiry about the relationship between the trajectories of 'politics of social justice' and 'mobilisation against poverty'.

- It has been argued that Bihar is exposed to five kinds of crisis, which are collectively contributing towards the growth of chronic poverty: economic crisis; political crisis; educational crisis; crisis for women and crisis for entrepreneurs. Is it correct to conclude on the basis of the micro-study of the Mushahari block that the people of Bihar are becoming debilitated owing to the cumulative consequences of a multidimensional crisis? Violent conflicts and migration are two poles of this.
- The last conclusion from the study is related to the remarkable absence of any inclusive approach regarding the poverty question by the sociopolitical leadership and movements of Bihar since the passing away of Jaiprakash Narayan and the fading away of the Gram Swaraj approach as well as the marginalisation of the politics of violence in Mushahari block. Bihar is continuously victimised by the politics of social splits (identity politics) in the search of 'vote banks' and the politics of class conflict (politics of interest). This is not helping society to make any progress in the eradication of poverty and destitution. Thus, it may be relevant to revisit the communitarian inclusive endeavour of conflict resolution through 'change' (and not 'revenge') on the lines of the Jaiprakash Narayan Gram Swaraj mission's response to Naxal terror, so as to make an outstanding impact on Mushahari, with a constructive role for the village elite and the state powers.

References

Almond, G. A., & Verba, S. (1963). *The civic culture: Political attitudes and democracy in five nations*. Princeton: Princeton University Press.

Amin, S. (2006). *Virus of liberalism*. Kolkata, India: Aakar Books.

Association of Voluntary Agencies for Rural Development (AVARD). (1971). *The Musahari Plan*. New Delhi: AVARD.

Avinash, B. (2006). 'Ve din, ve log'. *Jagran City* (Hindi). Muzaffarpur, India, 11 April.

Borooah, V. K. (2008). Deprivation violence, and conflict: An analysis of Naxalite activity in the districts of India. *International Journal of Conflict and Violence, 2*(2), 317–333.

Bottomore, T. B. (1975). *Marxist sociology*. London, UK: Macmillan.

Brady, D. (2003). Rethinking of sociological measurement of poverty. *Social Force, 81*(3), 715–752.

Collins, R. (1975). *Conflict sociology: Towards and explanatory science*. New York: New York Academic Press.

Coser, L. A. (1964). *The functions of social conflict*. Glencoe, IL: Free Press.

Dahrendorf, R. (1959). *Class and class conflict in industrial society*. Stanford: Stanford University Press.

Das, A. N. (1992). *The republic of Bihar*. New Delhi, India: Penguin Books.

Deb, D. (2009). *Beyond developmentality: Constructing inclusive freedom and sustainability* (pp. 514–515). Delhi: Daanish Books.

Eric, O. (2011). *How to change the world-tales of Marx and Marxism*. London: Abacus.

Feinstein, D. (Ed.). (1964). *Two worlds of change: Readings in economic development*. New York: Anchor Books, Double Day and Company.

Field, F. (1982). *Poverty and politics*. London, UK: Heinemann Educational Books.

Government of India. (2015). *Agriculture Census 2010–11*. Ministry of Agriculture and Farmers Welfare.

Johnson, A. G. (2000). *The Blackwell dictionary of sociology* (2nd ed.). Oxford: Blackwell Publishing.

Kumar, A. (2006). Naxalvad aur JP ka Mushahari. *Jagran City* (Hindi). Muzaffarpur, India, April 11.

Kumar, A. (2013). *Indian economy since independence: Persisting colonial disruption*. New Delhi: Vision Books. (Chap. 10).

Kymlicka, W. (2002). *Contemporary political philosophy: An introduction*. Oxford: Oxford University Press.

Lewis, C. (1964). *The functions of social conflicts*. Glencoe, IL: Free Press.

Louis, P. (2002). *Peoples power: The naxalite movement in Central Bihar*. New Delhi, India: Wordsmith.

Lucian, W. P., & Verba, S. (Eds.). (1965). *Political culture and political development*. Princeton: Princeton University Press.

Marks, Z. (2016). Poverty and conflict. GSDRC Professional Development Reading Pack No. 52. Birmingham, UK: University of Birmingham.

Mehta, A. K., Shepherd, A., Bhide, S., Shah, A., Kumar, A. (2011). India chronic poverty report. New Delhi: IIPA, CPRC.

Michel, F. (1980). *Power/knowledge: Selected interviews and other writings 1972–1977*. New York: Pantheon (Edited by Gordon, Colin).

Myrdal, G. (1968). *Asian drama: An enquiry into the poverty of a nation*. Harmondsworth, UK: Penguin.

Narayan, J. (1970a). *Face to face*. Varanasi, India: Sarva Sewa Sangh.

Narayan, J. (1970b). Open letter. July 17.

Osberg, L. (Ed.). (1991). *Economic inequality and poverty: International perspectives*. Armonk, NY: ME Sharpe.

Peter, B., & Thomas, L. (1967). *The social construction of reality*. Garden City, NY: Doubleday.

Radhakrishna, R., & Ray, S. (Eds.). (2005). *Handbook of poverty in India*. New Delhi: Oxford University Press.

Randall, C. (1975). *Conflict sociology: Toward an explanatory science*. New York: Academic Press.

Rao, H. C. H. (2006). Foreword. In R. Radhakrishna & S. Ray (Eds.), *Handbook of poverty in India*. New Delhi: Oxford University Press.

Skocpol, T. (1979). *States and social revolutions*. New York: Cambridge University Press.

Sridhar, V. (2007). Waiting for deliverance. *Frontline, 24*(03), 116.

Chapter 6
Changing Scenario of Migration and Poverty in India: Reflections and Issues

Amita Shah, Itishree Pattnaik and Animesh Kumar

1 Migration and Poverty in India: A Multi-patterned Reality

The Emerging Perspective

The recent discourse on migration in developing economies seeks to revisit the conventional binary approach where distress and development-induced migratory movements were seen as dichotomous situations. The new paradigm looks at migration, for economic motive, as an important exit route from poverty, including for the chronically poor, irrespective of the initial characteristics of distress influencing mobility. Recognizing the complex, multi-patterned and dynamic nature of migration, especially among developing economies with a large proportion of the labour force residing in rural areas, the new perspective tends to re-emphasize the positive role of migration, as an integral part of the diversified strategies adopted by the poor (de Hann 1999; Srivastava 2011; Deshingkar 2010; Shah 2009).

This is at variance with the policies adopted till recently in a large number of developing economies, such as India where the emphasis was mainly on prevent-

---

With necessary permissions this chapter draws on Shah and Kumar (2011)

A. Shah (✉)
Center for Development Alternatives, Ahmedabad, India
e-mail: amitagidr@gmail.com

I. Pattnaik
Gujarat Institute of Development Research (GIDR), Ahmedabad, India

A. Kumar
UNISDR Regional Office for Asia and Pacific, Bangkok, Thailand

---

"The views expressed herein are those of the author and do not necessarily reflect the views of the United Nations".

© Springer Nature Singapore Pte Ltd. 2018
A. K. Mehta et al. (eds.), *Poverty, Chronic Poverty and Poverty Dynamics*,
https://doi.org/10.1007/978-981-13-0677-8_6

ing, rather than supporting, migration. There is, however, counter-evidence from micro-level situations in India, which demonstrate that migration does help many poor (though not all and the poorest) to help improve the living conditions at the place of destination and/or origin, to make productive investments and also avert entry into poverty (Deshingkar and Farrington 2009; Shah 2009; Singh 2009; Shah and Shah 2005). This of course, intuitively confirms the basic economic rationale where the shift of labour force from backward to developed economies is expected to improve the economic and social status among migrants; in the absence of this, they may not have migrated or continued to stay away from their place of destination for economic reasons.

The recent discourse on migration seems to have moved away from the conventional neo-economic theories on the one hand and the structural theories of exploitative processes on the other. In doing so, it has taken a more nuanced, dynamic and context-specific approach to unravel the situations that trigger responses to the changing environment, and shape the outcomes within the short and long-term scenarios. An important feature characterizing the rich and growing literature on migration in the context of developing economies is the increasing focus on short-term or circular migration, as this stream of migration is particularly relevant from the viewpoint of poverty reduction.[1]

Based on a comprehensive review of the diverse and multi-patterned migration in India, Deshingkar and Farrington (ibid) highlight three important constraints that perpetuate poverty among migrants in the Indian situation. These are: poor education, discrimination, and a hostile policy environment (p. 25). This, by and large, is a correct depiction of what appears to be the proximate variables explaining the migration-poverty interface. The analysis, however, seems to have overlooked the deeper issues or ultimate factors that shape the extent, nature and outcomes of migration. These may refer to two major structural aspects concerning the Indian economy. The first is the more or less stagnant agricultural and rural economy combined with limited job expansion in non-farm activities in urban areas. And the second refers to sociocultural barriers resulting in high non-economic costs and hence low revealed preference for migration among certain segments of population. This implies structural barriers operating on both the demand and the supply side.

Whereas the first may get manifested in terms of limited demand and overcrowding, the latter may get reflected in limited supply and/or high reservation price despite the labour surplus situation prevailing in most parts of the rural economy in the country. The scenario of overcrowding has been reflected through a number of micro-level studies where non-availability (different from accessibility) of the expected type of work opportunity at the place of destination has been reported as the main reason for the individual or household abstaining from migration (Shah 2009). Similarly, there are situations where growing competition for the limited job opportunities has led to various forms of resistance sometimes subtle but at times

---

[1]This has been deliberated at length in the emerging framework of new economics of labour migration (NELM). For details see, Deshingkar and Farrington (2009).

violent as recently found in the case of resistance against Bihari migrants in Mumbai. Moreover, recession during 2008 has provided micro-level evidence of return migration from a number of major urban-industrial centres. On the other hand, migration, especially at the lower end of the income strata, is not *always* a preferred option, even if work opportunity is available on relatively moderate terms with respect to wages and other conditions of work owing to various non-economic factors. This suggests that even under an improved policy environment, migration as an option is likely to be: (a) available to a section of the population including the poor, and (b) preferred by some, but not all among those for whom the option is available.

It is therefore imperative to recognize the outer boundaries within which demand and supply side factors may operate. This is important because changing the policy constraint, by making it migration friendly, may still be bound by the outer limits set by the two structural issues influencing demand and supply of migrant labour as noted above. The contemporary discourse on migration thus needs to be located in the backdrop of some of these deeper processes that influence the mobility and the outcomes thereof; the policy framework needs to re-engage itself with the structural factors underlying the migration dynamics in developing economies like India.

Moving towards a comprehensive policy that addresses both the structural as well as intermediate constraints discussed above needs a nuanced understanding of the interface between migration and poverty in reality. The message that comes from some of the recent reviews of migration studies in India suggests that the reality is highly variable across time, space and sociocultural settings. In turn, the outcomes also vary across these categories. Similarly, the large body of empirical research, based on evidence from both secondary as well as primary data, presents different scenarios, suggesting thereby that generalization is difficult.

How do we move from this complex cobweb of situations and outcomes? An important way out is through continued field-level investigations across different typologies of migration scenarios with special focus on poverty linkages, and search for context-specific solutions that may work intermittently and also in the long run for helping a large number of the poor. This search, of course, has to cover newer grounds, not only in terms of the context specificity, but also in terms of raising relevant questions or redefining the questions already examined. This is particularly relevant in the light of the fact that (a) the official database provides limited leverage for addressing the issues of migration-poverty interface; (b) microstudies are too scattered and have limited comparability and (c) a large proportion of the existing studies, especially at macro-level, focuses on the scenarios obtaining at the place of destination rather than that of origin (Mitra and Murayama 2009).

The Focus

The main objectives of the paper are to:

(a) Review the existing evidence on migration-poverty interface in the light of the macro- and micro-level studies in India.
(b) Discuss the extent, patterns and correlates of short-term migration with the help a large set of data collected from all states by National Council of Applied

Economic Research (NCAER) and data collected from rural households in
Madhya Pradesh, which constitutes a large set of rural population in poverty.
(c) Discuss policy implications within the medium term and beyond.

2 Migration and Poverty: Select Review of Evidence and Perspective

Some of the more recent interstate analysis on migration (Mohanty et al. 2015)
highlighted that migration in a changing socio-economic context is essential for us
to move towards the next step in reducing poverty. As well recognized migration
prevents people from further sliding into poverty and helping some to escape
poverty (Mohanty et al. 2015; Bhandari and Reddy 2015; Agrawal and
Chandrasekhar 2015; Thomas 2012; Bhagat and Keshri 2010; Kundu 2009;
Deshingkar 2008) but at the same time there is significantly high level of inequality.
The ratio of state domestic products (SDP) of the poorest and richest states of India
has increased from 5.66 in 1991 to 9.22 in 2011 (also confirmed by Gini Index of
consumption) as noted by Mohanty et al. (2015). The academic understanding on
this issue is yet to get required attention. One of the important reasons for relatively
less link within the academic pool is quickly changing situation and lack of formal
data needed for the analysis.

The decision to move is complex as it depends upon factors like social relations,
culture and policy regimes of the migrants, apart from economic factors leading
towards expected higher income. Migrants do not like to leave their stake from
village completely because of social ties, lower costs, other safety net aspects, and a
long-term intention to pursue a better life in the village (Deshingkar 2008). This
reconfirms that understanding the complexity of rural–urban migration in India
requires detailed multifaceted analysis across regions and over time.

2.1 What Does the Official Data Show?

The recent survey by National Sample Survey Organisation (NSSO) brought home
some important aspects of migration in India as shown in Table 1. Some of the
important observations are: First, the proportion of migrants for the reason of
employment is significantly higher among urban as compared to rural areas.
Second, the rate of migration is higher among non-backward communities as
compared to the average; the rate is fairly low among tribal communities. Third,
return migration among male is fairly substantial, i.e. 237 and 117 out of 1000
migrants in rural and urban areas; among female, the rate is fairly low as much of
the female migration is on account of marriage. Fourth the average remittance in the
last year was Rs. 13,400 in rural areas as compared to Rs. 26,300 in urban areas; the

Table 1 Migration in India (2007–08): a snap shot[a]

Person-level characteristics						
Indicator	Rural			Urban		
	Male	Female	Person	Male	Female	Person
Migration rate (per 1000 population)	54	477	261	259	456	354
Scheduled tribe	47	440	238	288	430	356
Other (non-backward) communities	68	506	281	209	477	379
Proportion (per 1000) of migrants for employment related reasons	286	7	36	557	27	228
Return migration rate (per 1000 of migrants)	237	106	120	117	104	109
Number of remitter out-migrants during last 365 days (per 1000 out-migrants)	594	15	228	451	22	164
Average amount of remittance (Rs. 00) during the last 365 days by out-migrants residing India	134	60	130	277	134	263
Temporary migration (out of 1000)	28	05	17	06	01	04

[a]'A household member whose last usual place of residence (UPR), anytime in the past, was different from the present place of enumeration was considered as a migrant member in a household'

Source Government of India (2010)

proportion of migrants sending remittances accounted for only 58 and 41% of the male migrants in rural and urban areas, respectively. And fifth, the rate of temporary migration is fairly low, though these estimates are subject to underestimation.

Moreover, the NSSO estimates from the 64th round indicated that out-migration of a former member accounted for 30% of the rural households and 19% among urban households (page no. H-v). Remittances are mainly used for subsistence; only 10% reported use of remittances for debt repayment and 13% reported using that for saving/investment. Together these observations suggest that migration is yet to emerge as a major driver of economic betterment and accumulation of wealth among a large segment of the society and that low mobility combined with low outcomes are rooted in a number of structural factors such as class, social hierarchies and rural–urban gap in availability of economic opportunities.

2.2 Migration Over Time

As per the estimates from 55th Round, 245 million people were reported as migrants during 1999–2000. Migration rate (per 1000 population) in rural areas showed an increase from 21% in 1983 (38th Round) to 26.1% in 2007–08. Male migrants, migrate mainly for economic reasons. Between 1983 and 2007–08 male migration declined in both rural and urban areas, while female migration registered an increase (Table 2).

Table 2 Migration rates by categories, 1983–2007–08

	Rural			Urban		
	Male	Female	Person	Male	Female	Person
1983	7.2	35.1	20.9	27.0	36.6	31.6
1987–88	7.4	39.8	23.2	26.8	39.6	32.9
1993	6.5	40.1	22.8	23.9	38.2	30.7
1999–00	6.9	42.6	24.4	25.7	41.8	33.4
2007–08	5.4	47.7	26.1	25.9	45.6	35.4

Source National Sample Survey, various rounds

3   Migration and Rural Poverty: Some Perspectives

The evidence for India till the late eighties indicated that migration, especially long-term migration, was an important livelihood strategy among resource-poor farmers especially landless and pastoralists in large tracts of dry land regions in the country. On the other hand, those having medium to large land holdings and/or with access to irrigation did not have to move out for seeking subsistence livelihood (NIRD 2000). Migration from such relatively wealthy households was mainly for 'better prospects' rather than a 'distress move'. This was mainly due to the fact that most of the households with relatively better land holdings and access to irrigation had adopted cultivation of high-valued commercial crops like oilseeds, spices, horticulture. Similarly, areas with moderately good soil and groundwater table in other parts of the country could also escape 'distress migration'.

By and large long-term migration, especially into urban areas, has been associated mainly with better economic opportunities. Such opportunities are often obtained mainly by the relatively better-off population rather than the very rich or very poor in the rural areas. This has been borne out by a number of micro-level studies examining out-migration from rural areas. For instance, way back in the late eighties Oberai et al. (1989) had noted that in Kerala middle-level peasantry had migrated more as compared to the small farmers, while in Uttar Pradesh all landed farmers, except the highest size of landowners, have been found to have a higher propensity to migrate (Oberai et al. 1989). Similarly, migrant labourers from Bihar working on farms in Punjab have been seen to be 'little above the lowest rungs' and not the poorest at source (Singh 1995). Incidence of migration was seen to be lower among poorer segments as compared to the better-off within rural communities in the study regions of Madhya Pradesh and Andhra Pradesh (Deshingkar 2003). A similar observation has been made by a study of out-migration from dry land regions in Gujarat (Shah 2009) indicating long-term migration was confined mainly to the middle peasantry rather than landless and the rich farmers.

In terms of outcomes, the evidence suggests that long-term rural–urban migration has resulted in fairly positive outcomes. For instance, de Haan (1997) noted that the migrant population in cities is better-off than the original inhabitants. Similarly, Kundu and Sarangi (2007) observed that migrant population into urban areas is also found to be economically better-off than the non-migrants in a given urban location. This, in a sense, is quite obvious. For, in the absence of economic gains, the migrants would have returned to the place of origin unless non-economic factors such as severe social discrimination or political conflicts compelled them to stay away from where they belong. Beside these there could be other non-income motivations that may lead to rural–urban migration. These may refer to aspects like access to better amenities and services like health and education. Finally migration, especially from rural to urban areas, may also be motivated by precautionary reasons where the idea is to take care of the future risks of income loss in the place of origin. This is likely to be fairly prevalent in the agrarian society where land holdings are getting smaller and farming is becoming increasingly uncertain and/or non-viable (Shah 2009).

Based on a detailed analysis of the official statistics Singh (2009) notes that: *The relationship between poverty and migration is not clearly observed as middle and higher income groups show higher propensity to migrate.* The most successful group of migrants are the urban–urban migrants, where in terms of occupational category they are absorbed in higher paying jobs, on account of better education and skill. The influx of migrants towards metropolitan cities indicates that economic reforms have still not been able to provide employment opportunities in smaller and middle sized towns as well as in rural areas' (pp. 72–73).

The above phenomenon is further confirmed by the macro-level estimates by the NSSO, indicating that propensity to migrate is generally higher among the households with higher levels of economic well-being represented by monthly per capita expenditure (MPCE) (see Table 3). For instance, migration rate among rural males was the lowest (26) in the bottom-most decile of MPCE and increased consistently across the MPCE groups. Similarly, for urban males the average rate was 96% which increased from 462 per 1000 in the highest decile.

According to the estimates from the NSSO 64th round, migration rate in rural areas was found to be the lowest among STs and was highest among the other social groups. Nearly 36% of the rural male migrants were self-employed; this was 16% at the turn of the century. The rate of short-term migration was found to be nearly 17% among the rural population as already noted in Table 1 (Government of India 2010).

3.1 Short-Term Migration

The pattern of short-term migration, however, is just the opposite of what has been observed in the case of long-term migration captured by the official statistics. Not only that short-term migration is mainly concentrated among the resource-poor households like landless, marginal and small farmers, and at times, pastoralists, the outcomes at times, are not very encouraging as most of them continue to live under subsistence conditions even after having participated in short-term migration. A recent study in Bihar by Rodgers and Rodgers (2011) observed that: 'In addition

Table 3 Distribution of migrants by MPCE classes (per 1000 population)

MPCE decile class	Migration rate					
	Rural			Urban		
	Male	Female	Person	Male	Female	Person
0–10	26	388	209	96	357	229
10–20	31	423	227	142	414	277
20–30	34	437	235	160	412	284
30–40	34	445	237	175	429	298
40–50	37	472	250	238	455	342
50–60	45	482	257	267	478	368
60–70	41	481	252	301	478	385
70–80	53	522	279	347	500	419
80–90	70	540	294	373	501	432
90–100	166	592	366	462	555	505
All groups	54	477	261	259	456	354

Source Government of India (2010)

to the immediate effect on incomes, migration appears to have some developmental impacts but, less than one might expect' (p. 49).

Short-term migration in rural India has been one of the important and continuous processes in the recent understanding of rural development. Understanding the process however is not only faced by continuous changes taking place across issues, space and people, but also an important part of future development. The issue of short-term migration has changed in the last ten years when 27% of the farmers did not find farming profitable (Agrawal and Chandrasekhar 2015), which till now had been considered as the basic and quickly available process of rural development. The recent understanding by and large suggested that agriculture-based development has lost its importance in the changing rural environment. In reality, exiting from agriculture has proved to be difficult since adequate number of jobs have not been created in other sectors (Agrawal and Chandrasekhar 2015). At this stage it is important to note that the issue is not only about 'proportion' but mainly about 'where, how and for whom'.

Migration in the rural areas is yet to move beyond agriculture. The next sector in which migration in rural areas is observed to be prominent is in the construction sector (Thomas 2012). This perhaps may suggest that the shift in migration from agriculture to construction is yet to take a significant leap towards manufacturing and other economically strong sectors. Given the fact that short-term migration is yet to move towards a sustainable process of employment, the development process as of now, does not seem to be moving forward in this context.

Short-term migration by and large has been seen to improve the socio-economic status across a large number of States in India. Bhagat and Keshri (2010) also noted that in rural areas poor people are temporarily more mobile compared to people belonging to higher income groups. Nevertheless, the opposite is not true for urban areas (Bhagat and Keshri 2010; Kundu 2009; Gangopadhyay and Singh 2013). It is important to note here that seasonal migration may also help to bridge the existing socially defined caste hierarchies. It is important to keep this in mind while understanding the process of development.

It is important to note that the understanding till now has not taken deeper analysis of situation of rural–urban migration in hilly areas. A recent analysis by Bhandari and Reddy (2015) provides useful findings, based on a small-scale survey in Uttarakhand. The effort has been made to get a quick understanding of migration in agriculture and remittances. An important understanding from this survey is that although rural–urban migration in hilly areas has started declining over time and agriculture is losing its initial context; nevertheless, remittances and economic support through non-agricultural activities have started playing a significant role in the overall financial situation since 2013. This has increased women's workload in households where agriculture is still playing an important role. This analysis also points out that the unwillingness of the women of migrant households to undertake labour intensive agricultural work and spending of remittances on purchasing consumer durables might be the reason for less time being devoted for household work (Bhandari and Reddy 2015). It may be useful to understand the fact that the proportion of people working in agriculture itself has gone down, within which women from non-migrant households happen to take a larger share in workload in comparison to women from migrant households. This perhaps suggests changes in economic opportunities and approach in this area where economic earning is increasingly getting linked to non-agricultural rather than the agricultural activities. It is rather early to say whether and to what extent the process is helping overall economic growth in the region in the specific context of agricultural development and women's role within that.

A recent study by Mohanty et al. (2015) confirms the fact that incidence of poverty among migrant households has declined; indicative of the fact that it has a positive impact on poverty. Interstate migration is higher among the poverty induced states. This may be because economic inequality is higher in advanced states compared to less developed states, since migration in, by and large, less developed states is employment induced. This reconfirms the situation that poverty is more among interstate rather than intra-state migrants and non-migrants.

3.2 Short-Term Migration and Poverty Over Time Among Major States

It may be noted that poverty is directly linked with the size of the households; bigger households are found among interstate rather than intra-state migrants. The next process thus needs to take a closer note of the existing approach to reach out to

Table 4 Linkages between short duration migration and poverty

Poverty levels	Short-term migration levels		
	High	Medium	Low
High	West Bengal, Rajasthan, Odhisha, Madhaya Pradesh, Jharkhand, Gujarat, Chhattisgarh, Bihar, Assam, Uttar Pradesh	–	–
Medium	–	Karnataka, Maharashatra, TamilNadu, Andhra Pradesh	Haryana, Uttrakhand
Low	Jammu & Kashmir	Goa	Himachal Pradesh, Kerala, Punjab

the poor where migration is playing an important role. A state-focused approach by itself cannot provide the required understanding to move forward.

Taking the analysis further through comparing poverty levels and short-term migration from different states helps in understanding the linkages in the recent context. Table 4 provides insights regarding the inter-linkages between short-term migration and poverty in 21 major states.

Overall the information from these major states brings out the following:

Firstly, short-term migration continues to remain an integral part for insuring basic minimum financial support, covering as large as 10 out of 21 states. This is particularly notable because continued dependence for financial support remains a crucial part of livelihood across states having different levels of economic development. Second, six major states have relatively medium level of poverty and medium and low level of migration possibly because of relatively better economic earnings. Third, four states located mainly in high hills or closer to the ocean have low level of poverty and medium and high level of migration. This leaves Jammu Kashmir which has high level of migration (1.2%) and relatively low level of poverty (19.2%), suggesting a positive impact of migration on poverty. Overall, therefore, short-term migration continues to remain essential for meeting the basic needs of a large proportion of the population comprising 61.9% of India's population barring the 14 states and union territories. The relative share of 6 states (Karnataka, Maharashtra, Tamil Nadu, Andhra Pradesh, Haryana, Uttarakhand) constitutes 31.1% of the population which has relatively lower poverty and short-migration levels than the states mentioned above., The population in four states (Goa, Himachal Pradesh, Kerala, Punjab) is 5.9% and has comparatively the lowest level of poverty and short-term migration as well.

While the understanding on poverty-migration linkages is fairly well discussed and supported by our analysis noted here, an important lesson from the overview of analytical results, strongly suggest that the issue of migration and poverty is an ongoing process especially at this time not only because of the increasing proportion of population involved, but also because the issue of equity needs to be bought at the centre of the developmental process to which migration even with small space and population needs to be brought back as the central concern.

All this evidence substantiates the observation made earlier that migration as a coping or income augmenting mechanism is too costly for the very poor and the marginalized. For the poorest, migration is preceded by availing credit within the village, i.e., the poor households meet urgent needs through cash advances on migrant labour. Debt, in extreme cases, requires advance sale of labour through one or the other form of attached labour or bondage (Mosse et al. 2002).

The evidence presented above thus, reinstates the observation made earlier that long-term migration, driven mainly by better economic opportunities, especially in urban areas, is often accessed by the relatively better-off segment of population. On the other hand, short-term migration by the resource-poor segment of the rural communities often fails to enable exit from poverty or subsistence living conditions. The world of migrants thus comprises duality in terms of duration, destination, initial poverty condition and outcomes of migration. This duality is often characterized by high and low roads to the migration-development interface. It could therefore be argued that a dual pattern of mobility is likely to reinforce the existing socio-economic-spatial inequalities already existing within the country (de Haan ISS 2011), unless overall opportunities for work and migration improve in both rural as well as urban areas.

Counter-Narratives

Parallel to these not so encouraging realities, there is another body of literature that demonstrates that for many of the poor (if not the poorest) migration is an integral part of the strategy for livelihood support and labour allocation within households. Drawing upon a number of case studies Deshingkar and Farrington (2009) have highlighted that: (a) migration, especially circular migration is increasing in most parts of the country; (b) migration is least among the poorest but highest among the poor; (c) the poorest are disproportionately represented in short-term migration; (d) social networks have helped overcome some of the costs and entry barriers; (e) the income from migration has helped many of the poor in smoothening their consumption and (f) if structural as well as policy hurdles are mitigated, migration can help improve the outcomes, thereby enabling them to break out of poverty.

While there is no denial of the claim made by the authors that migration, as a coping and development mechanism, is not fully realized in countries that look at it as a necessary evil (at best), on balance it appears that the poverty-reducing impact of migration may continue to remain limited till the overall scenarios with respect to increased productive employment opportunities is significantly improved.

4 Short-Term Migration Among States: Evidence from Selected Villages

Short-Term Migration

In a major departure, the 55th round of the NSSO has tried to capture seasonal/circular migration by asking the non-migrants in rural households whether he/she had stayed away from the usual place of residence (and enumeration) for more than 60 days during the last 365 days for the reason of employment. Those responding positively were considered as 'temporarily staying away for employment' (TSAE). We have used these estimates to capture at least a part of the seasonal/circular migration believed to be fairly large among rural males in India. Similar data have been collected in the 64th round of NSSO for the year 2007–08. According to the estimates, the rate of temporary migration per 1000 population was fairly low; 17 in rural and 4 in urban areas. For the specific age group of 15–64 years, the rate was 26.4 in rural and 5.5 in urban areas.

It may, however, be noted that the extent of short duration migration captured through the official data system is and underestimate owing to a number of reason definitional as well as methodological (Srivastava 2011). According to Deshingkar and Farrington (2009) the number of such migrants is likely to be ten times higher than what has been captured by the official surveys. The numbers, of course, is subjected to variation over years; the variations are likely to be in terms of number of migrating persons within the households; duration and the income earned.

Compared to long-term migration, the pattern of temporary migration (TSAE) is quite different. A cross-classification of the rate of temporary migration (in the age group of 15–64 years) by monthly per capita expenditure (MPCE) groups suggests that the rate of temporary migration is as high as 45 among the lowest MPCE-group in rural areas and that the rate is more or less inversely associated with the MPCE as observed by Keshri and Bhagat (2012). The detailed analysis of temporary migration by the authors substantiated the widely acknowledged phenomenon that the rate is found to be highest in the case of scheduled tribes and other social groups and also those with very small landholdings among rural areas. Temporary migration was also found to be inversely associated with the level of education. Moreover, the incidence of temporary migration is found to be higher than the national average in major states like Jharkhand, Madhya Pradesh, West Bengal, Rajasthan, and Gujarat. The state wise-pattern could be influenced by both distresses as well as job opportunities created in the states.

Another important difference that emerged from the recent data pertains to the sharp difference in the share of tribal communities in long-term and short-term migration. As per the NSSO data for the year 2007–08, the rate of temporary migration among tribals is 45.2% as compared to 12.2% among 'other' social groups. This suggests that short-term migration is mainly concentrated among tribal communities, who also happen to coincide with those in the lowest MPCE category. Addressing this may, therefore, call for a much more comprehensive approach to redress the sustained high incidence of poverty among these socially, economically and spatially marginalized communities; migration, especially short-term migration, could hardly be seen as a solution for them to exit poverty.

The inverse relationship between rate of temporary migration and MPCE assumes special relevance in the context of migration-poverty interface. For, it suggests that whereas the poor are forced to undertake such temporary migration, their economic status may not have changed much since many of them continue to remain in the lower strata of MPCE. This, in turn, may suggest that the rural poor having to resort to temporary migration may still need support from the rural economies from which they migrate, as the poverty situation is hardly altered even after the low migration trajectory.

This brings us back to the point raised earlier that migration could be an important component of the livelihood strategy; it may nevertheless not work as an effective exit route from poverty. It is therefore imperative to see how the poor may find additional employment, possibly with higher level of productivity in the rural economies, which still holds the basis for obtaining livelihood support among a large proportion of the poor living in rural areas. In this context some of the region-/village-level indicators may also play important role in influencing migration decisions among rural households in addition to household or individual characteristics. For instance, agronomic potential reflected through rainfall and access to irrigation, even in small quantity, could be an important factor driving short-term migration. Similarly, social contacts matter a lot for short-term migration, which often operates like chain of migrant workers with one pulling the other from the same village or vicinity. Labour contractors play a significant role in creating segmentation within the potential market of migrant labour. This is why we find that the migrants are often concentrated in certain pockets within the large configuration of less developed regions or economies. Connectivity also matters for the migrants or contractors to draw labour from specific areas. Unfortunately ascertaining these aspects are difficult as the official statistics on short-term migration do not provide corresponding information of region/village specific indicators noted above.

Given this backdrop, in what follows we have tried to examine the impact of regional-/village-level indicators on short-term migration by using data from a large survey conducted by the NCAER during 2005–06. The survey was spread over all the major states in India, 1501 villages across 289 districts in the country.[2] While the main focus of the survey was to get a comprehensive picture of human and other related dimensions of development, the survey also included a few questions on population mobility at the village and household levels. Village-level data pertains to incidence of seasonal migration. This includes information on the number of households reporting such migration and number of persons taking up seasonal

---

[2] The survey was conducted jointly by National Council for Applied Economic Research, New Delhi, and University of Maryland, USA, for preparing a detailed analysis on human development in India (for details see, Desai et al. 2010). The specific question asked is – 'Do any persons from the village leave for seasonal work during the year? If yes, How many?'

migration from the village. In what follows, we present a brief picture of short-term migration across the major states covered by the survey.

Impact of Regional/Village-Level Indicators

At the outset it may be noted that the survey results indicated a fairly clear divide with respect to the incidence of seasonal migration across villages covered by the study. For instance, relevant information was available for 1460 villages (out of 1501 villages) across all the 31 states in the country. Of this, nearly 58% of the villages reported having seasonal migration during the year. The proportion is found to be particularly high among the states with predominance of hilly regions and/or economic backwardness except Orissa where the incidence of migration at village level was more or less on par with the all India average (see Table 5).

Explaining Short-Term Migration

We tried to examine some of the important correlates of short-term migration in the light of the village-/district-level indicators of development. Basically, the idea was to identify some of the area-specific factors that may have led to migration (or absence of that) from the village. A binomial logit regression has been used to estimate the probability of a village having seasonal migration by considering six independent variables.

Specification of the logit model used for the estimation is given below.

$$Vmi = f(BACKD; DISTANCE; EDU; VSIZE; GIA; PNCA), \tag{1}$$

where

Vmi	Denotes seasonal migration from the village (no migration = 0, migration = 1)
BACKD	Village belonging to backward district (backward district = 0; developed district = 1)
DISTANCE	Distance from the village to pucca (tarred) road (<1 km = 0; >3 kms = 1)
EDU	Level of secondary education captured by no. of secondary schools in the village (No or up to 3 secondary school = 0; >3 schools = 1)
VSIZE	Size of the village captured through no. of households (up to 500 households = 1; >500 households = 1)
GIA	Level of % gross irrigated area to gross sown area (up to 50% = 0; >50% = 1)
PNCA	Level of net sown area per household (Up to 10 acres = 0; >10 acres = 1; land)

It is hypothesized that of the six independent variables four variables viz; BACKD, EDU, GIA and PNCA have negative impact on probability of seasonal migration from the village; the remaining two, viz DISTANCE and VSIZE are expected to have positive impacts. The underlying rationale for the hypothesized negative impact rests on the widely prevalent perspective that: seasonal migration from rural areas is primarily a coping mechanism for subsistence livelihood hence is

Table 5 Incidence of seasonal migration across states

Major states	Villages surveyed	Households surveyed	% of villages reporting seasonal migration	% of HHs reporting seasonal migration
Himachal Pradesh	52	11,142	71.1	67.3
Punjab	61	33,756	6.9	6.6
Uttarakhand	20	5477	69.5	72.3
Haryana	79	48,939	41.8	35.5
Rajasthan	88	37,721	67.5	69.8
Uttar Pradesh	138	67,603	74.4	74.8
Bihar	61	50,001	96.3	91.8
Assam	38	10,552	71.8	69.5
West Bengal	66	50,674	58.5	61.0
Jharkhand	26	10,304	66.2	53.9
Orissa	84	24,435	47.3	47.0
Chhattisgarh	49	15,709	83.3	72.4
Madhya Pradesh	121	35,852	68.6	74.0
Gujarat	70	38,027	22.7	28.2
Maharashtra	115	56,427	49.9	53.5
Andhra Pradesh	94	100,209	77.3	74.5
Karnataka	142	79,908	53.9	57.1
Kerala	61	233,635	28.9	30.0
Tamil Nadu	62	71,737	68.3	59.9
Total	1427	982,108	59.2	58.4
All states	1501	1,964,216		57.8

Source Desai et al. (2010)

driven mainly by distress related factors. The results of the regression model are presented in Table 6.

Omnibus Test of Model Coefficients:

Step 1	Chi-square	df	Sign.
Model	52.627	6	0.000

It is observed that three out of the six independent variables exert significant influence on village-level seasonal migration. These are district-level backwardness (BACKD), distance from the pucca road (DISTANCE) and education (EDU). Besides these, two variables, viz irrigation (GIA) and size of the village (VSIZE) show limited impacts; the coefficient has fairly low significance. Net sown area per

Table 6 Short-term migration from the sample villages results of the logit model

Independent variables	B	Wald	Significance	Interpretation
BACKD	−0.643	19.158	0.000	Highly significant with higher probability of migration among backward districts
DISTANCE	0.328	13.436	0.000	Highly significant with higher probability of migration among remote villages
EDU	−0.161	3.369	0.066	Significant and inversely related to infrastructure of secondary school education
VSIZE	0.1	1.835	0.176	Low significance with higher probability among larger villages
GIA	−0.002	1.611	0.204	Low significance with lower probability among villages with better irrigation
PNCA	0.006	0.374	0.541	Not significant
Constant	1.062	11.039	0.001	Highly significant

household (PNCA) was not found have any impact on probability of seasonal migration at the village level. Overall the model is found to be highly significant.

It may be noted that all the variables in the model, except PNCA had the appropriate signs as hypothesized above. This implies that the seasonal migration from the village is higher among those in backward districts; in more remote villages and those with lower infrastructure for secondary education; having larger number of households and lower proportion of land under irrigation.[3]

These are, of course, some tentative results as village-wise information on indicator like proportion of irrigated area are often difficult to obtain from the village records, and that information on important variable such as proportion of landless households was not available. The idea, given the data limitations, is to get broad sense of direction with respect to a subset of variables that are likely to influence short-term migration across a cross section of villages in the country.

What is thus important is that: (i) such migration is limited to a subset of villages across the states, and (ii) economic backwardness continues to influence the larger pattern of short-term migration from rural areas. The second observation is further substantiated by the fact district-level backwardness has the largest influence, followed by distance or physical remoteness.

We also tried to examine the factors that influenced the extent of migration by looking into the subset of villages which had reported short-term migration. This has been examined with the help of a linear regression model with the dependent

---

[3]This analysis here reflects the results based on the one-to-one liner effects. This may not have reflected the entire scenario of the migration like in a non-liner function. In this may be taken as an initial analysis.

variable being proportion of households with short-term migration to total house-holds in the village. Two important observations emerged from the analysis: First, backwardness of the district no more remained a significant variable explaining the extent of short-term migration. This may imply that while being more or less concentrated in backward region, the intensity of short-term migration is found to be evenly spread across villages within the region. Second, the extent of short-term migration is higher among larger villages, distant villages and also villages with better educational infrastructure. On the other hand, the extent is lower among villages with better irrigation and higher net sown area per capita. This suggests that education facilitates migration if one is located within a backward region; however, favourable environment with respect to irrigation and land productivity would help contain short-term migration a widely acknowledged phenomenon in an agrarian society like India.

5   Migration Among Households in Select Villages: Understanding the Variations in a Micro-setting in MP

Given that the macro-level scenario confirms the continued importance of the coping or distress related migration from relatively backward and remote regions, the analysis, however, does not shed light on who among these less developed regions succeed in exercising the choice to migrate. Earlier, we had noted that whereas short-term migration is not particularly concentrated among the poorest, the poor by and large, constitute a significant majority among the migrants at the macro-level. The evidence, however, does help in gauging the perception as well as the preference for short-term migration among the poor.

This section tries to analyse the status of short duration migration and people's perception in the light of the recent survey conducted in 18 villages spread over three districts (Ujjain, Dhar and Hosangabad) in Madhya Pradesh.[4] Total 360 households covered in the survey.

The important observations from the Household survey are noted below:

1. Out of the total surveyed households around 34.4% witnessed incidence of short duration migration in MP Households with minimum one migrant covered around 53.3% in Dhar (tribal belt), 36.7% in Ujjain (relatively developed) and 13.3% in Hosangabad (irrigated and high rainfall zone). At a first instance, it shows that the level of migration is lower in the irrigated area compared to others.
2. Household-level analysis shows that, around 65.3% of households with unirri-gated land under cultivation migrate out in search of job compared to 35.7% of

---

[4]This survey is a part of the larger study focusing on examining the pattern of agriculture growth in Gujarat and Madhya Pradesh and the implications on poverty reduction in short and medium time frame.

households with irrigated land. Though there is no major difference in migrant jobs at place of destination for irrigated and unirrigated households.

3. Among the different caste groups, migration among the STs (60.2%) is highest. Among the other groups, migrating households among the OBCs (12.5%) is high.

4. Among the various landholding categories, evidence of migration was high among the marginal (32.1%) and small (56.4%) landholding groups. Evidence of migration was lowest among the big landholders (5.4%).

5. There is district-wise variation with respect to the migrants occupation at the place of destination. In Dhar, most of the migrants reported to work in non-farm sector like as drivers. Another major share work in others farm as agricultural labour and the share constituted around 20%. They migrate mainly to cities like Indore, Bhopal and Surat in search of jobs. Migrants in Ujjain reported to work as causal labours in construction sector (50%) and migrate to bigger cities like Bhopal and Ahmedabad. A major share of migrants from Ujjain also work as sharecroppers in other's farm (25%) and they mostly migrate to irrigated areas of Madhya Pradesh. Migrants from Hosangabad work as share croppers. During the monsoon due to heavy rain, most of years the villages suffer with flood, thus they prefer to migrate out and work in other farm, though the share of migrants is lowest in Hosanganad compared to other districts.

We have made an effort to examine the pattern of migration among the surveyed districts in Madhya Pradesh. An attempt has been made to examine the flow of migration from one sector to other, and whether there exist any region wise variation in the pattern (Table 7).

In Ujjain, for those whose main occupation is cultivators, they migrate mainly as sharecroppers and agricultural labour for short duration of about 6–8 months and come back to their own village for the cropping season. Causal labour mainly non-farm labour works as a construction worker after migration. This shows in Ujjain, there is a link between agriculture to agriculture sector and non-agriculture to non-agriculture. Similarly in Hosangabad, the cultivators either work as share-croppers or in industries as labour. Other non-farm labour migrates to irrigated districts as share croppers. This shows in Hosangabad there is a reverse migration, as there is a migration from non-farm sector to farm sector. However in Dhar, there is migration from farm sector to non-farm sector.

We have further tried to identify the major reasons for migration across districts and tried to examine whether there is any difference in reason behind migration across regions in Madhya Pradesh.

Though the incidence of migration was lowest in Hosangabad among other studied districts, but one of the major reasons for migration was due to flood and waterlogging among the surveyed villages.

In Ujjain, the major reason cited that mainly the young generation prefers to opt for non-farm activities rather than practicing agriculture. After the soyabean season, people prefer to migrate out in search of better opportunity in construction sector and to work as semi-skilled workers in construction sector.

Table 7 Flow of migration in Madhya Pradesh

Original occupation/occupation after migration		Agri labour	Construction	Share croppers	Diamond industry	Driver	Casual labour	Total
Ujjain	Cultivator	33.3	16.7	41.7	8.3	–	–	100
	Casual labour	–	100	–	–	–	–	100
	Total	20.0	50.0	25.0	5.0	–	–	100
Hosangabad	Cultivator	–	–	50.0	50.0	–	–	100
	Casual labour	–	–	100	–	–	–	100
	Self-employed	–	–	100	–	–	–	100
	Total	–	–	85.7	14.3	–	–	100
Dhar	Cultivator	–	30.0	10.0	–	40.0	20.0	100
	Animal husbandry	–	–	–	–	Insignificant sample	–	–
	Agri labour	100	–	–	–	–	–	100
	Service (pvt.)	–	–	–	–	100	–	100
	Casual labour	–	–	–	–	100	–	100
	Total	20.0	15.0	5.0		50.0	10.0	100

Source Field Survey, 2013–14

Dhar being the tribal belt, the unprofitability of agricultural crop production was noted as one of the major reason for migration. Dhar being the bordering district to Gujarat, we found cotton cultivation in Dhar, around 30% of the area out of the total gross cropped area, as total of gross cropped area across the surveyed households was under cotton and around 76% of the total surveyed households reported of cultivating cotton. The unprofitability of crop production due to increase in cost of cultivation of cotton leads to migrate people out of the village. The average size of land holding in Dhar being lowest, the earning from the small piece of land does not support the survival of the year long. However, among the six studied village in Dhar the incidence of migration was highest in the village Bhagiyapur, which is located near to the district headquarter. This is the only village among the surveyed villages in Dhar which has better connectivity compared to other studied villages.

6 Summing up and Way Forward

Despite being a widely adopted and critical strategy for coping and accumulation among poor and not so poor households, the existing literature on migration has not adequately explored the issue of migration-poverty interface and possibility of using migration as an exit route out of poverty. This is mainly because the macro-level data are not amenable to capturing the interface, and at the same time, micro-level studies are too scattered to draw larger picture across and within states in India. The limitations arise mainly because the official data do not provide adequate information regarding the extent, motivation and outcomes of migration. What is particularly serious is the data gap on short-term/seasonal migration, which has significant bearing on the well-being of the poor. Given this backdrop, the paper tries to review some of the existing evidence and examines the inter-relationships between migration and poverty in the light of the official statistics from the NSSO, a large-scale village survey conducted by NCAER and a survey conducted in Madhya Pradesh.

Evidence from a number of micro-level studies suggests that those having land and irrigation generally do not undertake such migration. However, those among the poor, who migrate for short duration, barely make a subsistence living in spite of migration. This pattern is further substantiated by the macro-level data on long and short-term migration in India. Data from the latest round of the NSSO clearly highlighted the dual pattern of poverty-migration interface. The estimates indicate that whereas incidence of migration is high among both rich and the poor, they often have fairly different trajectories. One of the most striking differences is with respect to the duration of migration across different expenditure strata. It is observed that while the rate of long-term migration is higher among the higher expenditure classes, the rate of short-term migration is higher among the poor. Hence, short and long-term migration remains disconnected within the overall dual scenario obtaining in the economy and society.

Apparently the poor, especially very poor, often do not have the option of long-term migration as they have very limited socio-economic-human resource base to build on for enhancing their economic well-being. The scenario on the demand side is also not very encouraging especially when employment opportunities in urban destinations are neither very substantial, nor certain, or continuous. Changing the demand scenario is challenging as the problem is rooted in the very structure of the macro-economy. At the same time, it is important to recognize that the flow of short-term migration is likely to increase in the short and medium term, given the declining (land) resource base among the ever-growing rural population. In this context, the two-legged approach, often flagged by researchers and policy makers, viz; increasing access to irrigation and improving the conditions of migrants- may serve as a short/medium term remedy. Of course, this is not to deny the role that migration, even short-term migration, plays in smoothening or retaining the given level of economic well-being among the poor migrants. Without support from income earned through migration, many of the poor households in rural areas would have suffered much more severe consequences in the form of multiple deprivations. But the above approach cannot be viewed as a long-term strategy whereby migration offers an effective route among the poor to exit severe or chronic poverty. For this to be realized, it is essential that the demand side scenario for non-farm work is improved dramatically. The need therefore is to address the very root cause of the existing dual structure of the economy while exploring the possibility of migration to work as an exit route out of poverty in general and chronic poverty in particular.

Way Forward

Rights-based Approach

One of the perspectives that have gained ground in the recent period is – it is neither desirable nor feasible to check migration from rural areas. Hence, the best way is to facilitate migrants by improving their work as well as living conditions at the place of destination. This is particularly important in the light of the fact that majority of these migrants are seasonal workers and/or engaged in the informal sectors, often live in slums and pavements. Since they do not have voting rights they are not covered under any formal systems of state support and legal protection. It is therefore important to first establish their identities as workers in temporary residence in cities and towns and enable them to claim for their rightful stake in the economy and community.

It is imperative to note that in 1991 the National Commission on Rural Labour had recommended changes in the existing Interstate Migrant Workmen (Regulation of Employment and Conditions of Service) Act, 1979. It suggested that the definition of migrant workmen should be expanded to cover all migrants – irrespective of the fact whether they came on their own or through contractors or changed their contractor (NCRL 1991). The National Commission for Enterprises in the unorganised sector has also recommended that the migrant workers should be treated at par with informal sector workers engaged in different activities in a region and recommended special provisions for these vulnerable sections of the unorganized sector (NCEUS 2007).

A number of voluntary groups have undertaken such initiatives in different parts of the country. For instance, Ajeevika Bureau is a voluntary initiative for providing support to rural migrants from Rajasthan into the neighbouring states. This includes a gamut of activities such as registration of migrant workers; issuing identity cards; skill upgradation; saving-credit facilities; legal support and policy advocacy; and extending help to their families back home in difficult times.

Several other initiatives have been undertaken by various organizations that fight for the rights of migrant workers who often depend on labour contractors and hence face additional exploitation within the informal labour markets. These are of course most needed interventions that may improve outcomes of migration. Do they influence the future flow of migration? This is a complex issue and is not within the ambit of intervention by such voluntary organizations. It is important to note that the ongoing work on the Global Compact for Safe, Orderly and Regular Migration also calls for collection and utilisation of disaggregated data on migration and addressing and reducing vulnerabilities in migration.

Redressing Urban Poverty and Promoting Urban Infrastructure

Following from the rights-based approach to protect the interests of migrant workers, a case has been made to improve living conditions for slum dwellers and homeless, many of whom are migrants. Similarly, a case has been made to extend employment guarantee scheme for the poor especially in the small towns who may not find adequate work/income in non-farm activities within urban areas. Public works in small towns could be linked to improvement in housing and other basic amenities in these towns and also in the urban areas.

In fact, the policies for slum clearance/development followed over a long period of time are often characterized by the dilemma of regularising 'illegal' residents and thereby attracting more of them. At the same time, shifting the locus of residents away from potential places of work has always met with limited success.

Notwithstanding these dilemmas, there has been an increasing concern about designing special schemes for helping the rural poor through self-employment and also wage-employment. It is in this context that some of the new initiatives such as Jawaharlal Nehru National Urban Renewal Mission (JNNURM) deserve special attention. The JNNURM is one of the several initiatives that have roots in the economic reforms-linked investments. This inter alia involves features of economic pricing, user fees, partnership with private sector, etc. The main focus of the Mission is to improve urban infrastructure and thereby directly influence the quality of life and human welfare. One of the important objectives is: 'provision of basic services to the urban poor including security of tenure at affordable prices, improved housing, water supply and sanitation, and ensuring delivery of other existing universal services of the government for education, health and social security' (Government of India 2005, p. 5).

While this opens up substantial scope for employment opportunities and welfare enhancement among the urban dwellers, the specific implications for the poor migrants already in the cities and/or likely to enter cities need further elaboration. This would necessitate that migrants, especially among the poor households, are made an integral part of the perspective on urban development plan, and that the focus on poor households should assume special significance in designing and actual execution of the plan. The fact that JNNURM is a vehicle to take forward the processes of economic reforms and makes it imperative to ensure that the focus on poverty and welfare of the poor is not lost sight of in the guise of efficiency, pricing and privatization.

It is likely that a more systemic response could be from the policies that address the issue of poverty and unemployment in both rural as well as urban economies. These approaches are discussed below.

Promoting Agricultural Growth

Notwithstanding the continued and marginally increasing dependence on rural–urban migration, making migration a means of income enhancement and/or poverty reduction, would essentially hinge on improvement of labour productivity and wages in the rural economy in general and agriculture in particular. Healthy growth in agriculture sector may enhance employment and/or returns to labour; promote opportunities for rural non-farm work and more importantly increase bargaining power of those who migrate outside the rural economies. This of course is too simplistic a description of the complex cobweb of highly segmented labour markets within which migration across sectors and space is shaped among workers from different socio-economic strata. With decline in per person land availability, it is a relevant question to address that what should be done to make people stay in agriculture.

Since agriculture growth has significant multiplier impact for boosting overall economic growth in the country (Ahluwalia 2009), it may either enhance incidence of migration and/or improve the outcome thereof. Whereas the former (i.e. out-migration) from rural areas may create labour shortage and additional demand for labour in agriculture, the latter (i.e. enhanced income) may help withdraw family labour from unskilled on-farm activities and thereby create space for those with lower reservation price. In both cases, the very poor who cannot manage to move out may stand to benefit.

Redistribution of land among the poor and landless households may enhance use of land by other non-agricultural use of lands like agro-processing units and small industries.

Strengthening Rural–Urban Linkages and Peri-Urban Areas

Clearly the perspectives discussed above are divided into two set of approaches; first focusing on supporting migrant workers to facilitate improvements in the outcomes of migration especially in urban areas; and the other focusing on checking distress related migration from rural areas. Whereas initiatives like JNNURM could help to enhance the welfare of the urban poor including migrants, MGNREGS may help to reduce out-migration and thereby reduce overcrowding and congestion in urban areas.

Essentially, the two perspectives seem to work in isolation without taking into consideration the continuum between rural and urban areas, economies and poverty. In fact, migration is the most crucial link in this continuum. It is therefore important that the discussion on migration, with special focus on the poor takes a dynamic view of the changing realities in both rural and urban areas. This in turn would help in resolving several of the dichotomies in the existing literature on migration, viz. migrants vs. non-migrants, distress vs. accumulation motives, lifetime vs. circular migration, rural vs. urban development, preventive vs. facilitating migration, and economic vs. human welfare, etc. Evolving this would necessitate deeper under-standing of the changing scenarios in both rural and urban areas and their influence on migration decisions and the outcomes thereof. In the absence of this, merely tracing the extent, pattern and streams of migratory flows may not help in addressing the issue of migration and development in a dynamic context.

References

Agrawal, T., & Chandrasekhar, S. (2015). *Short term migrants in India characteristics, wages and work transition.*, Working Paper No. 29 Mumbai: Indira Gandhi Institute of Development Research.

Ahluwalia, M. S. (2009). Growth, distribution and inclusiveness-reflections on India's experience. In M. Kaushik Basu & S. Ravi Kanbur (Ed.), *Arguments for a better world: Essays in honour of Amartya Sen.* Oxford: Oxford University Press.

Bhagat, R. B. & Keshri, K. (2010). Temporary and seasonal migration In India. *Genus, 19*, October–December.

Bhandari, G., & Reddy, B. C. (2015). Impact of out migration on agriculture and women work load: An economic analysis of hilly regions of Uttrakhand, India. *Indian Journal of Agricultural Economics, 70*(3), 395–404.

de Haan, A. (1997). Rural-urban migration and poverty: The case of India. *IDS Bulletin, 28*(2), 35–47.

de Hann, A. (1999). Livelihoods and poverty: The role of migration-a critical review of the migration literature. *The Journal of Development Studies, 36*(2), 1–47.

de Haan, A. (2011). Inclusive growth? Labour migration and poverty in India, International Institute of Social Studies, Working Paper No. 513.

Desai, S. B., Dubey, A., Joshi, B. I., Sen, M., Shariff, A., & Vanneman, R. (2010). *Human development in India: Challenges for a society in transition.* New Delhi: Oxford University Press.

Deshingkar, P. (2008). Circular internal migration and development. In Josh DeWind & Jennifer Holdaway (Eds.), *Migration and development within and across borders: Research and policy perspectives on internal and international migration.* New York: Social Science Research Council.

Deshingkar, P. (2010). Migration, remote rural areas and chronic poverty in India, Working Paper 323, CPRC Working Paper 163.

Deshingkar, P., & Daniel, S. (2003). *Seasonal migration for livelihoods in India: Coping, accumulation and exclusion.* Working Paper 220, London: Overseas Development Institute.

Deshingkar, P., & Farrington, J. (2009). *Circular migration and multilocational livelihood strategies in rural India.* New Delhi: Oxford University Press.

Gangopadhyay, K., & Singh, K. (2013). Extent of poverty in India, a different dimension. *Economic and Political Weekly, 48*(06), 75–83.

Government of India (2005). Jawaharlal Nehru Urban Renewal Mission: Overview. Available at http://mohua.gov.in/upload/uploadfiles/files/1Mission%20Overview%20English(1).pdf

Government of India (2010). Migration in India: 2007–08, NSSO Report No. 533, New Delhi: National Sample Survey Organisation.

Keshri, K., & Bhagat, R. B. (2012). Temporary and seasonal migration: Regional patterns, characteristics and associated factors. *Economic and Political Weekly, 47*(4), 81–87.

Kundu, A. (2009). Urbanisation and migration: An analysis of trend, pattern and policies in Asia. *Human Development Research Paper.*

Kundu, A., & Sarangi, N. (2007). Migration, employment status and poverty: An analysis across urban centres. *Economic and Political Weekly, 42*(4), 299–307.

Mitra, A., & Murayama, M. (2009). Rural to urban migration: A district level analysis for India. *International Journal of Migration, Health and Social Care, 5*(2), 35–52.

Mohanty, K. S., Mahapatro, S., Kastor, A., & Mahapatra, B. (2015). Does employment-related migration reduce poverty in India. *Journal of International Migration and Integration*, published online, May-2015.

Mosse, D., Gupta, S., Mehta, M., Shah, V., Rees J., & the KRIBP Project Team (2002). Brokered livelihoods: Debt, labour migration and development in tribal Western India. *Journal of Development Studies, 38*(5), June pp. 59–87.

NCEUS. (2007). *Report on conditions of work and promotion of livelihoods in the unorganised sector*. New Delhi: National Commission for Enterprises in the Unorganised Sector, Government of India.

NCRL. (1991). *Report of the National Commission on Rural Labour*. New Delhi: Ministry of Labour, Government of India.

NIRD. (2000). *India rural development report 1999: Regional disparities in development and poverty*. Hyderabad, India: National Institute of Rural Development.

Oberai, A. S., Prasad, P. H., & Sardana, M. G. (1989). *Determinants and consequences of internal migration in India: Studies in Bihar*. Kerala and Uttar Pradesh, New Delhi: Oxford University Press.

Rodgers, G., & Rodgers, J. (2011). Inclusive development? Migration, governance and social change in rural Bihar. *Economic and Political Weekly, 56*(23), 43–50.

Shah, A. (2009). Land degradation and migration in a dry land region in India: Extent, nature, and determinants, *Environment and Development Economics* pp. 1–24. Cambridge University Press (doi: https://doi.org/10.1017/S1355770X09990131).

Shah, A., & Kumar, A. (2011). *Migration and poverty in India: A multi-patterned and complex reality*. CPRC–IIPA, Working Paper 45, New Delhi.

Shah, D. C., & Shah, A. (2005). Migration in remote tribal areas: Evidence from South Western Madhya Pradesh. *Indian Journal of Agriculture Economics, 60*(2), 184–204.

Singh, Manjit. (1995). *Uneven development in agriculture and labour migration: A case of Bihar and Punjab*. Shimla: Indian Institute of Advanced Study.

Singh, D. P. (2009). Poverty and migration: Does moving help? *India urban poverty report 2009* pp. 50–75. New Delhi: Oxford University Press.

Srivastava, R. (2011). Labour migration in India: Recent trends, patterns and policy issues. *The Indian Journal of Labour Economics, 54*(3), 411–456.

Thomas, J. J. (2012). India's labour marker during the 2000s, surveying changes, *Economic and Political Weekly, 47*(51), 22 December 39–51.

Chapter 7
Ill Health and Poverty: Policy Imperatives for Achieving SDG3

Aasha Kapur Mehta and Sanjay Pratap

1 The Context

While there are strong interconnections between many of the SDGs, the strongest link is between SDG1 and SDG3, i.e., "end poverty in all its forms everywhere", and "ensure healthy lives and promote well-being for all at all ages".

Achievement of SDG3 requires a substantial reduction in the maternal mortality ratio, neonatal mortality, mortality from non-communicable diseases, deaths and injuries from road traffic accidents, and deaths and illnesses from hazardous chemicals and air, water and soil pollution and contamination. Other targets include ending the epidemics of AIDS, tuberculosis, malaria, and neglected tropical diseases and combating hepatitis, waterborne diseases and other communicable diseases. Also needed are strengthening of the prevention and treatment of substance abuse; universal health coverage; and universal access to sexual and reproductive healthcare services.

The state of health and health care in India is grim for many reasons. Extreme poverty, disease burden, morbidity and mortality levels are significant. More than half of Indian children and women are anaemic, and 36% of children below the age of five are malnourished. Government spending on health care in India is among the lowest in the world at only 1.15% of GDP. Financial support for medical emergencies is abysmal as 86% of Indians living in rural and 82% in urban areas lack health insurance (Government of India 2014). Access to public provisioning of health care is limited, and out-of-pocket expenditure on health is high.

The sudden onset of a long and expensive illness can drive households that are not poor into poverty due to high costs of accessing health care combined with loss of income due to inability to work. Ill health creates immense stress even among those who are financially secure. High healthcare costs force households to sell the

A. K. Mehta (✉) · S. Pratap
Indian Institute of Public Administration, New Delhi, India
e-mail: aasha2006@gmail.com

© Springer Nature Singapore Pte Ltd. 2018
A. K. Mehta et al. (eds.), *Poverty, Chronic Poverty and Poverty Dynamics*,
https://doi.org/10.1007/978-981-13-0677-8_7

meagre assets they own and additionally borrow money in order to try and save the lives of family members who suffer from a serious illness. Since most households do not have insurance, they are forced to borrow at usurious interest rates or sell meagre assets to cover expenses (Mehta and Gupta 2006; Government of India 2010: 15). This can lead to intergenerational transmission of poverty. It is in this context that public provisioning of good quality health care is extremely important.

Drawing attention to the link between poverty and health, the WHO (2015, p. 42) states:

> Every year, some 100 million people fall below the poverty line as a result of out-of-pocket expenditures on health, and a further 1.2 billion, already living in poverty, are pushed further into penury for the same reason.

It also notes that India has the largest share of the world's extreme poor estimated at 30% of people living on less than US$1.25 per day. In comparison, Nigeria has 10% and China 8% of the world's extreme poor (ibid.: 26).

WHO (1995: 1) classifies extreme poverty as the world's most ruthless killer and the greatest cause of suffering on earth. It notes that:

> Poverty is the main reason why babies are not vaccinated, clean water and sanitation are not provided and curative drugs and other treatments are unavailable and why mothers die in childbirth...It conspires with the most deadly and painful diseases to bring a wretched existence to all those who suffer it.

The Directive Principles of State Policy require the state to "regard the raising of the level of nutrition and the standard of living of its people and the improvement of public health as among its primary duties" (Article 47). Given this context, it is important to draw attention to the weaknesses in health provisioning that were identified by the Twelfth Plan (Government of India 2013). These are[1]:

- Severe shortfall in the availability of healthcare services both in public and private sectors.
- This is "exacerbated by a wide geographical variation in availability across the country" with rural areas being "especially poorly served".
- Variation in quality of healthcare services in both the public and private sectors, with lack of qualified doctors, inadequately defined regulatory standards and "ineffective" enforcement.
- Lack of affordability of health care for the vast majority of the population.
- Heavy out-of-pocket expenditures on services purchased from the private sector due to inadequately funded public health services.
- Very high financial burden on families in case of severe illness.
- Poor coverage of expenses by insurance schemes.
- Poor coverage of population by health insurance.

---

[1]See Twelfth Plan (2012–17), Volume III, page 1 to 3.

- Rising healthcare costs. Rising life expectancy implies increased vulnerability to chronic non-communicable diseases (NCDs), which typically require expensive treatment.
- Dual burden of disease due to rising cost of managing NCDs and injuries while still battling communicable diseases.
- Very low public expenditure on health.
- "Public expenditure on Core Health (both plan and non-plan and taking the centre and states together) was about 0.93% of GDP in 2007–08. It has increased to about 1.04% during 2011–12. It needs to increase much more over the next decade".

The National Health Policy 2002 was candid in acknowledging the unsatisfactory state of public health infrastructure at the time.

> For the outdoor medical facilities in existence, funding is generally insufficient; the presence of medical and para-medical personnel is often much less than that required by prescribed norms; the availability of consumables is frequently negligible; the equipment in many public hospitals is often obsolescent and unusable; and, the buildings are in a dilapidated state. In the indoor treatment facilities, again, the equipment is often obsolescent; the availability of essential drugs is minimal; the capacity of the facilities is grossly inadequate, which leads to over-crowding, and consequentially to a steep deterioration in the quality of the services. As a result of such inadequate public health facilities, it has been estimated that less than 20 percent of the population, which seek OPD services, and less than 45 percent of that which seek indoor treatment, avail of such services in public hospitals. This is despite the fact that most of these patients do not have the means to make out-of-pocket payments for private health services except at the cost of other essential expenditure for items such as basic nutrition. (Government of India 2002: 9 and 10)

Government of India (2017: 12) is equally candid in pointing out that government spending on health care in India is only 1.15% of GDP and stating that "it is unrealistic to expect achieving key goals in a Five Year Plan on half the estimated and sanctioned budget". It uses global evidence on health spending to argue that "unless a country spends at least 5–6% of its GDP on health with Government expenditure being a major part, basic healthcare needs are seldom met" (ibid.).

Section 2 of this chapter presents the comparative status of India's health outcomes and high disease burden as well as the relative contribution of different categories of diseases to disability-adjusted life year (DALY[2]). It provides an overview of national and state-wise morbidity and spatial differences in health outcomes. Section 3 draws attention to the extremely low spending on health by the Government of India (centre and states) – far lower than most countries, despite commitments to raise it substantially. This must be viewed in the context of the impact of health shocks on creating impoverishment and the non-existent health insurance coverage of most Indian households.

Section 4 briefly reviews the targets set for NRHM in 2005 against achievements in 2012 and 2015–16 in the context of health provisioning and disease burden. NITI Aayog is the nodal agency for monitoring progress towards achieving

---

[2]Years lost due to ill health, disability or early death.

the SDGs and for mapping the ministries and departments responsible for achievement of specific targets and indicators. It has identified NRHM (as a part of NHM) and ICDS as important interventions for achieving SDG3. Hence, Sect. 5 draws lessons regarding what does and does not work in the context of these schemes so that better health and nutrition outcomes can be achieved.

2 India's Health Outcomes and Disease Burden: A Comparison with Selected Countries

India's mortality rates and disease burden are unacceptably high in both absolute and relative terms compared with countries in the WHO South-East Asian Region,[3] BRICS countries and a few selected nations (Table 1). India's maternal mortality ratio (MMR) at 174 per 100,000 live births (167 according to the Registrar General of India) compares poorly with estimates of 54 for Vietnam, 44 for Brazil, 40 for Malaysia, 30 for Sri Lanka, 27 for China and 20 for Thailand.

India's neonatal mortality rate (NMR) of 27.7 per 1000 live births not only exceeds the global average of 19.2 but is more than two times the neonatal mortality rate in Indonesia, Vietnam and South Africa; three times that in Brazil; four times that for Thailand; five times that for China, Sri Lanka, Russian Federation and Maldives; seven times that for Malaysia; and a massive 17 times that for Republic of Korea. The only countries that have a neonatal mortality rate higher than India among those listed above are Pakistan and Afghanistan. India's under-5 mortality rate (UMR) is 47.7 per 1000 live births and exceeds the global average. It is more than four times the under-five mortality rate for Thailand at 12.3, China at 10.7, Sri Lanka at 9.8 and Malaysia at 7.

Life expectancy at birth at 68.3 years is the same as that for Timor-Leste and is 3 years less than the global average. In comparison, LEB is 76.1 in China, 76 in Vietnam and 75 in Brazil, Malaysia, Sri Lanka and Thailand.

2.1 State of Health

2.1.1 Disease Burden

The global average incidence of tuberculosis is 142 per 100,000 population. However, the incidence is far higher in India at 217. In comparison, it is 156 in Nepal, 67 in China and 41 in Brazil. Malaria incidence per 1000 population at risk is also extremely high in India at 18.6, while it is 0.8 in neighbouring Bangladesh,

---

[3]WHO South-East Asia Region comprises Bangladesh, Bhutan, Democratic People's Republic of Korea, India, Indonesia, Maldives, Myanmar, Nepal, Sri Lanka, Thailand, Timor-Leste.

Table 1 Comparing achievements on life expectancy at birth, maternal mortality ratio, under-5 mortality rate and neonatal mortality rate for selected countries in 2015

	LEB male	LEB female	LEB persons	Healthy life expectancy at birth (years)	Maternal mortality ratio (per 100,000 live births)	Under-5 mortality rate (per 1000 live births)	Neonatal mortality rate (per 1000 live births)
Afghanistan	59.3	61.9	60.5	52.2	396	91.1	35.5
Bangladesh	70.6	73.1	71.8	62.3	176	37.6	23.3
Bhutan	69.5	70.1	69.8	61.2	148	32.9	18.3
Brazil	71.4	78.7	75	65.5	44	16.4	8.9
China	74.6	77.6	76.1	68.5	27	10.7	5.5
India	66.9	69.9	68.3	59.5	174	47.7	27.7
Indonesia	67.1	71.2	69.1	62.2	126	27.2	13.5
Kenya	61.1	65.8	63.4	55.6	510	49.4	22.2
Malaysia	72.7	77.3	75	66.5	40	7	3.9
Maldives	76.9	80.2	78.5	69.6	68	8.6	4.9
Myanmar	64.6	68.5	66.6	59.2	178	50	26.4
Nepal	67.7	70.8	69.2	61.1	258	35.8	22.2
Pakistan	65.5	67.5	66.4	57.8	178	81.1	45.5
Republic of Korea	78.8	85.5	82.3	73.2	11	3.4	1.6
Russian Federation	64.7	76.3	70.5	63.3	25	9.6	5
South Africa	59.3	66.2	62.9	54.5	138	40.5	11
Sri Lanka	71.6	78.3	74.9	67	30	9.8	5.4
Thailand	71.9	78	74.9	66.8	20	12.3	6.7
Timor-Leste	66.6	70.1	68.3	60.7	215	52.6	22.3
Vietnam	71.3	80.7	76	66.6	54	21.7	11.4
Global	69.1	73.7	71.4	63.1	216	42.5	19.2

Source World Health Statistics (2017)

1.9 in Malaysia and 2.7 in Thailand. Of the countries for which data is presented in Table 2, only Afghanistan, Indonesia and Kenya have a higher incidence of malaria than India.

Clearly, therefore, concerted efforts are required to substantially reduce poverty, disease burden and mortality rates in India if SDG1 and SDG3 are to be achieved nationally and globally. Universal health coverage and universal access to health-care services are needed. For this, substantial increases in budgetary allocation to health care must be prioritized.

India's per person disease burden remains high. Although the per person disease burden (DALYs rate) declined between 1990 and 2016, it is 72% higher than either

Table 2 Tuberculosis, malaria and HIV: comparing India with selected countries

	TB incidence (per 100,000 population)	Malaria incidence (per 1000 population at risk)	New HIV infections among adults 15–49 years old (per 1000 uninfected population)
Afghanistan	189	23.6	0.06
Bangladesh	225	0.8	0.01
Bhutan	155	0.1	–
Brazil	41	7.9	0.39
China	67	<0.1	–
India	217	18.6	0.11
Indonesia	395	26.1	0.5
Kenya	233	166	3.52
Malaysia	89	1.9	0.27
Maldives	53	–	–
Myanmar	365	11.8	0.41
Nepal	156	3.3	0.08
Pakistan	270	8.6	0.16
Republic of Korea	80	0.8	–
Russian Federation	80	–	–
South Africa	834	3.1	14.4
Sri Lanka	65	0	0.05
Thailand	172	2.7	0.2
Timor-Leste	498	0.2	–
Vietnam	137	0.3	0.28
Global	142	94	0.5

Source World Health Statistics (2017)

China or Sri Lanka (ICMR et al. 2017: 17).[4] During this period, the relative contribution of communicable, maternal, neonatal and nutritional diseases (CMNNDs) to DALYs decreased from 61% to 33% while that of non-communicable diseases (NCDs) increased from 31% to 55%. The relative contribution of CMNNDs to deaths decreased from 54% to 28% while that of NCDs increased from 38% to 62%, respectively (Table 3).

---

[4]DALYs is the sum of years of potential life lost due to premature mortality and the years of productive life lost due to disability. One DALY represents the loss of the equivalent of one year of full health.

Table 3 Contribution of disease categories to DALYs and to deaths, 1990 and 2016 (%)

	Contribution of disease categories to DALYs		Contribution of disease categories to deaths	
Disease categories	1990	2016	1990	2016
Communicable, maternal, neonatal and nutritional diseases	60.9	32.7	53.6	27.5
Non-communicable diseases	30.5	55.4	37.9	61.8
Injuries	8.6	11.9	8.5	10.7

Source ICMR et al. (2017). India: Health of the Nation's States

The largest reduction in relative contribution to DALYs was due to diarrhoea, lower respiratory and other common infectious diseases followed by neonatal disorders. The largest increase in relative contribution to DALYs was due to cardiovascular diseases followed by injuries, diabetes, urogenital, blood and endocrine diseases, cancers and mental and substance use disorders (Table 4).

ICMR et al. (2017) draw attention to the fact that for India as a whole, "the disease burden or DALY rate for diarrhoeal diseases, iron-deficiency anaemia and tuberculosis was 2.5–3.5 times higher than the average globally for other geographies at a similar level of development".

2.1.2 Morbidity, Anaemia and Malnutrition

Government of India (2014) estimates the prevalence of morbidity[5] to be 8.9% persons in rural and 11.8% in urban areas. Estimates of prevalence of morbidity for the last three surveys conducted by NSSO are presented in Table 5. Morbidity rates are higher for females relative to males. A large proportion of ailing persons suffered from chronic ailments (Table 6).

However, these estimates do not capture the true extent of morbidity in India for the following reasons:

1. Estimates of morbidity in different states are presented in Table 7. While morbidity is reportedly as high as 31% in Kerala and 16% in rural and 20% in urban Andhra Pradesh, it is only 3–6% in Assam, Bihar and Chhattisgarh. These estimates cannot be taken at face value and need further investigation.
2. With half of India's women and children suffering from anaemia and 36% children suffering malnourishment (Table 8), it is unlikely that morbidity levels are only 8.9% in rural and 11.8% in urban areas.

[5]Prevalence of morbidity is measured as the number of persons reporting ailments during the last 15 days per thousand persons.

Table 4 Contribution of disease categories to DALYs, 1990 and 2016 (%)

Disease categories	1990 Population 864 million	2016 Population 1316 million
Communicable, maternal, neonatal and nutritional diseases	**60.9**	**32.7**
HIV/AIDS and tuberculosis	5.1	4.2
Diarrhoea, lower respiratory and other common infectious diseases	33.2	12.7
Neglected tropical diseases and malaria	2.1	1.5
Maternal disorders	1.4	0.6
Neonatal disorders	13.9	7.9
Nutritional deficiencies	3.8	4.6
Other communicable, maternal, neonatal and nutritional diseases	1.5	1.1
Non-communicable diseases	**30.5**	**55.4**
Cancers	2.3	5
Cardiovascular diseases	6.9	14.1
Chronic respiratory diseases	4.5	6.4
Cirrhosis and other chronic liver diseases	0.9	1.6
Digestive diseases	1.3	1.5
Neurological disorders	2.0	3.6
Mental and substance use disorders	2.9	5.6
Diabetes, urogenital, blood and endocrine diseases	2.6	5.6
Musculoskeletal disorders	2.3	4.6
Other non-communicable diseases	4.9	7.4
Injuries	**8.6**	**11.9**
Transport injuries	1.7	3.3
Unintentional injuries	4.6	5.4
Suicide and interpersonal violence	2.1	3.1
Other	0.1	0.0

Source ICMR et al. (2017) p. 46

3. NFHS 4 shows that 9.2% of children under 5 suffered from diarrhoea during the 2 weeks preceding their survey in 2014 (Table 8). Diarrhoea is only one of the many diseases that lead to morbidity.
4. Data that is captured is very sensitive to the way that it is collected, the tools that are used and the way the questions are asked. Micro-studies provide far higher estimates of morbidity.
5. Centre for Multi-disciplinary Development Research (CMDR) conducted a health-related survey covering 4,500 households in three states, i.e. Maharashtra, Karnataka and Odisha during July–August 2001. Analysing the results of the survey, Panchamukhi and Puttaswamaiah (2004) found that 5,662

Table 5 Proportion (per 1000) of ailing persons (PAP) during last 15 days: rural and urban

Gender	PAP in NSS rounds		
	52nd	60th	71st
	(1995–1996)	(January–June 2004)	(January–June 2014)
	Rural		
Male	54	83	80
Female	57	93	99
All	55	88	89
	Urban		
Male	51	91	101
Female	58	108	135
All	54	99	118

Source Government of India (2014), page 27

Table 6 Number (per 1000) of persons reporting ailment during last 15 days by gender

Sector	Ailment	Male	Female	All
Rural	Short duration	44	54	49
	Chronic	36	45	40
	Any	80	99	89
Urban	Short duration	45	56	51
	Chronic	56	79	67
	Any	101	135	118

Source Government of India (2014)

out of 23,973 persons surveyed in the three states suffered morbidity during the reference period. Around 27% of those surveyed in Maharashtra, 18.16% in Karnataka and 27% in Odisha reported morbidity and said they had been ill during the previous 30 days (Singh et al. 2006: 9).

Despite the decline in both malnutrition and stunting among children under 5 years of age over the 10 years between NFHS3 and NFHS4, the levels are still very high and call for urgent action. Malnutrition declined from 42.5% in 2005–06 to 35.7% in 2015–16 and stunting from 48 to 38.4% during the same period (Table 8). However, the percentage of children under 5 who were wasted and severely wasted increased from 19.8% to 21% and 6.4% to 7.5% respectively. While 9.2% of children under 5 suffered from diarrhoea during the 2 weeks preceding their survey, the percentage of children suffering from this who received ORS doubled from 26% in 2005–06 to 50.6% in 2015–16. Children with diarrhoea who were taken to the health facility increased from 61.3% to 67.9% between NFHS 3 and NFHS 4.

Table 7 Proportion (number per 1000) of ailing persons in selected states by gender

States	PAP (per thousand) for					
	Rural			Urban		
	Male	Female	All	Male	Female	All
Andhra Pradesh	154	156	155	190	217	204
Assam	23	41	31	42	53	47
Bihar	52	64	57	66	57	62
Chhattisgarh	45	34	40	36	53	44
Gujarat	88	95	92	93	115	103
Haryana	48	65	56	77	72	75
Jharkhand	47	57	52	69	125	96
Karnataka	85	102	93	84	125	103
Kerala	305	315	310	277	332	306
Madhya Pradesh	50	56	53	59	84	71
Maharashtra	73	88	80	66	74	70
Odisha	90	119	103	86	108	97
Punjab	124	203	161	143	196	170
Rajasthan	44	64	54	82	84	83
Telangana	133	158	146	148	221	184
Tamil Nadu	84	110	97	80	112	95
Uttar Pradesh	66	88	77	82	143	111
West Bengal	139	184	161	147	214	179
All	80	99	89	101	135	118

Source Government of India (2014)

While 58.4% of children aged 6–59 months were anaemic in 2015–16, this percentage had decreased by 11% since 2005–6. Also, cause for concern is the fact that more than half of all women and 22.7% of all men aged 15–49 years suffer from anaemia (Table 9).

2.1.3 Contribution of Different Diseases to Death

Cardiovascular diseases were the largest cause of death in India (28.1%) in 2016. Diarrhoea, lower respiratory and other common infectious diseases accounted for 15.5%, chronic respiratory diseases 10.9%, cancers 8.3%, diabetes, urogenital, blood and endocrine diseases 6.5% and HIV/AIDS and tuberculosis 5.4% (Table 10). It is important to note that many of these can be prevented with adequate access to health care.

Table 8 Treatment of childhood diseases (children under age 5 years)

Indicators	NFHS-3	NFHS-4		
	2005–06	2015–16		
	Total	Urban	Rural	Total
Prevalence of diarrhoea (reported) in the last 2 weeks preceding the survey (%)	9.0	8.2	9.6	9.2
Children with diarrhoea in the last 2 weeks who received oral rehydration salts (ORS) (%)	26.0	58.5	47.9	50.6
Children with diarrhoea in the last 2 weeks who received zinc (%)	na	23.7	19.1	20.3
Children with diarrhoea in the last 2 weeks taken to a health facility (%)	61.3	74.1	65.8	67.9
Total children age 6–23 months receiving an adequate diet (%)	na	11.6	8.8	9.6
Children under 5 years who are stunted (height-for-age) (%)	48.0	31.0	41.2	38.4
Children under 5 years who are wasted (weight-for-height) (%)	19.8	20.0	21.5	21.0
Children under 5 years who are severely wasted (weight-for-height) (%)	6.4	7.5	7.4	7.5
Children under 5 years who are underweight (weight-for-age) (%)	42.5	29.1	38.3	35.7

Source NFHS 4

Table 9 Anaemia among children and adults

Indicators	NFHS-3 2005–06	NFHS-4 2015–16		
	Total	Urban	Rural	Total
Children age 6–59 months who are anaemic (<11.0 g/dl) (%)	69.4	55.9	59.4	58.4
Non-pregnant women age 15–49 years who are anaemic (<12.0 g/dl) (%)	55.2	50.9	54.3	53.1
Pregnant women age 15–49 years who are anaemic (<11.0 g/dl) (%)	57.9	45.7	52.1	50.3
All women age 15–49 years who are anaemic (%)	55.3	50.8	54.2	53.0
Men age 15–49 years who are anaemic (<13.0 g/dl) (%)	24.2	18.4	25.1	22.7

Source NFHS 4

Table 10 Contribution of different disease categories to death in 2016

Disease categories	2016 (population 1316 million)
Communicable, maternal, neonatal and nutritional diseases	**27.5**
HIV/AIDS and tuberculosis	5.4
Diarrhoea, lower respiratory and other common infectious diseases	15.5
Neglected tropical diseases and malaria	0.8
Maternal disorders	0.5
Neonatal disorders	3.8
Nutritional deficiencies	0.5
Other communicable, maternal, neonatal and nutritional diseases	0.9
Non-communicable diseases	**61.8**
Cancers	8.3
Cardiovascular diseases	28.1
Chronic respiratory diseases	10.9
Cirrhosis and other chronic liver diseases	2.1
Digestive diseases	2.2
Neurological disorders	2.1
Mental and substance use disorders	0.4
Diabetes, urogenital, blood and endocrine diseases	6.5
Musculoskeletal disorders	0.1
Other non-communicable diseases	1.1
Injuries	**10.7**
Transport injuries	2.9
Unintentional injuries	4.9
Suicide and interpersonal violence	2.8
Other	0

Source ICMR et al. (2017) p. 36

2.2   Spatial Differences in Outcomes

2.2.1   Status of Health Outcomes in Large States: 2014–15 and 2015–2016

Not only are the health outcomes for India poor, but additionally spatial inequalities are extremely high with some states performing well and most states lagging behind.

There was "an almost twofold difference" in the disease burden rate or DALY rate "between the states in 2016, with Assam, Uttar Pradesh, and Chhattisgarh having the highest rates, and Kerala and Goa the lowest rates" (ICMR et al. 2017: 17). The report highlights the fact that "range of disease burden or DALY rate among the states of India was ninefold for diarrhoeal disease, sevenfold for lower respiratory infections and ninefold for tuberculosis in 2016". Further, "the burden also differed between the sexes, with diarrhoeal disease, iron-deficiency anaemia, and lower respiratory infections higher among females, and tuberculosis higher among males" (ICMR et al. 2017: 18). Hence, the ICMR report stresses the importance of evidence-based targeted efforts to meet healthcare needs in each state.

A study on health outcomes in India's states conducted by Ministry of Health and Family Welfare, World Bank and NITI Aayog (2018) with 2014–15 as the base year and 2015–16 as the reference year shows a 5.8-fold difference between the best and worst performing states on NMR per thousand live births in 2015–16. NMR ranges from only 6 in Kerala to between 30 and 35 in Rajasthan, Uttar Pradesh, Madhya Pradesh and Odisha. Similarly, under-5 mortality rate ranges from 13 in Kerala to 56 in Odisha and 62 in Assam and Madhya Pradesh (Table 11; Fig. 1).

Sex ratio at birth is highest in Kerala at 967, followed by 961 in Chhattisgarh, 951 in West Bengal and 950 in Odisha. The discrimination against women and girls is reflected in the extremely low sex ratio at birth of 831 in Haryana, 844 in Uttarakhand, 854 in Gujarat, 861 in Rajasthan and 878 in Maharashtra.

Kerala, Punjab, Maharashtra and Tamil Nadu have the lowest mortality rates for NMR and UMR. West Bengal has low mortality on NMR and Jammu and Kashmir on UMR. Kerala, Gujarat, Andhra Pradesh, Maharashtra and Tamil Nadu have the lowest MMR. Rajasthan, Uttar Pradesh, Madhya Pradesh and Odisha perform very poorly on NMR, UMR and MMR.

TFR fell to 1.6 in Jammu and Kashmir, Tamil Nadu and West Bengal and to 1.7 in Andhra Pradesh, Himachal Pradesh and Punjab. However, population was yet to stabilize in the more populous states with TFR as high as 3.2 in Bihar, 3.1 in Uttar Pradesh, 2.8 in Madhya Pradesh and 2.7 in Jharkhand and Rajasthan.

2.3 Positive and Negative Trends in Health Outcomes in Large States: 2014–15 and 2015–16

Not only was the sex ratio at birth extremely low in in Haryana, Uttarakhand, Gujarat, Rajasthan and Maharashtra but between the base year (2014–15) and the reference year (2015–16) this worsened by a massive 53 points in Gujarat, 35 in Haryana, 32 in Rajasthan, 27 in Uttarakhand, 18 in Assam and Maharashtra, 14 in Himachal Pradesh, 12 in Chhattisgarh and 11 in Karnataka. It also worsened by 10 in Tamil Nadu, 8 in Jharkhand and Madhya Pradesh, 7 in Kerala, 3 in Odisha and 1 each in Telangana, Andhra Pradesh and West Bengal. It improved only in three large states, i.e. Punjab by 19, Uttar Pradesh by 10 and Bihar by 9. There was no change in Jammu and Kashmir.

Table 11 Performance of large states on neonatal mortality rate (NMR), under-5 mortality rate (UMR), total fertility rate (TFR), low birth weight (LBW) and sex ratio at birth (SRB) in base year (BY) 2014–15 and reference year (RY) 2015–16

States	NMR		UMR		TFR		LBW		SRB	
	BY	RY	BY	RY	BY	RY	BY	RY	BY	RY
Andhra Pradesh	26	24	40	39	1.8	1.7	5.62	6.73	919	918
Assam	26	25	66	62	2.3	2.3	18.19	16.68	918	900
Bihar	27	28	53	48	3.2	3.2	6.7	7.22	907	916
Chhattisgarh	28	27	49	48	2.6	2.5	11.61	12.15	973	961
Gujarat	24	23	41	39	2.3	2.2	10.58	10.51	907	854
Haryana	23	24	40	43	2.3	2.2	14.61	14.9	866	831
Himachal Pradesh	25	19	36	33	1.7	1.7	8.66	12.63	938	924
Jammu and Kashmir	26	20	35	28	1.7	1.6	6.33	5.93	899	899
Jharkhand	25	23	44	39	2.8	2.7	7.81	7.42	910	902
Karnataka	20	19	31	31	1.8	1.8	10.76	11.49	950	939
Kerala	6	6	13	13	1.9	1.8	10.81	11.72	974	967
Madhya Pradesh	35	34	65	62	2.8	2.8	14.16	14.1	927	919
Maharashtra	16	15	23	24	1.8	1.8	14.57	13.74	896	878
Odisha	36	35	60	56	2.1	2	20.1	19.16	953	950
Punjab	14	13	27	27	1.7	1.7	5.95	6.88	870	889
Rajasthan	32	30	51	50	2.8	2.7	27.43	25.51	893	861
Tamil Nadu	14	14	21	20	1.7	1.6	10.46	13.03	921	911
Telangana	25	23	37	34	1.8	1.8	6.11	5.7	919	918
Uttar Pradesh	32	31	57	51	3.2	3.1	11.74	9.6	869	879
Uttarakhand	26	28	36	38	2	2	7.77	7.26	871	844
West Bengal	19	18	30	30	1.6	1.6	15.48	16.45	952	951

Source Ministry of Health and Family Welfare, World Bank and NITI Aayog. Healthy States Progressive India (2018)

Between 2014–15 and 2015–16, there was a worsening of the NMR by 1 in Bihar and Haryana and by 2 in Uttarakhand. In comparison, there was a significant improvement by 6 in Himachal Pradesh, Jammu and Kashmir, and by 2 in Andhra Pradesh, Jharkhand and Telangana. NMR also improved by 1 in Assam, Chhattisgarh, Gujarat, Karnataka, Madhya Pradesh, Odisha, Punjab, Uttar Pradesh and West Bengal. There was no change in Kerala and Tamil Nadu.

Under-five mortality rate improved in Jammu and Kashmir by 7 points; Uttar Pradesh by 6; Bihar and Jharkhand by 5; Assam and Odisha by 4, Himachal Pradesh, Madhya Pradesh and Telangana by 3; Gujarat by 2; and Tamil Nadu,

	NMR (per '000 live births)	U5MR (per '000 live births)	TFR*	LBW (percentage)	SRB (No. of Girls Born for Every 1,000 Boys Born)	MMR
5 Best Performers	Kerala	Kerala	Jammu & Kashmir	Telangana	Kerala	Kerala
	Punjab	Tamil Nadu	Tamil Nadu	Jammu & Kashmir	Chhattisgarh	Maharashtra
	Tamil Nadu	Maharashtra	West Bengal	Andhra Pradesh	West Bengal	Tamil Nadu
	Maharashtra	Punjab	Andhra Pradesh	Punjab	Odisha	Gujarat
	West Bengal	Jammu & Kashmir	Himachal Pradesh	Bihar	Karnataka	Andhra Pradesh
5 Worst Performers	Uttarakhand	Rajasthan	Jharkhand	Haryana	Haryana	Bihar /Jharkhand
	Rajasthan	Uttar Pradesh	Rajasthan	West Bengal	Uttarakhand	Madhya Pradesh / Chhattisgarh
	Uttar Pradesh	Odisha	Madhya Pradesh	Assam	Gujarat	Odisha
	Madhya Pradesh	Assam	Uttar Pradesh	Odisha	Rajasthan	Rajasthan
	Odisha	Madhya Pradesh	Bihar	Rajasthan	Maharashtra	Uttar Pradesh /Uttarakhand

Fig. 1 Selected health outcome indicators: five best and worst performing large states in 2015–16. *Source* Based on Table 11

Rajasthan, Andhra Pradesh and Chhattisgarh by 1. It worsened by 3 in Haryana, 2 in Uttarakhand and 1 in Maharashtra. There was no change in Karnataka, Kerala, Punjab and West Bengal.

Interventions are needed in states where health indicators are poor and in those where they are worsening.

3 Health Financing

Government health expenditure as a per cent of total health expenditure in India is far lower than most countries. While the proportion of health expenditure in total expenditure by government (centre + states) is only 30.5% in India in 2011, it is 42–50% in Sri Lanka, Brazil, South Africa and USA; 56% in China; 60% in Russia; and 76–85% in Germany, France, Thailand, Sweden, Japan, UK, Norway and Denmark (Table 12). Correspondingly, life expectancy at birth is higher in all the countries listed in Table 12, with several of them experiencing 8 to 18 years higher life expectancy.

Budgetary allocation of funds to the health sector is far short of commitments that have been made. Estimates presented in the National Health Accounts

Table 12 Health outcomes and health expenditures in selected countries

Country	Total health expenditure per capita (USD) – 2011	Total health expenditure as % of GDP – 2011	Government health expenditure as % of total health expenditure 2011	Life expectancy at birth (years) 2012
India	$62	3.9	30.5	66
Thailand	$214	4.1	77.7	75
Sri Lanka	$93	3.3	42.1	75
BRICS countries				
Brazil	$1119	8.9	45.7	74
China	$274	5.1	55.9	75
Russia	$803	6.1	59.8	69
South Africa	$670	8.7	47.7	59
OECD countries				
USA	$8467	17.7	47.8	79
UK	$3659	9.4	82.8	81
Germany	$4996	11.3	76.5	81
France	$4968	11.6	76.8	82
Norway	$9908	9.9	85.1	82
Sweden	$5419	9.5	81.6	82
Denmark	$6521	10.9	85.3	80
Japan	$4656	10	82.1	84

Source National Health Policy 2017

(Table 13) show that government health expenditure was only 29% of total health expenditure in 2014–15, while out-of-pocket expenses were as high as 63%.

The 71st Round of the Governement of India (2014) found that "as high as 86% of rural population and 82% of urban population were still not covered under any scheme of health expenditure support" (see Governement of India 2014 page ii and Table 14).

The Report observes that "the poorer households appear unaware or beyond the reach of such coverage, both in rural and urban areas. Government, however, was able to bring about 12% urban and 13% rural population under health protection coverage through Rashtriya Swasthya Bima Yojana (RSBY) for unorganized workers and those below poverty line, ESI for organized workers, CGHS for government employees and other state levels insurance plans that cover the below poverty line population. Only 12% households of 5th quintile class of urban area had some arrangement of medical insurance from private provider. For all others, this share of private medical insurance is negligible" (Government of India 2014: 46).

However, it is important to note that medical insurance provided by private insurance agencies is not only exorbitant but also provides very limited cover with exemptions for any pre-existing conditions. This leaves individuals who have

Table 13   Key health financing indicators for India across NHA rounds

Sl. No.	Indicator	NHA 2014–15	NHA 2013–14	NHA 2004–05
1	Total health expenditure as per cent of GDP	3.9	4	4.2
2	Total health expenditure per capita (Rs.)	3826	3638	1201
3	Current health expenditures as per cent of total health expenditure	93.4	93	98.9
4	Government health expenditure as a per cent of total health expenditure	29	28.6	22.5
5	Out-of-pocket expenditures (OOPE) as per cent of total health expenditure	62.6	64.2	69.4
6	Social security expenditure on health as per cent of total health expenditure	5.7	6	4.2
7	Private health insurance expenditures as per cent of total health expenditure	3.7	3.4	1.6
8	External/donor funding for health as per cent of total health expenditure	0.7	0.3	2.3
9	Government spending on health as % of GDP	1.15	1.15	
10	Total health expenditure per capita (Rs.)	3826		
11	Per capita government health expenditure (Rs.)	1108		
12	Per capita out-of-pocket expenditures (Rs.)	2394		

Source National Health Accounts Estimates Report 2014–15. Page 11

insurance "uncovered" in the eventuality of being struck by a chronic and expensive disease.

The average medical expenditure for treatment per hospitalization case was estimated to be Rs. 18,268 (Table 15).

4   National Rural Health Mission (NRHM), State of Health Provisioning and Disease Burden[6]

NITI Aayog is the nodal agency for monitoring progress towards achieving the SDGs and for mapping the ministries and departments responsible for achievement of specific targets and indicators. The two-core centre schemes through which

---

[6]With necessary permission, this section draws on Mehta and Pratap (2014a) Policies and Programmes: Analysing ICDS and NRHM to understand what has worked, what has not and why? CPRC IIPA Working Paper 48 and Mehta and Pratap (2014b). Addressing Poverty and Malnutrition: Key Issues for Better Outcomes, Yojana, August.

Table 14 Percentage distribution of persons by coverage of health expenditure support for each quintile class of usual monthly per capita consumption expenditure in 2014

| Quintile class of MPCE | Percentage of persons having coverage of health expenditure support | | | | | |
	Not covered	Government-funded insurance scheme	Empl. (not government) supported health protection	Arranged by % of hh covered by insurance company	Others	All
	Rural					
1	89.1	10.1	0.7	0	0	100
2	88.8	10.7	0.4	0.1	0	100
3	87.4	11.9	0.6	0.1	0	100
4	83.3	15.9	0.5	0.1	0.1	100
5	81.1	17	0.8	0.9	0.2	100
All	85.9	13.1	0.6	0.3	0.1	100
	Urban					
1	91.4	7.7	0.6	0	0.2	100
2	87.5	10.6	1.3	0.5	0.2	100
3	84.7	12.9	1.3	1	0.1	100
4	79.7	13.5	3.3	3.4	0.1	100
5	66.6	15.1	5.6	12.4	0.3	100
All	82	12	2.4	3.5	0.2	100

Source Governement of India (2014)

Table 15 Average total medical expenditure (Rs) for treatment per hospitalization case (EC) during stay at hospital

| Gender | Average total medical expenditure for treatment (Rs) per hospitalization case | | |
	Rural	Urban	All
Male	17,528	28,165	21,223
Female	12,295	20,754	15,292
All	14,935	24,436	18,268

Source Government of India (2014)

SDG3 is to be achieved[7] are National Health Mission (including National Rural Health Mission) and Integrated Child Development Services. Hence, NRHM (and briefly ICDS) is reviewed below to identify some of the key implementation issues that need attention. Many of the identified issues are applicable in the context of improved delivery of other programmes and schemes as well.

---

[7]NITI Aayog (2017). Sustainable Development Goals (SDGs), targets, CSS, interventions, nodal and other ministries. August.

About NRHM: Context and Brief Background[8]

The National Rural Health Mission (2005–12) was launched in 2005 with the vision of providing effective health care to improve the availability of and access to quality health care for all those residing in rural areas, especially the poor, women and children. It has a special focus on 18 states, which have weak public health indicators and/or weak infrastructure so as to address existing interstate and inter-district disparities. These 18 states are Arunachal Pradesh, Assam, Bihar, Chhattisgarh, Himachal Pradesh, Jharkhand, Jammu and Kashmir, Manipur, Mizoram, Meghalaya, Madhya Pradesh, Nagaland, Odisha, Rajasthan, Sikkim, Tripura, Uttarakhand and Uttar Pradesh. It aims to undertake "architectural correction of the health system to promote policies that strengthen public health management and service delivery in the country". It is an articulation of the commitment of the government to raise public spending on health from 0.9% of GDP to 2% to 3% of GDP and was set up in recognition of the massive challenges faced with regard to the state of public health.

Recognizing the linkages between ill health, hospitalization and poverty, the Government of India (2005) or NRHM Mission Document 2005 draws attention to the existence of skewed provisioning with curative services favouring the non-poor: for every Re. 1 spent on the poorest 20% population, Rs. 3 is spent on the richest quintile; health insurance covers only 10% Indians; hospitalized Indians incur an average 58% of their total annual expenditure on health care; over 40% of hospitalized Indians borrow money or sell assets to cover medical expenses; over 25% of hospitalized Indians fall below the poverty line because of hospital related expenses; there are striking regional inequalities.

The Mission Document also draws attention to the decline in public health expenditure in India from 1.3% of GDP in 1990 to 0.9% of GDP in 1999; the impact of lack of community ownership of public health programmes on levels of efficiency, accountability and effectiveness; and the lack of integration of sanitation, hygiene, nutrition and drinking water issues.

The goals of NRHM are reduction in infant mortality rate (IMR) and maternal mortality ratio (MMR); providing universal access to public health services such as women's health, child health, water, sanitation and hygiene; immunization and nutrition; prevention and control of communicable and non-communicable diseases, including locally endemic diseases; providing access to integrated comprehensive primary health care; population stabilization, gender and demographic balance; revitalization of local health traditions and mainstreaming AYUSH; and the promotion of healthy lifestyles.

---

[8]Information regarding NRHM is from the NRHM Mission Document 2005 and the MoHFW website.

Table 16 NRHM: targets and achievement on IMR, MMR and other indicators[a]

Targets to be achieved by 2012 (as per NRHM Mission Document 2005)	Achievements
Infant mortality rate reduced to 30/1000 live births by 2012	58 in 2005 (CBHI 2006) 42 in 2012 (SRS 2013), 46 in rural and 28 in urban 37 in 2015 (SRS 2015) 41 in Rural and 25 in Urban
Maternal mortality ratio reduced to 100/100,000 by 2012	254 in 2004–06 (SRS 2011) 212 in 2007–09 (SRS Bulletin 2011) 167 in 2011–13 (MMR Bulletin 2011–13)
Total fertility rate reduced to 2.1	2.9 in 2005 (SRS 2011) 2.4 in 2012 (PIB website accessed on 12 April 2018) 2.3 in 2015 (SRS 2015)
Malaria mortality reduction rate −50% up to 2010, additional 10% by 2012	1707 deaths due to malaria in 2006; 519 deaths in 2012 and 331 deaths in 2016 (NVBDCP website accessed on 12 April 2018)
Kala-azar mortality reduction rate: 100% by 2010 and sustaining elimination until 2012	187 deaths due to kala-azar in 2006, 203 in 2007, 29 in 2012, 10 in 2013 and 11 deaths in 2014 (Gupta et al. 2015)
Filaria/microfilaria reduction rate: 70% by 2010, 80% by 2012 and elimination by 2015	Average microfilaria rates (%) were 1.02 in 2005, 0.43 in 2012 and 0.44 in 2014 (NVBDCP website accessed on 12 April 2018)
Dengue mortality reduction rate: 50% by 2010 and sustaining at that level until 2012	184 deaths were reported due to dengue in 2006, 110 in 2010, 169 in 2011, 242 in 2012, 39 in 2013, 220 in 2015 and 245 in 2016 Dengue cases reported were 12,561 in 2008, 15,535 in 2009, 28,292 in 2010, 18,860 in 2011, 50,222 in 2012, 11,013 in 2013, 99,913 in 2015 and 129,166 in 2016 (NVBDCP website accessed on 12 April 2018)
Japanese encephalitis mortality reduction rate: 50% by 2010 and sustaining at that level until 2012	663 deaths in 2006, 995 in 2007, 684 in 2008, 779 in 2009, 112 in 2010, 181 in 2011, 140 in 2012, 202 in 2013, 283 in 2016 (NVBDCP website accessed on 12 April 2018)
Cataract operation: increasing to 46 lakh until 2012	5,404,406 in 2007–08, 5,810,336 in 2008–2009, 5,810,684 in 2009–2010, 6,032,724 in 2010–2011, 6,349,205 in 2011–2012, 6,302,894 in 2012–13 and 6,481,435 in 2016–17 (NPCB website accessed on 12 April 2018)
Leprosy prevalence rate: reduce from 1.8/10,000 in 2005 to less than 1/10,000 thereafter	Prevalence rate reported at 1.3 in 2005, 0.68 in 2012 and 0.69 in 2015 (NLEP website accessed on 12 April 2018)

(continued)

Table 16 (continued)

Targets to be achieved by 2012 (as per NRHM Mission Document 2005)	Achievements
Tuberculosis DOTS services: maintain 85% cure rate through entire mission period	86% success rate of new smear-positive patients June 2013. RNTCP has achieved global benchmark of case detection and treatment success. Annually more than 1.5 million TB patients are placed on DOTS treatment under RNTCP. In 2011, RNTCP has achieved the NSP CDR of 71% and treatment success rate of 88% which is in line with the global targets for TB control (TB India 2010, TB India 2012 and India TB Report 2018)
Upgrading community health centres to Indian public health standards	146,026 sub-centres; 23,236 PHCs; and 3346 CHCs in 2005. 148,366 sub-centres; 24,049 PHCs; and 4833 CHCs in 2012 155,069 sub-centres; 25,354 PHCs; and 5510 CHCs on 31 March 2016. (RHS 2015–16 NRHM website accessed on 12 April 2018)
Increase utilization of first referral units from less than 20 to 75%	Number of FRUs has increased significantly from 940 in 2005 to 2641 in June 2013, 2724 in 2016 and 3076 in 2017 (NHM website accessed on 12 April 2018)
Engaging 250,000 female Accredited Social Health Activists (ASHAs) in 10 states	128,855 during 2005–06 and 870,089 ASHAs selected across 31 states and union territories in 2013 (NHM website accessed on 12 April 2018)

Source Government of India (2005) for targets; achievements are based on specific official documents as mentioned in each case

Note [a]Data pertaining to disease burden reported by national agencies such as NVBDCP, NPCB, TB India is for both rural and urban areas

NRHM: National-Level Targets and Achievements

Government of India (NRHM 2005) specifies targets for 14 indicators at the national level. Each of these is listed in Column 1 of Table 16. Progress towards achieving the 14 targets is presented against it, with data sources indicated for each.

While there has been progress towards meeting the targets, there are concerns with regard to achieving many of them.

The shortfall in the case of IMR and MMR remains significant. The NRHM Mission Document 2005 targeted a reduction in total fertility rate to 2.1. While there has been reduction in TFR, the target has still not been achieved due to high fertility in some of the more populous states such as Bihar, Uttar Pradesh, Madhya Pradesh, Jharkhand and Rajasthan.

The worsening of the child sex ratio and sex ratio at birth is alarming. It is no longer limited to a few states and has spread to areas which have no prior history of adverse sex ratios. This highlights both the increasing magnitude and seriousness of the problem (Twelfth Plan Volume 3, pages 165 and 183, Eapen and Mehta 2012).

NRHM: Disease Burden and Disease Control

The communicable and non-communicable disease burdens in India are high. The Twelfth Plan (Volume 3, page 7) draws attention to the fact that "India bears a high proportion of the global burden of TB (21%), leprosy (56%) and lymphatic filariasis (40%)". Further, multi-drug resistance to TB is being increasingly recognized. Six of the major National Disease Control Programmes have been integrated under NRHM. While significant reduction has been achieved on mortality caused by several diseases, there is deterioration in others. Targets and achievements of some of these are discussed below.

National Vector Borne Disease Control Programme (NVBDCP) includes six diseases. These are malaria, filaria, dengue, chikungunya, Japanese encephalitis and kala-azar. Taking note of the increasing incidence of vector-borne diseases, the Twelfth Plan stresses avoidance of mosquito breeding conditions in homes and workplaces and minimizing human–mosquito contact.

The Twelfth Plan goal for **malaria** was annual malaria incidence of <1/1000. While the annual parasite incidence (API) rate has decreased, confirmed deaths due to malaria have fluctuated between 1707 and 519. There were 313 deaths due to malaria in 2016. Reported cases of malaria and Pf are highest in Odisha, Chhattisgarh, Jharkhand and Madhya Pradesh, while deaths caused by malaria and Pf are highest in Maharashtra, Odisha and Meghalaya.

Filaria/microfilaria was to be eliminated by 2015. Reduction is significant from 1.02% in 2005 to 0.43% in 2012. Twenty-one states/UTs and 256 districts are endemic for lymphatic filariasis. Five states (Assam, Tamil Nadu, Goa, Puducherry, and Daman and Diu) have stopped mass drug administration after achieving elimination status and are observing post-MDA surveillance activities. Ninety-seven districts have cleared the first transmission assessment survey and stopped mass drug administration, while 27 districts have cleared the first and second assessment. Mass drug administration is proposed in 143 districts as of January 2018 (NVBDCP website 14 April 2018).

The number of **dengue** cases reported increased massively from 12,561 in 2008 to 99,913 in 2015 and 129,166 in 2016. While deaths due to dengue have fluctuated, 184 deaths were reported in 2006, 242 in 2012, 39 in 2013, 220 in 2015 and 245 in 2016, and there is a huge rise in reported cases of dengue. Suspected cases of chikungunya increased significantly in 2008 and 2009. The target for Japanese encephalitis mortality reduction rate was 50% by 2010 and was to be sustained at that level until 2012. There were 663 deaths due to JE in 2006 and 112 in 2010. However, there was an increase to 181 deaths in 2011 fluctuating thereafter from 140 in 2012 to 291 in 2015 and 283 in 2016. Suspected cases of JE increased from 555 in 2010 to 1214 in 2011 fluctuating thereafter and reaching 1676 in 2016.

Public health measures have been launched against this disease such as strengthened surveillance through sentinel laboratories and JE vaccination for all children between 1 and 15 years of age, in high prevalence districts. With the rise in suspected cases and the high proportion of case fatality, the containment and elimination of JE need urgent attention.

The target for **kala-azar** requires a mortality reduction rate of 100% by 2010 with sustained subsequent elimination. Fatality has decreased to 11 cases in 2014.

While improvement has occurred, concerted efforts are needed in the worst affected blocks if elimination is to be achieved.

Leprosy

The leprosy prevalence rate reported by NLEP is 0.68/10,000 in 2012 and 0.69/10,000 in 2015. Government of India (2017) mentions that though leprosy is significantly reduced it is "stagnant at current levels of new infective cases and disabilities" (ibid.: 6).

Since elimination of leprosy is declared at a rate of less of 1 case per 10,000 population, elimination was achieved at the national level. However, active case detection reveals that there are a large number of previously undetected leprosy cases in the population (Katoch et al. 2017 and Kumar and Husain 2013). The findings of Katoch et al. (2017) need special attention since they are based on a nationwide survey that detected 2,161 new cases of leprosy out of a population of 14,725,525 (10,302,443 rural; 4,423,082 urban) that was screened. In other words, **just the new cases** of leprosy that were detected are 1.47/10,000 population. This has important implications for policy as depending on self-reporting will not enable either elimination or eradication.

Cataract Operations

The target for cataract operations was to increase these to 46 lakhs per year until 2012. The number of cataract operations performed was 64.8 lakh in 2016–17.

Tuberculosis

The Revised National TB Control Programme (RNTCP), based on the internationally recommended directly observed treatment short-course (DOTS) strategy, was launched in 1997 and then expanded across the country. The programme seeks to achieve and maintain a cure rate of at least 85% among new sputum positive (NSP) patients and a case detection of at least 70% of the estimated NSP cases in the community. RNTCP achieved these targets in 2007 and is maintaining them since then. Challenges due to persistence of TB transmission and multi-drug-resistant tuberculosis need to be addressed (Government of India 2017).

Government of India (2015) draws attention to the slower pace of reduction in mortality due to tuberculosis and measles in India compared with neighbouring countries. The decline in mortality due to TB was 43.6% in India relative to 63.1% in China, while the decline in mortality due to measles was only 58.5% in India relative to 87.3% in Bangladesh and 81.4% in China (Table 17).

State of Health Provisioning: Rural Infrastructure

As per norms, there should be one sub-centre for 3000–5000 people, one Primary Health Centre (PHC) for 20,000–30,000 people and one Community Health Centre (CHC) for 80,000–120,000 people. Tables 18 and 19 show that despite a 6%

Table 17 Mortality rates due to tuberculosis and measles in India, China and Bangladesh

	Tuberculosis			Measles		
	2000[a]	2012[a]	% decline	2000[a]	2012[a]	% decline
India	38.7	21.8	43.6	8.2	3.4	58.5
China	8.6	3.2	63.1	0.3	0.06	81.4
Bangladesh	56.8	44.9	21.0	10.2	1.3	87.3

[a]Mortality rate per 100,000
Source Government of India (2015) NITI Aayog Working Paper

Table 18 Coverage of rural health infrastructure (as on 31 March 2016)

	Norm (population per facility)	Status (2016)
Sub-centre	3000–5000	5377
Primary Health Centre (PHC)	20,000–30,000	32,884
Community Health Centre (CHC)	80,000–120,000	151,316

Source Government of India, Ministry of Health & Family Welfare (2008), p. v

Table 19 Number of sub-centre, PHCs and CHCs functioning in India

Year	Sub-centre	PHCs	CHCs
2005	146,026	23,236	3346
2012	148,366	24,049	4833
2016	155,069	25,354	5510

Source Government of India, Ministry of Health & Family Welfare (2008)

increase in the number of sub-centres, 9% increase in PHCs and 65% increase in CHCs, there is a shortfall on each of these relative to norms.

While one sub-centre covers less than 4,000 people in rural Gujarat, Kerala, Chhattisgarh and Rajasthan, it covers almost 9,500 people in rural Bihar and 7,500 people in rural Uttar Pradesh. Similarly, while there is one PHC for between 21,000 and 27,000 people in Andhra Pradesh, Telangana, Tamil Nadu, Karnataka, Gujarat, Kerala, Chhattisgarh and Rajasthan, a PHC covers thrice as many people at 76,621 people in Jharkhand and 68,408 in West Bengal (Government of India, Ministry of Health & Family Welfare 2008).

One area in which improvement needs to be noted is that between 2005 and 2012, the percentage of sub-centres, PHCs and CHCs functioning in government buildings in rural areas increased from 50% to 64.4%, 78% to 90.2% and 91.6% to 97%, respectively (Rural Health Statistics 2012: ix and x).

Despite a 55.8% increase in the number of ANMs at sub-centres and PHCs and a 42.7% increase in the number of allopathic doctors at PHCs during the period 2005–2012 (Rural Health Statistics 2012: ix and x), the shortfall in medical personnel remains significant. Not only are there vacant positions of health workers/ANMs and of doctors and specialists, but more than 8,963 sub-centres in rural areas do not have a female health worker/ANM, 73,849 do not have a male health worker and 5,258 do not have either of them. Vacancies are especially high in Rajasthan, Uttar Pradesh and Gujarat (Tables 20 and 21).

Table 20 Doctors at PHCs

Year	In position	Vacant	Shortfall
2005	20,308	4282	1004
2012	28,984	6493	2489
2016	26,464	8774	3244

Source Government of India, Ministry of Health & Family Welfare (2008)

A study conducted by MoHFW, World Bank and NITI Aayog also draws attention to the massive shortfall in availability of medical officers at Primary Health Centres (PHCs), staff nurses (SNs) at PHCs and Community Health Centres (CHCs) and Auxiliary Nurse Midwife (ANMs) at health sub-centres (MoHFW 2018). Table 22 shows that vacant posts of medical officers were especially high in PHCs in Bihar (63.6%), Madhya Pradesh (57.81%), West Bengal (48.43%), Jharkhand (45.29%) and Chhattisgarh (41.83%) in 2014–15. Vacancies of SNs at PHCs and CHCs were more than 86% in Bihar, 70% in Jharkhand and 48% in Rajasthan in this year. Bihar had the highest vacancies of ANMs in sub-centres (67.86%). It is important to note that there was no vacancy of either ANMs or SNs in Odisha. Between the base year 2014–15 and the reference year 2015–16, while a large number of vacancies of ANMs in SCs were filled in Rajasthan, Uttar Pradesh and Bihar, there was an increase in vacancies of ANMs at the SCs level in Gujarat by 10.95%, Haryana 5.57%, Madhya Pradesh 5.65%, Tamil Nadu 4.15%. Maximum vacancies of SNs at PHCs and CHCs level were filled in Bihar (35.87%) and Karnataka (19.23%). There was no change in percentage of SNs appointed between the base year and the reference year in Odisha, Telangana and Uttar Pradesh.

Uttarakhand and Haryana are the two states where the appointment of medical officers at PHCs level was as high as 24.97 and 13.29% between the base and reference year. There were a high number of vacancies of specialists in district hospitals. This was highest in Chhattisgarh (77.68%), Bihar (60.58%), Uttarakhand (60.33%), Gujarat (55.5%), Telangana (54.81%), Madhya Pradesh (50.98%) and Jharkhand (50.32%).

An existing facility (district hospital, Sub-divisional Hospital, Community Health Centre, etc.) can be declared a fully operational first referral unit (FRU) only if it is equipped to provide emergency obstetric care including surgical interventions like caesarean sections; newborn care; and blood storage facility on a 24 hour basis. At present, there are 3,076 FRUs functioning in the country. Out of these total 94.2% of the FRUs are having operation theatre facilities, 96.3% of the FRUs are having functional labour room, while 68.9% of the FRUs are having blood storage/linkage facility.

Table 23 shows that the percentage of functional first referral units (FRUs) was extremely low in Bihar (12.5%) and Uttar Pradesh (15.25%). Less than 6% of 24 × 7 PHCs were functional in West Bengal and Himachal Pradesh. Only 3% of districts in Odisha and Rajasthan, 4% in Chhattisgarh and 10% in Madhya Pradesh had functional CCUs in 2014–15. Further, Assam, Bihar, Jharkhand, Telangana,

Table 21 Number of sub-centres without ANMs or health workers (as on 31 March 2016)

State/UT	Sub-centres functioning	Without HW[F]/ ANMs	Without HW [M]	Without both
Andhra Pradesh	7659	0	3734	70
Arunachal Pradesh	304	284	166	90
Assam	4621	0	1621	39
Bihar	9729	354	3325	323
Chhattisgarh	5186	524	1336	141
Goa	212	0	13	0
Gujarat	8801	1903	1830	1123
Haryana	2576	30	1172	29
Himachal Pradesh	2071	214	1129	121
Jammu and Kashmir	2805	0	1531	0
Jharkhand	3953	60	2839	39
Karnataka	9332	717	2574	638
Kerala	4575	0	0	0
Madhya Pradesh	9192	0	5434	0
Maharashtra	10,580	393	2471	140
Manipur	421	29	89	12
Meghalaya	431	2	145	1
Mizoram	370	0	58	0
Nagaland	396	3	396	0
Odisha	6688	253	3246	115
Punjab	2951	138	1200	100
Rajasthan	14,408	2161	10,917	1754
Sikkim	147	8	15	2
Tamil Nadu	8712	1391	1722	374
Telangana	4863	0	3407	0
Tripura	1033	298	187	0
Uttarakhand	1847	176	1304	122
Uttar Pradesh	20,521	0	14,291	0
West Bengal	10,369	25	7517	25
A & N Islands	123	0	74	0
Chandigarh	17	0	16	0
D & N Haveli	56	0	2	0
Daman and Diu	26	0	8	0
Delhi	26	0	26	0
Lakshadweep	14	0	0	0
Puducherry	54	0	54	0
All India/total	155,069	8963	73,849	5258

Source Government of India, Ministry of Health & Family Welfare (2008)

Table 22 Vacancies of medical officers and staff

States	Vacancy: ANMs at SCs (%)		Vacancy: SNs at PHCs and CHCs (%)		Vacancy: MOs at PHCs (%)		Vacancy: Specialists at DHs (%)	
	BY	RY	BY	RY	BY	RY	BY	RY
Andhra Pradesh	20.56	15.67	17.33	20.48	17.97	12.76	40.55	30.41
Assam	10.93	8.99	4.57	8.95	19.92	17.77	62.91	41.72
Bihar	67.86	59.3	86.15	50.28	63.6	63.6	64.96	60.58
Chhattisgarh	12.35	9.23	44.27	37.28	41.83	45.02	77.98	77.68
Gujarat	17.13	28.08	37.71	36.46	39.78	32.03	51.02	55.5
Haryana	9.66	15.23	45.95	43.24	38.64	25.35	0	0
Himachal Pradesh	12.57	9.87	21.51	27.19	16.19	21.73	NA	NA
Jammu and Kashmir	17.65	10.28	42.88	27.48	34.92	30.15	24.52	22.22
Jharkhand	19.57	19.73	71.8	74.94	45.29	48.67	55.37	50.32
Karnataka	27.85	22.59	45.2	25.97	13.35	11.48	20.9	21.53
Kerala	4.88	4.49	5.54	5.3	5.59	5.86	22.15	21.48
Madhya Pradesh	8.58	14.23	36.45	33.5	57.81	58.34	50.56	50.98
Maharashtra	8.25	9.46	16.74	15.67	16.82	16.96	19.47	30.34
Odisha	0	0	0	0	23.17	26.91	43.53	19.04
Punjab	7.17	8.48	36.22	33.98	9.83	7.77	21.74	47.72
Rajasthan	36.12	19.24	48.12	47.26	14.93	14.86	41.47	45.77
Tamil Nadu	11.82	15.97	21.78	19.09	7.56	7.58	17.86	16.73
Telangana	20.2	18.01	12.79	12.79	22.31	22.31	59.83	54.81

(continued)

Table 22 (continued)

States	Vacancy: ANMs at SCs (%)		Vacancy: SNs at PHCs and CHCs (%)		Vacancy: MOs at PHCs (%)		Vacancy: Specialists at DHs (%)	
	BY	RY	BY	RY	BY	RY	BY	RY
Uttar Pradesh	14.06	0	1.89	1.89	36.83	26.73	35.74	32.41
Uttarakhand	15.47	16.88	13.11	20.02	37.16	12.19	38.3	60.33
West Bengal	2.16	0.77	25.72	9.7	48.43	41.23	22.97	20.18

Source Ministry of Health and Family Welfare, World Bank and NITI Aayog. Healthy States Progressive India (2018)

Table 23 Functional FRUs, 24 × 7 PHCs and CCUs

States	Functional FRUs (%)	Functional FRUs (%)	Functional 24 × 7 PHCs (%)	Functional 24 × 7 PHCs (%)	Districts with functional CCUs (%)	Districts with functional CCUs (%)
	BY	RY	BY	RY	BY	RY
Andhra Pradesh	48.48	57.58	33.2	29.15	53.85	53.85
Assam	67.74	72.58	169.55	176.92	0	0
Bihar	12.5	11.54	70.89	73.58	0	0
Chhattisgarh	21.57	23.53	36.47	40.39	3.7	3.7
Gujarat	32.23	42.98	27.81	31.46	57.69	48.48
Haryana	52.94	50.98	73.62	77.56	19.05	19.05
Himachal Pradesh	107.14	121.43	5.8	5.8	91.67	91.67
Jammu and Kashmir	180	196	53.6	45.6	18.18	27.27
Jharkhand	15.15	22.73	33.03	33.03	0	0
Karnataka	105.74	116.39	78.07	69.23	43.33	43.33
Kerala	120.9	120.9	0	0	64.29	64.29
Madhya Pradesh	44.83	49.66	58.4	56.47	9.8	9.8
Maharashtra	31.11	32.44	48.04	46.71	22.86	22.86
Odisha	61.9	65.48	30	30	3.33	3.33
Punjab	138.18	141.82	35.74	26.35	63.64	63.64
Rajasthan	23.36	29.2	67.3	68.03	2.94	70.59
Tamil Nadu	129.17	122.92	54.23	34.95	56.25	56.25
Telangana	80	80	26.99	26.99	0	0
Uttar Pradesh	15.25	15.75	17.92	17.42	0	0
Uttarakhand	100	95	56.44	54.46	0	0
West Bengal	45.36	49.18	5.7	5.91	76.92	76.92

Source Ministry of Health and Family Welfare, World Bank and NITI Aayog. Healthy States Progressive India (2018)

Uttar Pradesh and Uttarakhand did not have any districts with functional CCUs. While there was a massive improvement in Rajasthan with 71% districts reporting functional CCUs, there was no change in any of the other nine states.

NRHM led to improved implementation of processes as can be seen from NFHS 3 and NFHS 4 estimates regarding a significant increase in the proportion of mothers who had the requisite check-ups, mother and child protection card, etc. (Table 24). Indicators pertaining to institutional births and immunization of children show a significant improvement (Tables 25 and 26).

Table 24 Maternal and child health

Indicators	NFHS-3	NFHS-4		
	2005-06	2015-16		
	Total	Urban	Rural	Total
Maternity care (for last birth in the 5 years before the survey)				
Mothers who had antenatal check-up in the first trimester (%)	43.9	69.1	54.2	58.6
Mothers who had at least four antenatal care visits (%)	37.0	66.4	44.8	51.2
Mothers whose last birth was protected against neonatal tetanus (%)	76.3	89.9	88.6	89.0
Mothers who consumed iron-folic acid for 100 days or more when they were pregnant (%)	15.2	40.8	25.9	30.3
Mothers who had full antenatal care (%)	11.6	31.1	16.7	21.0
Registered pregnancies for which the mother received mother and child protection (MCP) card (%)	na	87.7	90.0	89.3
Mothers who received post-natal care from a doctor/nurse/LHV/ANM/midwife/other health personnel within 2 days of delivery (%)	34.6	71.7	58.5	62.4
Mothers who received financial assistance under Janani Suraksha Yojana (JSY) for births delivered in an institution (%)	na	21.4	43.8	36.4
Average out-of-pocket expenditure per delivery in public health facility (Rs.)	na	3913.0	2947.0	3198.0
Children born at home who were taken to a health facility for check-up within 24 h of birth (%)	0.3	3.2	2.4	2.5
Children who received a health check after birth from a doctor/nurse/LHV/ANM/midwife/other health personnel within 2 days of birth (%)	na	27.2	23.0	24.3

Source NFHS4

Table 25 Delivery care (for births in the 5 years before the survey)

Indicators	NFHS-3	NFHS-4		
	2005–06	2015–16		
	Total	Urban	Rural	Total
Institutional births (%)	38.7	88.7	75.1	78.9
Institutional births in public facility (%)	18.0	46.2	54.4	52.1
Home delivery conducted by skilled health personnel (out of total deliveries) (%)	8.2	3.0	4.9	4.3

Source NFHS4

Table 26 Immunization

Indicators	NFHS-3	NFHS-4		
	2005–06	2015–16		
	Total	Urban	Rural	Total
Children age 12–23 months fully immunized (BCG, measles, and three doses each of polio and DPT) (%)	43.5	63.9	61.3	62.0
Children age 12–23 months who have received BCG (%)	78.2	93.2	91.4	91.9
Children age 12–23 months who have received three doses of polio vaccine (%)	78.2	73.4	72.6	72.8
Children age 12–23 months who have received three doses of DPT vaccine (%)	55.3	80.2	77.7	78.4
Children age 12–23 months who have received measles vaccine (%)	58.8	83.2	80.3	81.1
Children age 12–23 months who have received three doses of Hepatitis B vaccine (%)	na	63.3	62.5	62.8
Children age 9–59 months who received a vitamin A dose in last 6 months (%)	16.5	62.9	59.1	60.2
Children age 12–23 months who received most of the vaccinations in public health facility (%)	82.0	82.1	94.2	90.7
Children age 12–23 months who received most of the vaccinations in private health facility (%)	10.5	16.7	3.4	7.2

Source NFHS4

However, the programme focus is on maternal and child health or as the Government of India (2017: 7) notes

"much of the increase in service delivery was related to select reproductive and child health services and the national disease control programme." Further, NRHM was "intended to strengthen State health systems to cover all health needs. The progress however remained confined to a few indicators only, like mortality and disease prevalence. Such selective focus and facility development is clearly not efficient. Strengthening health systems for providing comprehensive care requires higher levels of investment and human resources, than were made available. The budgetary support and the expenditure was only about 40% of what was envisaged for a fully revitalised NRHM Framework."

Given the state of public provisioning, shortfall in medical personnel and health infrastructure, it is not surprising that there is high dependence on private hospitals with 68% of those hospitalized in urban areas and 58% in rural areas getting treatment in private facilities. While dependence on public hospitals is high in Assam, Bihar, MP, Odisha, Rajasthan, West Bengal, rural Telangana, rural Chhattisgarh, urban Kerala and urban Punjab, dependence on private hospitals is high in Andhra Pradesh, Gujarat, Karnataka, Maharashtra, Tamil Nadu, rural Punjab, rural Uttar Pradesh, urban Haryana and urban Jharkhand (Table 27).

184

A. K. Mehta and S. Pratap

Table 27 Percentage distribution of cases of hospitalized treatment received from public sector and private sector hospitals for rural and urban areas

State	% of persons hospitalized in			
	Private hospital		Public hospital	
	Rural	Urban	Rural	Urban
Andhra Pradesh	77.5	78.2	22.5	21.8
Assam	10.8	48.5	89.2	51.5
Bihar	57.4	61.2	42.6	38.8
Chhattisgarh	50.6	70.6	49.4	29.4
Gujarat	76.6	76.7	23.4	23.3
Haryana	66.7	81.7	33.3	18.3
Jharkhand	60.4	73.6	39.6	26.4
Karnataka	73.2	81.7	26.8	18.3
Kerala	65.3	66.7	34.7	33.3
Madhya Pradesh	46.5	58.3	53.5	41.7
Maharashtra	80.8	80	19.2	20
Odisha	18.7	42	81.3	58
Punjab	70.7	69.8	29.3	30.2
Rajasthan	45.8	45.6	54.2	54.2
Telangana	59.6	70.7	40.4	29.3
Tamil Nadu	71.4	78.8	28.6	21.2
Uttar Pradesh	69.8	71.7	30.2	28.3
West Bengal	22.8	47.4	77.2	52.6
All	58.1	68	41.9	32

Source Government of India (2014)

About ICDS: A Brief Background[9]

ICDS is one of the world's largest outreach programmes for early childhood care and development. It was launched on 2 October 1975. It is centrally sponsored and implemented through all 36 state governments and UTs. Care and health services are provided in an integrated manner at the grass-roots level through *Anganwadis*. The Anganwadi Centre (AWC) or village courtyard is the main platform for delivering ICDS. The programme reaches out to children below 6 years and to expectant and nursing mothers and now to young adolescent girls as well. The objectives of ICDS are to improve the nutritional and health status of children below the age of six; lay the foundation for proper psychological, physical and social development; reduce incidence of mortality, morbidity, malnutrition and school dropout; achieve effective coordination of policy and implementation among various departments to promote child development; and enhance the capability of mothers to address the normal health and nutritional needs of children, through proper health and nutrition education to lactating and nursing mothers aged 15–45 years.

[9]This section uses information available on the MWCD website http://wcd.nic.in/icds/icds.aspx.

The above objectives are achieved through a package of interdependent services comprising supplementary nutrition, immunization, health check-up, referral services, preschool non-formal education and nutrition and health education. Three of the six services, namely immunization, health check-up and referral services, are delivered through public health infrastructure under the Ministry of Health and Family Welfare with the support of the *Anganwadi* worker who assists the Auxiliary Nurse Midwife in identifying the target group. Supplementary nutrition includes supplementary feeding and growth monitoring, and prophylaxis against vitamin A deficiency and control of nutritional anaemia. All families in the community are surveyed to identify children below the age of six and pregnant and nursing mothers. They avail of supplementary feeding support for 300 days in a year. Children below the age of 3 years of age are weighed once a month, and children 3-6 years of age are weighed quarterly. Weight-for-age growth cards are maintained for all children below 6 years. This helps to detect growth faltering and helps in assessing nutritional status. Severely malnourished children are given special supplementary feeding and referred to medical services.

The ICSD team comprises the *Anganwadi* worker, *Anganwadi* helpers, supervisors, Child Development Project Officers (CDPOs) and District Programme Officers (DPOs). The Anganwadi worker is selected from the local community and is a community-based frontline honorary worker of the ICDS programme. The medical officers, Auxiliary Nurse Midwife (ANM) and Accredited Social Health Activist (ASHA) form a team with the ICDS functionaries to achieve convergence of different services.

Most children going to *Anganwadis* belong to BPL families and relatively vulnerable sections of the population. However, in view of the high levels of malnutrition among children in India, and especially among children belonging to poor families, in 2001, the Supreme Court ordered that ICDS is "geographically universalized"; that is, there must be an *Anganwadi* in every habitation. Every child under six, adolescent girl, pregnant woman and lactating mother are entitled to supplementary nutrition under ICDS.

The ICDS administrative unit is the community development block in rural areas, the tribal block in tribal areas and the ward or slum in urban areas. The existing norm of 1 lakh population for sanction of urban project continues. However, the population norms for setting up an *Anganwadi* centre and mini-centre have been lowered in an effort to increase reach. In rural and urban areas, the norm is now one AWC for a population size of 400–800 and a mini-AWC for 150–400 persons. In tribal/riverine/desert, hilly and other difficult areas, the norm is lower with one AWC for a population size of 300–800 persons and a mini-AWC for 150–300 persons.

Information regarding coverage by ICDS[10] shows that as on 31 March 2015, 7072 projects and 1,346,186 AWCs were operational across 36 states/UTs,

---

[10]http://icds-wcd.nic.in/icds.aspx.

covering 1022.33 lakh beneficiaries under supplementary nutrition and 365.44 lakh 3–6 years children under preschool component. The programme has recently been revamped and strengthened.

Malnutrition is caused by a large number of factors that include weak public health measures; lack of access to medical attention due to non-availability of health services, such as access to doctors, medical staff and medicines due to non-functioning or distant sub-centres, PHCs and CHCs; lack of immunization, ante- and post-natal care and emergency care; low levels of institutional delivery; ill health due to high disease load due to infections such as diarrhoea, dysentery, fever and malaria; lack of access to food, nutrition and health education; early marriage and pregnancy, non-spacing/anaemia among women, low birth weight babies; poor cultural practices regarding feeding of colostrum, breast and complementary feeding, poor quality of water; poor sanitation, migration and mothers having to go for work leaving children at home.[11] While recognizing that several interventions are required to address malnutrition, it is important to point out that both Integrated Child Development Services (ICDS) and NRHM have a critical role in addressing malnutrition.

5 Implementing Programmes for Better Outcomes[12]

How can better health and nutrition outcomes be achieved through NRHM and ICDS? What are the lessons that can be drawn from the implementation of these two major programmes that try to address critical dimensions of poverty? What can be learnt from their successes and failures?

What works, what does not work and why?

Spatial mapping: Spatial mapping works as it can be used to identify where facilities are located and where shortfalls exist. Based on this, corrective follow up action can be taken. Spatial mapping of facilities is important not just at the level of the district or block but also within each village. How many AWCs should there be in a village or slum based on population norms? If the number of existing AWCs is below this norm, new AWCs should be set up on priority in the poorest areas of each village or slum.

For instance, if a village with a population of 5,000 has only 2 Anganwadi Centres (AWCs), then there is a shortfall of AWCs in the village as per norms. Two

---

[11]This is based on a presentation made by Dr. N. C. Saxena at a UN Women-IIPA workshop held at IIPA on 29 February 2012. Some of these important issues are highlighted in Chap. 4 in this book.

[12]With necessary permission, this section draws on Mehta and Pratap (2014a) Policies and Programmes: Analysing ICDS and NRHM to understand what has worked, what has not and why? CPRC IIPA Working Paper 48 and Mehta and Pratap (2014b). Addressing Poverty and Malnutrition: Key Issues for Better Outcomes, Yojana, August. It also builds on Mehta et al. (2012).

issues need attention: (a) why does the village have one-third the AWCs that it should have as per norms and (b) where are the two AWCs located and what determined the choice regarding location?

While interviewing women and men in different households in Bisalpur village near Jodhpur, it was found that the children of the more deprived households of the village were not being sent to the AWCs as they were located too far away. Both the AWCs were located in the richer part of the village, near the houses of those who were influential. The village could have had four additional AWCs, and if these were located in the poorer areas of the village, this would have enabled access for children of vulnerable households.

Similarly, spatial mapping is very useful for determining where health facilities are located and what gaps in provisioning need to be bridged. If a health sub-centre should be provided for a population of 3000–5000, a PHC for population size of 20,000–30,000 and a CHC for a population size of 80,000–120,000 shortfalls based on these norms should be corrected.

High burden or worst affected blocks and panchayats: Concentrating resources and efforts in high-burden pockets in each panchayat, block and district is important. Unless concerted efforts are made to improve performance in the worst affected blocks, it will be difficult to achieve targets with regard to either reduction in malnutrition or elimination or control of specific diseases.

For instance, reduction in prevalence rate of several diseases may have been achieved at the national level. However, this has not been achieved in all blocks. Increased emergence of multi drug resistant tuberculosis in India is cause for serious concern. Areas that are especially vulnerable need to be identified and effective strategies for prevention, treatment and cure must be implemented urgently.

The boat clinic in Assam and Kerala is an innovative response to meeting the health needs of the people living in geographically isolated inaccessible areas (Government of Assam, undated). Mobile Medical Units can be used effectively to rapidly deliver healthcare services to areas that are remote. However, it must be ensured that availability of MMUs is primarily where the need is greatest and that they are used for the intended purpose.

Include the poorest households while taking decisions

Mechanisms are needed for ensuring that women from the poorest households in the village are included while taking decisions regarding functioning of the AWCs, health sub-centres, PHCs, timings, etc., as well as while reviewing the functioning of these facilities and schemes.

Infrastructure: Poor infrastructure or location of Anganwadi Centres and health sub-centres in dilapidated spaces that do not have toilets or water or are located near dirty drains does not work. Lack of clean surroundings, toys, play kits, weighing scales and charts affects the demand for AWC services (Mehta and Ali 2008). Efforts are underway to rectify this by re-positioning AWCs as places of "joyful learning" and locate AWCs in government schools and permanent structures with improved facilities and infrastructure (Twelfth Five-Year Plan, Volume III: 190). This is important for AWC services to be demand led rather than supply driven.

If NRHM and ICDS centres that are delivering such critical services cannot be housed in permanent structures and clean surroundings, adequate allocations for rent must be provided. As noted above, a large proportion of sub-centres, PHCs and CHCs are now housed in government buildings. Priority in resource allocation should be for making sub-centres and PHCs functional in high-burden districts and blocks as problems of inadequate availability of healthcare services and shortfall of doctors, nurses and staff are "exacerbated" by a wide geographical variation in availability across the country. Lack of public health services leads to out-of-pocket expenditures and high financial burden in case of ill health. Shortfalls in essential infrastructure and drugs need to be corrected. No individual should fail to secure adequate medical care because of inability to pay. The state must take responsibility for access to quality health care (preventive, promotive and curative) for all, with special responsibility for vulnerable groups.

Workload, motivation and training: The motivation and commitment of staff are critical to the success of both NRHM and ICDS. Vacant posts need to be filled, workload rationalized, supportive supervision provided and issues of vulnerability and exploitation addressed. Burdening functionaries with non-programme-related tasks and participation in non-NRHM or ICDS events takes time away from the primary duties of the functionaries.

Persistent shortage of service providers such as doctors, nurses, health workers, Auxiliary Nurse Midwife (ANMs) and severe shortage of specialist doctors at Community Health Centres (CHCs) need attention.

The ICDS programme assumes that each supervisor will be able to monitor the functioning of 20 to 25 AWCs, scattered over a large geographical area. Expecting that supervisors will regularly visit far-flung AWCs located in areas with little or no public transport is a design flaw that leads to failure to achieve requisite outcomes in malnutrition reduction. Where AWCs are located in remote areas with poor connectivity, safety concerns of supervisors must be addressed and transport arrangements made. The number of AWCs to be monitored by a supervisor must be reduced significantly for successful implementation.

Regular training and upgradation of skills of ICDS and NRHM staff are important.

Voluntary work and poor payments: So-called voluntary workers – whether AWW, AWH or Accredited Social Health Activist (ASHA) worker – are the pivot on which effective delivery of the ICDS and NRHM depends. They are paid an honorarium and lack job security. In the interest of better delivery of the ICDS as well as gender justice, long-standing unmet demands for secure work for those appointed as AWWs, AWHs and ASHA workers must be met.

Outreach: Assuming that once an AWC or PHC exists, people will automatically use the facility, does not work. Efforts at reaching out to the target population make a difference. Malnutrition decreased significantly in Odisha and Chhattisgarh through the Mitanins chosen by the local community and trained and supported by a block training team, the Auxiliary Nurse Midwife and the AWW. "What has worked in the Mitanin model has been its outreach – rather than a centre-based approach which helped provide services at the doorstep of all rural families of the state" (Saxena and Srivastava 2009).

Early detection of tuberculosis or leprosy or malnutrition cannot wait for the disease to manifest itself. Door to door outreach, campaigns and surveys are needed for prevention, early detection and treatment.

Community ownership, PRIs and PPP: The Bachpan model implemented by the Naandi Foundation to strengthen ICDS in Ratlam district in Madhya Pradesh used a five-pronged strategy to significantly reduce malnutrition. This includes raising community awareness to create demand for ICDS services; initiation of community-based monitoring mechanisms such as the formation of *Ekta Samuha* comprising elected panchayat members, village-level government service providers and citizens as well as development of user-friendly community monitoring tools for collecting, collating and analysing data; building convergence between government departments and PRIs in planning and service delivery through establishment of district, block and cluster-level forums for collectively identifying gaps in services; forums for interface among CBO representative, PRIs and service providers; and promoting a cadre of change agents at the village level (*Gram Mitra*) and felicitation of the best performing *Gram Mitras*, Anganwadi workers, ANMs, supervisors and communities.[13]

Similarly, the constitution of *jaanch* (enquiry) committees for local (village)-level monitoring of ICDS in Odisha as well as decentralized purchase of grains and preparation of meals by village communities, self-help groups and *Mahila Mandals* has led to greater ownership of the ICDS and improved outcomes.[14]

Budgets: Inadequate budgets and lack of timely fund flow constrain performance. Delays occur in the flow of funds from the centre to the states for several reasons that include the need to furnish budgetary proposals and provide utilization certificates. If states are unable to contribute their share of funds, this leads to problems in utilizing centre grants.

The malnutrition and the communicable and non-communicable disease burdens in India are high. Juxtaposed against this high disease burden is low public sector provisioning for health and unfulfilled commitments regarding providing access to care. Public expenditure on health care in India is among the lowest in the world, both as a proportion of total expenditure on health care and as a percentage of

---

[13]This is based on a presentation made by Shri Sushanta Kumar at a UN Women-IIPA workshop held at IIPA on 29 February 2012.

[14]This is based on a presentation made by Shri Rajkishor at a UN Women-IIPA workshop held at IIPA on 29 February 2012.

GDP. The budget for health has to increase significantly for delivery of equitable health care of a high-quality. NRHM was set up to undertake "architectural correction" of the health system to strengthen public health service delivery as well as articulate the commitment of the government to raise public spending on health from 0.9% of GDP to 2–3% of GDP (NRHM Mission Document 2005–2012). However, allocation of funds to the health sector is far short of these commitments. Allocations for clean drinking water, sanitation, etc., are being included to create a "broad" definition of health sector-related resources so as to seem to fulfil these commitments. This must be stopped.

Unmet targets and skewed priorities: Targets set for reduction in malnutrition, IMR, MMR have not been achieved. The malnutrition burden and disease burden remain high despite ICDS and NRHM. Several diseases are not included in NRHM. Data shows that reported morbidity is higher among women than men. Differentials in morbidity and mortality and differential access to treatment and care for women are a cause for concern. However, disease-wise information is sporadic.

NRHM is overwhelmingly directed towards institutional delivery and maternal health. While reducing maternal mortality and providing reproductive health care are important, the focus of health provisioning for women has to be on planning for women's survival and health throughout the life cycle. This requires that data on disease burden and health-seeking behaviour must be presented separately for males and females. Strategies are needed for identification of specific barriers to access to health care and removal of these constraints.

Accurate data: There are massive gaps between data reported from the field through the government system and data that is generated through independent evaluations. Therefore, systems must be established for regular verification of the data reported from the field. This is applicable to malnutrition as well as to mortality and morbidity.

Death reviews: Learning from infant, maternal and other death reviews and audits must be followed by rapid corrective action and dissemination (Mehta and Pratap 2014a, b: 83).

Training: Training given to ASHA workers in Odisha in malaria control in high endemic blocks works as it enables them to identify cases, facilitate referral of the cases to the fever treatment depots (FTDs) and thereby contribute to progress in malaria control. However, poor availability of rapid diagnostic test kits, etc., led to an unnecessarily high referral rate and potential delays in the treatment (6th Common Review Mission 2012).

Convergence: Malnutrition, mortality and morbidity are a function of a large number of variables that include food and nutrition, access to preventive, promotive and curative health care, nutrition counselling, safe water and sanitation. Convergence within and across programmes and schemes implemented by ministries and departments such as health, education, WCD, rural development and water and sanitation is needed.

References

Das Gupta, R. K., Dhariwal, A. C., Roy, N., & Gupta, A. (2015). Kala-azar: Roadmap for elimination. *Journal of the Indian Medical Association, 113*(12). Available at http://www.nvbdcp.gov.in/Doc/jima_december2015.pdf. Accessed on April 12, 2018.

Eapen, M., & Mehta, A. K. (2012). Gendering the twelfth plan: A feminist perspective. *Economic and Political Weekly*, 47(17), 28 April.

Government of Assam. (undated). National Health Mission, Department of Health & Family Welfare. Available at http://www.nrhmassam.in/boatclinic_report.php.

Government of India. (2002). Ministry of Health and Family Welfare. *The National Health Policy-2002*. Available at https://www.nhp.gov.in/sites/default/files/pdf/NationaL_Health_Pollicy.pdf. Accessed on April 15, 2018.

Government of India. (2005). Ministry of Health and Family Welfare. 'National Rural Health Mission (NRHM) Mission Document 2005–2012.' New Delhi.

Government of India. (2010). *Engendering Public Policy: Report of the Working Group of Feminist Economists during the Preparation of the Five Year Plan. Planning Commission*. New Delhi. Available at: http://planningcommission.nic.in/reports/genrep/rep_engpub.pdf.

Government of India. (2012). National Rural Health Mission, Ministry of Health & Family Welfare, 6th Common Review Mission Report. New Delhi.

Government of India (2012). Ministry of Finance. Expenditure Budget 2014–15, Volume I: 39

Government of India. (2013). Planning Commission, Twelfth Five Year Plan (2012–2017), Social Sectors Volume III.' New Delhi.

Government of India. (2014). Ministry of Statistics and Programme Implementation. *Health in India*. Report No. 574. NSS 71 Round. January-June. New Delhi. Available at: http://mospi.nic.in/sites/default/files/publication_reports/nss_rep574.pdf. Accessed on April 15, 2018.

Government of India. (2016). *Tenth Common Review Mission Report*. New Delhi: Ministry of Health and Family Welfare.

Government of India. (2017). *National Health Policy*. New Delhi: Ministry of Health and Family Welfare.

Government of India. Ministry of Health and Family Welfare. (2013). *Rural Health Statistics in India 2012*. New Delhi. Available at http://nhm.gov.in/images/pdf/publication/RHS-2012.pdf. Accessed on April 15, 2018.

Government of India. Ministry of Health & Family Welfare. (2008). *Rural health statistics bulletin tables March 2008*. Available at: https://nrhm-mis.nic.in/Pages/RHS2017.aspx%3fRootFolder%3d%252FRURAL%20HEALTH%20STATISTICS%252F%2528F%2529%20RHS%20-%202008%26FolderCTID%3d0x01200057278FD1EC909F429B03E86C7A7C3F31%26View%3d%7b9029EB52-8EA2-4991-9611-FDF53C824827

Government of India. Ministry of Health and Family Welfare. (2010). *TB India 2010: RNTCP status report*. Available at https://tbcindia.gov.in/showfile.php?lid=2922. Accessed on April 12, 2018.

Government of India. Ministry of Health and Family Welfare. (2012). *TB India 2012: Revised national TB control programme annual status report*. Available at https://tbcindia.gov.in/showfile.php?lid=3141. Accessed on April 12, 2018.

Government of India. Ministry of Health and Family. (2017). *National health accounts estimates for India 2014–15*. National Health Accounts Technical Secretariat, National Health Systems Resource Centre. New Delhi. Available at: https://mohfw.gov.in/sites/default/files/National%20Health%20Accounts%20Estimates%20Report%202014-15.pdf accessed on 15.04.2018

Government of India. Ministry of Health and Family Welfare. (2017a). *Situation analyses: Backdrop to the national health policy-2017*. New Delhi. Available at https://mohfw.gov.in/sites/default/files/71275472221489753307.pdf. Accessed on April 15, 2018.

Government of India. Ministry of Health and Family Welfare. (2017b). *National health and family survey-4. 2015–16*. Available at http://rchiips.org/NFHS/pdf/NFHS4/India.pdf. Accessed on April 15, 2018.

Government of India. Ministry of Health and Family Welfare. (2018a). *India TB report 2018*. Available at https://tbcindia.gov.in/showfile.php?lid=3314. Accessed on April 12, 2018.

Government of India. Ministry of Health and Family Welfare. (2018b). *Healthy states, progressive India: Report on the ranks of states and union territories.* World Bank and NITI Aayog.

Government of India. Ministry of Health and Family Welfare. *Update on the ASHA programme 2013.* National Rural Health Mission. Available at http://nhm.gov.in/images/pdf/communitisation/asha/Reports/Update_on_ASHA_Program_July_2013.pdf. Accessed on April 12, 2018.

Government of India. Ministry of Health and Family Welfare. Central Bureau of Health Intelligence (CBHI). Mortality Statistics in India 2006: Status of Mortality Statistics Reporting in India. (2007). New Delhi. Available at http://www.cbhidghs.nic.in/writereaddata/mainlinkfile/File976.pdf. Accessed on April 12, 2018.

Government of India. Ministry of Health and Family Welfare. Health Management Information System. Available at https://nrhm-mis.nic.in/Pages/RHS2017.aspx. Accessed on April 12, 2018.

Government of India. Ministry of Health and Family Welfare. Health Management Information System. New Delhi. Available at https://nrhm-mis.nic.in/Pages/RHS2016.aspx?&&p_SortBehavior=0&p_S_x002e_No_x002e_=176%2e000000000000&&RootFolder=%2fRURAL%20HEALTH%20STATISTICS%2f%28A%29RHS%20-%202016&PageFirstRow=1&&View={3EF44ABD-FC77-4A1F-9195-D34FCD06C7BA. Accessed on April 12, 2018.

Government of India. Ministry of Health and Family Welfare. National Health Mission. Available at http://nhm.gov.in/nrhm-components/health-systems-strengthening/infrastructure.html. Accessed on April 12, 2018.

Government of India. Ministry of Health and Family Welfare. National Leprosy Eradication Programme (NLEP). Available at http://nlep.nic.in/pdf/Progress%20report%2031st%20March%202014-15%20-.pdf. Accessed on April 12, 2018.

Government of India. Ministry of Health and Family Welfare. National Programme for Control of Blindness. Available at http://www.npcb.nic.in/writereaddata/mainlinkfile/File287.pdf and http://www.npcb.nic.in/writereaddata/mainlinkfile/File324.pdf. Accessed on April 12, 2018.

Government of India. Ministry of Health and Family Welfare. National Vector Borne Disease Control Programme. Available at http://nvbdcp.gov.in/den-cd.html. Accessed on April 12, 2018.

Government of India. Ministry of Health and Family Welfare. National Vector Borne Disease Control Programme. Available at http://nvbdcp.gov.in/Doc/je-aes.pdf. Accessed on April 12, 2018.

Government of India. Ministry of Health and Family Welfare. National Vector Borne Disease Control Programme. Available at http://nvbdcp.gov.in/fil-rate.html. Accessed on April 12, 2018.

Government of India. Ministry of Health and Family Welfare. National Vector Borne Disease Control Programme. Available at http://nvbdcp.gov.in/malaria3.html. Accessed on April 12, 2018.

Government of India. Ministry of Home Affairs. Registrar General, India. (2011). *Sample registration system. SRS Bulletin 2011.* New Delhi. Available at: http://censusindia.gov.in/vital_statistics/SRS_Bulletins/SRS_Bulletin-September_2013.pdf. Accessed on April 12, 2018.

Government of India. Ministry of Home Affairs. Registrar General, India. (2011). *Sample registration system. MMR Release 2011.* Available at http://censusindia.gov.in/vital_statistics/SRS_Bulletins/MMR_release_070711.pdf. Accessed on April 12, 2018.

Government of India. Ministry of Home Affairs. Registrar General, India. (2011). *Sample Registration System. SRS Bulletin 2011.* New Delhi. Available at http://censusindia.gov.in/vital_statistics/SRS_Bulletins/Final-MMR%20Bulletin-2007-09_070711.pdf. Accessed on April 12, 2018.

Government of India. Ministry of Home Affairs. Registrar General, India. (2011). *Sample registration system. MMR release* (2011). Available at http://censusindia.gov.in/vital_statistics/SRS_Bulletins/MMR_release_070711.pdf. Accessed on April 12, 2018.

Government of India. Ministry of Home Affairs. Registrar General, India. (2013). *Sample registration system. MMR Bulletin (2011–13).* Available at http://www.censusindia.gov.in/vital_statistics/mmr_bulletin_2011-13.pdf. Accessed on April 12, 2018.

Government of India. Ministry of Home Affairs. Registrar General, India. (2015). *Sample registration system. SRS Report 2015.* New Delhi. Available at: http://www.censusindia.gov.in/vital_statistics/SRS_Report_2015/9.SRS%20Statistical%20Report-Detailed%20tables-2015.pdf. Accessed on April 12, 2018.

Government of India. Ministry of Home Affairs. Registrar General, India. (2015). *Sample registration system. SRS report 2015.* New Delhi. Available at http://www.censusindia.gov.in/vital_statistics/SRS_Report_2015/7.Chap%203-Fertility%20Indicators-2015.pdf. Accessed on April 12, 2018.

Government of India. Press Information Bureau. (2015). New Delhi. Available at http://pib.nic.in/newsite/PrintRelease.aspx?relid=123670. Accessed on April 12, 2018.

Government of India. *Sample Registration System (SRS) 2015.* Ministry of Home Affairs, Registrar General & Census Commissioner, India. New Delhi.

Indian Council of Medical Research, Public Health Foundation of India, and Institute for Health Metrics and Evaluation. (2017). India: Health of the Nation's States—The India State-level Disease Burden Initiative. New Delhi, India: ICMR, PHFI, and IHME.

Katoch, K., Aggarwal, A., Yadav, V. S., & Pandey, A. (2017). National sample survey to assess the new case disease burden of leprosy in India. *Indian Journal of Medical Research, 146,* 585–605.

Kumar, A., & Husain, S. (2013). The burden of new leprosy cases in India: A population-based survey in two states. *Tropical Medicine*, 2013.

Mehta, A. K., & Ali, A. (2008). *Functioning and universalisation of the ICDS in Delhi.* Report submitted to the Government of NCT Delhi.

Mehta, A. K., & Gupta, S. (2006). *The impact of HIV/AIDS on women care givers in situations of poverty: Policy issues.* New Delhi: United Nations Development Fund for Women South Asia and Institute of Public Administration.

Mehta, A. K., & Pratap, S. (2014a). *Policies and programmes: Analysing ICDS and NRHM to understand what has worked, what has not and why?* CPRC IIPA Working Paper 48. New Delhi: Chronic Poverty Research Centre, University of Manchester and Indian Institute of Public Administration.

Mehta, A. K., & Pratap, S. (2014b). *Addressing poverty and malnutrition: Key issues for better outcomes.* Yojana, August.

Mehta, A. K., Pratap, S., & Ali, A. (2012). *Reviewing flagship programmes from a gender lens: ICDS.* UN Women.

Mehta, A. K., Shepherd, A., Bhide, S., Shah, A., & Kumar, A. (2011). *India Chronic Poverty Report.* New Delhi: CPRC and IIPA.

NITI Aayog. (2017). Sustainable development goals (SDGs), targets, CSS, interventions, nodal and other ministries. Development Monitoring and Evaluation Office. Government of India. New Delhi

Panchamukhi, P. R., & Puttaswamaiah, S. (2004). *Morbidity status, utilisation and cost of treatment: A comparative study in the selected states.* Dharwad: Centre for Multi Disciplinary Development Research.

Saxena, N. C., & Srivastava, N. (2009). ICDS in India: Policy, design and delivery issues. *IDS Bulletin, 40*(4).

Singh, S., Mehta, A. K., & Tiwary, R. K. (2006). *Economic reforms in India: Pro-poor dimensions-health, agriculture, services and infrastructure.* New Delhi: IIPA and UNDP.

World Health Organisation. (2015). *Health in 2015: From MDGs millennium development goals to SDGs sustainable development goals.* World Health Organisation. Available at http://www.who.int/gho/publications/mdgs-sdgs/en/.

World Health Organisation. (2017). *World health statistics 2017: Monitoring health for the SDGs sustainable development goals.* World Health Organisation. Available at http://apps.who.int/iris/bitstream/handle/10665/255336/9789241565486-eng.pdf?sequence=1.

World Health Organization. (1995). *The world health report: 1995: Bridging the gaps/report of the Director-General.* Geneva: World Health Organization. Available at http://apps.who.int/iris/handle/10665/41863.

Chapter 8
Interface Between Education and Poverty in India: Eluding Goals and Search for New Perspectives?

Amita Shah, Kiran Banga Chhokar, Sanjay Pratap and Itishree Pattnaik

There is hardly any 'well educated literate population that is poor, (and) there is no illiterate population that is other than poor' (Galbraith 1994).
Education Poverty and Income Poverty are closely related and mutually reinforcing. Hence, it is difficult to fix the genesis and direction of causality. It is therefore imperative that the vicious cycle be first broken by redressing education poverty since that has intrinsic value for enhancing the quality of human life beyond income and economic well-being.
The question is how to attain educational security that also ensures the intrinsic value of education, which is an important dimension of amelioration of poverty.

Education is an important dimension of development and an indicator of human development and well-being. It is also an important vehicle for attaining higher and sustained economic growth, which may in turn help expand economic opportunities and enhance returns to work and workers, especially among those with higher education and technical skills. In addition, education provides a direct premium in terms of higher earnings at least among a subset of workers at any given level of

With necessary permissions the paper draws on Shah et al. (2011) CPRC-IIPA Working Paper 46. The authors would like to thank Dr. Shiddalingaswami for his contribution to an earlier version of this paper.

A. Shah (✉)
Center for Development Alternatives, Ahmedabad, India
e-mail: amitagidr@gmail.com

K. B. Chhokar
Independent Consultant, Education for Sustainable Development,
New Delhi, India

S. Pratap
Indian Institute of Public Administration, New Delhi, India

I. Pattnaik
Gujarat Institute of Development Research (GIDR), Ahmedabad, India

© Springer Nature Singapore Pte Ltd. 2018
A. K. Mehta et al. (eds.), *Poverty, Chronic Poverty and Poverty Dynamics*,
https://doi.org/10.1007/978-981-13-0677-8_8

195

economic growth. Above all, education has been found to help broaden people's ability to comprehend complex socio-cultural-political realities, thereby strengthening democratic processes that eventually may lead to empowerment, which represents the intrinsic value of education, independent of its income or economic impact (Cohen 1998).

1 Education and Expectations

1.1 Relationship between Education and Poverty

Our understanding of the relationship between education and poverty has so far been based on the existing evidences revolving around the interlinkages between the two. What is, however, missing in most studies is an alternative scenario that may potentially get created through different approaches where education gets directly linked with poverty reduction, equity and human dignity across space and people. This may require a different approach to analysis based not only on the outcomes but also on a deeper understanding of the various processes. The ongoing analysis, thus, should be taken as a part of a changing rather than a static process.

There is a growing recognition of the fact that while universalizing primary education, a constitutional commitment in India, can at best help ameliorate poverty in the short run, preventing a potential relapse into poverty may require widening the base of at least secondary education, which at present is limited only to about one-third of the children in the age group of 14–17 years enrolled in secondary education (Tilak 2005). It has been argued that it is only at this level of educational attainment that people can actually achieve 'freedom' or 'capability' – the notions advocated by Sen (1999). Raising the net of secondary and higher education thus assumes special relevance in the context of redressing chronic poverty in a sustained manner. Also, higher education plays a significant role in terms of economic, human and gender development as it helps enhance upward mobility, increase life expectancy and reduce infant mortality (ibid.).

While a fairly rich body of literature looks at the linkages between education, economic growth and poverty and also assesses economic returns to education in the Indian context (Rao 1964, 1970; Governement of India 1966; Haq and Haq 1998; Loh 1995; Tilak 1994, 2007; Duraisamy 2002), very few studies have systematically looked at the impact of education on overall development at individual as well as at societal levels. This is mainly due to the dynamic nature of the circular causation where conditions of poverty influence education and in turn get impacted by it. The linkage is also contextualized within the stratified socio-cultural-spatial milieu characterizing most communities in India.

Breaking the vicious cycle of lack of education and poverty is a critical challenge, and the onus lies primarily on the state. This is reflected by fairly progressive policy statements accompanied by large-scale supply-side responses by the state since independence. Although this is commendable, the goal of universal primary education is yet to be achieved. Moreover, serious challenges exist in making the Indian educational system inclusive and empowering. At the same time, while new opportunities and threats are emerging from the changing demographic composition, global competition too is growing. The link between poverty and education thus gets shaped within a dynamic socio-cultural-economic setting.

Two decades ago, the gap in attendance rate between children from the richest and the poorest expenditure quintiles was more than 40% points. Over the years, as more and more children from the lowest monthly per capita expenditure quintiles have started to attend school, the gap between the richest and the lowest MPCE quintiles has been narrowing. However, in the lowest quintile children are still not attending higher grades (Sankar 2008, p. 9).

Given this backdrop, this paper tries to revisit the discourse on education through the lens of poverty reduction, especially among those facing severe income poverty over a long duration.

1.2 Constitutional Obligations and State Response: The Education Miracle in India

Soon after independence, in accordance with Article 45 of its Constitution, India embarked upon the policy of providing free and compulsory education to all children up to the age of 14 years. It was hoped that all children would be provided with elementary education in ten years, but seven decades later this remains an unfulfilled target. From the beginning, the country's Five-Year Plans have laid special emphasis on education. The First Five-Year Plan focused on the creation of many more schools, which policymakers believed would be the key to providing universal access to education (Little 2010). Education was initially seen as the vehicle for building the right kind of values and attitudes for attaining economic development within a democratic set-up (Second Five-Year Plan), then for promoting economic growth and quality of the society (Fourth Five-Year Plan), and more recently for facilitating social and economic progress, leading to both individual and group entitlements (Eleventh Five-Year Plan).

To achieve these goals, the government has made requisite amendments to the Constitution and has set up a number of important committees and task forces (see Appendix Table 12). Some of the important landmarks include the 42nd Amendment (in 1976) whereby the responsibility of providing educational services was shifted from the state governments to being the joint responsibility of the state governments and the central government. Subsequently, the 73rd and 74th Amendments made in 1993 brought the emphasis on educational initiatives to local bodies, namely the Panchayati Raj Institutions (PRIs). In 2002, the 86th Amendment to the Constitution made elementary education (i.e. up to class VIII) a constitutional commitment.

Subsequently, the Right to Education Act was enacted in 2009, which made elementary education a fundamental right.

Literacy and education are seen as important instruments for poverty reduction of the world over, as suggested by a number of publications by various international agencies such as The World Bank, UNDP and UNESCO. Whereas the Government of India does recognize a close link between education and poverty reduction, the former has not been explicitly made part of poverty reduction programmes.[1] This could be due to two reasons: first, education, as noted earlier, is an important basic need (Planning Commission 2008, p. 11); hence, it goes beyond the realm of redressing income poverty. Second, and perhaps more important, literacy or education by itself may not ensure exit from poverty among a large mass of poor and chronic poor in the country; its impact is likely to be mediated through a complex interplay of factors such as socio-cultural-spatial stratification, labour market dynamics and, above all, the quality of education itself.

Creating a system of free and compulsory elementary education aiming at larger objectives of enhancing the quality of life of society on the one hand and promoting economic growth on other has been a herculean task. Over time, however, India has made major strides in terms of creating a huge infrastructure catering to a large population cutting across class, caste, ethnicity, language and regions. Literacy has increased from barely 18% during 1950–51 to almost 75% over a span of roughly 60 years (Census of India 1951 and 2011). There has also been a huge increase in the number of specialized institutions of excellence rendering critical services to some of the core areas of the economy, defence and scientific knowledge, thereby enabling the country to be labelled as a knowledge economy, not only within South Asia but the world over. There are, of course, major gaps in reaching out to certain segments of the population that still remain excluded from even basic literacy. Gaps also exist in creating an actual knowledge base and/or skills that may have a direct bearing on economic development and individual earnings, if not on the quality of society referred to in the Fourth Plan, and increased entitlement to individuals as well as groups, mentioned in the Eleventh Plan.

1.3 Economic Growth and Returns to Education: Does It Help the Poor and Chronic Poor?

A number of studies in the early phase of India's planned development had gone into examining the contribution of the expansion of education to economic growth.

---

[1]The government's poverty reduction programmes directly address income poverty. These include self-employment programmes such as the *Swarnajayanti Gram Swarojgar Yojana* for the rural poor, wage employment programmes such as the *Mahatma Gandhi National Rural Employment Guarantee Scheme*, social security programmes like the *National Old Age Pension Scheme*, area development programmes such as the *Drought Prone Area Programme* and other programmes such as the *Indira Awaas Yojana,* a housing scheme for the poor.

The estimates vary widely, from 34 to 27 and 6.8%, depending on the methodology and the data used (Tilak 2007). Education was also found to have impacted poverty, income distribution, health outcomes and demographic changes (ibid.). More recently, Mathur and Mamgain (2004) also observed a significant impact of education on per capita net state domestic product (NSDP).

A lot of research has gone into examining the impact of education on social and private returns (Psacharopoulos 1973, 1994; Psacharopoulos and Tilak 1992; Psacharopoulos and Patrinos 2004; Heyneman 1980; Schultz 1988; Duraisamy 2002). For example, calculations were sought to be made to find the relationship between schooling and earnings, level of economic development, etc. Tilak (1987) found that social returns to primary, secondary and higher education were 23, 28 and 11%, respectively. Compared to this, private returns were found to be significantly higher and also increasing along with higher levels of educational attainment.

While these findings appear to be intuitively valid, little is known about the benefits reaching the poor and the chronic poor. The issue is how many of the poor and the very poor children could actually break through the threshold level of education that could fetch them better income and earnings in the labour market? The labour market is fairly overcrowded and also segmented in favour of the not-so-poor. While there are methodological difficulties in clearly addressing these issues, the empirical evidence, by and large, suggests a positive impact on poverty reduction, particularly if at least a subset of the poor children could break the entry barrier into the educational system.

There is, however, a limited understanding of what type of education helps realize the more basic goals of education, namely freedom, capability, entitlement and the quality of society per se, and how. Notwithstanding these limitations, one frequently comes across situations where people, even the poor, tend to value and demand educational services, which in turn could be a testimony of the positive impact that education has exerted or is expected to exert on the lives of the poor. The demand for and value of education also reflect the changing social norms and aspirations for shifting out of agriculture or primary occupations in rural areas. It is likely that an element of distress contributes to shaping such aspirations among the rural youth. The fact still remains that education is increasingly being seen as a necessary (if not a sufficient) precondition for shifting out of the stagnant rural economy and actually attaining upward economic mobility.

1.4 Unfinished Agenda and Policy Initiatives

The issue of physical access to elementary schools has been addressed by the government very vigorously since it started on the path of planned development. As a result, the number of schools across the country, as also within one kilometre of most habitations, has increased vastly in the past seven decades, and so have gross enrolment ratios at different levels of education. However, challenges of student retention, overcrowding, inadequate numbers of teachers as well as of well-trained teachers, teacher absenteeism and poor learning outcomes persist.

A number of initiatives have been undertaken in the recent past for addressing the issue of making the education system inclusive and also empowering. The most important among these is the umbrella programme of Sarva Shikhsha Abhiyan (SSA) initiated in 2002 (during the Tenth Five-Year Plan) to universalize elementary education. It is also India's response to the international call for Education for All and to meeting the Millennium Development Goal of achieving universal primary education. The main objectives of SSA were:

- All 6- to 14-year-old children to be in regular schools, educational guarantee scheme (EGS) centres, alternative and innovative education (AIE), or 'Back-to-School' camps by 2005;
- Bridging all gender and social category gaps at the primary stage by 2007 and at the elementary education level by 2010;
- Universal retention by 2010;
- Focus on elementary education of satisfactory quality with emphasis on education for life.

Although the goals stated above have not been achieved so far, SSA has resulted in improvements in the following educational indicators:

- As per the Unified District Information System for Education (U-DISE), in 2015–16, enrolment in elementary schools was 19.67 crore children (the 2011 Census had estimated 20.78 crore children in the 6–13 age group) in 14.49 lakh elementary schools.
- The number of out-of-school children in the 6–14 years age group had gone down from 134.6 lakh in 2005 to 81 lakh in 2009 and further to 61 lakh in 2014.
- The annual average dropout rate at the primary level had come down from 9.11% in 2009–10 to 4.13% in 2015–16.
- The transition rate from primary to upper primary went up from 83.53% in 2009–10 to 90.14% in 2015–16.
- The pupil–teacher ratio (PTR) improved from 32 in 2009–10 to 24 in 2015–16.
- SSA had made significant progress in achieving near universal access and equity.
- Department of School Education and Niti Aayog are jointly developing a School Education Quality Index (SEQI) in consultation with all States and UTs. This index aims to institutionalize a focus on improving education outcomes (learning, access, equity) as the principle aim of school education policy in India. http://pib.nic.in/newsite/PrintRelease.aspx?relid=155999.

The unfinished agenda items thus need urgent attention. These include moving from universal enrolment to effective retention of children at least up to the elementary level. The Right to Education (RTE) Act 2009 is a significant development as it makes free and compulsory education for children between 6 and 14 years of age a fundamental right. SSA has now become the primary mode of helping achieve the goals of RTE. More crucial than just access is the challenge of enhancing the quality of elementary education so as to avoid wastage and at the same time to create the requisite stock of skills, knowledge and attitudes that in turn could feed into higher growth not only for the economy but also for the mass of poor individuals and groups. The task is to achieve this without losing sight of affordability of education among the poor. In this context, in addition to seeking to provide state-run schools within a kilometre of all habitations, RTE requires all private schools to ensure intake of 25% children from poor and disadvantaged families in every incoming class, whose education will be subsidized by the state.

The Approach Paper to the Twelfth Five-Year Plan underlined the need to address teacher absenteeism and accountability, and to build their capacity, so as to better target uncovered and under-covered populations, to strategically reach out-of-school children including street children and those with special needs, and to strengthen the monitoring and evaluation of SSA (Planning Commission 2011). It also called for promoting adult literacy through the Sakshar Mission.

While the focus of poverty reduction programmes of governments, international development agencies and donors around the world has been on elementary education, it is being increasingly recognized that enabling exit from poverty also needs the simultaneous expansion of secondary and higher education (Tilak 2005; World Bank 1997, 2006). In March 2009, the Government of India launched the Rashtriya Madhyamik Shiksha Abhiyan (RMSA), a scheme to enhance access and enable improvement of quality of secondary education, and to ensure greater socio-economic and gender equity (http://mhrd.gov.in/rashtriya_madhyamik_ shiksha_abhiyan). The Planning Commission (2011, pp. 127–128) had recommended that during the Twelfth Plan, the RMSA "be made a single comprehensive scheme to address issues of coverage and quality in secondary education in a holistic manner".

1.5 Objectives

The paper aims to (a) present a brief overview of the approaches adopted for promoting universal and relevant education in India; (b) examine the link between education and poverty; (c) critically revisit the evidence on returns to education and identify the impact on the poor; and (d) discuss policy implications.

The paper is divided into five sections, including this introduction. The subsequent sections deal with each of the four objectives mentioned above. The analysis is based mainly on secondary data and associated literature. The paper is expected to feed into the larger discourse on addressing the issues of chronic poverty where education is both an important dimension as well as a factor influencing exit from income poverty which engulfs a large proportion of the population in the country.

2 Education for Income and Empowerment: Setting the Context

Attainment of literacy and basic education among all has been one of the most difficult challenges of development in India. Educational attainment may be viewed as having significant intrinsic value just as health does. It could be argued that given the status of human well-being with respect to economic and health outcomes, educational attainment has the potential for opening up wider horizons of life, besides reinforcing the other two dimensions of well-being. It is therefore not surprising that educational attainment, especially universal primary education, has been accorded a high priority in the developmental discourse right from the initial phase of planned development in the country.

While there has not been much debate on the intrinsic value of education for societal development, much of the discourse on education and development in India, especially since 1960, has centred on its instrumentalist value in terms of promoting income, hence economic growth and also health outcomes; the latter may result directly or indirectly from income enhancement. Prior to this the dominant understanding was that people in a large agrarian economy such as India may not seek or demand educational services owing to factors such as limited economic returns, high opportunity cost and low social premium. Promoting education therefore would hold a fairly low priority, especially among the poor who tend to be preoccupied with their struggle for ensuring basic needs–food, fodder, shelter and the minimum health care for the family. This, in turn, implied that promoting education, at least at the primary level, is purely a welfare function or a social service to be performed by the state.

The welfare-oriented approach to education led to important features that have continued to remain more or less intact till the time that Sen (1983) brought to the fore the capability perspective to education and human development. The two closely interrelated features are supply driven (since people are not likely to demand educational services), and focused mainly on reducing opportunity cost (as a means of promoting demand) as against enhancing the quality of life per se among the people, irrespective of the income gains resulting from a different kind of education. Importantly, the state became the sole provider, rather than facilitator, of educational services, devoid of any direct involvement of parents and the community at large. A vital outcome of such an approach was that though promoting primary education was an important goal for the state, it was treated as if it could be attained slowly and sequentially in tandem with the stages of economic growth. The implication was that education could wait but economic growth must proceed. A financial resource crunch in the initial phase of development in the country gave further legitimacy to this perspective.

A major breakthrough, however, came in the mid-1970s when economic analyses indicated that education may have significant pay-offs, individually as well as economy-wide, even at an early stage of a country's economic development. In what could be considered as path-breaking contributions by several economists, it was demonstrated that investment in education had significant pay-offs both for the national economy as well as for individual workers (Heyneman 1980; Kothari 1970; Tilak 1987). This in fact set off an important branch of economics, which tended to look at education almost entirely as an economic good or commodity to be analysed through the market framework of demand and supply. Whereas this perspective made a major contribution in breaking the stereotyped welfare-oriented and supply-driven approach, it also brought into its fold another stereotyping, namely, commodification of education accompanied by almost complete neglect of the intrinsic value that education holds over other attainments. The lopsided emphasis on higher/technical education, as part of the growth strategy adopted during the Second Five-Year Plan, is more or less part of the same syndrome where such skills and specialized scientific knowledge were considered critical given their multiple economic pay-offs, especially in the long run.

To an extent the strategy has worked well especially in the wake of globalization since the early 1990s when a large army of skilled and technical/scientific man-power along with institutional infrastructure helped give the Indian economy a competitive edge over several other developing economies. As a result, the eco-nomic rationale continued to overpower other considerations for promoting edu-cation. This has led to a scenario where investment in education has come to be justified in terms of its potential contribution to the economy; this in turn has cast its shadow on the contemporary discourse on issues such as: What kind of education should be provided, by whom and at what cost? The recent upsurge of the 'de-mographic dividend' provides yet another justification for promoting the income-oriented approach to education.

The growing recognition of the capability approach propagated by Sen (1983) brought back the emphasis on the intrinsic value of education, irrespective of the purely economic outcomes associated with it. Sen's capability approach also made clearer the link between poverty and education. The Human Development Report 1997, making a distinction between income poverty and human poverty, observed that human poverty is "a denial of choices and opportunities for living a tolerable life" (UNDP 1997, p. 2). Therefore the denial of opportunities, education being one, to enhance human capabilities to lead a tolerable life represents human poverty.

The intrinsic value of education may vary along an array of valued states of one's being, ranging from elementary to a complex personal state. Capability is thus expressed as an individual's access to 'adequate resources to achieve' what one may aspire to in terms of different states or levels of being. According to Sen what matters more is the freedom to achieve the aspired states of being rather than the actual achievement. With respect to education, this may imply ensuring 'agency and freedom to make up one's mind about schooling as valued end and convert one's aspirations about schooling into valued achievement' (Unterhalter 2003, p. 3).

While there is no clear indicator prescribed for assessing the various capabilities to function, prior education of parents could probably be one such indicator that may potentially lead to greater freedom for making the choice and actually convert that into functioning. In this sense, education could be viewed as both a resource (means) and the aspired achievement of the various states of being (i.e. end). Of course the 'adequate resource' may entail a number of entitlements besides education, namely, economic, socio-cultural and political. The important point at this juncture is to highlight the dual role of education, that is, as an initial resource that may lead to freedom or capability to function and achieve the aspired states of being. This may imply circular causality–a phenomenon that has been discussed elaborately in the literature (Duraisamy and Duraisamy 2005).

An important fallout of the dual role of education is that it brings back the emphasis on the state's responsibility for provisioning of education, especially elementary education, which in turn may facilitate capabilities among people across different class, caste, ethnicity and regions to demand (or make choices) for acquiring educational services, ideally, of a desired quality. Therefore the discourse on education till now has remained focused mainly on improving the supply-side mechanisms particularly in order to include the (income) poor. The evolution of SSA is largely a reflection of the revived emphasis on the supply-side mechanism where the focus is primarily on reaching out to the hitherto excluded communities; improving the content and pedagogy is seen as a means to attract those, most of them poor and chronically poor, who have been left out of the state-run primary education system.

In this context, the focus of the discourse has started shifting towards criticality of secondary and higher education for attaining the positive economic outcomes from education. Tilak (2005), among others, has demonstrated that while 'basic education may take people out of poverty, this can be sustained well by secondary and higher education which help upward mobility and offer better economic opportunities' (p. 43). The bulk of research looking at the impact of education has remained confined to asking how much is the economic return from education; does education help ameliorate poverty; how to make education keep pace with the changing market demand for skilled labour, etc. Although valid, these are empirically difficult questions to investigate and the issue of intrinsic value of education remains relatively less explored. In that context the relevant questions to be probed are: Does a person, having attained at least primary education, behave and feel differently about one's self? Does educational attainment change the aspirations of life other than that pertaining to income enhancement? Does that lead to empowerment among individuals as well as communities to 'decide' what kind of education they would want rather than merely choosing whether they should demand the type of education that is already being supplied through the state-supported systems? These are some of the important questions that need increasing attention in the next phase of discourse that may engage more intensely with the notion of intrinsic value of education and people's capability to acquire that.

The recent debate on 'demographic dividend' further sharpens the emphasis on skill formation and market orientation. The demographic transition resulting from a fall in fertility rates changes the age structure, creating a predominance of population in the working age group of 15–60 years. In the next 20 years, India's labour force is expected to increase by 32%, while during the same period it is expected to decline by 4% in several industrialized countries and by 5% in China (Planning Commission 2011, p. 9).

Although findings from an empirical exercise suggest positive growth impact emanating purely from demographic factors (James 2008), the counter argument is that in the absence of adequate stock of skilled manpower at the cutting edge, and the expansion of good quality employment and livelihood opportunities, expected benefits from the growing proportion of young population may not be realized (Chandrasekhar et al. 2006; James 2008). It has been argued that 'while primary education serves as threshold level of human capital development for economic growth, it is secondary and higher education including investment in science and technology that accelerates and sustains high economic growth and development' (Tilak 2005, p. 58). The question is whether the present educational system generates the expected human capital and the requisite driving force for economic growth. What about enhancing the aspirations of life and being, independent of the economic improvement that may or may not be realized by all attaining education at some level?

Given this backdrop, the following two sections try to examine the education gap among states and communities within the country, and to recapitulate the major findings on the link between education and poverty based on a select set of studies carried out in the recent past.

2.1   Mapping the Education Gap Among States and Communities

With over a million educational institutions and about 250 million students enrolled, India represents one of the world's largest educational systems (Tilak 2003: p. 24). Starting with a dismal base of educational infrastructure at the time of independence, India has made major strides in horizontal expansion of its educational system over the past seven decades.

Table 1 presents a bird's eye view of the progress made on educational attainments in the country. The literacy rate has been steadily increasing and has now reached almost 75%. The adult literacy rate (for age 15 years and above) too has been rising – from 41% in 1981, to more than 70% in 2014, but it still lags far behind the world average of 83.7% (www.cia.gov/library/publications/the-world-factbook/fields/2103.html). The focus on adding more schools has been visible since independence, and as the data shows, this trend has continued over the past thirty years. While about 1.5 lakh schools were added in the twenty years between 1981 and 2001, a similar number got added in the next 10 years, between 2001 and 2011, taking the total to more than 8 lakh schools, and to almost 8.5 lakh by 2014.

Table 1 Broad indicators of education

Broad indicators	1981	2001	2009–2011	2014
Literacy rate	43.6	64.84	74.04	...
Adult literacy rate	40.8	61.0	67.3	70.5
Number of primary schools	4,94,503	6,38,738	8,09,974	8,47,118
Gross enrolment ratio primary (I–V)	80.5	95.7	115.47	100.1
Gross enrolment ratio upper primary (VI–VIII)	41.9	58.6	81.52	91.2
Gross enrolment ratio elementary (I–VIII)	67.5	81.6	102.47	96.9
Gross enrolment ratio primary of SC (I–V)	..	96.8	128.25	111.9
Gross enrolment ratio upper primary of SC (VI–VIII)	..	65.3	88.63	101.0
Gross enrolment ratio elementary of SC (I–VIII)	..	86.8	113.45	108.0
Gross enrolment ratio primary of ST (I–V)	..	101.1	138.62	109.4
Gross enrolment ratio upper primary of ST (VI–VIII)	..	60.2	83.43	94.1
Gross enrolment ratio elementary of ST (I–VIII)	..	88.0	118.85	104.0
Dropout rates (I–V)	58.7	40.7	28.86	4.34
Dropout rates (VI–VIII)	72.7	53.7	42.39	3.77
Dropout rates (I–X)	82.5	68.58	52.76	...
Teacher–pupil ratio primary	1:38	1:43	1:42	1:24
Teacher–pupil ratio upper primary	1:33	1:38	1:34	1:17
Teacher–pupil ratio high/hr. secondary	1:27	1:32	1:39	1:24
Per capita public budgetary expenditure on education	53	605	1395	...
Budgetary expenditure on education as a share of GDP (For 1981 its Education 2.6 + Scientific research 0.8)	3.4	4.28	2.6%	4.13[a]

Sources (i) Data tables of Planning Commission; (ii) Statistics of School Education, 2009–10, MHRD; (iii) Selected Socio-economic Statistics India, 2011, MOSPI; (iv) website: www.indiabudget.nic.in; (v) Elementary Education in India, Progress towards UEE, 2011, NUEPA; (vi) Census of India
Sources For column 5, Educational Statistics at a Glance. Available at http://mhrd.gov.in/sites/upload_files/mhrd/files/statistics/ESG2016_0.pdf
[a]Statement indicating the Public Expenditure on Education. Available at: http://mhrd.gov.in/sites/upload_files/mhrd/files/statistics/PubExpdt-2013.pdf

2.2   Enrolment and Dropout

The latest figures for gross enrolment ratio (GER) for 2009–11 in the primary and upper primary school are 115 and 81%, respectively (see Table 1). Despite the more than 100% GER (mainly because of enrolment of children of different ages in the various grades), a rough estimates put the number of out-of-school children in the age group 6–14 years at nearly 30–40 million children (Tilak 2007).

Findings from the Public Report on Basic Education (PROBE), based on a survey conducted in 2006 covering 96 schools in 277 villages in Rajasthan, Bihar, Madhya Pradesh and Uttar Pradesh observed that about 5% of children in the age group of 6–12 years were out of school (De et al. 2011). This proportion was 26% during an earlier survey conducted in 1996 (Shiva Kumar et al. 2009). This is certainly a significant achievement. The proportion was found to be more or less the same across all social groups except for tribals where the proportion of out-of-school children was 89%.

The report, however, noted that enrolment in school does not mean attendance, and attendance does not mean learning! Only 66% of the children enrolled were marked present and the actual attendance was even lower at the time of the survey. It was found that whereas 80% of students in class 4 and 5 (in government schools), could do simple addition and subtraction, almost the same percentage of students could not write an answer to a simple question and about 62% could not read a simple story (Shiva Kumar et al. 2009). A recent study by Pratham Education Foundation (2017) highlighted the increase in reading ability especially in early grades in government schools. However the reading level of class 5 students has not changed much over the period.

Apart from presenting a dismal picture of the actual learning during the primary level of schooling, the evidence reinstates the point noted earlier about the low quality of education during this stage, which in turn, gets reflected in a scenario where economic returns to primary education are almost negligible. The case for secondary education thus, at least partly, reflects the syndrome of wastage during the early phase of education.

The low level of learning (not to mention capability and empowerment) coupled with only a limited chance of getting economic opportunities for income enhancement is most likely to result in withdrawal of children from school. This holds good particularly when the actual cost and/or the opportunity cost of sending children to school is fairly substantial among poor households.

According to Table 1, in 2009–2011, 29% of the children enrolled in primary schools dropped out, whereas the dropout rate was much higher at the upper primary level with 42% children discontinuing their education. According to an NSSO (2010) survey, the major reasons for dropping out of school were:

Financial constraints	21%
Child not interested in studies	20%
Unable to cope or failure in studies	10%
Completed desired level or class	10%
Parents not interested in studies	9%

Although the data for 2014 shows a drastic reduction in the dropout rates (4.3% at the primary and 3.7% at the upper primary level), India is still far from achieving universal elementary education, The decline in school dropout rate might be due to an increase in attention to the improvement of elementary education. Increase in expenditure on the new government policies like District Primary Education

Programme (DPEP) and Sarva Shiksha Abhiyan (SSA), too, may have led to the improvement of retention of students. (Govind and Bandyopadhyay 2011).

While economic pressures are the leading cause, poor quality of education and its lack of relevance have an important bearing on the poor performance of children and the lack of interest of children as well as their parents. In the case of SC and ST children, discrimination and humiliation which they are subjected to by the other children is another leading cause of dropping out (Sedwal and Kamat 2008). Retention in school thus remains the most critical challenge especially for children of poor, socially and spatially disadvantaged communities.

Among factors responsible for discontinuance of education, gender discrimination may be important in leading to higher dropout rates among girls. According to estimates for 2004–05, 15.5% of boys in the age group 5–14 years were out of school as compared to 20.7% girls in the same age group (NCEUS 2007). Similarly, there are gender differences, though not very significant, in terms of attending school (Unni 2009). Whereas about 80 and 87% of rural boys in the age groups 5–9 and 10–14 years attended school, the figure among rural girls was 77% in both the age groups. In urban areas the difference is much less; the proportion of boys attending school is around 89–90% as compared to 87–88% among girls.

2.3 Literacy Rates and Educational Attainment

By 2010–11, 75% of India's population was literate. When India became independent, the literacy rate was nearly 18% which increased to 52% in 1991 and then to almost 65% in 2001 (Table 2). This is not a mean achievement considering the vastness of the population, physical remoteness and, above all, almost negligible infrastructure, especially in rural areas at the time of independence.

Table 2 Literacy rate in India

Year	Literacy rate	(% change)
1900–01	9.01	..
1940–41	16.42	..
1950–51	18.33	11.63
1960–61	28.31	54.45
1970–71	34.45	21.69
1980–81	43.56	26.44
1990–91	52.21	19.86
2000–01	64.8	24.11
2010–11	74.04	14.26

Source Economic survey, various issues. Table 2(3) literates and literacy rates by sex: 2011, Census of India. http://censusindia.gov.in/2011-prov-results/data_files/india/Table-2(3)_literacy.pdf.http://planningcommission.nic.in/data/datatable/0904/tab_160.pdf

Table 3 Percentage distribution of persons of age 15 years and above by completed level of education

Level of education	Rural			Urban			Rural + Urban		
	Female	Male	Total	Female	Male	Total	Female	Male	Total
(1)	(2)	(3)	(4)	(5)	(6)	(7)	(8)	(9)	(10)
Not literate	52.5	28.2	40.3	25.4	11.3	18.0	45.1	23.3	34.0
Literate									
Without formal education[a]	0.8	1.1	1.0	0.9	0.9	0.9	0.9	1.1	1.0
Below primary	7.8	9.4	8.6	5.9	5.5	5.7	7.3	8.3	7.8
Primary	14.4	17.7	16.0	13.2	13.3	13.2	14.0	16.4	15.3
Middle	12.3	19.9	16.2	15.9	18.8	17.4	13.3	19.6	16.5
Secondary	7.2	12.6	9.9	15.6	18.4	17.0	9.5	14.3	11.9
Higher Secondary	3.1	6.4	4.7	10.0	12.1	11.1	5.0	8.0	6.5
Diploma	0.3	0.8	0.6	0.8	2.4	1.7	0.5	1.3	0.9
Graduation	1.3	3.0	2.2	9.3	13.3	11.4	3.5	6.0	4.8
Post-graduation and above	0.3	0.8	0.5	3.0	3.9	3.5	1.1	1.7	1.4
Total	100	100	100	100	100	100	100	100	100

Source NSS report no. 532: education in India, 2007–08: participation and expenditure, p. 14, May 2010
[a]It is possible that there might be some who have completed primary education but remain illiterate. However, national level disaggregated data for that category is not available

Literacy however, varies by class, gender, ethnicity and rural–urban locations across states in India. Table 3 presents estimates of literacy rates and educational attainment among male and female population during 2007–8. The data in Table 3 clearly indicates the gender gap in both illiteracy and educational attainments, which gets accentuated as one moves along the ladder of higher levels of education in rural areas. The gender gap is not as stark in the urban areas except in the case of illiteracy.

Table 4 presents changes in literacy rates across major states in India. In 2001, the poorest performers were Bihar (47% literate) and Uttar Pradesh (57% literate), while Kerala was the best with 91% of its population being literate. The only other states having higher than 70% literacy were Maharashtra (22.3%) and Tamil Nadu (73.5%). The rest of the states had literacy rates ranging between 61 (Andhra Pradesh and Rajasthan) and 69% (West Bengal). By 2011, the situation had improved considerably. Bihar and UP had attained 64 and 70% literacy, respectively. Rajasthan and Andhra Pradesh were the only other states with literacy around 67%. Literacy in all other states ranged between 70 and 80%. Kerala retained its lead with 93% literacy.

Table 4 State-wise literacy rate

States/UTs	1981	1991	2001	2011
Andhra Pradesh	35.66	44.08	60.47	67.66
Assam	–	52.89	63.25	73.18
Bihar	32.32	37.49	47.00	63.82
Gujarat	44.92	61.29	69.14	79.31
Haryana	37.13	55.85	67.91	76.64
Karnataka	46.21	56.04	66.64	75.60
Kerala	78.85	89.81	90.86	93.91
Madhya Pradesh	38.63	44.67	63.74	70.63
Maharashtra	57.24	64.87	76.88	82.91
Odisha	33.62	49.09	63.08	73.45
Punjab	43.37	58.51	69.65	76.68
Rajasthan	30.11	38.55	60.41	67.06
Tamil Nadu	54.39	62.66	73.45	80.33
Uttar Pradesh	32.65	40.71	56.27	69.72
West Bengal	48.65	57.70	68.64	77.08
All India	43.57	52.21	64.84	74.04

Source National Human Development Report, Table 2(3) Literates and literacy rates by sex: 2011, Census of India. http://planningcommission.nic.in/data/datatable/0904/tab_160.pdf

3   Income and Education Poverty

Whereas income poverty and education poverty work in a mutually reinforcing manner, the evidence by and large suggests that the negative impact of poverty on educational attainment is far more widespread than the positive impact that educational attainment exerts in terms of reducing poverty. However, in a labour-surplus economy such as India, it may be reasonable to treat the evidence of linkages as indicators of association rather than causation.

This is so because the evidence, as we shall see later in this paper, pertains mainly to the fact that those with better educational attainment get higher income in the form of wages and salaries. It is not quite clear as to what extent chances of getting a wage/salaried job in an otherwise labour-surplus economy such as India is in the first place (positively) influenced by initial higher socio-economic status. This makes it difficult to ascertain the extent to which educational attainment among initially poor persons has helped in exiting/mitigating poverty, other things remaining same. A number of studies have indicated significant negative correlation between poverty and the extent of literacy across households as well as states. A simple correlation, using household consumption expenditure data, suggested an inverse relationship between monthly per capita income and the highest level of education attained by a member of the household (Shah and Yagnik 2004). Similar observations are also found from micro-level studies, especially in relatively less-developed states in the country. It is, however, likely that deprivation, especially at the level of primary education, may be influenced by a combination of income poverty and social-spatial-cultural marginalization faced by SCs, STs and religious minorities, the point already made earlier.

Notwithstanding the complexity, an important point that emerges quite clearly is the close positive association between income poverty and illiteracy. It is likely that most of the illiterates are located in households facing income poverty, notwith-standing the policy of free universal primary education in the country. As noted earlier, to a large extent, this could be due to relatively higher direct cost as well as opportunity cost of sending children to school among poor as compared to not-so-poor households. At the same time one needs to recognize the fact that educational attainment or enrolment does not necessarily lead to literacy but as the illiterate educated are difficult to isolate in the macro-level data, education has been used here as an indicator for literacy.

Table 5 Two-way link of literacy and poverty

Classification	1981	1991	2001	2011
Virtuous high literacy and low poverty	Kerala, Maharashtra, Gujarat, Karnataka	Kerala, Tamil Nadu, West Bengal, Karnataka, Haryana, Gujarat	Kerala, Maharashtra, Tamil Nadu, Punjab, Haryana, Karnataka, Gujarat	Kerala, Tamil Nadu
Vicious low literacy and high poverty	Odisha, Bihar, Madhya Pradesh, Uttar Pradesh	Odisha, Bihar, Madhya Pradesh, Uttar Pradesh	Odisha, Bihar, Madhya Pradesh, Uttar Pradesh, Assam	West Bengal, Karnataka, Uttar Pradesh, Bihar, Odisha, Rajasthan, Madhya Pradesh
Lop sided high literacy and high poverty	Tamil Nadu, West Bengal	Assam, Maharashtra	West Bengal	Maharashtra, Gujarat
Lop sided EG low literacy and low poverty	Rajasthan, Andhra Pradesh, Punjab, Haryana	Rajasthan, Punjab, Andhra Pradesh	Rajasthan, Andhra Pradesh	Punjab, Haryana, Andhra Pradesh

Note Literacy rate for Assam for 1981 not available. Therefore only 14 states for 1981
Source Based on Appendix Table 13

3.1 Link Between Literacy and Poverty Across States

We tried to examine the link between literacy and poverty by classifying the states across four categories using the All-India estimate as the cut-off for identifying high and low status with respect to the two variables. Table 5 presents the scenario that obtained during 2001, for which data is available. It is observed that seven of the 16 major states were in the "virtuous" category with higher (than All-India) level of literacy with low levels of poverty. These states include Kerala, Maharashtra, Tamil Nadu, Punjab, Haryana, Karnataka and Gujarat. Of these, Kerala and Gujarat had been in this category throughout since 1981. The states of Bihar, Madhya Pradesh, Uttar Pradesh (all three undivided, including the newer states of Jharkhand, Chhattisgarh and Uttarakhand), Odisha and Assam belonged to the "vicious" category, with low literacy and high levels of poverty.

A similar attempt was made to examine poverty and proportion of population with different levels of education across states in India. The results in Table 6 show a somewhat mixed picture: that (a) poverty and illiteracy have a positive association; (b) poverty and post-primary schooling have a negative association; and (c) poverty and primary schooling have almost no association. 'Mere literacy' too has a positive association with poverty. This seems to suggest that income poverty is a critical barrier for attaining even literacy per se. Conversely, higher attainment of education beyond primary level is a prerogative of those with relatively better income levels.

The positive association between literacy and per capita state domestic product (PCSDP) has been examined by working a typology consisting of four categories of states (see Table 7). The link was further examined through a regression analysis (Tilak 2005, p. 45). It is however noted that whereas coefficient of education as an independent variable is fairly significant, the analyses by and large indicate association between the two rather than establishing a causal relationship (ibid., p. 46).

The phenomenon of negative association between poverty and higher level of educational attainments is found to be fairly systematic as one goes up the ladder. Table 8 presents a fairly clear picture of how income works as an enabling factor for attaining higher education.

Table 6 Coefficient of correlation between education and poverty

Coefficient of correlation between poverty ratio (1999–00) and	
% of Population (1995–96) having	r
Illiteracy	0.21242
Literacy	0.48595
Primary	0.05105
Middle/upper primary	−0.35790
Secondary and above	−0.55952

Source Based on Table no. 13, Tilak (2005)

Table 7 Two way link of literacy and PCNSDP

Classification	1981	1991	2001	2011
Virtuous high literacy and high PCNSDP	Kerala, Maharashtra, Karnataka, Gujarat	Punjab, Kerala, Haryana, Maharashtra, Tamil Nadu, Karnataka	Punjab, Kerala, Haryana, Maharashtra, Gujarat, Tamil Nadu, Karnataka	Kerala, Maharashtra, Tamil Nadu, Gujarat, Punjab, Haryana, Karnataka
Vicious low literacy and low PCNSDP	Bihar, Madhya Pradesh, Uttar Pradesh, Odisha, Rajasthan, Andhra Pradesh	Bihar, Madhya Pradesh, Uttar Pradesh, Odisha, Rajasthan	Bihar, Madhya Pradesh, Uttar Pradesh, Odisha, Rajasthan, Assam	Odisha, Assam, Chhattisgarh, Madhya Pradesh, Uttar Pradesh, Jharkhand, Rajasthan
Lop sided high literacy and low PCNSDP	Tamil Nadu, West Bengal, Karnataka	West Bengal, Assam, Gujarat	West Bengal	Bihar, West Bengal
Lop sided EG low literacy and high PCNSDP	Haryana, Punjab	Andhra Pradesh	Andhra Pradesh	Andhra Pradesh

Source Based on Appendix Table 13

4   Poverty and Education among Social Groups

Based on the consumption expenditure data from the 61st Round of the National Sample Survey Organisation (NSSO), Sengupta et al. (2008) have worked out educational gaps between poor and vulnerable (i.e. those in danger of becoming poor in the face of risks such as drought, price rise, illness or death of the main breadwinner in the household) and those in the middle and high income groups. According to the study about 73% of India's population belonged to the category of poor and vulnerable and the remaining 27% to the middle and high income group category. Table 9 presents a detailed account of the educational gap between these two categories of households' income across different social groups.

As expected, the proportion of illiterate population among the poor and vulnerable is higher than their share in the total population in the case of each social group. For example, poor and vulnerable among SCs/STs account for 85% of their population; 91% of whom are illiterate. It is, however, noteworthy that nearly 30% of the "other" social group in the middle and high income category are illiterate. This suggests that poverty matters, although to a different extent, depending on the social category. But a more significant observation that emerges from Table 9 is

Table 8 Adult population (age 15 years and above) with secondary and higher education, by economic groups, 1995–96

Income quintile groups	Secondary	Higher secondary	Diploma/ certificate	Graduate	Post graduate and above	Total
Rural						
00–20	2.4	0.8	0.0	0.6	0.0	3.8
20–40	3.9	1.3	0.1	0.6	0.1	6.0
40–60	4.9	1.8	0.1	0.7	0.1	7.6
60–80	7.3	3.0	0.1	1.4	0.1	11.9
80–100	12.2	5.1	0.6	3.4	0.8	22.1
Total	6.5	2.6	0.2	1.4	0.2	10.9
Urban						
00–20	6.4	2.9	0.3	1.5	0.3	11.4
20–40	11.4	5.0	0.4	3.8	0.5	21.1
40–60	15.5	7.3	0.6	5.5	0.9	29.8
60–80	20.0	11.4	1.1	10.1	1.9	44.5
80–100	20.8	15.5	1.9	21.8	5.4	65.4
Total	15.4	8.9	0.9	9.2	2.0	36.4
Total						
00–20	3.4	1.3	0.1	0.8	0.1	5.7
20–40	5.9	2.3	0.2	1.5	0.2	10.1
40–60	7.6	3.2	0.2	2.0	0.3	13.3
60–80	10.6	5.2	0.4	3.6	0.6	20.4
80–100	14.4	7.7	0.9	8.1	2.0	33.1
Total	8.8	4.2	0.4	3.5	0.7	17.6

Source Based on Table no. 7, Tilak (2005)

that the extent of illiteracy disproportionately varies by group (i.e. in 'SC/ST', illiteracy among the poor is 7% higher than it would be if it mirrored the poor/rich divide; however, for 'others', illiteracy among the poor is 20% higher than it would be if it mirrored the population).

To the extent income poverty and social marginalization are interspersed, income poverty is likely to have a compounding impact on education poverty–first through the income effect and then through socio-cultural marginalization. It is difficult to gauge the impact on education poverty independent of each other. The next section tries to partly deal with the issue while reviewing the evidence on returns to education.

Table 9 Poverty and education among social groups

Social category	Poverty status	Illiterate	Up to primary	Middle	Secondary and above but below graduate	Graduate and above	Total
SC/ST	Poor and vulnerable	91.2	89.7	80.7	65.4	47.8	85.0
	Middle and HIG	8.8	10.3	19.3	34.7	52.2	15.0
	All	100.0	100.0	100.0	100.0	100.0	100.0
Muslims	Poor and vulnerable	89.5	87.2	76.5	63.1	43.4	81.3
	Middle and HIG	10.6	12.8	23.6	36.9	56.6	18.7
	All	100.0	100.0	100.0	100.0	100.0	100.0
OBC	Poor and vulnerable	85.6	83.6	74.3	59.9	39.4	76.3
	Middle and HIG	14.5	16.4	25.7	40.1	60.6	23.7
	All	100.0	100.0	100.0	100.0	100.0	100.0
Others	Poor and vulnerable	70.6	66.9	57.7	39.5	21.6	50.9
	Middle and HIG	29.4	33.1	42.3	60.5	78.4	49.1
	All	100.0	100.0	100.0	100.0	100.0	100.0
All	All poor and vulnerable	86.1	83.3	71.2	52.4	29.7	72.6
	Middle and HIG	13.9	16.7	28.8	47.6	70.3	27.4
	All	100.0	100.0	100.0	100.0	100.0	100.0

Source Based on Table no. 9, Sengupta et al. (2008)

4.1 Education and Chronic Poverty

Bhide and Mehta (2006) examined the link between education and chronic poverty using a panel data set. Table 10 presents the distribution of households by educational level of the head of the households and the status of poverty among the sample households. The pattern in Table 10 supports the positive link between educational level and proportion of households in the category of chronic poverty. This, once again, does not indicate a causal link between the two. Moreover, the variable capturing education refers only to the head of the household, irrespective of age and gender.

This section highlights the fact that both literacy and enrolment at all levels of education have seen significant gains since independence, and dropout rates have decreased. However, retaining students within the education system remains a

Table 10 Education level of household head and dynamics of poverty

Education	Distribution of Sample HHDs (%)				Distribution of poor HHDs (%)		
	CP	TP	NP	Total	CP	TP	Total
Period: 1970–81; sample 3996							
Illiterate	34.66	36.51	28.82	100	48.7	51.3	100
Primary education	34.03	46.57	19.4	100	42.22	57.78	100
Above primary	14.56	36.21	49.23	100	28.69	71.31	100
Total	28.43	37.26	34.31	*100*	43.28	56.72	100
Period: 1981–98; sample 3996							
Illiterate	27.03	50	22.97	100	35.09	64.91	100
Primary education	29.69	38.82	31.5	100	43.34	56.66	100
Above primary	16.7	37.25	46.06	100	30.95	69.05	100
Total	24.27	38.59	37.14	100	39.61	61.39	100

Note CP Chronic Poor in both the periods; *TP* Transient Poor in one of the periods; *NP* Non-poor in both the periods
Source Based on Table no. 3, Bhide and Mehta (2006)

challenge. Financial constraints imposed on parents by poverty are the leading cause of both non-enrolment and withdrawal of children from school, often to put them to work. Another is the poor quality and lack of relevance of education to the lives, especially of the poor, and to the needs of the market. In addition, the uninspiring, non-stimulating and even humiliating experiences of children in school often lead them to drop out.

Literacy and schooling in India vary by class, gender, ethnicity, geography and rural–urban locations. As expected, Scheduled Tribes lag behind other categories of population as do the Scheduled Castes, although the difference for the latter is less owing to several government programmes targeting education among SCs. Whereas income poverty and education poverty impact each other, evidence tends to suggest that the negative impact of poverty on educational attainment is more widespread than the positive impact of educational attainment on poverty. This link is evident across 15 major states of India where, by and large, those that have high literacy tend to have low poverty whereas those with low literacy levels tend to have high poverty. While one may not cause the other, these two parameters of development do display an association.

Notwithstanding the limited evidence, the general perception, as noted earlier, is that given the households' assets and other characteristics, primary education may help households exit poverty; it may however not help sustain improvement in economic status and/or prevent a relapse into poverty. Higher levels of education, thus, are essential for sustained exit from poverty over a long period of time (Tilak 2005; p. 13).

5   Returns to Education: A Review of Evidence and Issues

The growing numbers of educated unemployed and the continued dominance of self-employment as a major source of income in India have led to questioning the economic justification of education especially among the vast majority of the poor in the country. Earlier, national level estimates had indicated that private returns to education in urban areas ranged between 9 and 17% (Blaug et al. 1969). For rural areas, Duraisamy (1992) revealed that education among farmers (4 years and above) led to an increase in the gross value of output by 4%, and that these farmers attain higher allocative efficiency as compared to their uneducated counterparts.

Subsequently a number of studies have examined private returns of education focusing on those engaged in salaried and wage employment, regular as well as casual. Most of the studies found that returns to education increase along with an increase in educational attainment. Based on micro-level data, Tilak (1990) found that earnings of male workers nearly doubled if they had higher than secondary education. Among women, the wage increase was found to be as high as 90%. The phenomenon of higher returns of education among women as compared to men was also observed by Kingdon and Unni (1998). They found that the wage disadvantage effect of lower educational attainment among women was compensated by higher returns to their education. Observing a 'U' shaped association between education and participation in wage and salaried employment among both men and women, they found that the coefficient of wage/salaried employment declined till the level of middle school and rose thereafter, becoming positive after graduation. Their analyses also highlighted the fact that the wealth of the households, captured through ownership of land, was inversely associated with participation in wage/salaried employment. The authors therefore point to the limitation of omitted family background bias that may have an important bearing on examining the impact among the poor. This subsequently was noted by Unni (2001) who observed that households deriving major income from salaried employment had the highest average household income; that they were the least likely to be poor and had the highest educational attainment. These were followed by the households in agriculture and the self-employed in non-agriculture activities. Those engaged in wage employment were more likely to be poor.

There are, however, also instances of educated youth who have completed at least secondary education (in some cases even graduation and masters) but can find work only as daily wage manual labourers. A study by Aajeevika Bureau (2009) among tribal migrant youth from Rajasthan found that this is mainly because education does not equip them with the skills needed in the job market and also because they have only limited exposure to employment options. The Aajeevika study found that several such youth were frustrated at having wasted years in school.

As most of the studies on returns to education cover those with salaried and wage employment, they often face the problem of sample selection bias (Duraisamy 2002, p. 613). Using a simultaneous equation framework for estimating wage function, he noted that 'the less productive men are likely to be in wage work than others' thereby indicating influence of the sample selection bias.

Notwithstanding the significant impacts of education on wage/salary incomes, these results suffer from limited generalizability given the fact that workers with higher education constitute only a small proportion of the labour force in India, and hence are not representative. Also finding wage and salaried employment is a privilege for the few in an economy that has experienced jobless growth over a couple of decades. According to recent estimates, nearly two-thirds of the workforce in India has no education or less than five years of it. Given this scenario, posing education as a panacea for economic growth may sound problematic (D'Souza 2008). It is therefore stressed that the link between education and output is context specific where creation of employment is a precursor to realization of increased returns to education. This issue is further substantiated by Duraisamy (2002) who found that returns to education among the younger age cohorts had declined. He attributes this to increased supply of workers with education up to secondary level owing to expansion of schooling over time.

More recently Roy (2008) has cautioned against the expected increase in returns to skills and education in the contemporary context of the Indian economy. She notes that fluctuations in skill premia occur mainly because of changes in the relative supply of labour. Hence technology-driven demand for skilled labour is not likely to outpace rising supply of educated workers owing to the large size of reserve labour in the economy (ibid., p. 789).

This brings us back to the issue of how many among the poor households could attain higher education? Even if they do so, how likely would they be to actually enter salary or wage employment, especially when supply of such labour force with increased educational attainment is on the rise? While evidence shows that higher secondary and above level of education for men and graduation among women increases the chances of entering wage/salaried employment, the question is: would this in itself help enhance productivity and thereby earnings among a large proportion of the poor and less educated workforce engaged as self-employed and/or casual labour? If the answer is in the negative, the findings indicating increasing returns along with increasing educational attainments may hold limited relevance in addressing the issue of income poverty at least in the short and medium term.

In the same vein, the plea for promoting post-primary education as a means of poverty reduction may also appear to be somewhat misplaced especially for two reasons. First, persons attaining higher education and obtaining wage/salaried jobs with sustained increase in earnings may constitute only a small proportion of the poor. And second, low return to primary education is primarily a reflection of its low quality (Duraisamy 2002). In this scenario secondary education may serve as a substitute for good quality of primary education. Hence the solution, essentially, may lie in improving the quality of primary education rather than shifting the focus on secondary and higher education, which not only has limited outreach but may also imply compounding wastage of education.

This is not to undermine the importance of promoting higher levels of education. The point however is that the case for higher education should not be made purely on the ground of economic returns and certainly not at the cost of improving the quality of education at all levels starting from primary education. It is the quality–both in terms of effective delivery as well as content–that matters for building up human capital, capability and society that forms the core of education, besides its impact on income and earnings.

6 The Unfinished Tasks and Future Options: Discussion of Selected Policy Issues

The critical challenge therefore is to complete the unfinished agenda of universal and free elementary education of requisite quality to be fed into healthy, broad-based and affordable systems of secondary and higher education with relevant skills. This essentially would mean strengthening the supply-side mechanisms with respect to infrastructure and availability of teachers who actually teach. On the demand side the necessary actions would be improving the environment of schools and imparting skills and values-based education that may have intrinsic value for children of all classes, castes, regions, ethnicity and gender. While increasing investment in education is an important starting point, by itself it may not bring improvement in influencing demand-side constraints unless the issue of corruption, high cost and social discrimination are resolved simultaneously.

Till then the familiar scenario of elementary education may continue to remain as:

> Even...where teachers were present, they were not necessarily teaching. In one instance, the head-teacher was on leave and three of the remaining five teachers were standing in the playground talking among themselves.... Some children were sitting on benches and chatting while others were roaming around the school campus.
>
> Shiva Kumar et al. (2009)

Revived emphasis on SSA during the Eleventh Plan was aimed at accomplishing the unfinished agenda by addressing some of the issues raised above. With the passage of the RTE Act in 2010, the Approach Paper to the Twelfth Plan states that the right to education "requires that the mandate under the RTE is aligned with the vision, strategies and norms of SSA (Planning Commission 2011, p. 125)

This section briefly discusses the strengths and limitations of the approach during the Eleventh Plan. "Inclusiveness" was the catchword of the Eleventh Plan which was expected to result in substantial reduction in poverty, improvement in health outcomes and universal access for children to elementary education, and increased access to secondary education and higher education as well as to opportunities of skill development. According to government documents, "India is well poised to meet the Millennium Development Goal (MDG) target of 50% reduction of poverty between 1990 and 2015" (Planning Commission 2011, p. 6). The other MDG that India has been trying to meet is Goal 2 of providing universal elementary education to its children.

(a) **Increasing investment and widening the net through privatization**

Under-investment in education has been seen as one of the most important lacunae causing education poverty in the country. This is reflected in the severe shortage of teachers in schools. While there has been a massive drive to increase the number of teachers, the teacher–pupil ratio has registered only a marginal improvement over the past 10 years (Table 11). A substantially large proportion of schools still have only one teacher; the issue of frequent absenteeism of teachers would therefore mean a virtual collapse of teaching activities in such schools. Recent reports indicate that there is substantial under-spending of budgetary allocation in a number of states. At the same time there are reports suggesting that appointment of school teachers have been virtually frozen for several years in a number of states.

While this issue needs further probing, the case for increasing the budgetary allocation and also effective utilization of the allocated funds could hardly be overemphasized. The official estimates indicate that whereas total spending on education has increased over time, the increase is not commensurate with the rising student population and other needs for improving basic infrastructure, etc. Investment in secondary and higher education thus becomes the most critical casualty. As per the official estimates, investment in education sector has continued to remain in the range of 3.5% of the gross domestic product (GDP). This is far below the historically set norm of 6% of GDP.

Government spending on education has increased by 790 times from Rs. 344.4 crore in 1960–61 to Rs. 227,137.44 crore in 2010–11. The share of education in gross domestic product, which was 2.1% in 1960–61, increased to 4.28 in 2001 but went down to 3.80% in 2010–11. Per capita expenditure on education increased considerably from Rs. 7.8 in 1960–61 to Rs. 942.23 in 2006–07. Per pupil expenditure also increased significantly from Rs. 53 in 1960–61 to Rs. 3957.1 in 2000–01.

Notwithstanding the need for increased investment in education, an important aspect that needs attention is the corruption that has crept into the vital parts of the education system, especially at the primary level. One of the reasons why teachers are often absent and abstain from teaching is that many of them got their jobs

Table 11 Government expenditure on education, 1960–61 to 2010–11

Head	1960–61	2001	2010–11
Government spending on education (Rs. crore)	344.4	78,236.5	272,137.44[a]
Share of education in gross domestic product (per cent)	2.1	4.28	3.80[a]
Per capita expenditure on education (Rs.)	7.8	761.8	942.23[b] (2006–07)
Per pupil expenditure (Rs.)	53	3957.1	5269[c]

Sources [a]http://mhrd.gov.in/sites/upload_files/mhrd/files/ABE_2008-11_1.pdf
[b]http://planningcommission.nic.in/reports/genrep/tilak.pdf
[c]Per student public expenditure on elementary education. *Source* Dongre et al. (2014)

through unscrupulous channels; therefore making them work is quite difficult within the given system (The Economist 2017; Azim Premji Foundation 2017).

The government sees partial privatization of education as an effective solution. While this may involve higher private cost to the parents, the recent policy proposes to circumvent the problem by reimbursement of the cost to private schools by introducing education coupons. As private schools vary in quality and cost, the less expensive ones may not be very different from the government schools Also, as long as the poor have to pay for the education of children, girls will continue to be at a disadvantage (Shiva Kumar et al. 2009). Privatization of the elementary school system may prove fatal for poor children who, even if they are able to bear the indirect cost attached to schooling in such institutions, may face severe entry barriers based on social discrimination and also suffer humiliation and discrimination at the hands of teachers as well as other students.

The RTE Act mandates that all private schools, even if they do not receive any financial aid from the government, must reserve 25% seats for economically disadvantaged children. This mandate will need intelligent and sensitive implementation to ensure that the existing social inequalities of class, caste and gender do not continue. It is not clear to what extent this arrangement would help check corruption, especially in a scenario where the schools are not directly accountable to the parents or the communities. An attempt has been made under SSA to promote community involvement by setting up different committees such as Village Education Committees, School Monitoring Committees and School Education Committees. Although there are instances of such committees having been able to improve the physical infrastructure in schools, select contract/para-teachers and supervise school lunch programmes, they have not been able to influence the quality of teaching (De et al. 2011).

The crucial question is whether a move towards partial privatization may help improve the efficacy of the public system or would it prove to be a serious assault on this very vital aspect of a welfare state? Increased state investment thus needs to be seen in this context of making education inclusive for the poor. At the same time, increased investment should be accompanied by increased accountability to the local communities.

(b) **Shiksha Karmis: The issue of quality**

To deal with the issue of shortage of teachers without having to make the large financial investment required to pay their salaries, a mechanism used by several states is the involvement of para-teachers (also called Shiksha Karmis). Shiksha Karmis are, by and large, local youth who undergo intensive training (in Rajasthan, where the programme was started, it is 37 days followed by a month-long in-service training each year). The intention of this approach was to provide assistance to the many single-teacher schools in the country, of which there are still many, while also helping provide access to education to deprived communities in remote and difficult areas where regular teachers either did not want to go or remained absent for long periods. Para-teachers have also been used to fill up teacher vacancies in schools.

It is estimated that 220,000 para-teachers are employed in full-time schools all over the country, of which about 54% are in Madhya Pradesh. If those teaching in part-time schools is also added, the total works out to 500,000 by 2015–16 (www. educationforallinindia.com/page154.html).

Prima facie, the approach seems to hold substantial promise though it has been severely criticized for further diluting the concern for quality in primary education. Quality is of course a non-negotiable aspect of education as it is a means of helping achieve freedom and empowerment. Nevertheless, recruitment of properly trained teachers, given the corruption syndrome, does not guarantee quality of teaching.

The involvement of para-teachers may also be accompanied by requisite support in terms of training, infrastructural facilities and above all involvement of the local communities. An initiative by the Social Work Research Centre (SWRC) at Tilonia in Rajasthan provides an encouraging example in this context. The innovative approach adopted for extending the outreach of primary schooling among working children and/or those located in geographically remote areas consisted of an active role of the education committee for demanding such support and later on provisioning of accommodation as well as basic amenities for the para-teacher who would be invariably selected from the same region and trained by the Centre. This approach seems to have attained reasonably good success; more such initiatives with CBOs' involvement may help expedite the pace of promoting primary education among less privileged children and areas.

Besides this, the system of para-teachers could be opened up to many more potential initiatives from communities at large. This may also include some of the voluntary/traditional institutions evolved through various streams of social/religious agencies such as Gandhian basic education and Madrasas.

The need therefore is to open the gates for active participation from a large number of well-meaning and experienced educational agencies rather than leaning merely on privatization.

(c) **Mid-Day Meal: Implications for retention and effective learning**

The Mid-Day Meal programme represents, at least in outreach, one of the most successful government interventions in recent years, having now become universal across the country (Singh 2008). Its aim was to end hunger in the classroom and to be an incentive to the poor and chronically poor families to send their children, including girls, to school, thereby leading to a reduction in child labour. Under the scheme, on every school day, all students in primary classes in government, local body and government-aided schools are to be provided a hot cooked meal consisting of no less than 300 kcal and 8–12 grams of protein. Though officially started in 1995, the National Mid-Day Meal Scheme (MDMS) remained unimplemented in most states till 2002. Following a Supreme Court ruling in November 2001, most states started providing school meals by 2003.

Tracing the impact of the mid-day meal programme on enrolment, attendance and retention however is difficult because many states also introduced other incentivizing schemes when the mid-day meals scheme was being implemented. For example, Shiksha Apke Dwar in Rajasthan and Bicycles to VIII Standard

Students in Karnataka were introduced during the same period. Furthermore, prior to the implementation of mid-day meals was a scheme that distributed dry rations to schoolchildren. Besides, to study the impact of the mid-day meal programme, the enrolment, attendance and retention data provided by schools is of little help because teachers tend to mark most pupils as 'present' irrespective of the actual attendance' (Dreze and Goyal 2003). The reason for the fudging of data is that teachers are offered various incentives to do so (PROBE Team 1999).

Notwithstanding these limitations several studies have been undertaken for evaluating the scheme. A study by Shankar and Natasha (2001) by Centre for Equity Studies (CES) examined the impact of the scheme in three states, namely, Chhattisgarh, Rajasthan and Karnataka. The study, conducted in 27 randomly selected villages from each state, estimated that the scheme is associated with a 50% reduction in the number of out-of-school girls. Teachers reported that the programme makes it easier to retain children in school after the lunch break, as children who went home for lunch often did not return to school, especially if the distance from home was great. Since the introduction of the scheme, according to a large majority (78%) of the teachers interviewed, afternoon attendance is roughly the same as morning attendance.

Sethi (2003), who studied 10 years of school enrolment and retention for classes I–V in Odisha, found that after the introduction of MDMS, enrolment and retention had increased and the dropout rate had decreased considerably. A study by Josephine (1998) on the impact of MDMS on girls' enrolment in West Garo Hills of Meghalaya found that the enrolment had increased from 9.1 to 25% in Dalu and from 10.9 to 25.3% in Rongram block. Seetharaman (2006) found that while the Mid-Day Meal programme did not make a significant impact on improving the nutritional status of the children, it did result in a reduction of the dropout rate of girls in sample villages in Uttar Pradesh and Rajasthan. Jayaraman (2009) found that the introduction of school lunch in Tamil Nadu and Karnataka was associated with a 25% increase in class 1 enrolment, but that there was no evidence to suggest that it helped bridge the overall gender or caste gaps in enrolment. Chaudhuri (2007) found that direct cash payments to the working families instead of the mid-day meal programme are likely to be more effective in eradicating the problem of child labour.

Mid-day meals are loosely supervised and formal monitoring arrangements are sparse. The lack of supervision opens the door to a range of problems such as petty corruption, logistic delays and poor hygiene (Dreze and Goyal 2003). To overcome such problems, Jharkhand has sought the involvement of the community through Sarasvati Vahini, an association of schoolchildren's mothers. Two of the mothers take the responsibility of cooking while the others take turns in supervising the cooking and distribution of meals. Children's involvement is also sought through the formation of Bal Sansad in each school whose members oversee health and hygiene by ensuring that students wash their hands before and after the meal, wash their plates, wait in queue to be served and that the cooks wear their aprons while cooking (http://mdm.nic.in/BestPractices/Jharkhand.pdf).

(d) **Revitalizing Vocational Education: Is there a role for basic education?**

Vocational education, or *Vocational Education and Training* (VET), prepares learners for jobs that are based on manual or practical activities. The Industrial Training Institutes (ITIs) and Industrial Training Centres (ITCs) have provided training to students after Class X, mainly technical trades like motor mechanics, plumbing, refrigeration and air-conditioning repairs. Vocational education has, however, diversified, in the past few decades and now covers areas such as retail, tourism, information technology, funeral services and beauty services, as well as in the traditional crafts and cottage industries. The government recognizes the need for improved training and skill development in order to provide employment opportunities for a fast-growing young population.

Since the late 1980s, skill training and vocational education have been mainstreamed into formal education and is offered in school classes 11 and 12 under a centrally sponsored scheme called 'Vocationalisation of Secondary Education'. Its purpose is to enhance individual employability, reduce the mismatch between demand and supply of skilled manpower and provide an alternative for those pursuing higher education without particular interest or purpose (World Bank 2006).

According to targets set by the Government of India, vocational education was to reach out to 25% of the students in higher education by 1995. The target is far from being achieved. The plan now is to ensure that 25% of the workforce should have received formal skills through vocational education and training by the end of the XII Plan (Planning Commission 2011). For this, skill creation outside the formal system too was being co-ordinated, and the National Skill Development Mission was launched during the XI Plan period.

Among the various factors responsible for under-achievement of targets set for vocational education are high cost, low quality and a lack of links with the productive sectors on the one hand and higher education on the other. Lack of effective demand for such skills in the productive sectors led to relatively low preference being attached to such training. An unwarranted fallout of this is that vocational education is viewed as being meant for the poor and perhaps a poor substitute for higher education (Tilak 2005; p. 26). Although fresh efforts have been made to introduce vocational/technical courses at higher (undergraduate) level of education; one does not find any major breakthrough in terms of addressing the demand-side barriers. More recently there has been a revival of emphasis on skill training in the wake of a growing concern for productivity enhancement among the vast army of informal sector workers especially in the secondary and tertiary sectors, and also in the context of the debate on demographic divided as noted earlier.

The current government launched, in July 1915, the Pradhan Mantri Kaushal Vikas Yojana (PMKVY), India's largest Skill Certification Scheme. The scheme seeks to impart Short Term Training at PMKVY Training Centres (TCs), to those who are either school/college dropouts or unemployed. Apart from providing training according to the National Skills Qualification Framework (NSQF), the TCs are meant to also impart training in Soft Skills, Entrepreneurship, Financial and Digital Literacy. Upon successful completion of their training, candidates should receive placement assistance. Of the 22.5 lakh enrolled in the various training programmes, 7.39 had been certified by early January 2018, of whom 3.38 lakh had been placed as of 2 April 2018. In addition to training first-time learners, the scheme also recognizes and certifies those with prior learning (GOI 2015)

The economy is facing a shortage of specialized skills and expertise across a large number of productive sectors, including agriculture and education, as there is a shortage of good teachers at all levels. This should be viewed as part of a larger phenomenon of the distortions between the kind of knowledge that is generated and what should be delivered. In fact the phenomenon is intrinsically linked to the issue of quality of education at all levels, especially at primary levels where a majority of poor children have the only chance of learning. Is there a way to address the issue of mismatch between demand for and supply of skilled labour in the economy and the society?

An important aspect that often gets neglected while looking for solutions is the issue of almost complete disjuncture between academic and vocational training; between different disciplines; and also between informal and formal processes of skill formation. As a result, society/economy is faced with a scenario where agricultural scientists do not know how to actually undertake cultivation; a simple graduate may not know how to deal with the day-to-day business of personal life; a science graduate also does not necessarily know enough mathematics that is imparted even at the lower levels of schooling. So while there are a number of educated unemployed, a number of sectors including education are facing a severe shortage of teachers with relevant skills and commitment. On the other hand, a large number of employers in industry and service sectors end up choosing those with substantial on-the-job training and/or those with an academic qualification and invest in in-house training for their workers.

India has a rich tradition of evolving alternative pedagogy especially for basic education. One such example is the approach of Nai Taleem, a complete education propagated by the erstwhile Gandhian institutions in the country. There is a need to revisit this and several other alternative approaches to education that combine academic knowledge with life skills as they may have a better chance for improving both employability as well as social and individual empowerment of persons who may have attained only elementary education.

(e) **Learning from state-level initiatives**

A number of initiatives have been undertaken at the state level that may offer useful insights for future policies. Some of these initiatives have been described here.

Madhya Pradesh education guarantee scheme

One of the outstanding success stories in elementary education during the past 20 years comes from Madhya Pradesh. Through its Education Guarantee Scheme (EGS), the state set out to address the issue of lack of access to primary education for children of very poor households, including those in the scattered settlements of its vast tribal areas. It was able to do so by linking with local self-government institutions. The state government pledged its own resources without depending on grants from either the central government or foreign donor agencies. A large-scale appointment of teachers (mostly local youth) was done where the communities identified the prospective teachers who were then trained by the state education department.

The EGS, from the outset, was meant to be a large-scale programme. In just three years (July 1997–July 2000) 26,571 schools were created with an enrolment of more than 12 lakh children, of which 47% were girls. Of the total number of children, 91% belonged to SC, ST and other socially disadvantaged communities. Within a few years the EGS programme showed a sharp drop in the number of out-of-school children and, within a decade, a sizable increase in female literacy. The gross enrolment ratios increased and did not show any significant disparities between different social groups (Ramachandran 2004). Data for 2011–12 shows a further improvement in female–male ratio in education in the state. In primary and upper primary education, the girls to boys enrolment ratio were 0.95 and 1.01, respectively, in urban areas and 0.97 and 1.04 in rural areas. This shows that girls enrolment is given equal weightage in rural areas. Also the recent data reveals a decline in dropout rates among the SC and ST students (Gupta 2012).

A significant feature of this programme is that the state government created administrative and legislative provisions to entrust the local communities and local self-government institutions with the powers and responsibility of managing, running and supervising the schools. The schools are accountable to the Parent Teacher Associations and the Village Education Committees set up for the purpose.

As part of another initiative, 16,000 government schools in Madhya Pradesh (Government of Madhya Pradesh 2016), most of them catering to children of the poor and chronically poor, have adopted innovative, activity-based learning (based on Rishi Valley's RIVER approach (Rishi Valley Institute for Educational Resources) with remarkable success. The learning in these schools is teacher supported, peer supported as well as involves self-learning, where each child learns at his/her own pace and level of competency (Brara 2012). The RIVER approach has now been adopted by more than 250,000 schools in 16 states, enriching more than 10 million children (Source: http://tidelearning.com/river-tide/).

Akshaya Patra

Karnataka introduced hot cooked meals in primary schools in June 2002. The state was able to involve the private sector to participate in this programme. One of the successful ventures is called Akshaya Patra, which started with leadership from both ISKCON and secular leaders in Bangalore. The programme, which is completely secular, is run by an independent organization that cooks and distributes lunch to children in Bangalore Municipal Corporation schools. The organization gets a grant from the state government but meets a major share of its costs from corporate and individual donations.

An ultramodern, centralized kitchen for the programme is operated through a public/private partnership. The hygienically prepared and tasty food, which comprises sambar, rice, vegetables and often some curd, is delivered just before lunch break to schools in sealed and heat retaining containers.

As a result of the success of this programme, private sector participation in mid-day meals has increased considerably. Software companies such as Infosys, Bharti and Jindal are major donors to the programme. This model has been successfully replicated in rural Karnataka, Delhi, Hyderabad and other cities.

Akshay Patra is currently serving mid-day meals to almost 1.6 million children every day in 13,839 schools across 12 states, and hopes to feed more than 20 million children by 2020 (https://www.akshayapatra.org/).

Bicycles to students

Some states, such as Jharkhand, Karnataka and Odisha, have launched schemes to provide free bicycles to girl students from families who are below the poverty line and have enrolled for Class VIII in government and government-aided schools. The aim is to encourage and enable girls to continue their schooling and improve their attendance. Although most habitations have primary schools within a one-kilometre radius, not all villages have middle schools, nor do they have transport facilities for girls to travel to the villages that have the schools. As a result girls tend to drop out after primary school.

In Jharkhand and Odisha this scheme is also available to girls belonging to SC, ST and minority communities. In Karnataka this scheme has been extended to boys as well. During 2007–08, 2.14 lakh boys and 2.21 lakh girls were provided with bicycles. During 2008–09, the government proposed that it would provide free bicycles to around 7 lakh students (Economic Survey of Karnataka, 2008–09). However in 2015–16 the number reached 5.18 lakh, of which 2.55 lakh recipients were girls (Government of Karnataka 2016).

Kalinga Institute

Kalinga Institute of Social Science (KISS) in Bhubaneswar, Odisha, is a residential institution that provides free education, from class 1 to post-graduation, to tribal children in the state. The institute started in 1993 with 125 tribal children. By 2018 it had 27,000 tribal children from very poor families enrolled in different classes of the institute. The mission of KISS is to eradicate poverty and empower the poor, disadvantage tribal sections of the society through holistic, quality education, to provide them with sustainable livelihoods. It seeks to prepare the underprivileged children and youth as 'change agents' for their community while working to preserve their tribal culture, heritage and values.

The innovative pedagogy and curriculum adopted by the institute ensures zero dropout, whereas schools in the tribal hinterland suffer widespread dropout. Ample opportunities to live and interact with the mainstream population has been providing the children the much needed confidence and acquaintance with skills of mainstream life. Sports are an important part of education at the institute which instils in the students confidence and team spirit. Several students have proved to be high achievers and have represented India in international sports events. All student undergo vocational education in one of the 50 trades offered according to their individual talent. The training is designed to impart necessary occupational skills to the tribal students prepare them for the job market and to mould them into successful entrepreneurs. Several students have found placement in the government, private and corporate sectors (https://cdn.kiss.ac.in/wp-content/uploads/2018/03/KISS-Annual-Report-2017.pdf).

The institute plans to educate 2,00,000 tribal children over the next decade at its different branches to be set up in all 30 districts of Odisha and also in other states (https://kiss.ac.in/).

7 Concluding Remarks

India has made remarkable progress in improving access to primary education and increasing enrolment rates over the past two decades. But the issue of quality still eludes education at every level. The concern in this paper is with access for the chronically poor to education that is inclusive and empowering and that can enable them to exit poverty.

An issue that may deserve careful investigation is whether the proposed upward shift in the critical minimum level of education to exit poverty implies more of the same quality of education. If so, it may amount to extending the duration of education for attaining skills and knowledge of the primary level; apparently the extension could be a necessary corrective measure in order to overcome absence of the requisite quality (in terms of both effective delivery as well as content) of education at the primary level. Also, the issue of skill formation can hardly be overlooked at this juncture of India's economic growth. This, in fact, further supports the case for simultaneously promoting secondary and higher education without waiting for universalization of elementary education to be achieved.

Increased privatization, as envisaged by the recent policy approach, could hardly be an effective solution when it comes to including poor children in quality education on a mass scale (Juneja 2011). At the same time the state alone may not be able to reach out to the educationally deprived communities. Legislation and statutes are essential, but they need to be accompanied by an empowered community, especially of parents, to demand for the rights of their children. In fact communities could help in various ways other than just being a watchdog for the state machinery to perform and deliver. Identifying and creating space for spontaneous yet latent force within the communities may help generate such dynamism from within. This may call for changing the value system of what matters in education; increasing the scope for local innovation and initiatives; and above all, creating their agency for making education inclusive and relevant.

There are several outstanding examples of successful educational experiments in enabling learning among children of the poorest by nongovernmental organizations, institutions and governments from around the country (Janadhyala and Ramachandran 2007) from which administrators, policy makers and implementers can draw inspiration and valuable lessons.

The discussion in this paper highlights the need to go beyond the dominant perspective on education consisting of a purely economistic framework and value system, straitjacket pedagogy and the state's role as provider to it being stimulator to promote community initiatives; and to the importance of a focus on quality. The purpose of education has to be to empower through attainment of a sense of well-being rather than suffering exclusion at the start of the schooling system. A paradigm shift such as this may help redress income as well as educational poverty simultaneously.

Appendix

Table 12 Education: Important laws, policies, commissions, constitutional provisions and programmes

(a) Important laws, policies and commissions on education

Name of the Committee	Year	Objectives
University Grants Commission, modified on 1985	1956 and 1985	Coordination, determination and maintenance of standards of university education in India, in order to ensure effective region-wise coverage throughout the country The UGC has the unique distinction of being the only grant-giving agency in the country which has been vested with two responsibilities: that of providing funds and of coordination, determination and maintenance of standards in institutions of higher education http://www.ugc.ac.in
The Institutes of Technology Act, 1961	1961	An Act to declare certain institutions of technology to be institutions of national importance and to provide for certain matters connected with such institutions. The Act was amended in 1963, 1994, 2002 and 2012 http://www.iitg.ac.in/rti/links/IITG_1961Act_14.08.2012_intranet_P1.pdf
National Policy on Education, 1968	1968	It aimed to promote national progress, a sense of common citizenship and culture, and to strengthen national integration. It laid stress on the need for a radical reconstruction of the education system, to improve its quality at all stages, and gave much greater attention to science and technology, the cultivation of moral values and a closer relation between education and the life of the people
National Policy on Education, 1986	1986	Universal access and enrolment Universal retention of children up to 14 years of age A substantial improvement in the quality of education to enable all children to achieve essential levels of learning

(continued)

Table 12 (continued)

(a) Important laws, policies and commissions on education

Name of the Committee	Year	Objectives
All India Council of Technical Education Act 1987	1987	To provide for the establishment of an All India Council for Technical Education with the view to ensure proper planning and co-ordinated development of the technical education system throughout the country, the promotion of qualitative improvements of such education in relation to planned quantitative growth, regulation and proper maintenance of norms and standards in the technical education system, and for matters connected therewith
National Policy on Education, 1986 as modified in 1992	1992	Establishment of new institutions, especially in backward area Expansion of intake in existing institutions Opening new branches and courses, especially in emerging area Grant of incentives for establishment of bonafide non-government institutions of good quality and non-commercial nature Programme of quality improvement of technical education Improvement and expansion of secondary education
The National Council of Teacher Education Act, 1993	1993	Enacted with a view to achieving planned and co-ordinated development of the teacher education system throughout the country, the regulation and proper maintenance of norms and standards in the teacher education system and for matters connected therewith http://www.ncte-india.org/noti/act.htm
The Persons with Disabilities (Equal Opportunities, Protection of Rights and Full Participation) Act, 1995	1995	This law is to ensure equal opportunities for people with disabilities and their full participation in nation building. The Act provides for both preventive and promotional aspects of rehabilitation like education, employment and vocational training, reservation, research and manpower development, creation of barrier-free environment, rehabilitation of persons with disability, unemployment and establishment of homes for persons with severe disability, etc. http://www.rehabcouncil.nic.in/pdf/pwdact1995.pdf
The National Council for Minority Educational Institutions Act, 2004	2004	An Act to constitute a National Commission for Minority Educational Institutions and to provide for matters connected therewith or incidental thereto http://ncmei.gov.in/writereaddata/filelinks/1f24301a_NCMEI%20Act,%20as%20amended.pdf

(continued)

Table 12 (continued)

(a) Important laws, policies and commissions on education

Name of the Committee	Year	Objectives
National Knowledge Commission	2006	Transforming India into a knowledge society. It covers sectors ranging from education to e-governance in the *five focus areas* of the knowledge paradigm, namely access to knowledge, knowledge concepts, knowledge creation, knowledge application and knowledge services
National Institutes of Technology Act, 2007	2007	The Government of India introduced the *National Institutes of Technology (NIT) Act 2007* to bring 20 such institutions within the ambit of the act and to provide them with complete autonomy in their functioning. The NITs are deliberately scattered throughout the country in line with the government norm of an NIT in every major state of India to promote regional development http://www.aicte-india.org/nit.htm
The School of Planning and Architecture Act	2014	To establish and declare Schools of Planning and Architecture as Institutions of national importance in order to promote education and research in architectural studies including planning of human settlements

(b) Provisions in the Constitution

The Constitution of India is the ultimate document which guides State policy in all sectors, including Education. Some of the important feature of provisions contained in the Constitution, which have a bearing on Education, are:

- Provision of free and compulsory education to all children up to the age of fourteen years
- Education, in general, is the concurrent responsibility of the Union and the States. However, (a) coordination and determination of standards in higher and technical education, and (b) institutions declared by Parliament by law to be institutions of national importance, are the responsibility of the Union
- Local authorities (Panchayats and Municipalities) are to be assigned a suitable role in education (especially School, Adult and Non-Formal Education) through individual State legislations
- State Governments and Local Authorities are expected to provide facilities for instruction in the mother tongue at the primary stage of education

(c) Programmes

Programme	Year	Objectives	Remarks
Operation Blackboard	1987	Improving the school environment and enhancing retention and learning achievement of children by providing minimum essential facilities in all primary schools	The scheme brought about both quantitative and qualitative improvements in primary education. In all, 523,000 primary schools were covered as originally envisaged. These schools have been provided with central assistance

(continued)

Table 12 (continued)

(c) Programmes

Programme	Year	Objectives	Remarks
National Programme of Nutritional Support to Primary Education (School Meal Programme)	1995	To give a boost to UEE in terms of increasing enrolment, retention and attendance in primary classes by supplementing nutritional requirements of children attending primary schools. It is an ambitious scheme that was sought to be operationalized throughout the country in a very short period. The programme envisaged provision of nutritious and wholesome cooked meal of 100 gm of food grains per school day, free of cost, to all children in classes I–V by 1997–98	Universal coverage of the scheme, achievement of social equity The scheme has been successful in eliminating classroom hunger. It was able to bring together children from different communities in almost all the states and was thus able to achieve the objective of social equity to a considerable extent *Source* http://planningcommission.nic.in/reports/peoreport/peoevalu/peo_cmdm.pdf
District Primary Education Programme	1994	To provide all children with access to primary education either in the formal system or through the non-formal education (NFE) programme To reduce differences in enrolment, dropout rates and learning achievement among gender and social groups to less than 5% To reduce overall primary dropout rates for all students to less than 10% To raise average achievement levels by at least 25% over measured baseline levels and ensuring achievements of basic literacy and numeracy competencies and a minimum of 40% achievement levels in other competencies by all primary school children	DPEP has so far opened more than 1,60,000 new schools, including almost 84,000 alternative schooling (AS) centres. The AS centres cover nearly 3.5 million children, while another two lakh children are covered by bridge courses of different types The gross enrolment ratio (GER) for Phase-I states was around 93–95% for the last three years. After the adjustment for the Alternative Schools/Education Guarantee Centres enrolment, the GER in the 2001–02 works out above 100%. In the districts covered under subsequent phases of DPEP, the GER including enrolment of AS/EGS was above 85% The enrolment of girls has shown significant improvement. In DPEP-I districts, the share of girls enrolment in relation to total enrolment has increased

(continued)

Table 12 (continued)

(c) Programmes

Programme	Year	Objectives	Remarks
			from 48 to 49%, while this increase in the subsequent phases of DPEP districts has been from 46 to 47% The total number of differently abled children enrolled is now more than 420,203 which represents almost 76% of the nearly 553,844 differently abled children identified in the DPEP states *Source* http://india.gov.in/sectors/education/index.php?id=14
Bihar Education Project (BEP)	1991	Bringing about quantitative and qualitative improvement in the elementary system in Bihar	The project lays emphasis on the education of deprived sections of society, such as SCs, STs and women. Participatory planning and implementation are crucial ingredients of the project
Uttar Pradesh Basic Education Programme (with World Bank assistance)	1993	(a) improving access; (b) improving quality; and (c) building institutional capacity to manage elementary education	Primary enrolments have increased dramatically, particularly for all girls and for SC girls, with the overall GER ranging between 93 and 102% Enrolment growth in the project districts is estimated to have been around 33% points higher than in non-project districts Total out-of-school girls aged 6–14 years are reported to have decreased from 1.48 million in 1993 to 0.58 million in 2000, a reduction of 61% *Source* World Bank (2002). Report no: 21754
Andhra Pradesh Primary Education Project	1984 and 1996 two phases	The APPEP adopted a two-pronged strategy of improving classroom transaction by training teachers. Construction activities	The project has trained an estimated 80,000 teachers in 23 districts and more than 3000 teachers' centres have become operational for the professional growth of teachers *Source* http://www.cgg.gov.in/StrategyforGirlChildEducationforthestateofAP.pdf

(continued)

Table 12 (continued)

(c) Programmes

Programme	Year	Objectives	Remarks
Shiksha Karmi Project	1987	Universalization and qualitative improvement of primary education in the remote and socio-economically backward villages of Rajasthan, with primary focus on girls	The project covers 202,000 students (84,000 girls). 20 day schools upgraded to upper primary schools. Approximately 1% children in Shiksha Karmi schools were disabled. 13 residential training schools for women were established and 349 women Shiksha Karmi were trained. 2137 Village education committees were activated. As on March 1998, the project employed 6085 Shiksha Karmi (5390 males and 695 females) *Source* http://www.sida.se/Documents/Import/pdf/No7-Rajasthan-Shiksha-Karmi-Project-An-overall-appraisal.pdf
Right to Free and Compulsory Education (RTE) Act, 2009 had been enacted in 2010	2010	Aims at providing justiciable legal framework entitling all children between the ages of 6–14 years free and compulsory admission, attendance and completion of elementary education Norms – Pupil Teacher Ratios (PTRs), buildings and infrastructure, school-working days, teacher-working hours in both primary and upper primary schools	Most of the States reported an improvement in schools complying with PTR norms of RTE Act during 2009–10 to 2015–16. *Source* http://data.uis.unesco.org/ on 18 January, 2018
Nation Early Childhood Care and Education (ECCE) Policy	2013	Right of the child to survival, growth and holistic development, and the right to inputs that will make such development possible – care, love, nurturing, protection, health, nutrition, stimulation, play and learning	The policy focuses on restructuring the Integrated Child Development Services (ICDS) scheme and integrating early childhood education with the Right to Education Act to ensure a smooth transition into formal schooling. All service providers will have to be registered with the state governments to ensure quality of services provided *Source* http://lawcommissionofindia.nic.in/reports/Report259.pdf

Table 13 State-wise poverty ratio, literacy rate and per capita net state domestic product

	Literacy (%)				Poverty (%)				Per Capita NSDP (Rs.)[a]			
	1981	1991	2001	2011	1983	1993	2004	2011	1981	1991	2001	2011
Andhra Pradesh	35.66	44.08	60.47	67.02	28.91	22.19	15.8	9.2	19,815	26,951	40,057	69,000
Assam	NA	52.89	63.25	72.19	40.47	40.86	19.7	32	24,471	27,490	28,531	41,142
Bihar	32.32	37.49	47	61.8	62.22	54.96	41.4	33.7	9618	11,223	11,587	21,750
Gujarat	44.92	61.29	69.14	78.03	32.79	24.21	16.8	16.6	20,841	23,811	38,559	87,481
Haryana	37.13	55.85	67.91	75.55	21.37	25.05	14	11.2	28,198	41,128	54,526	106,085
Jharkhand	35.03	41.39	53.56	66.41	NA	NA	40.3	37	NA	NA	24,545	41,254
Karnataka	46.21	56.04	66.64	75.36	38.24	33.16	25	20.9	24,340	34,780	51,294	90,263
Kerala	78.85	89.81	90.86	94	40.42	25.43	15	7.1	24,474	30,422	48,594	97,912
Madhya Pradesh	38.63	44.67	63.74	69.32	49.78	42.52	38.3	31.6	16,296	18,428	24,906	38,550
Maharashtra	57.24	64.87	76.88	82.34	43.44	36.86	30.7	17.4	23,568	32,818	48,853	99,173
Odisha	33.62	49.09	63.08	72.87	65.29	48.56	46.4	32.6	19,486	23,112	27,529	47,632
Punjab	43.37	58.51	69.65	75.84	16.18	11.77	8.4	8.3	34,425	45,800	56,960	85,577
Rajasthan	30.11	38.55	60.41	66.11	34.46	27.41	22.1	14.7	17,186	23,471	33,628	57,391
Tamil Nadu	54.39	62.66	73.45	80.09	51.66	35.03	22.5	11.3	19,648	27,195	42,083	92,984
Uttar Pradesh	32.65	40.71	56.27	67.68	47.07	40.85	32.8	29.4	15,077	19,224	21,352	32,002
West Bengal	48.65	57.70	68.64	76.26	54.85	35.66	24.7	20	9404	12,622	20,144	32,164
All India	43.57	52.21	64.84	74.04	44.48	35.97	27.5	21.9	24,022	25,260	34,922	63,462

Note Share of population below poverty line – for the year 1983, 1993 and 2004 calculated in terms of Lakdawala methodology. For the year 2011 – Tendulkar methodology

Per capita NSDP presented, in constant price with base 2011–12. For West Bengal the base year is 2004–05

Source Literacy – Primary census abstract, Census of India, various issues

Poverty – Government of India Planning Commission (2014)

Per capita NSDP – Economic survey, various issues

[a]In constant price 2011–12 base year

References

Aajeevika Bureau. (2009). *Does formal schooling matter? Exploring the disconnect between education and employment for rural youth (unpublished)*. Udaipur: Aajeevika Bureau.

Azim Premji Foundation. (2017). Teacher absenteeism study. http://azimpremjiuniversity.edu.in/SitePages/pdf/Field-Studies-in-Education-Teacher-Absenteeism-Study.pdf

Bhide, S. & Mehta, A. K. (2006). Tracking poverty through panel data: Rural poverty in India, 1970–98. *Margin, 38*(4) and 39(1), 29–40.

Blaug, M., Layard, P. R. G., & Woodhal, M. (1969). *The causes of graduate unemployment in India*. London: Allen Lane the Penguin.

Brara, S. (2012). Pedagogy at even pace, *The Hindu*. October 10, 2012.

Chandrasekhar, C. P., Ghosh, J., & Roychowdhury, A. (2006). The demographic dividend and young India's economic future. *Economic and Political Weekly, 41*(49), 5055–5064.

Chaudhuri, S. (2007). *Mid-day meal program and incidence of child labour in developing economy*. MPRA paper no. 4367 posted 07, November 2007/0352.

Cohen, D. (1998). *The wealth of the world and the poverty of nations*. Cambridge, MA: MIT Press.

De, A., Khera, R., Samson, M., & Shivakumar, A. K. (2011). *PROBE revisited*. New Delhi: Oxford University Press.

D'Souza, E. (2008). Self-employment and human capital. *The Indian Journal of Labour Economics, 4*, 783–787.

Dongre, A., Kapur, A., & Tewary, V. (2014). *How much does india spend per student on elementary education?*. Dharam Marg, Chanakyapuri, New Delhi: Accountability Initiative, Centre for Policy Research.

Dreze, J., & Goyal, A. (2003). Future of mid-day meals. *Economic and Political Weekly, 38*(44), 4673–4683.

Duraisamy, P. (1992). Effects of education and extension contacts on agricultural production. *Indian Journal of Agricultural Economics, 47*(2), 201–205.

Duraisamy, P. (2002). Changes in returns to education in India, 1983–94: By gender, age-cohort and location. *Economics of Education Review, 21*(6), 609–622.

Duraisamy, P., & Duraisamy, M. (2005). Regional difference in wage premia and returns to education by gender in India. *Indian Journal of Labour Economics, 48*(2), 335–347.

Galbraith, J. K. (1994). Beyond contentment. *The Telegraph*, June 14, 1994 [Reprint from The Guardian].

Government of India. (1966). *Report of the education commission 1964–66, education and national development*. Ministry of Education.

Government of India. National Sample Survey Organization NSSO (2010). *Education in India, 2007–08: Participation and expenditure* (pp. H-1 and H-4). NSS report no. 532. May 2010.

Government of India. *Report of the secondary education commission, (October 1952 to June 1953)* (Vol. 1). India: Secondary Education Commission. Ministry of Education.

Government of India. *Various issues of national account statistics*. Ministry of Statistics and Programme Implementation. New Delhi.

Government of India. *Various issues of national sample survey*. Ministry of Statistics and Programme Implementation. New Delhi.

Government of India Planning Commission. (2014). Report of the expert group to review the methodology for measurement of poverty. http://planningcommission.nic.in/reports/genrep/pov_rep0707.pdf.

Government of Karnataka. (2016). *Men and women in Karnataka 2015–16*. Available at: http://des.kar.nic.in/sites/Report%20on%20Men%20and%20Women%20in%20Karnataka%20year%20[2009...2012]/2015-16pdf%20%20final%20Men%20and%20Women.pdf.

Government of Madhya Pradesh. (2016). *Economic Survey 2016–17*.

Govind, R., & Bandyopadhyay, M. (2011). Access to elementary education in India. In R. Govind (Ed.), *Who Goes to School? Exploring exclusion in Indian education*. New Delhi: Oxford University Press.

Gupta, A. (2012). *State education report—Madhya Pradesh primary, middle, and secondary education*. India: Catalyst Management Services (CMS) and Center for Education Innovation. http://www.educationinnovations.org/sites/default/files/India%20-%20State%20Education%20Report%20-%20Madhya%20Pradesh.pdf

Haq, M., & Haq, K. (1998). *Human development in South Asia 1998*. Karachi: Oxford University Press.

James, K. S. (2008). Glorifying malthus: Current debate on demographic dividend in India. *Economic and Political Weekly, 43*(25), 63–69.

Janadhyala, K., & Ramachandran, V. (2007). *Enabling most deprived children to learn: Lessons from promising practices*. Report Commissioned by Department of Elementary Education, MHRD, Government of India and International Labour Organisation. New Delhi: Final Revised Version. July 2007.

Jayaraman, R. (2009). The impact of school lunches on school enrolment: Evidence from an exogenous policy change in India. In *Proceedings of the German Development Economics Conference* (Vol. 15), Frankfurt. M. http://hdl.handle.net/10419/39926.

Josephine, Y. (1998). *Impact of mid-day meals programme on enrolment and retention of girls in primary schools of West Garo Hills in Meghalaya*. Research report. New Delhi: Educational Administration Unit, National Institute of Educational Planning and Administration.

Juneja, N. (2011). Access to what? Diversity and participation. In R. Govind (Ed.), *Who goes to school? Exploring exclusion in Indian education*. New Delhi: Oxford University Press.

Kingdon, G. G., & Unni J. (1998). *Education and women's labour market outcomes in India: An analysis using NSS household data*. Applied economics discussion paper series. Oxford: Institute of Economics and Statistics, University of Oxford.

Kothari, V. N. (1970). Disparities in relative earnings among different countries. *Economic Journal, 80*(319), 605–616.

Kumar, S., De, A., Dreze, J., Samson, M., & Shyamshree, D. (2009). Report card. *Frontline*, 88–92.

Little, A. W. (2010). *Access to elementary education in India: Policies, politics and progress*. CREATE research monograph (Vol. 44). London: CREATE.

Loh, J. (1995). *Education and economic growth in India: An aggregate production function approach, in school effectiveness and learning achievement at primary stage*. New Delhi: National Council of Educational Research and Training.

Mathur, A., & Mamgain, R. P. (2004). Human capital stocks, their level of utilization and economic development in India. *Indian Journal of Labour Economics, 47*(4), 655–675.

NCEUS. (2007). *Report on conditions of work and promotion of livelihoods in the unorganised sector*. New Delhi: National Commission for Enterprises in the Unorganised Sector.

Planning Commission. (2008). *Eleventh five year plan 2007–2012, volume II, social sector*. New Delhi: Government of India.

Planning Commission. (2011). *Faster, sustainable and more inclusive growth: An approach to the twelfth five year plan*. New Delhi: Government of India.

Pratham Education Foundation. (2017). The eleventh annual status of education report (ASER 2016).

PROBE Team. (1999). *Public report on basic education*. Oxford: Oxford University Press.

Psacharopoulos, G. (1973). *Returns to education: An international comparison*. Amsterdam: Elsevier.

Psacharopoulos, G. (1994). *Returns to investment in education: A global update*. World Development, 22(9), 1325–1343.

Psacharopoulos, G., & Patrinos, H. (2004). Returns to investment in education: a further update. *Education Economics, 12*(2), 111–134.

Psacharopoulos, G., & Tilak, J. B. G. (1992). Education and wage earnings. In M. C. Alkin (Ed.), *The encyclopedia of educational research* (pp. 419–423). New York: Macmillan, for the American Educational Research Association.

Ramachandran, V. (2004). *Education guarantee scheme: A community—government partnership that gets millions into school in Madhya Pradesh*. Washington, DC: The World Bank.

Rao, V. K. R. V. (1964). *Education and economic development*. New Delhi: National Council for Educational Research and Training.

Rao, V. K. R. V. (1970). *Education and human resource development*. Bombay: Allied.

Reserve Bank of India (RBI). *Bulletin various issues*.

Roy, S. (2008). Skill premium: What caused the 'mismatch'? *The Indian Journal of Labour Economics, 4*, 789–802.

Sankar, D. (2008). *What is the progress in elementary education participation in India during the last two decades? An analysis using NSS education rounds. South Asia sector for human development*. World Bank. Available at: http://documents.worldbank.org/curated/en/679791468041070340/pdf/421120REVISED01C10NSS0paper1Oct1111.pdf

Schultz, T. P. (1988). Education investments and returns. *Handbook of Development Economics, 1*, 544–621.

Sedwal, M., & Kamat, S. (2008). *Education and social equity with a special focus on scheduled castes and scheduled tribes in elementary education*. CREATE Research Monograph (Vol. 19). New Delhi: NEUPA.

Seetharaman, S. (2006). Impact of mid day meal on the nutritional status of school going children. NIRD. Hyderabad. Available at http://educationforallindia.com.

Sen, A. (1983). Poor, relatively speaking. *Oxford Economic Papers, 35*, 153–169.

Sen, A. (1999). *Development as freedom*. Oxford University Press.

Sengupta, A., Kannan K. P., & Raveendran, G. (2008). India's common people: Who are they, how many are they and how do they live? *Economic and Political Weekly, 43*(11), 49–63.

Sethi, B. (2003). *Mid-day meal programme and its impact in improving enrolment in Rayagada district*. Mimeo. Mussoorie: Lal Bahadur Shastri National Academy of Administration.

Shah, A., Chhokar, K. B., Pratap, S., & Shiddalingaswami. (2011). *Interface between education and poverty in India: Eluding goals and search for new perspectives?* CPRC-IIPA Working Paper no. 46, New Delhi.

Shah, A., & Yagnik, J. (2004). *Estimates of BPL-households in rural Gujarat: Measurement, spatial pattern and policy imperatives*. Ahmedabad: Gujarat Institute of Development Research.

Shankar, P., & Natasha, S. K. (2001). *Interrogating 'best practices' for the implementation of school nutrition programmes in urban India', A report for the office of the commissioners to the supreme court in CWP 196/2001*. Delhi: Centre for Equity Studies.

Singh, A. (2008). Do school meals works? Treatment evaluation of the midday meal scheme in India. Paper submitted in part fulfilment of the requirements for the degree of M.Sc. in Economics for Development at the University of Oxford, November 2008.

The Economist. (2017). Why the world's biggest school system is failing its pupils. https://www.economist.com/news/asia/21723137-more-indians-are-attending-school-ever-they-are-not-learning-much-why-worlds.

Tilak, J. B. G. (1987). *Economics of inequality in education*. New Delhi: Sage.

Tilak, J. B. G. (1990). Education and earnings: Gender differences in India. *International Journal of Development Planning Literature, 5*(4), 131–39.

Tilak, J. B. G. (1994). *Education for development in Asia*. New Delhi: Sage Publications.

Tilak, J. B. J. (Ed.). (2003). *Financing education in India: Current issues and changing perspectives*. New Delhi: Ravi Books, for National Institute of Educational Planning and Administration.

Tilak, J. B. G. (2005). *Post-elementary education, poverty and development in India*. Working paper series no. 6. New Delhi: National Institute of Educational Planning and Administration.

Tilak, J. B. G. (2007). Inclusive growth and education: On the approach to the eleventh plan. *Economic and Political Weekly, 42*(38), 3872–3877.

UNDP. (1997). *Human development report 1997*. New York: Oxford University Press.

Unni, J. (2001). Earnings and education among ethnic groups in rural India. Working paper no. 124. Ahmedabad: Gujarat Institute of Development Research.

Unni, J. (2009). Women workers in the new economy. *The Indian Journal of Labour Economics,* *52*(4), 657–674.

Unterhalter, E. (2003). *Education, capabilities and social justice.* Background paper prepared for the Education for all Global Meeting Report, 2003–04, Gender and Education for All: The Leap to Equality, 2004/ED/EFA/MRT/PI/76, UNESCO.

World Bank. (1997). *Primary education in India.* Washington DC: The World Bank.

World Bank. (2002). *Secondary education and the New Agenda for economic growth.* Mimeo. New Delhi: The World Bank.

World Bank. (2006). *Skill development in India: The vocational education and training system.* Document of the World Bank, Human Development Unit South Asia Region, January 2006.

Chapter 9
Conclusions

Aasha Kapur Mehta and Shashanka Bhide

Poverty elimination is often noted as a core policy objective in India as well as globally. If poverty elimination "alone" is used to measure success[1], then India's report card on poverty is dismal. Despite rapid economic growth and improvement on a range of development indicators, a large proportion of India's population continues to suffer extreme poverty in multiple dimensions.

In the various chapters of this volume, we have attempted to present data and analyses on different dimensions of poverty and poverty alleviation programs in India, with an underlying focus on the dynamics of poverty – a strand of literature that provides insights on how the poor escape poverty or how the non-poor fall into poverty. Prevalence of "chronic poverty" or "persistent poverty" of households over long periods of time is particularly a failure of the development programs and requires multiple coordinated instruments to address the challenge of overcoming chronic poverty.

NITI Aayog is the nodal agency for monitoring progress towards achieving all the SDGs in India and for mapping the Ministries and Departments responsible for achievement of specific targets and indicators. The nodal ministry for achieving SDG1 is the Ministry of Rural Development (see Table 1).

Two schemes, Mahatma Gandhi National Rural Employment Guarantee Scheme (MGNREGS) and National Social Assistance Programme (NSAP), are regarded as the Core of the Core interventions by Government for achieving an end to poverty in all its forms everywhere. The third scheme, Deen Dayal Antyodaya Yojana (DAY) – National Rural Livelihood Mission (NRLM) and National Urban

---

[1]As was stated in the Cabinet Secretariat press note while constituting NITI Aayog.

A. K. Mehta (✉)
Indian Institute of Public Administration, New Delhi, India
e-mail: aasha2006@gmail.com

S. Bhide
Madras Institute of Development Studies, Chennai, India

© Springer Nature Singapore Pte Ltd. 2018
A. K. Mehta et al. (eds.), *Poverty, Chronic Poverty and Poverty Dynamics*,
https://doi.org/10.1007/978-981-13-0677-8_9

Table 1 SDG1 – end poverty in all its forms everywhere

Centrally sponsored schemes/central sector schemes (CSS)	Related interventions	Targets	Other concerned ministries/departments
1. National rural employment guarantee scheme (MGNREGA) **(Core of the Core)** 2. Deen Dayal Antyodaya Yojana (DAY) – National Rural Livelihood Mission (NRLM) and National Urban Livelihood Mission (NULM) **(Core)** 3. National Social Assistance Programme (NSAP) **(Core of the Core)**	1. Pradhan Mantri Jan Dhan Yojana 2. Pradhan Mantri Jeevan Jyoti Bima Yojana 3. Atal Pension Yojana (APY)	1.1 By 2030, eradicate extreme poverty for all people everywhere, currently measured as people living on less than $1.25 a day	RD, HUPA, Skill Development and Entrepreneurship
		1.2 By 2030, reduce at least by half the proportion of men, women and children of all ages living in poverty in all its dimensions according to national definitions	RD, HUPA Skill Development and Entrepreneurship
		1.3 Implement nationally appropriate social protection systems and measures for all, including floors, and by 2030 achieve substantial coverage of the poor and the vulnerable	Social Justice and Empowerment, RD, Labour, WCD, Minority Affairs, Tribal Affairs
		1.4 By 2030, ensure that all men and women, in particular the poor and the vulnerable, have equal rights to economic resources, as well as access to basic services, ownership and control over land and other forms of property, inheritance, natural resources, appropriate new technology and financial services, including microfinance	Agriculture and Cooperation, Land Resources, Drinking Water and Sanitation, HUPA, RD, Panchayati Raj, Urban Development
		1.5 By 2030, build the resilience of the poor and those in vulnerable situations and reduce their exposure and vulnerability to	Home Affairs

(continued)

Table 1 (continued)

Centrally sponsored schemes/central sector schemes (CSS)	Related interventions	Targets	Other concerned ministries/departments
		climate-related extreme events and other economic, social and environmental shocks and disasters	
		1.a Ensure significant mobilization of resources from a variety of sources, including through enhanced development cooperation, in order to provide adequate and predictable means for developing countries, in particular least developed countries, to implement programmes and policies to end poverty in all its dimensions	RD, HUPA
		1.b Create sound policy frameworks at the national, regional and international levels, based on pro-poor and gender-sensitive development strategies, to support accelerated investment in poverty eradication actions	External Affairs, RD

Nodal Ministry Ministry of Rural Development
Source Government of India (2017)
Note RD is Rural Development; HUPA is Housing and Urban Poverty Alleviation; WCD is Women and Child Development

Livelihood Mission (NULM) is regarded as a Core Scheme. While it is promising its coverage is very limited so far. A brief analysis of NSAP and MGNREGA as Core of the Core interventions is given below to draw attention to the fact that the design, implementation and funding for programmes such as these are crucial in India's efforts towards poverty elimination and will determine whether or not India will achieve SDG1.

1 Achieving SDG1 Through Core of the Core Schemes: NSAP and MGNREGS

1.1 National Social Assistance Programme (NSAP)

The Preamble to the NSAP Guidelines on the Ministry of Rural Development Website[2] mentions Article 41 of the Constitution of India:

> The State shall, within the limits of its economic capacity and development, make effective provision for securing the right to work, to education and to public assistance in cases of unemployment, old age, sickness and disablement, and in other cases of undeserved want.

Hence, the Ministry states on the Website that[3]

> "The National Social Assistance Programme (NSAP) which came into effect from 15th August 1995 represents a significant step towards the fulfilment of the Directive Principles in Article 41 of the Constitution. The programme introduced a National Policy for Social Assistance for the poor and aims at ensuring minimum national standard for social assistance in addition to the benefits that state are currently providing or might provide in future. NSAP at present comprises Indira Gandhi National Old-Age Pension Scheme (IGNOAPS), Indira Gandhi National Widow Pension Scheme (IGNWPS), Indira Gandhi National Disability Pension Scheme (IGNDPS), National Family Benefit Scheme (NFBS) and Annapurna."

Assistance under the sub-schemes of NSAP is applicable to persons belonging to Below Poverty Line (BPL) category. The other eligibility criteria and the scale of assistance under the sub-schemes of NSAP are as follows:

- Indira Gandhi National Old-Age Pension Scheme (IGNOAPS) – at Rs. 200/- per month for persons aged 60–79 years. For persons, who are 80 years and above the pension, is Rs. 500/- per month.
- Indira Gandhi National Widow Pension Scheme (IGNWPS) – at Rs. 300/- per month for widows aged 40–79 years. After attaining the age of 80 years, the beneficiary will get Rs. 500/- per month.

---

[2]Available at http://nsap.nic.in/Guidelines/nsap_guidelines_oct2014.pdf accessed 16th April 2018.
[3]http://nsap.nic.in/ (accessed 16th April 2018).

- Indira Gandhi National Disability Pension Scheme (IGNDPS) – at Rs. 300/- per month for disabled aged 18–79 years. After attaining the age of 80 years, the beneficiary will get Rs. 500/- per month.
- National Family Benefit Scheme (NFBS) – One-time assistance of Rs. 20,000/- on the death of primary breadwinner.
- Annapurna Scheme – Provision of 10 kg foodgrains per month for the old who could not be covered under Old-Age Pension Scheme.

The members of the First Common Review Mission (CRM), constituted by the Ministry of Rural Development to review the implementation of its schemes, visited eight States in May 2016. The Mission found that the amount received per month as pension in the eight States varied considerably (see Table 2). While the amount released by the Centre to all State Governments for old-age pension was constant at Rs. 200/- per month, the old-age pension received by a citizen who was Below Poverty Line and lived in Madhya Pradesh was Rs. 275/-, in Odisha Rs. 300/-, in Karnataka, Rajasthan and Tripura Rs. 500/-, in Jharkhand Rs. 600/- and in Andhra Pradesh Rs. 1000/-.

It is important to note that the eligibility norms and amounts for pension provided by the Centre are the same for all States and UTs (see row 3 of Table 2). However, the pension received by beneficiaries depends on the extent to which a State supplements the amount provided by the Centre. This needs to be viewed in the context of the following:

(a) Achievement of SDG1 – End poverty in all its forms everywhere – will not be possible unless all those who are Below Poverty Line and above the age of 60 or widows or disabled are able to move out of poverty.
(b) The official poverty line was Rs. 816/- per capita per month for rural and Rs. 1000/- per capita per month for urban areas for 2011–12. It would be higher for subsequent years. Clearly, therefore, the old-age pensions provided as per

Table 2 Variation in monthly pension reaching the vulnerable (in Rs)

Centre/state	Old-age pension		Widow pension	Disability pension
	60–79 years	80 + years	40–59 years	
Central funds	**200**	**500**	**300**	**300**
Andhra Pradesh	1000	1000	1000	1000–1500
Jharkhand	600	700	600	600
Karnataka	500	750	500–800	500–1500
Madhya Pradesh	275	500	300	300
Maharashtra	600	600	600	600
Odisha	300	500	300	500
Rajasthan	500	750 (at 75)	500–750	500–750
Tripura	500	700	500	500–1100

Source Government of India (2016), p. 70. The information is based on data reported by CRM Teams visiting States and information from Ministry of Rural Development

Table 2 above are not adequate for moving the 3,20,29,352 persons mentioned as beneficiaries on the NSAP dashboard, out of poverty.

Hence, among other recommendations, the first CRM urged the Government to increase old-age, widow and disability pensions "substantially in line with the directions provided by Article 41 of the Constitution". It also recommended that pensions be increased annually based on linkage with inflation.

Additionally, "where eligible beneficiaries are left out, they should be identified and included by the local administration. All eligible persons (widows, elderly, disabled) need to be mapped and facilitated in filing applications for pension. The Panchayat Secretary, Gram Rozgar Sewak and/or other social capital like SHG leaders, Anganwadi Workers may be motivated to facilitate this process".[4]

Delays in disbursement of pensions must be avoided and this should follow a fixed monthly schedule. Resources required for NSAP should be estimated by identifying the number of men and women who are vulnerable, based on SECC data.

Clearly, therefore, the present approach to implementing NSAP, which is regarded as Core of the Core interventions for ending poverty, requires considerable strengthening in order to achieve SDG1.

2 MGNREGS

While there are a large number of programmes and schemes that are being implemented by Government of India, none of the schemes commits the State to providing a minimum level of subsistence to either individual citizens or households. For instance, MGNREGA aims at enhancing livelihood security of households in rural areas of the country by providing one hundred days of guaranteed wage employment in a financial year to every household whose adult members volunteer to do unskilled manual work. However, MGNREGA is not designed to provide work that generates an adequate annual income for a household to cross the poverty line. The 100-day entitlement is for a household and not for each adult who needs and demands unskilled work. In practice, there are a large number of implementation challenges that prevent households from accessing even the 100 days of work. Only 7.8% households in 2016–17 and 5.7% households in 2017–18 completed 100 days of wage employment (Table 3). Further, on average only 46 days of employment were provided to a household in 2016–17 and 45.65 days in 2017–18. Unless there are other avenues of income for the households, the employment guarantee scheme alone would not lead to poverty elimination. Monitoring the impact of the employment guarantee scheme towards poverty elimination is necessary to make required corrections to the scheme.

---

[4]See Government of India (2016).

Table 3 Employment and wages under MGNREGA in recent years

	FY 2017–2018	FY 2016–2017	FY 2015–2016	FY 2014–2015
Average days of employment provided per household	45.65	46	48.85	40.17
Average wage rate per day per person (Rs.)	169.49	161.65	154.08	143.92
Total No of HHs completed 100 days of wage employment	29,10,340	39,91,202	48,47,975	24,92,654
Total households worked [in Cr]	5.11	5.1224	4.8134	4.14
Total individuals worked [in Cr]	7.58	7.6693	7.2261	6.2

Source MoRD Website accessed on 16 April 2018
http://mnregaweb4.nic.in/netnrega/all_lvl_details_dashboard_new.aspx

Delayed payments, shortfalls in fund flow, low-wage rates and overloading of the Gram Rozgar Sevak with non-MGNREGS tasks are among the many reasons for this. Average employment of 45.65 days per household at a wage rate of Rs. 169.49 per day translates into Rs. 7737/- per household per year or Rs. 645 per household per month. This is obviously very inadequate for enabling 5.11 crore households who worked under MGNREGS in 2017–18 to move out of poverty just through this work. Earning from other sources would be required to enable them to cross the poverty line.

3 What Needs to Be Done to End Poverty[5]

A large number of programmes and schemes have been implemented over decades to directly attack poverty through generating work, provide health care, education, nutrition and support to backward areas and vulnerable groups. Although poverty has declined, the outcomes are well below expectations as a massive number of India's population continues to live in poverty. There are several reasons for this and some of these are outlined below.

While a large number of poverty alleviation programmes have been initiated, it is recognised that their implementation is not integrated with one another. Systematic attempts to identify people who are in poverty in each village and slum and determine their needs are at a nascent stage. This systematic approach is needed to identify the households that require assistance as well as the type of assistance that is required.

There are exclusion errors even in the case of programmes such as old-age pension. The effort that is needed to ensure that pensions reach all those who are

---

[5]With necessary permissions, this section draws on Mehta (2017).

eligible, as soon as they become eligible, is missing. Entitlement does not automatically translate into benefit.

The resources allocated to anti-poverty programmes are inadequate and expenditure is often curtailed according to availability of funds. In the process of planning budgetary expenditure and allocating resources to different programmes, the highest priority needs to be given to programmes and processes that will end poverty. Funds needed for this should be estimated on the basis of identifying priorities, related tasks and outcomes at the village, block, district, state and national levels. Preference in fund allocation should be given to improve outcomes in the most backward geographic locations.

While our plans have taken cognisance of the literature on chronic poverty and dynamics of poverty, programmes and schemes have not used this understanding to address this issue. To address poverty effectively, alleviation programmes need to understand and address chronic poverty and the dynamics of poverty. We know, for instance, that poverty is especially prevalent among certain occupational groups. Casual agricultural labour is the largest group that is stuck in poverty. These are the "working poor", for whom the state has not been able to secure the right to an adequate means of livelihood. Similarly, there is a geographical dimension to poverty – concentration of poverty in certain parts of the country. The focus of programmes and schemes should be on ensuring that the poorest households, villages, blocks and districts come out of poverty. Poverty has persisted among marginalised groups, especially the Scheduled Tribes. Hence, inclusion of tribal girls or women in programmes in the poorest blocks and villages should be used as an indicator of performance.

We also know that chronic ill health is a cause of entry into poverty for all those who are not financially secure or fully insured. Full cover for ill health is available only to beneficiaries of the CGHS and beneficiaries of a few other schemes. The private health cover available is limited to expenses of around Rs. 1 to 5 lakh. Most of India's population does not have access to even this. Yet, public provisioning for health care remains lower than in many countries. The budget for public provisioning of health has to increase significantly for delivery of equitable health care of a high quality that is accessible to all.

TheHead Count Ratio (HCR), or percentage of population below the poverty line, is an important indicator of the extent of poverty in a country. The HCR is used to track progress in reducing poverty as well as design programmes to alleviate it.

The Socio-Economic Caste Census (SECC) for rural areas has provided us with evidence regarding the deprivation suffered by 6.89 crore out of 17.98 crore (38.36%) rural households[6] that are landless and depend on manual casual labour for their survival. Among these are a large number of households identified by the SECC that have no adult member, or that have a disabled member and no able

[6]See http://secc.gov.in/stateSummaryReport. Accessed 19th May 2018.

bodied adult member or no literate adult or that are houseless or have one room with kucha walls and roof.

Achievement of SDG1 and 2 would require that we ensure access to food, shelter, basic income support to children in all rural households identified by the SECC that have no adult member.

Hence, unless we try to understand the drivers, maintainers and interrupters of poverty and strengthen the processes that address them, many of those living in poverty today will remain poor over time and may pass their poverty to their children. This, combined with the size of the problem, demands that we address the poverty challenge on priority.

References

Government of India. (2016). *Report of the First Common Review Mission, Ministry of Rural Development, New Delhi* (p. 77). Available at: http://ruraldiksha.nic.in/writereaddata/Circulars_Rural/63_Latest_Compiled_CRM_Thematic_Report_3June2016.PDF. Accessed May 19, 2018.

Government of India. (2017). *Sustainable Development Goals (SDGs), Targets, CSS, Interventions, Nodal and other Ministries.* New Delhi: NITI Aayog. August.

Mehta, A. K. (2017). Poverty eradication: Why do we always fail? In Richard Mahapatra & Sunita Narain (Eds.), *State of India's Environment 2017.* Centre for Science and Environment: New Delhi.

Index

A

Above Poverty Line (APL), 3, 14, 18, 33, 39, 45, 50, 115
Accredited Social Health Activists (ASHAs), 173, 185, 188, 190
Agricultural labour, 12, 31, 40, 73, 103, 112, 114–117, 144
Agricultural productivity, 22, 96, 98
Akshaya Patra, 226
Assetlessness, 45
Augmented Human Development Index (AHDI), 23
Automatic inclusion, 26, 28
Auxiliary Nurse Midwife (ANM), 176–180, 182, 185, 188, 189

B

Backward districts, 23, 140, 142
Bands of vulnerability, 10, 32
Below Poverty Line (BPL), 10–12, 20, 24–26, 28, 30, 61, 78, 113, 114, 154, 168, 171, 185, 227, 235, 244, 245, 248
Body Mass Index (BMI)
    stunted, 58, 67
    under-nourished, 57, 67
    underweight, 58, 67
BPL Census, 24–26
Brazil, Russia, India, China, South Africa (BRICS), 156, 168

C

Calorie consumption, calorie deficiency, 55, 57–59, 63, 64, 68, 113
Cash transfer/direct cash transfers, 49, 80, 81

Caste Census, 26
Caste status, 45, 99, 104
Casual employment, 40
Casual labour
    casual agricultural labour, 27, 45, 248
    casual rural labour, 61, 149
Centrally Sponsored Scheme (CSS), 170, 224, 242, 243
Child mortality, 57, 69, 70
Chronically poor, chronic poor, 7, 19, 23, 25, 26, 37, 39, 42–45, 127, 198, 199, 204, 216, 222, 226, 228
Chronic Energy Deficiency (CED), 66
Chronic food insecurity, 56
Chronic poverty, 2–5, 25, 37, 38, 40, 41, 44, 45, 48, 50, 93, 99, 104, 108, 115, 118, 121, 124, 147, 196, 201, 215, 241, 248
Chronic Poverty Research Centre (CPRC), 37, 93, 169, 186, 195
Citizenship deficit, 5, 97, 98
Class related destitution, 94
Clean fuels, 37
Common Review Mission (CRM), 190, 245, 246
Communicable and non-communicable diseases, 171
Compounded poverty, 94
Consumption expenditure, 10, 12, 13, 15, 30, 42, 45, 60, 170, 210, 213
Consumption inequality, 49
Coping mechanism, 5, 140
Core of the core schemes, 244
Correlates of poverty, 33, 50, 51
Crop shocks, 44, 47

© Springer Nature Singapore Pte Ltd. 2018
A. K. Mehta et al. (eds.), *Poverty, Chronic Poverty and Poverty Dynamics*,
https://doi.org/10.1007/978-981-13-0677-8

D
Deen Dayal Antyodaya Yojana (DDAY), 17, 241, 242
Democracy deficit, 5, 97
Demographic dividend, 67, 203, 204
Deprivation criteria, 27
Destitution, 5, 56, 94, 106, 124
Development deficit, 5, 97
Direct Cash Transfer (DCT), 80, 81
Disability-Adjusted Life Years (DALY), 155, 157–160, 164, 165
Disease burden, 6, 7, 153, 155–157, 159, 164, 165, 169, 173, 174, 189, 190
Diversification of income, 41, 46
Diversification opportunities, 46
Drinking water, 17, 21, 22, 37, 69, 84, 87, 96, 109, 111, 171, 190, 242
Drivers, maintainers and interrupters of poverty, 4, 249
Dynamics of poverty/poverty dynamics, 3, 4, 8, 37–39, 40–43, 47, 48, 50, 51, 241, 248

E
Economic growth, 4, 18, 31–33, 39, 48, 49, 55, 60, 63, 68, 71, 89, 135, 149, 195–198, 202, 205, 218, 228, 241
Economic infrastructure, 21
Economic polarisation, 94
Economic shocks, 47, 48
Educational attainment, 26, 48, 196, 199, 202, 204, 205, 208–212, 216–218
Elementary education, 67, 197, 198, 200, 201, 204, 206, 207, 219, 225, 228, 233, 234
Employment growth, 32
Ending poverty
anti poverty programmes, 94, 248
elimination of poverty, 16
Enrolment ratio, 199, 206, 226
Entry into poverty, 26, 43, 47, 48, 128, 248
Escape from poverty, 3, 25, 39, 40, 42, 43, 46, 51
Exit from poverty, 25, 46, 50, 137, 198, 201, 216
Extreme poverty, 3, 6, 16, 17, 49, 103, 153, 154, 241, 242

F
Factors leading to migration, 130
Fair price shops, 78
Falling into poverty, 3, 42, 51
Female literacy, 31, 226
Financial inclusion, 24
Financial shocks, 48

Food
insecurity, 4, 56, 60, 68
security, 25, 55, 57, 68, 75, 79, 80, 88

G
Gandhian, 94, 98, 100–102, 104–106, 108, 117, 123, 222, 225
Gender Development Index (GDI), 20
Geography of poverty, 40
Global Hunger Index (GHI), 30, 56, 57, 70, 71
Governance deficit, 5, 97
Gram Swaraj, 102, 105, 106, 108–111, 122–124
Gross Enrolment Ratio (GER), 199, 206, 226, 232
Gross State Domestic Product (GSDP), 49

H
Hashim Committee, 26
Head Count Ratio (HCR), 10, 17, 39, 248
Healthcare facilities, 22, 40, 41
Health insurance, 6, 51, 153, 154, 169, 171
Health shocks, 48, 155
High disease burden, 6, 155, 189
High disease burden blocks, 189
High poverty states, 20
Household size, 30, 41, 45, 47, 115, 116
Human Development Index (HDI), 20, 22, 49
Human Immunodeficiency Virus (HIV) acquired immune deficiency syndrome (AIDS), 56, 162
Hunger
chronic hunger, 58
endemic hunger, 4, 56–58, 62
explicit hunger, 57
self reported hunger, 57–59
subjective hunger, 58

I
Ill health, 2, 4, 6, 14, 41, 47, 58, 153, 171, 186, 188, 248
Ill health and entry into poverty/health shock and impoverishment, 33, 37, 41, 47, 155, 248
Incidence of poverty, 10, 13, 16, 18–21, 29–31, 33, 38, 39, 42, 46, 48–51, 135, 138
Income inequality, 49
Income mobility, 30, 38, 41, 42, 47, 49, 51
Income transfers, 31
Indebtedness, 40, 41, 73
India Human Development Survey (IHDS), 29, 44, 45
Infant mortality, 31, 196
Infant Mortality Rate (IMR), 69, 171, 172

Infrastructure, 1, 23, 24, 30, 40, 41, 46, 48, 51, 78, 82, 122, 142, 143, 155, 171, 176, 183, 185, 187, 188, 198, 203, 205, 208, 219–221
Initial conditions, 10, 31, 46, 49
Integrated Child Development Scheme (ICDS), 7, 57, 87–89, 156, 169, 170, 184, 185, 188–190
  Anganwadi Centres (AWCs), 83, 86, 184–187
  Anganwadi Helper (AWH), 185, 188
  Anganwadi Worker (AWW), 83, 86, 185, 188, 189, 246
Integrated Child Development Services (ICDS), 83–86, 186
Intergenerational transmission of poverty, 6, 154
International Food Policy Research Institute (IFPRI), 30, 56, 70, 71
Interrupters of poverty, 4, 38, 40, 249
Investment in education, 203, 219, 220
Irrigation, 22, 26, 30, 31, 40, 46–48, 72, 74–77, 110, 111, 122, 132, 139, 141–143, 146, 147

J
Jaiprakash Narayan, 100, 102–104, 106, 108–110, 113, 114, 117, 123, 124
Janani Suraksha Yojana (JSY), 182

L
Landlessness, 45, 73, 118
Legitimacy deficit, 5, 97
Livelihood opportunities, 40, 205
Livelihood security, 246
Longitudinal surveys/panel surveys, 30, 50
Longitudinal village studies, 43

M
Macroeconomic shocks, 48
Mahatma Gandhi National Rural Employment Guarantee Scheme (MGNREGS), 198, 241
Maintainers of poverty, 4, 40, 249
Malnourished
  malnourishment, 89, 159
  stunted, 55, 58, 62
  under-nourished, 55, 63, 87
  underweight, 55, 58, 87
Malnutrition, 37, 57, 60, 67–71, 79, 83–89, 122, 161, 184–190
Maternal Mortality Ratio (MMR), 153, 156, 157, 171, 172
Mid-Day meal scheme, 82, 222

Migration-poverty interface, 128, 129, 139, 146
Millennium Development Goals (MDGs), 2, 9, 49, 69
Mixed Recall Period (MRP), 13
Mobile Medical Units (MMUs), 187
Monthly Per Capita Consumption Expenditure (MPCE), 13, 15, 170
Morbidity, 6, 153, 155, 159–161, 184, 190
Mortality rates, 6, 156, 157, 165
Most backward and poorest districts, 21
MPCE categories, 138
Multidimensional deprivation, 1, 19, 22
Multidimensional Index of Poverty (MPI), 29
Multidimensional poverty, 24, 29
Multidimensional wellness, 26
Mushahari and Mushahari Plan, 104–106, 109, 110, 123

N
National Commission for Enterprises in the Unorganised Sector (NCEUS), 10, 32, 147
National Council of Applied Economic Research (NCAER), 42
National Rural Health Mission (NRHM), 6, 7, 14, 155, 156, 169–173, 181, 183, 186, 188, 190
National Social Assistance Programme (NSAP)
  Indira Gandhi National Disability Pension Scheme (IGNDPS), 244, 245
  Indira Gandhi National Old Age Pension Scheme (IGNOAPS), 244
  Indira Gandhi National Widow Pension Scheme (IGNWPS), 244
Nation building deficit, 5, 97
NITI Aayog, 2, 7, 16, 24, 81, 155, 165, 166, 169, 176, 177, 181, 241
Nutrition, 7, 14, 15, 17, 24, 30, 55, 58, 66, 68, 69, 76, 82–85, 87, 88, 155, 171, 184–186

O
Official poverty line, 3, 12, 17, 245
Omnibus test, 141
Out of pocket expenditure on health, 6, 153
Oxford Poverty and Human Development Initiative, 29

P
Panel data, 40, 42, 43, 45, 47, 49, 215
Participatory solutions, 5
Pathway out of poverty, 7
Pattern of migration, 144

Peri-urban areas, 149
Persistent deprivation, 22, 23
Political sociology of poverty, 5, 95
Post conflict trajectories, 94
Poverty band, 32
Poverty-based conflicts, 5, 97
Poverty conflict nexus, 94
Poverty incidence/incidence of poverty, 9, 10,
    14, 19, 20
Poverty Line Basket (PLB), 12, 113
Poverty persistence/persistence of poverty, 3,
    5, 10, 25, 26, 33, 42
Poverty reduction, 1, 3, 8, 10, 30–32, 39,
    47–50, 128, 143, 149, 196–199, 201,
    218
Primitive tribal group, 26
Public Distribution System (PDS), 57, 78
Public provisioning for health care, 248
Purchasing Power Parity (PPP), 17, 189

Q
Qualitative techniques, 44

R
Radicalisation of economic conflict, 5
Regional concentration of poverty, 20
Remittance, 130, 131, 135
Return migration, 129–131
Road density, 49
Rural electrification, 31
Rural infrastructure, 40, 72, 175

S
Safety nets, 41, 43, 73
Sanitation, 17, 25, 28, 37, 69, 84, 87, 88, 148,
    154, 171, 186, 190, 242
Sarva Shiksha Abhiyan (SSA), 208
Sarvodaya
    Gandhian reform process in response to the
        Maoist approach, 98
Saxena Committee, 26
Scoring index, 28

Skill development, 24, 219, 224, 242
Social fragmentation, 94
Social infrastructure, 21, 98
Social protection, 3, 242
Social security, 88, 96, 148, 169, 198
Socio-Economic Caste Census (SECC), 27,
    248
Sociology of poverty, 40, 99
Spatial inequalities, 22, 137, 164
Spatial mapping, 186, 187
Starvation, 4, 56, 79
State-wise seasonal migration, 135, 139–142,
    146
Sustainable development Goals (SDG), 2–4, 9,
    18, 51, 153, 156, 170

T
Temporary migration, 131, 138, 139
Tendulkar committee, 2, 11, 13–15, 113, 114
Transient poor, 25, 39, 216
Trickle-down effects, 31

U
Under-5 mortality rate, 30, 156, 157, 165, 166
Uniform recall period (URP), 13
Union Cabinet, 26
Unskilled workers, 31
Upward income mobility, income mobility, 38
Urbanisation/urban growth, 31, 46–51, 96

V
Victims of poverty, 5, 94, 97, 98
Village infrastructure/village level
    infrastructure, 30, 46, 47
Village size, 30
Vulnerability/vulnerabilities, 3, 10, 28–31, 40,
    48, 98, 148, 155, 188, 242

W
Working poor, 8, 27, 60, 248

Printed in the United States
By Bookmasters